Proportionality, Reasonableness and Standards of Review in International Investment Law and Arbitration

ELGAR INTERNATIONAL INVESTMENT LAW

Series Editors: Andrea K. Bjorklund, *McGill University, Montreal, Quebec, Canada* and August Reinisch, *University of Vienna, Austria*

This monograph series provides a point of convergence for authoritative, original works focused specifically on international investment law in all its forms. Works will be single or co-authored, theoretically rigorous and analytically precise, often considering the intersection of investment law with other fields of law such as trade, intellectual property, environment or public international law. The series will comprise works from established authors as well as from younger scholars whose work is genuinely innovative and challenging. Proposals are encouraged that primarily engage with new and previously under-developed themes in the field, draw on other disciplines in order to further thinking in the field, or alternatively attempt to offer a definitive statement on areas of uncertainty in the existing law.

The development of original thinking in international investment law and research of the highest quality is the main emphasis of the series. Both international and comparative in its approach, it aims to include some of the best theoretical and empirical work from both well-established researchers and the next generation of scholars.

Titles in this series include:

International Investment Law and the Environment
Saverio Di Benedetto

Intellectual Property Rights as Foreign Direct Investments
From Collision to Collaboration
Lukas Vanhonnaeker

Performance Requirements and Investment Incentives Under International Economic Law
David Collins

The ASEAN Comprehensive Investment Agreement
The Regionalisation of Laws and Policy on Foreign Investment
Julien Chaisse and Sufian Jusoh

Non-Discrimination and the Role of Regulatory Purpose in International Trade and Investment Law
Andrew D. Mitchell, David Heaton and Caroline Henckels

Regulatory Autonomy in International Economic Law
The Evolution of Australian Policy on Trade and Investment
Tania Voon, Andrew D. Mitchell and Elizabeth Sheargold

Proportionality, Reasonableness and Standards of Review in International Investment Law and Arbitration
Valentina Vadi

Proportionality, Reasonableness and Standards of Review in International Investment Law and Arbitration

Valentina Vadi

Professor of International Economic Law, Lancaster University Law School, UK

ELGAR INTERNATIONAL INVESTMENT LAW

Edward Elgar PUBLISHING

Cheltenham, UK • Northampton, MA, USA

Published by
Edward Elgar Publishing Limited
The Lypiatts
15 Lansdown Road
Cheltenham
Glos GL50 2JA
UK

Edward Elgar Publishing, Inc.
William Pratt House
9 Dewey Court
Northampton
Massachusetts 01060
USA

A catalogue record for this book
is available from the British Library

Library of Congress Control Number: 2017959518

This book is available electronically in the **Elgar**online
Law subject collection
DOI 10.4337/9781785368585

MIX
Paper from responsible sources
FSC
www.fsc.org
FSC® C013056

ISBN 978 1 78536 857 8 (cased)
ISBN 978 1 78536 858 5 (eBook)

Typeset by Columns Design XML Ltd, Reading
Printed and bound in Great Britain by TJ International Ltd, Padstow

For Ester

Contents

Preface

The façade of the church of Santa Maria Novella in Florence has been considered as the perfect expression of the golden proportion, and as 'the most important of the Renaissance', setting the example that architects would follow for centuries to come.[1] Its architect, the humanist Leon Battista Alberti (1404–1472), was credited with having elaborated the 'first great example of eurhythmia' and a remarkable system of proportions.[2]

Yet, on a closer look, the façade of Santa Maria Novella presents irregular patterns, uneven structural elements and visible asymmetries that were typical in the Middle Ages.[3] In fact, for quintessentially economic and legal reasons, the architect had to include 'extensive portions of the existing medieval façade into his new design'.[4] Alberti could not simply develop an entirely new façade relying on abstract theories of proportion; rather, he had to build upon the existing gothic elements, still visible in the lower section of the façade, devise new elements, and combine old and new features in an orderly fashion. Abstract theories had to be combined with concrete realities. Yet, Alberti combined the various 'imperfections' with sufficient elasticity to form an elegant façade that transcended the medieval origins of the church and led to the Renaissance.

In international investment law and arbitration something similar is happening.[5] Like the façade of Santa Maria Novella in the fifteenth

---

[1] R. Wittkower, *Architectural Principles in the Age of Humanism* (Warburg Institute 1949) 45–7.

[2] Ibid.

[3] M. Selzer, *The Symmetry Norm and the Asymmetric Universe* (Keep Ahead 2015) 10, 17.

[4] Ibid. 10; F. Borsi, *Leon Battista Alberti* (Harper & Row 1977) 80.

[5] Admittedly, this is not the first piece of international law scholarship that analogizes the debate on the functioning of international courts and tribunals to some architectural debate. See for instance D. Shelton, 'Form, Function, and the Powers of International Courts' (2009) 9 *Chicago JIL* 537–71, 537 (on the debate raised by the construction of the first skyscrapers in Chicago). International law scholars have also analogized the international community to some architectural

century, the arbitral jurisprudence remains a work in progress, and there are ongoing attempts to create order out of the existing chaos, systematize the field and enhance its perceived legitimacy. The proportionality concept has been seen as one of the available tools to calibrate investment law and its jurisprudence to emerging circumstances and make the system a more equilibrate one. Yet, the past cannot but influence some of the available choices. The proportionality analysis is an abstract theory 'with a propensity for the best possible [option]'.[6] Despite its best intentions, it can remain ineffective as the search for 'the right proportion' or perfection can prove to be elusive and remain 'ideal'.[7]

This is not to say, however, that the ongoing efforts of scholars, arbitrators and policy makers cannot, or will not achieve a sound, valuable and enduring outcome. International investment law is rising up over its old horizon, and gradually assuming a new shape. This book aims to contribute to this renaissance, examining the role that the concepts of proportionality and reasonableness, on the one hand, and standards of review, on the other, can play in devising the new architecture of international investment law and arbitration, thus contributing to its effectiveness, perceived legitimacy and justice.

Valentina Vadi

---

elements. See e.g. E. Benvenisti, 'Sovereigns as Trustees of Humanity: On the Accountability of States to Foreign Stakeholders' (2013) 107 AJIL 295–333, 295, 298 (analogizing the international community to 'a global condominium' and state sovereignty to 'a small apartment in one densely packed high-rise'); A. Gentili, *De iure belli* [1598], J.C. Rolfe trans. (Clarendon Press 1933) Book I, Chap. XV, 67–9 ('All the universe, which you see, in which things divine and human are included, is one … the whole world is one body, … all men [and women] are members of that body, [and] … the world is their home … And this union of ours is like an arch of stones, which will fall unless the stones … hold one another up').

6 G. Nolte, 'Thin or Thick? The Principle of Proportionality in International Humanitarian Law' (2010) 4 LEHR 245–55, 254.

7 Ibid.

Acknowledgments

In May 2013, during my appointment as a Marie Curie Post-doctoral Fellow at Maastricht University in the Netherlands, I was invited to present a paper on proportionality analysis in international investment law and arbitration at the British Institute for International and Comparative Law (BIICL), in London. In preparing my presentation, I soon realized that there seemed to be an almost unchallenged consensus as to the pros of using proportionality analysis in international investment law and arbitration. I started wondering whether the use of such concept – of domestic origin, but having successfully migrated to several domestic, regional and international regimes – could be woven into international investment law and arbitration, and/or whether there could be alternatives. Without questioning the benefits of proportionality analysis in various fields of law, I wondered whether, in addition to certain merits, such methodology also presented pitfalls, and whether alternative methodologies were available.

In September 2013, I moved to New York City as I was awarded an Emile Noël Postdoctoral fellowship at the Jean Monnet Center for International and Regional Economic Law, New York University (NYU). The intense interdisciplinary environment of the Center fueled my interest in the topic. I started investigating the application of the concept of proportionality in various areas of international and regional economic law. If proportionality was successful in a number of legal fields, could it also be successful in international investment law and arbitration? In the migration of constitutional ideas from one field to another, context matters, and what can be successful in one field, may not be as successful in another.

At Lancaster University, where I am currently a Professor of International Economic Law, I developed the idea of writing a book on the use of proportionality, reasonableness and standards of review in international investment law and arbitration. While a number of books have focused on the use of proportionality in various fields of law, none of them has included reasonableness as a possible alternative; moreover – to date – the linkage between proportionality and/or reasonableness, on the one hand, and standards of review, on the other, has not been addressed in full. Far from having a mere theoretical relevance, the migration of constitutional ideas from the domestic realm to the international one can have a profound impact on the field. Therefore, such migration deserves to be investigated for both its theoretical and practical implications. This book seeks to address the question as to whether proportionality, reasonableness and standards of review can improve the quality of legal reasoning, thus helping to solve the alleged 'legitimacy crisis' of the field, and aiding in the development of international investment law in conformity with public international law.

This book is part of a tetralogy of literary works dedicated to the interplay between international investment law and other fields of law, such as public health law (V. Vadi, *Public Health in International Investment Law and Arbitration* (Routledge 2012)), cultural heritage law (V. Vadi, *Cultural Heritage in International Investment Law and Arbitration* (CUP 2014)) and comparative law (V. Vadi, *Analogies in International Investment Law and Arbitration* (CUP 2016)). It focuses on some aspects of the interplay between constitutional law and international law. In particular, it explores the migration of constitutional ideas – such as proportionality, reasonableness and standards of review – to international investment law and arbitration. While these books can be read together in order to gather some complementary views of the complex mosaic of international investment governance, each one can also be read separately, having its own aims and objectives.

In developing my thinking on the theme of this book, earlier versions of some of the chapters were first published by OUP, such as 'Proportionality, Reasonableness and Standards of Review in Investment Treaty Arbitration', in A.K. Bjorklund (ed.), *Yearbook on International Investment Law and Policy* (2013–2014) 201–28; 'The Migration of Constitutional Ideas: The Strange Case of Proportionality in International Investment Law and Arbitration', in Andrea K. Bjorklund (ed.), *Yearbook on International Investment Law and Policy* (2013–2014) 337–60; with revised versions published, such as 'The Migration of Constitutional Ideas to Regional and International Economic Law: The Case of Proportionality' (2015) 35 *Northwestern Journal of International Law and Business* 557–89, and 'A History of Success? Proportionality in International Economic Law', in Antonio Segura Serrano (ed.), *The Reform of International Economic Governance* (Routledge 2016) 171–92. Research undertaken for this book was also published in two pieces co-authored with Lucas Gruszczynski, and entitled 'Standards of Review in International Investment Law and Arbitration: Multilevel Governance and the Commonweal' (2013) 16 JIEL 613–33 and 'Standards of Review and

Scientific Evidence in WTO Law and International Investment Arbitration: Converging Parallels?', in L. Gruszczynski and W. Werner (eds), *Deference in International Courts and Tribunals* (OUP 2014) 152–72. While the book relies on these earlier works, its sheer length makes it a better format for a sustained exploration of the subject.

Parts of the book were presented at conferences and seminars held in Coimbra, Granada, Lancaster, London, New York and Warwick. I greatly benefited from the comments received from colleagues on these occasions. In particular, I would like to thank N. Jansen Calamita, Judy Carter, Caroline Foster, Lukasz Gruszczynski, Caroline Henckels, Ester Herlin-Karnell, Catherine Kessedjian, Christopher McCrudden, Martins Paparinskis, Stephan Schill, Sivan Shlomo-Agon, Fiona Smith, Muthucumaraswamy Sornarajah and Joseph Weiler for their comments on various occasions. I also thank Andrea Bjorklund and August Reinisch for their guidance, encouragement and support. I particularly thank José Alvarez, Bruno De Witte, Antonietta Di Blase, Alisdair Gillespie, Francesco Francioni, Moshe Hirsch, Vaughan Lowe, Gus Van Harten, Ana Vrdoljak and Steve Wheatley for their inspiring work, guidance and mentorship. The opinions expressed in this book are my own and the usual disclaimer applies. Finally, I thank Ben Booth, Michaela Doyle, Glynis Dyson, Laura Mann, Iram Satti and Amber Watts of Edward Elgar for helping steer this book through the publication process.

On a personal note, I would like to thank my parents, Lidiana and Carlo, and my aunt Ester, who have encouraged and supported me in every possible way. I also thank my husband, Gianluca and my daughter, Ester Susanna, for being a source of love, joy and wonder.

Valentina Vadi

Abbreviations

AJCL	*American Journal of Comparative Law*
AJIL	*American Journal of International Law*
ASEAN	Association of Southeast Asian Nations
BIT(s)	Bilateral investment treaty(ies)
BYIL	*British Yearbook of International Law*
CETA	EU–Canada Comprehensive Economic and Trade Agreement
CJEU	Court of Justice of the European Union
CJICL	*Cambridge Journal of International and Comparative Law*
CUP	Cambridge University Press
DCF	Discounted cash flow
ECHR	European Convention on Human Rights
ECtHR	European Court of Human Rights
ECT	Energy Charter Treaty
EEC	European Economic Community
EJIL	*European Journal of International Law*
EJLS	*European Journal of Legal Studies*
EU	European Union
FCN	Friendship, Commerce and Navigation
FDI	Foreign direct investment
FET	Fair and equitable treatment
FIPA	Foreign Investment Protection Agreement
FTA(s)	Free trade agreement(s)
GATS	General Agreement on Trade in Services
GATT	General Agreement on Tariffs and Trade
IAR	Investment Arbitration Reporter

IBRD	International Bank for Reconstruction and Development
ICJ	International Court of Justice
ICESCR	International Covenant on Economic, Social and Cultural Rights
ICLQ	*International and Comparative Law Quarterly*
ICS	Investment Court System
ICSID	International Centre for the Settlement of Investment Disputes
ICSID Review–FILJ	*ICSID Review Foreign Investment Law Journal*
IJCL	*International Journal of Constitutional Law*
IIA(s)	International investment agreement(s)
ILC	International Law Commission
ILJ	*International Law Journal*
ILM	International Legal Materials
ILR	International Law Reports
IMF	International Monetary Fund
ITN	*Investment Treaty News*
JIDS	*Journal of International Dispute Settlement*
JIEL	*Journal of International Economic Law*
JIL	*Journal of International Law*
JWIT	*Journal of World Investment and Trade*
JWT	*Journal of World Trade*
LCIA	London Court of International Arbitration
LDCs	Least developed countries
LEHR	*Law and Ethics of Human Rights*
MAI	Multilateral Agreement on Investment
MFN	Most favoured nation
MIT	Massachusetts Institute of Technology
MLR	*Modern Law Review*
NAFTA	North American Free Trade Agreement
NYU	New York University
NYULR	*New York University Law Review*

NZJPIL	*New Zealand Journal of Public and International Law*
NZLR	*New Zealand Law Review*
OECD	Organization for Economic Co-operation and Development
OP-ICESCR	Optional Protocol to the ICESCR
OUP	Oxford University Press
PCB	Polychlorinated biphenol
PCIJ	Permanent Court of International Justice
PMRA	Pest Management Regulatory Agency
RECIEL	*Review of European Community and International Environmental Law*
RIIA	*Reports of International Arbitral Awards*
SCC	Stockholm Chamber of Commerce
TDM	*Transnational Dispute Management*
TRIMS	Agreement on Trade-Related Investment Measures
TRIPs	Agreement on Trade-Related Aspects of Intellectual Property Rights
TTIP	Transatlantic Trade and Investment Partnership
UN	United Nations
UNCITRAL	United Nations Commission on International Trade Law
UNCTAD	United Nations Conference on Trade and Development
UNSC	United Nations Security Council
UNTS	United Nations Treaty Series
VCLT	Vienna Convention on the Law of Treaties
VJTL	*Vanderbilt Journal of Transnational Law*
WIR	World Investment Report
WTO	World Trade Organization
YIL	*Yearbook of International Law*

Introduction

Once the domain of elitist scholars and practitioners, international investment law has come to the forefront of legal debate. Under most investment treaties, states have agreed to give arbitrators a comprehensive jurisdiction over what are essentially regulatory disputes. Some scholars and practitioners have expressed concern regarding the magnitude of decision-making power allocated to investment treaty tribunals. Many of the recent arbitral awards have determined the boundary between two conflicting values: the legitimate sphere for state regulation in the pursuit of public goods on the one hand, and the protection of private interests from state interference on the other. Although international investment law is one of the most dynamic and thriving fields of international law, it has been criticized for failing to strike a fair balance between the promotion of foreign direct investments and the regulatory autonomy of host states.

Can constitutional ideas such as proportionality, reasonableness and standards of review help arbitrators in interpreting and applying broad and open-ended treaty provisions? Can they help facilitate the consideration of the commonweal in investment treaty arbitration? Can they contribute to the perceived legitimacy and effectiveness of international investment governance? Are there rules to govern the 'migration' of constitutional ideas to other legal fields? What are the limits, if any, of the use of domestic law concepts in the international realm?

This book examines the role of criteria such as proportionality, reasonableness and standards of review in the balancing of private and public interests in investment disputes, and addresses the question as to whether such tools can, and/or do, help arbitral tribunals adjudicate such disputes. Proportionality and reasonableness are legal tools traditionally used in domestic, regional and even some international courts and tribunals for resolving conflicts between private and public interests through a process of balancing. This book analyses the migration of these constitutional ideas from the domestic realm to the international one. It then examines the promises and pitfalls of the use of such concepts in international investment law and arbitration.

While comparative reasoning can play an important role in shaping the field of international investment governance, before importing elements from other fields we should consider whether the given transplant will work well and what its implications will be in the investment law context. This book shows that the use of proportionality and reasonableness in investment arbitration can be appropriate, provided that one adopts appropriate standards of review, that is, appropriate procedural mechanisms indicating the extent to which the adjudicator re-examines state conduct.

While some scholars consider that arbitral tribunals should adopt proportionality analysis as the applicable method of review,[1] others have adopted a more cautious stance.[2] This book adopts a moderate position between the two poles, by not excluding the use of proportionality and/or reasonableness, but providing a reflection on whether it is desirable to use these concepts in the first place and, if so, how best to use them, adopting appropriate standards of review. In short, by adopting appropriate standards of review the use of proportionality and reasonableness in investment arbitration can contribute to the further development of the field in a manner compatible with the more general evolution of public international law.

The book aims to fill a significant gap in the current literature: to date there is no comprehensive study to cover the interplay between proportionality, reasonableness and standards of review in international investment law and arbitration. This study aims to contribute to the ongoing debate as to whether these concepts can help arbitral tribunals contribute to international justice and peaceful and prosperous relations among nations. While the interrelationship between proportionality, reasonableness and standards of review may be studied from a variety of different perspectives and institutional settings, this book adopts an 'internal' approach with respect to international investment law and arbitration. The choice of this approach is not meant to imply that the institutional setting of international investment law is to be preferred to others to reconcile

---

1 See, for instance, G. Bücheler, *Proportionality in Investor–State Arbitration* (OUP 2015); C. Henckels, *Proportionality and Deference in Investor–State Arbitration: Balancing Investment Protection and Regulatory Autonomy* (CUP 2015) 21.

2 See N.J. Calamita, 'The Principle of Proportionality and the Problem of Indeterminacy in International Investment Treaties', in A. Bjorklund (ed.), *Yearbook of International Investment Law and Policy* (2013–2014) 157–200.

public and private interests.[3] Instead, looking at the interplay between proportionality, reasonableness and standards of review from an inside view of international investment law allows a reflection on this emerging field of public international law in particular and its contribution to the development of international law more generally.

At the same time, the book presents some lines of continuity with the available literature, which can be placed in five broad categories: (1) literature on international investment law;[4] (2) literature on international investment law and other values;[5] (3) literature on proportionality in various

---

[3] Clearly, arbitral tribunals are not the only available fora, let alone the superior fora for this kind of dispute. Other fora are available such as national courts, human rights courts, regional economic courts and the traditional state-to-state fora such as the International Court of Justice or even inter-state arbitration.

[4] The existing literature on international investment law is too vast to be mentioned here exhaustively; it suffices to say that international investment law has become a topical issue and the literature on this matter is booming. See e.g. M. Sornarajah, *Resistance and Change in the International Law on Foreign Investment* (CUP 2015); Eric De Brabandere, *Investment Treaty Arbitration as Public International Law: Procedural Aspects and Implications* (CUP 2014); Z. Douglas, J. Pauwelyn and J.E. Viñuales (eds), *The Foundations of International Investment Law: Bringing Theory into Practice* (OUP 2014); R. Dolzer and C. Schreuer, *Principles of International Investment Law*, 2nd edn (OUP 2012); J.E. Alvarez, *The Public International Law Regime Governing International Investment* (Hague Academy of International Law 2011); M. Sornarajah, *The International Law on Foreign Investment*, 3rd edn (CUP 2010); J.W. Salacuse, *The Law of Investment Treaties* (OUP 2010); S.W. Schill, *The Multilateralization of International Investment Law* (CUP 2009); C. Binder, U. Kriebaum, A. Reinisch and S. Wittich (eds), *International Investment Law for the 21st Century* (OUP 2009); C. Dugan, N. Rubins, D. Wallace and B. Sabahi, *Investor–State Arbitration* (OUP 2008); A. Reinisch, *Standards of Investment Protection* (OUP 2008).

[5] On international investment law and other values, see e.g. S. Subedi, *International Investment Law: Reconciling Policy and Principle*, 3rd edn (Hart Publishing 2016); G. Sacerdoti (ed.), *General Interests of Host States in International Investment Law* (CUP 2014); G. Van Harten, *Sovereign Choices and Sovereign Constraints: Judicial Restraint in Investment Treaty Arbitration* (OUP 2013); F. Baetens (ed.), *Investment Law within International Law: Integrationist Perspectives* (CUP 2013); P.-M. Dupuy, F. Francioni and E.-U. Petersmann (eds), *Human Rights in International Investment Law and Arbitration* (OUP 2009); and G. Van Harten, *Investment Treaty Arbitration and Public Law* (OUP 2007).

legal fields;[6] (4) literature on reasonableness in various legal fields;[7] and (5) literature on standards of review in international law.[8]

The book complements the existing literature in several ways. First, although there is flourishing literature on international investment law and arbitration, only recently have scholars and practitioners focused on specific theoretical aspects. Second, the book contributes to the existing literature on international investment law and other values, addressing the question as to whether constitutional law benchmarks, such as proportionality, reasonableness and standards of review, can help arbitrators achieve a better balance between public and private interests in investor–state arbitration. Third, while there is a growing amount of literature on proportionality in a variety of fields of law, only in the past decade have investment law scholars started investigating the specific application of proportionality analysis to international investment law and arbitration. Fourth, this study complements the existing literature on reasonableness by offering a critical assessment of the role that this concept can (and does) play in international investment law and arbitration. Although reasonableness plays a significant role in investor–state arbitration it has received limited, if any, attention by international investment law scholars.[9] Fifth, the book contributes to the existing literature on standards of review by exploring the linkage between standards of review and proportionality, on the one hand, and standards of review and reasonableness, on the other, in international investment law and arbitration.

Finally, the book complements the existing literature providing the reader with a useful analytical framework of the role proportionality, reasonableness and standards of review play in investor–state arbitration. The author has explored this interplay in earlier contributions but this has been done in a piecemeal fashion; to date there is no comprehensive study to cover the interplay between proportionality, reasonableness and

---

[6] On proportionality in investor–state arbitration, see e.g. G. Bücheler, *Proportionality in Investor–State Arbitration*; C. Henckels, *Proportionality and Deference in Investor–State Arbitration*. For additional references, see Chapter 3 below.

[7] On reasonableness in different fields of law and legal theory, see e.g. G. Bongiovanni, G. Sartor and C. Valentini (eds), *Reasonableness and Law* (Springer 2009). For additional references see Chapter 4 below.

[8] On standards of review in international law, see e.g. L. Gruszczynski and W. Werner (eds), *Deference in International Courts and Tribunals* (OUP 2014). For additional references see Chapter 5 below.

[9] But see V. Vadi, 'Proportionality, Reasonableness and Standards of Review in Investment Treaty Arbitration', in A.K. Bjorklund (ed.), *Yearbook of International Investment Law and Policy* (2013–2014) 201–28.

standards of review in international investment law and arbitration. Therefore, such theoretical framework offered by the book may be of help to both practitioners and scholars alike, who are interested in the legitimacy, effectiveness and justice of international investment law and arbitration.

The book adopts an interdisciplinary approach, principally relying on the international law literature, but also taking into account the existing literature on legal theory and comparative constitutional law. The use of interdisciplinary sources is not aimed at diluting the quality of the classical types of public international law analysis, or integrating the logic of public law into international investment law.[10] Rather, the adoption of an interdisciplinary approach aims at deepening the public international law analysis, making it more nuanced and responsive to current debates.[11] The book does not suggest reading international investment law as a constitutional system; rather, it highlights that international investment law is part and parcel of international law.

The intended readership for this book is that of specialists in the field of international investment law, international economic law and public international law. The book will also appeal to policy makers, arbitrators and practitioners. In order to make the analysis relevant to the different targeted audiences, the language will deliberately be kept technical, but efforts will be taken to achieve clarity and cohesion. As a result, this study will be of relevance for a wide audience, including but not limited to: international (investment) law scholars, arbitrators and practitioners, government departments, as well as other interested audiences.

The book is structured into three parts. The first part has a general/introductory character and sets out the overall legal and analytical foundations upon which to build an original study of the concepts of proportionality, reasonableness and standards of review in international investment law and arbitration. In this first part, Chapter 1 examines the international regime governing foreign direct investments. Chapter 2

---

[10] For a different approach, see, among others, J. Kleinheisterkamp, 'Investment Treaty Law and the Fear of Sovereignty: Transnational Challenges and Solution' (2015) 78 MLR 793–825, 795 (arguing that 'the perceived clash between investment treaty law and sovereignty can and must be resolved by integrating the logic of public law, as a proxy for sovereignty, into investment treaty law').

[11] In this sense, see V. Lowe, 'The Politics of Law-Making: Are the Method and Character of Norm Creation Changing?', in M. Byers (ed.), *The Role of Law in International Politics: Essays in International Relations and International Law* (OUP 2000) 207–226, 218.

explores the phenomenon of the migration of constitutional ideas from domestic law to international (investment) law, its promises and pitfalls. The second part analyses and critically assesses the use and/or eventual desirability of the notions of proportionality, reasonableness and standards of review in international investment law and arbitration. This starts with Chapter 3, which explores the notion, origins and structure of proportionality, and its successful migration from constitutional law to different fields of domestic and international law. After discussing the successful migration of proportionality from domestic law to EU law and international trade law, the chapter investigates whether and, if so, to what extent, proportionality has migrated to international investment law and arbitration, analysing the relevant jurisprudence. Chapter 4 investigates the notion of reasonableness and its pros and cons, as well as its application in various areas of domestic and international law. It then examines its use in international investment law and arbitration. Chapter 5 discusses the concept of standards of review and examines the standards that have been adopted by international courts and tribunals and investment arbitration tribunals respectively. The final part concludes by examining the interactions between proportionality, reasonableness and standards of review. Here, Chapter 6 proposes a more critical use of proportionality and reasonableness in conjunction with appropriate standards of review. The conclusions sum up the key findings of the study.

1. International investment law as a field of international law

INTRODUCTION

Once deemed to be an 'exotic and highly specialised' domain,[1] international investment law is now moving mainstream.[2] Due to economic globalization and the rise of foreign direct investments, the regulation of the field has become a key area of international law. Under international investment agreements (IIAs), states parties agree to provide a certain degree of protection to investors who are nationals of contracting states, or their investments. Such protection generally includes compensation in case of expropriation, fair and equitable treatment, non-discrimination and full protection and security, among others.

Most contemporary investment treaties include investor–state arbitration for the settlement of disputes that may arise between the foreign investor and the host state. Under this mechanism, foreign investors may bring claims directly against the host state before international arbitral tribunals. Investors are not required to exhaust local remedies and no longer depend on diplomatic protection to defend their interests against the host state. Investor–state arbitrations are heard by ad hoc or institutionalized arbitral tribunals whose arbitrators are selected by the disputing parties and/or appointing institutions. The internationalization of investment disputes has been conceived as an important valve for guaranteeing a neutral forum and depoliticizing investment disputes.[3]

---

[1] ILC, *Fragmentation of International Law: Difficulties Arising from the Diversification and Expansion of International Law*, Report of the Study Group (Martti Koskenniemi) UN Doc. A/CN.4/L.682 (13 April 2006) para. 8.

[2] S.W. Schill, 'W(h)ither Fragmentation? On the Literature and Sociology of International Investment Law' (2011) 22 EJIL 875–908.

[3] I.F.I. Shihata, 'Toward a Greater Depoliticization of Investment Disputes: The Roles of ICSID and MIGA' (1986) 1 *ICSID Review–FILJ* 1–25.

Arbitral tribunals have reviewed state conduct in key sectors including but not limited to water services, cultural heritage, environmental protection and public health.[4] Consequently, many of the recent arbitral awards have determined the boundary between two conflicting values: the legitimate sphere for state regulation in the pursuit of the public interest, on the one hand, and the protection of private interests from state interference, on the other. With awards that have reached as high as $50 billion,[5] the field has attracted the increasing attention of states, investors and the media, as well as the public at large.

Despite its flourishing, investment treaty law and arbitration is facing a 'legitimacy crisis'.[6] Concerns have arisen regarding the magnitude of decision-making power allocated to investment treaty tribunals.[7] Some scholars contend that investor–state arbitration lacks democratic insight.[8] Others lament that investor–state arbitration operates as a self-contained regime, privileging the interests of foreign investors while 'structural[ly] disregard[ing]' those of 'more weakly organized and less powerful groups, and of vulnerable individuals'.[9] There is uncertainty over the relevance or irrelevance of norms external to investment law, such as human rights law, within investment treaty arbitration.[10] The debate has focused not so much on the question as to whether international investment agreements limit state sovereignty – at the end of the day, this is what international agreements do, limiting state sovereignty in order to

---

[4] See e.g. A.M. Daza-Clark, *International Investment Law and Water Resources Management* (Brill 2016); V. Vadi, *Public Health in International Investment Law and Arbitration* (Routledge 2012); J.E. Viñuales, *Foreign Investment and the Environment in International Law* (CUP 2012); V. Vadi, *Cultural Heritage in International Investment Law and Arbitration* (CUP 2014).

[5] See e.g. *Yukos Universal Ltd (Isle of Man) v. The Russian Federation*, UNCITRAL, PCA Case No. AA227, Final Award, 18 July 2014, para. 1827.

[6] S.D. Franck, 'The Legitimacy Crisis in Investment Treaty Arbitration: Privatizing Public International Law Through Inconsistent Decisions' (2005) 73 *Fordham LR* 1521–625.

[7] See generally M. Waibel, A. Kaushal, K.-H.L. Chung and C. Balchin (eds), *The Backlash against Investment Arbitration* (Kluwer Law International 2010).

[8] B. Choudhury, 'Recapturing Public Power: Is Investment Arbitration's Engagement of the Public Interest Contributing to the Democratic Deficit?' (2008) 41 *Vanderbilt Journal of Transnational Law* 775–832.

[9] R.B. Stewart, 'Remedying Disregard in Global Regulatory Governance: Accountability, Participation, and Responsiveness' (2014) 108 AJIL 211–70, 211, 221.

[10] B. Simma, 'Foreign Investment Arbitration: A Place for Human Rights?' (2011) 60 ICLQ 573–96.

provide states with perceivably greater benefits – but 'over the extent to which IIAs delimit state sovereignty' and its ability to regulate.[11]

While developing countries have deemed investment treaty arbitration politically biased against them,[12] emerging economies and industrialized countries alike have expressed some concerns about this mechanism.[13] For instance, Bolivia, Ecuador and Venezuela sent a formal notice to the International Centre for the Settlement of Investment Disputes (ICSID) declaring their withdrawal from the Convention on the Settlement of Investment Disputes between States and Nationals of Other States (ICSID Convention).[14] Brazil has never ratified the ICSID Convention, nor has it ratified any treaty that provides for investor–state arbitration.[15] South Africa, India and Indonesia 'have announced that they will not conclude any more investment treaties'.[16] Ecuador has denounced all of its bilateral investment treaties (BITs).

Against this background, this chapter aims to briefly illustrate the fundamental features of international investment law and arbitration. A preliminary investigation of the field seems not only appropriate but also essential to assess whether notions such as proportionality, reasonableness and standards of review can (or do) help solve the investment regimes' pressing challenges. The chapter proceeds as follows. First, after providing some historical background, it explores the normative framework that governs foreign direct investment. Second, it highlights the most salient features of investor–state arbitration. Third, it explores the backlash against investment treaty law and arbitration. It then concludes that this area of law remains under-theorized, and that more theoretical studies of the same are needed in order for it to develop in conformity with and contribute to international law.

---

[11] E. Guntrip, 'Self-Determination and Foreign Direct Investment: Reimagining Sovereignty in International Investment Law' (2016) 65 ICLQ 829–57, 829–30.

[12] A. Shalakany, 'Arbitration and The Third World: A Plea for Reassessing Bias Under the Specter of Neoliberalism' (2000) 41 *Harvard ILJ* 419–68.

[13] K. Miles, 'Investor–State Dispute Settlement: Conflict, Convergence and Future Directions' (2016) *European Yearbook of International Economic Law* 273–308.

[14] M. Clark, 'Venezuela's Withdrawal from the ICSID Convention', *Association for International Arbitration Bulletin*, October 2012, 2.

[15] J. Kalicki and S. Medeiros, 'Investment Arbitration in Brazil' (2008) 24 *Arbitration International* 423–45.

[16] M. Sornarajah, *Resistance and Change in the International Law on Foreign Investment* (CUP 2015) 1.

1.1 MULTILATERAL FAILURES AND BILATERAL SUCCESSES

International investment law constitutes an important part of public international law governing foreign direct investments.[17] Defined as 'the transfer of tangible or intangible assets from one country into another for the purpose of their use in that country to generate wealth under the total or partial control of the owner of the assets',[18] foreign direct investment (FDI) is an all-encompassing concept, including almost any kind of business activity. While there is still no comprehensive global treaty governing foreign investments, there are over 3,304 IIAs.[19] IIAs include BITs, regional investment treaties, free trade agreements (FTAs) or sectoral agreements with investment provisions, such as the Energy Charter Treaty.[20]

Efforts to establish global rules to protect foreign investments and a World Investment Court to settle potential disputes between host countries and investors have been pursued by industrialized countries for a long time.[21] A first attempt to create a unified global investment law was made at the Bretton Woods conference in 1944. Agreeing on the importance of promoting economic relations to foster peace and economic growth, the conference participants established the International Monetary Fund (IMF)[22] to secure financial stability and facilitate international trade, and the International Bank for Reconstruction and Development (IBRD)[23] to finance the post-war reconstruction of Europe. The conference participants also considered establishing an International

---

[17] J.E. Alvarez, *The Public International Law Regime Governing International Investment* (Hague Academy of International Law 2011). For an historical overview, see A. Newcombe and L. Paradell, *Law and Practice of Investment Treaties* (Kluwer Law International 2009) 3–57.

[18] M. Sornarajah, *The International Law on Foreign Investment*, 3rd edn (CUP 2010) 8.

[19] UNCTAD, *World Investment Report 2016* (UN 2016) xii.

[20] Energy Charter Treaty, opened for signature 17 December 1994, in force 16 April 1998, 34 ILM 360.

[21] See e.g. R. Dattu, 'A Journey from Havana to Paris: The Fifty-Year Quest for the Elusive Multilateral Agreement on Investment' (2000–2001) 24 *Fordham ILJ* 275–316.

[22] Articles of Agreement of the International Monetary Fund (IMF), 22 July 1944, in force 27 December 1945, 2 UNTS 40.

[23] Articles of Agreement of the International Bank for Reconstruction and Development (IBRD) as amended in 1965, 606 UNTS 294.

Trade Organization (ITO), governing both trade and investment. However, the Havana Charter never came into force.[24]

Although the World Trade Organization (WTO),[25] which came into being in 1995, in some ways has become 'the missing leg' of the Bretton Woods 'stool',[26] the moves to adopt multilateral investment rules initiated at the Doha Ministerial Conference in 2001 had to be abandoned at the Ministerial Conference in Cancun in 2003, due to the growing opposition from developing countries and strong criticism from civil society. Following the 2015 Ministerial Conference in Nairobi, the EU suggested that investment could form part of the new issues for negotiation in the WTO,[27] but it remains to be seen whether the suggestion will be broadly endorsed.

When the Organization for Economic Co-operation and Development (OECD), a group of 30 industrialized countries, attempted to launch a Multilateral Agreement on Investments (MAI),[28] this effort collapsed. Civil society opposed the MAI, perceiving it to be a one-sided instrument, unilaterally prepared by OECD countries to ensure higher standards of protection and legal security for foreign investors. It did not adequately take into account the developmental needs of the host states, omitting crucial environmental and social issues.[29]

However, some authors contend that global rules on foreign investment exist already.[30] On the one hand, some multilateral instruments, such as the Energy Charter Treaty, govern foreign investments albeit in specific sectors. The ICSID Convention constitutes a multilateral procedural instrument establishing the ICSID. Several WTO instruments deal

---

[24] Charter for an International Trade Organization ('Havana Charter'), Final Act of the United Nations Conference on Trade and Employment, held at Havana, Cuba from 21 November 1947 to 24 March 1948, UN Document E/Conf. 2/78.

[25] Agreement Establishing the World Trade Organization, 15 April 1994, 33 ILM 1994.

[26] See J. Jackson, *The World Trading System* (MIT Press 2002) 32.

[27] European Commission, 'Joint Statement by Commissioners Malmström and Hogan ahead of the 10th WTO Ministerial Conference in Nairobi', *News item*, 14 December 2015.

[28] OECD Multilateral Agreement on Investment, Consolidated Text and Commentary, Draft DAFFE/MAI/NM(97)2.

[29] See S. Picciotto, 'Linkages in International Investment Regulation: The Antinomies of the Draft Multilateral Agreement on Investment' (1998) 19 *University of Pennsylvania JIEL* 731–68.

[30] S.W. Schill, *The Multilateralization of International Investment Law* (CUP 2009).

directly with aspects of foreign investments. For instance, the Agreement on Trade-Related Aspects of Intellectual Property Rights (TRIPS)[31] covers intellectual property, which can be a form of investment.[32] The General Agreement on Trade in Services (GATS)[33] covers the provision of services through a commercial presence in another country. In addition, the Agreement on Trade-Related Investment Measures (TRIMS)[34] deals with performance requirements associated with foreign investment. On the other hand, although never ratified, the Havana Charter inspired many investment provisions.[35] Because of the similarities among these different investment treaties and the fact that they tend to be negotiated from a limited set of model BITs, it has been argued that investment treaties are incrementally building a de facto global investment regime.[36] Some even consider these recurring provisions as evidence of customary law.[37]

In parallel, the current absence of a World Investment Court does not necessarily indicate that this will always be the case. The EU–Canada Comprehensive Economic and Trade Agreement (CETA)[38] and the EU–Vietnam FTA include an Investment Court System (ICS), a standing bilateral court and an appellate tribunal for settling the investment disputes arising from the implementation of the agreements. Both Canada

---

[31] Agreement on Trade Related Aspects of Intellectual Property Rights (TRIPS), 15 April 1994, Marrakesh Agreement establishing the World Trade Organization, Annex 1C, 33 ILM 1997 (1994).

[32] See generally L. Vanhonnaeker, *Intellectual Property Rights as Foreign Direct Investments* (Edward Elgar 2015).

[33] General Agreement on Trade in Services (GATS), 15 April 1994, Marrakesh Agreement Establishing the World Trade Organization, Annex 1B, 33 ILM 1167 (1994).

[34] Agreement on Trade-Related Investment Measures (TRIMS), 15 April 1994, Annex 1A to the Marrakesh Agreement Establishing the World Trade Organization (WTO Agreement), 1868 UNTS 186.

[35] Havana Charter, Article 12.

[36] See generally Schill, *The Multilateralization of International Investment Law*.

[37] J.E. Alvarez, 'A BIT on Custom' (2010) 42 *NYU JIL & Policy* 17–80, 63. Contra see M. Sornarajah, 'A Coming Crisis: Expansionary Trends in Investment Treaty Arbitration', in K.P. Sauvant (ed.), *Appeals Mechanism in International Investment Disputes* (OUP 2008) 39–80, 44.

[38] 2016 EU-Canada Comprehensive Economic and Trade Agreement (CETA). The European Commission proposed the signature of the CETA to the Council of the EU in July 2016. The European Parliament voted in favour of CETA on 15 February 2017. The EU national parliaments must approve CETA before it can take full effect.

and the EU have also informally discussed the establishment of a World Investment Court, analogous to the World Trade Organization Appellate Body or the European Court of Human Rights.[39] They propose the inception of a standing court with judges nominated by the treaty parties, and an appellate body.[40] Finally, discussions are taking place on a global scale at the United Nations Commission on International Trade Law (UNCITRAL).[41]

Notwithstanding the persistent failures at the multilateral level, states have successfully negotiated IIAs at the bilateral and regional levels. Most IIAs are BITs.[42] Comprehensive economic cooperation agreements, FTAs and mega-regionals also include provisions on investments.[43] Whether regional agreements can provide a platform for future multilateral investment rules or undermine multilateralism remains to be seen.[44]

States sign IIAs for both economic and political reasons. States generally expect that the conclusion of such treaties will encourage FDI.[45] Therefore, both developed and developing countries strategically push IIAs albeit for different reasons. On the one hand, host countries – generally developing and least developed countries – compete to attract

---

[39] See C. Malmström, 'In Davos, Discussing Investment Disputes', *European Commission Blog*, 19 January 2017; A. Roberts, 'The Shifting Landscape of Investor–State Arbitration: Loyalists, Reformists, Revolutionaries and Undecideds', *International Economic Law and Policy Blog*, 15 June 2017.

[40] Ibid.

[41] G. Kaufmann-Kohler and M. Podestà, 'Challenges on the Road toward a Multilateral Investment Court', 201 *Columbia FDI Perspectives*, 5 June 2017.

[42] UNCTAD, *World Investment Report 2016*, 101 (reporting 2,946 BITs by the end of 2015).

[43] Ibid.

[44] T. Voon, 'Consolidating International Investment Law: The Mega-Regionals as a Pathway towards Multilateral Rules' (2017) *World Trade Review* 1–30, 6 (arguing that regional agreements can gradually lead to multilateralism). But see W. Alschner, 'Regionalism and Overlap in Investment Treaty Law: Towards Consolidation or Contradiction?' (2014) 17 JIEL 271–98, 284 (arguing that regionalism constitutes an obstacle to multilateralism).

[45] Some works doubt IIAs' positive impact on investment flows. See M. Hallward-Driemeier, 'Do Bilateral Investment Treaties Attract Foreign Direct Investment? Only a Bit … And They Could Bite', Policy Research Working Paper No. 3121 (World Bank 2003). However, other research suggests that IIAs can have a positive impact on investment flows. See J. Tobin and S. Rose-Ackerman, 'Foreign Direct Investment and the Business Environment in Developing Countries: The Impact of Bilateral Investment Treaties' (2005) *Yale Law and Economics Research Paper* No. 293, 1–52.

FDI and assume broad obligations for the protection of foreign investors in order to attract foreign investments. According to Guzman, LDCs 'face a prisoner's dilemma': while, as a group, they would be better off if they did not ratify IIAs, 'each individual LDC is better off "defecting" from the group by signing a BIT that gives it an advantage over other LDCs in the competition to attract foreign investment'.[46] Most developing countries adopting BITs overestimated the economic benefits of BITs, signed them because of 'foreign policy considerations',[47] and 'entirely ignored' their costs, including the risk of investment treaty claims, 'until their own country was hit by a claim'.[48]

On the other hand, industrialized countries sign IIAs to obtain favourable standards. In the aftermath of World War II, the customary international law governing foreign investment was ambiguous and lacked adequate enforcement mechanisms.[49] These flaws in the international investment regime hindered foreign investments; risk-adverse investors did not invest where there was little predictability regarding the protection of foreign investments under international law.[50] Consequently, capital exporting states began to fill this legal gap by negotiating BITs.[51]

Nowadays, the traditional distinction between capital importers and capital exporters has become blurred. Not only do industrialized countries compete to attract FDIs, but emerging economies also pursue their own investment treaty-making agenda.[52] The emerging awareness that both industrialized and developing countries compete for FDIs (and can be respondent in investment arbitration) has entailed a gradual

46 See A. Guzman, 'Explaining the Popularity of Bilateral Investment Treaties: Why LDCs Sign Treaties that Hurt Them' (1997) 38 *Virginia JIL* 639–88, 667.

47 C. Dupont and T. Schultz, 'Towards a New Heuristic Model: Investment Arbitration as a Political System' (2016) 7 JIDS 3–30, 16.

48 L.N. Skovgaard Poulsen, 'Bounded Rationality and the Diffusion of Modern Investment Treaties' (2014) 58 *International Studies Quarterly* 1–14, 2 (noting, at 5, that 'decision-makers tend either to exaggerate or entirely to ignore low-probability, high-impact risks').

49 J.W. Salacuse, 'The Emerging Global Regime for Investment' (2010) 51 *Harvard ILJ* 427–74, 439.

50 J.W. Salacuse and N.P. Sullivan, 'Do BITs Really Work? An Evaluation of Bilateral Investment Treaties and Their Grand Bargain' (2005) 46 *Harvard ILJ* 67–130, 76.

51 Ibid. 68–70.

52 V. Vadi, 'Converging Divergences: The Rise of Chinese Outward Foreign Investment and Its Implications for International (Investment) Law' (2012) *Yearbook of International Investment Law* 705–724.

recalibration of investment treaties. Nowadays, IIAs tend to reflect a more balanced approach to the protection of foreign investments than that taken in past decades.[53] In fact, recent IIAs include preambles, exceptions and carve-outs that restate the importance of non-economic concerns in international investment law and arbitration.

1.2 CONTENTS OF INVESTMENT TREATIES

While investment treaties differ in their details, their scope and content have become standardized over the years, as negotiations have been characterized by an ongoing sharing and borrowing of concepts.[54] The inclusion of the most favoured nation clause in most BITs also drives convergence in treaty interpretation. Moreover, arbitral tribunals have constantly drawn upon earlier cases – which, albeit not binding, constitute persuasive precedents – leading to the coalescence of a *jurisprudence constante*.[55] This section briefly examines this *common lexicon* of investment treaty law.[56]

Typically, after defining foreign investors and their investments, IIAs include provisions on non-discrimination (both national treatment and most favoured nation treatment), minimum standards, and fair and equitable treatment. Other common provisions in investment treaties concern the repatriation of profits and other investment-related funds or the promise to freeze the existing regulatory regime for the duration of the investment (stabilization clauses). A small number of investment treaties also include provisions prohibiting certain forms of performance requirements – i.e. obligations on investors to act in ways considered

---

[53] J.E. Alvarez, 'The Return of the State' (2011) 20 *Minnesota JIL* 223–64.

[54] C. McLachlan, 'The Principle of Systemic Integration and Article 31(3)(c) of the Vienna Convention' (2005) 54 ICLQ 279–320.

[55] See F.G. Sourgens, 'Law's Laboratory: Developing International Law on Investment Protection as Common Law' (2014) 34 *Northwestern JIL & Business* 181–247 (providing a theory of persuasive precedent in investor–state arbitration); A.K. Bjorklund, 'Investment Treaty Arbitral Decisions as Jurisprudence Constante', in C. Picker, I. Bunn and D. Arner (eds), *International Economic Law: The State and Future of the Discipline* (Hart Publishing 2008) 265–80. But see G. Kaufmann-Kohler, 'Arbitral Precedent: Dream, Necessity or Excuse?' (2007) 23 *Arbitration International* 357–78; Z. Douglas, 'Can a Doctrine of Precedent be Justified in Investment Arbitration?' (2010) 25 *ICSID Review – FILJ* 104–110.

[56] C. McLachlan, L. Shore and M. Weiniger, *International Investment Arbitration* (OUP 2007) 6.

beneficial for the host economy, mostly relating to local content, joint ventures, technology transfer and employment of nationals.

Protection against unlawful expropriation and guarantees of compensation in the event of nationalization, expropriation or indirect expropriation constitute the core of investment treaties. In general terms, states can expropriate private property; such expropriations are lawful provided certain conditions are met.[57] For instance, according to Article 1110 of the North American Free Trade Agreement (NAFTA):

> No Party may directly or indirectly nationalize or expropriate an investment of an investor of another Party in its territory or take a measure tantamount to nationalization or expropriation of such an investment, except: (a) for a public purpose; (b) on a non-discriminatory basis; (c) in accordance with due process of law and Article 1105(1); and (d) on payment of compensation.[58]

The concept of expropriation is broadly construed in investment treaties that not only protect foreign assets from the direct and full taking of property, but also from de facto or *indirect* expropriation. *Indirect expropriation* refers to measures that do not directly take investment property, but that interfere with its use, depriving the owner of its economic benefit.[59] Interference in the use of property or with the enjoyment of its benefits can constitute indirect expropriation even where the property has not been seized and the legal title of the property has not been affected.[60] If a host state targets a foreign investor by imposing very high taxes or regulatory requirements that may make the foreign investment economically unviable, this can constitute an indirect expropriation.

In particular, the central question raised by the so-called indirect expropriation is how to draw the line between legitimate regulations that do not give rise to compensation and regulatory takings that do.[61] States have an inherent right to regulate domestic affairs, including business activities.[62] Moreover, due to the rise of international treaties, 'states are

---

[57] P. Comeaux and N. Kinsella, *Protecting Foreign Investment under International Law* (Oceana Publications 1997) 77–8.

[58] NAFTA, Article 1110.

[59] B. Stern, 'In Search of the Frontiers of Indirect Expropriation', in A. Rovine (ed.), *Contemporary Issues in International Arbitration and Mediation* (Martinus Nijhoff 2008) 29–51.

[60] *Starrett Housing Corp. v. Iran*, 16 Iran–US CTR (1983) 112, 154.

[61] V. Lowe, 'Regulation or Expropriation?' (2002) 55 *Current Legal Problems* 447–66.

[62] *ADC Affiliate Ltd and ADC & ADMC Management Ltd v. Hungary*, ICSID No. ARB/03/16, Award, 2 October 2006, para. 423.

increasingly becoming subject to international obligations that require [them] to regulate'.[63] There is no settled approach to cases where investors allege that certain regulatory measures constitute a compensable form of expropriation. Thus, as Professor Schreuer points out, today, the most difficult question for an arbitrator faced with an allegation of expropriation is not so much whether the requirements for a legal expropriation have been met, but whether there has been an expropriation in the first place.[64]

Because IIAs include vague standards of investment protection, they do not give arbitral tribunals 'clear guidance as to the scope of obligations assumed under the treaties'.[65] Such vagueness can be an added value as it can 'accommodate new facts that the lawmaker might not be able to foresee or some valuable aims that might be involved in the situation'.[66] Moreover, 'too detailed a regulation might be difficult, if not impossible, to apprehend and apply'.[67] Therefore, some vagueness 'leav[es] some room for adjustment when necessary and avoid[s] unnecessary complexity'.[68] However, such vagueness has raised the question as to whether criteria such as proportionality and reasonableness can help the arbitrators to interpret and apply investment treaty provisions.

1.3 INVESTOR–STATE ARBITRATION

Investor–state arbitration has moved 'from a matter of peripheral academic interest to a matter of vital international concern'.[69] Since the 1980s, investor–state arbitration has become a standard feature in international investment treaties for the settlement of disputes that arise

---

63 S. Olynyk, 'A Balanced Approach to Distinguishing Between Legitimate Regulation and Indirect Expropriation in Investor-State Arbitration' (2012) 15 *International Trade and Business LR* 254–96.

64 C. Schreuer, 'The Concept of Expropriation under the ETC and other Investment Protection Treaties' (2005) 2 TDM 1–10.

65 S.W. Schill, 'Enhancing International Investment Law's Legitimacy: Conceptual and Methodological Foundations of a New Public Law Approach' (2011) 52 *Virginia JIL* 57–102, 66–7.

66 F.J. Urbina, 'A Critique of Proportionality' (2012) 57 *American Journal of Jurisprudence* 49–80, 63.

67 Ibid.

68 Ibid.

69 S.D. Franck, 'Development and Outcomes of Investment Treaty Arbitration' (2009) 50 *Harvard ILJ* 435–89, 435.

between the foreign investor and the host state.[70] Under this mechanism, foreign investors may bring claims against the host state before international arbitral tribunals. This differs from the traditional paradigm of states as the only subjects of international law and the only ones having the capacity to raise international claims against other states in legal proceedings.[71] Not only is the number of investment treaty arbitrations continuously rising, reaching a total of 696 publicly known cases by the end of 2015,[72] but the high profile of several investment disputes in key areas has caused investor–state arbitration to attract the sustained interest of policy makers, scholars and the public at large. Investor–state arbitration is a truly global phenomenon: 124 states were sued via investor–state arbitration between 1990 and 2014[73] and 'investors from over 70 countries have filed investment arbitrations representing increasingly diversified industries'.[74]

Investor–state arbitration depoliticizes disputes between foreign investors and the host states.[75] It constitutes a rule-based dispute-settlement mechanism for resolving investment disputes[76] that shield such disputes from power politics[77] and insulates them from the diplomatic relations between states.[78] The depoliticization of investment disputes benefits: (1) foreign investors; (2) the host state; and (3) the home state.[79] First, foreign investors no longer have to rely on the vagaries of diplomatic protection;[80] they no longer depend on the discretion of their home states as to whether a claim can be raised against another state.[81] Rather, they

---

[70] D. Sedlak, 'ICSID's Resurgence in International Investment Arbitration: Can the Momentum Hold?' (2004) 23 *Penn State International LR* 147–71.

[71] A. Newcombe and L. Paradell, *Law and Practice of Investment Treaties* (Kluwer Law International 2009) 44–5.

[72] UNCTAD, *World Investment Report 2016*, 104.

[73] R. Wellhausen, 'Recent Trends in Investor–State Dispute Settlement' (2016) 7 JIDS 117–35, 126.

[74] Dupont and Schultz, 'Towards a New Heuristic Model', 22.

[75] S. Puig, 'No Right without a Remedy: Foundations of Investor–State Arbitration' (2013–2014) 35 *University of Pennsylvania JIL* 829–61, 848.

[76] Ibid.

[77] Ibid. 853.

[78] S. Puig, 'Recasting ICSID's Legitimacy Debate: Towards a Goal-Based Empirical Agenda' (2013) 36 *Fordham ILJ* 465–504, 485–7.

[79] A. Roberts, 'Triangular Treaties: The Extent and Limits of Investment Treaty Rights' (2015) 56 *Harvard ILJ* 353–417, 390.

[80] Puig, 'No Right without a Remedy', 844.

[81] M. Sornarajah, *The Settlement of Foreign Investment Disputes* (Kluwer Law International 2000) 61–84.

can bring direct claims and make strategic choices in the conduct of the proceedings.[82] In this regard, investor–state arbitration can facilitate access to justice for foreign investors[83] and provides a neutral forum for the settlement of investment disputes.[84] It is perceived to be necessary to render meaningful the more substantive investment treaty provisions.[85] Second, the depoliticization of investment disputes protects the host state,[86] by reducing the interference of the home country in the domestic affairs of the host state. It prevents or 'limit[s] unwelcome diplomatic, economic and perhaps military pressure from strong states whose nationals believe they have been injured'.[87] Third, the depoliticization of investment disputes also protects the home state in that it no longer has 'to become embroiled in investor–state disputes'.[88]

While investor–state arbitration has become increasingly popular among investors, and the number of investment treaty arbitrations has grown significantly, the regime has attracted criticism by scholars, states and society. The principal concern is that international investment law and arbitration can adversely affect state regulatory autonomy in important public policy-related fields, and even prevent regulation in such fields (the so-called regulatory chill).[89] Some scholars contend that the investment regime is facing a 'legitimacy crisis'.

1.4 THE 'LEGITIMACY CRISIS' OF INTERNATIONAL INVESTMENT LAW

Is international investment law and arbitration facing a 'legitimacy crisis'? A multidimensional concept used in different fields of study, legitimacy indicates the acceptance of a legal system.[90] A system is

---

82 Puig, 'Recasting ICSID's Legitimacy Debate', 485.

83 F. Francioni, 'Access to Justice, Denial of Justice and International Investment Law' (2009) 20 EJIL 729–47.

84 Puig, 'No Right without a Remedy', 846.

85 T. Wälde, 'The "Umbrella" (or Sanctity of Contract/Pacta sunt Servanda) Clause in Investment Arbitration' (2004) 1 TDM 1–13.

86 Roberts, 'Triangular Treaties', 389–90.

87 J. Pauwelyn, 'At the Edge of Chaos? Foreign Investment Law as a Complex Adaptive System' (2014) 29 *ICSID Review* 372–418, 404.

88 Roberts, 'Triangular Treaties', 390.

89 G. Van Harten and D.N. Scott, 'Investment Treaties and the Internal Vetting of Regulatory Proposals: A Case Study from Canada' (2016) 7 JIDS 92–116.

90 J.M. Coicaud, *Legitimacy and Politics* (CUP 2002) 10.

considered to be legitimate when it operates in a manner that is consistent with widely held values, norms and beliefs. The legitimacy of the international legal system in general and the investment treaty regime in particular has been discussed intensively.[91] Scholars have questioned whether international (investment) law lacks input legitimacy, criticizing how arbitrators are selected, the procedures by which arbitral awards are rendered and the power exercised.[92] They have questioned whether international investment law lacks output legitimacy, that is, reasonable performance.[93] They have also questioned whether international (investment) law has yielded to power struggles, neglected non-economic interests in favour of economic ones and privileged foreign investors over states.[94]

Legitimacy concerns relate to both substantive and procedural aspects of the investment regime.[95] From a substantive perspective, international investment law in general, and investor–state arbitration in particular, are seen as having an increasing impact on sovereign policy objectives.[96] States sign and ratify IIAs to attract FDIs and promote (sustainable) development.[97] However, they do not surrender their ability to govern.[98] Yet, investment arbitrations can (and have) touch(ed) upon key public

[91] On the legitimacy of international investment law see e.g. D. Schneiderman, 'Legitimacy and Reflexivity in International Investment Arbitration: A New Self-Restraint?' (2011) 2 JIDS 471–95; C.N. Brower and S.W. Schill, 'Is Arbitration a Threat or a Boom to the Legitimacy of International Investment Law?' (2008) *Chicago JIL* 471–98.

[92] J. Bonnitcha, L.N. Skovgaard Poulsen and M. Waibel, *The Political Economy of the Investment Treaty Regime* (OUP 2017) Ch. 9.

[93] Ibid.

[94] R. Wolfrum, 'Legitimacy of International Law from a Legal Perspective: Some Introductory Considerations', in R. Wolfrum and V. Roeben (eds), *Legitimacy in International Law* (Springer 2008) 1–24, 2.

[95] D.D. Caron, 'Investor–State Arbitration: Strategic and Tactical Perspectives on Legitimacy' (2009) 32 *Suffolk Transnational LR* 513–24, 514–15.

[96] Guntrip, 'Self-determination and Foreign Direct Investment', 829–30.

[97] G. Scelle, 'Essai sur les sources formelles du droit international', in *Recueil d'Etudes sur les sources du droit en l'honneur de François Gény* (vol. III) (Sirey 1934) 400–430, 410 (highlighting the *dédoublement fonctionnel* of states).

[98] C.M. Ryan, 'Meeting Expectations: Assessing the Long-Term Legitimacy and Stability of International Investment Law' (2008) 29 *University of Pennsylvania JIL* 725–62, 752.

interests, ranging from access to water[99] to tobacco control,[100] and from environmental protection[101] to cultural heritage management.[102] As a result, both scholars and practitioners contend that international investment law and arbitration is constraining the regulatory autonomy of the state.[103] Concerns have arisen that IIAs 'become a charter of rights for foreign investors, with no concomitant responsibilities or liabilities, no direct legal links to promoting development objectives, and no protection for public welfare in the face of environmentally or socially destabilizing foreign investment'.[104]

Alongside these substantive concerns, several procedural factors feed into the perception of a legitimacy crisis. Investor–state tribunals are constituted ad hoc, under different arbitral rules. The fact that arbitrators are untenured can fuel the perception of conflicts of interest within or between arbitral tribunals. While the selection of arbitrators can lead to requests for disqualification, such requests are rarely successful, fuelling a presumption of bias. There is no appellate court to ensure consistency in their rulings. Inconsistent awards have caused concern,[105] leaving many observers with the impression that international investment arbitration lacks coherence.[106] Lack of transparency may preclude public awareness of the very existence of investor–state arbitrations. Forum-shopping – either by using the most-favoured-nation (MFN) clause, or by

---

[99] See A.M. Daza-Clark, *International Investment Law and Water Resources Management* (Brill 2016).

[100] See V. Vadi, *Public Health in International Investment Law and Arbitration* (Routledge 2012).

[101] See J.E. Viñuales, *Foreign Investment and the Environment in International Law* (CUP 2012).

[102] See V. Vadi, *Cultural Heritage in International Investment Law and Arbitration* (CUP 2014).

[103] See generally M. Waibel, A. Kaushal, K.-H.L. Chung and C. Balchin, 'The Blacklash against Investment Arbitration: Perceptions and Reality', in M. Waibel, A. Kaushal, K.-H.L. Chung and C. Balchin (eds), *The Blacklash against Investment Arbitration: Perceptions and Reality* (Kluwer Law International 2010) xxxviii.

[104] H. Mann, 'The Right of States to Regulate and International Investment Law: A Comment', in UNCTAD, *The Development Dimension of FDI: Policy and Rule-Making Perspectives* (UN 2003) 212–23.

[105] Compare *Lauder v. Czech Republic*, UNCITRAL, Final Award, 3 September 2001 and *CME Czech Republic BV v. Czech Republic*, UNCITRAL, Partial Award, 13 September 2001 and Final Award, 14 March 2003.

[106] S. Franck, 'The Legitimacy Crisis in Investment Treaty Arbitration: Privatizing Public International Law through Inconsistent Decisions' (2005) 73 *Fordham LR* 1521–625, 1537–8.

corporate restructuring in order to be protected by a given IIA – risks altering 'the delicate equilibrium between the complainant's freedom of choice … and protection to the defendant', in addition to increasing the risk of conflicting awards.[107]

In response to growing unrest about the international investment law regime, states have increasingly felt the need to protect their regulatory space and to limit arbitral discretion. While a few developing countries withdrew from the ICSID system,[108] other countries moved away from the Energy Charter Treaty. While several countries terminated existing IIAs,[109] others omitted investor–state arbitration from the provisions of their treaties.[110] Finally, several states are revising their model BITs, reducing the level of protection provided by such templates, and expanding the scope of exception clauses.[111] States have also shown growing reluctance to comply with orders and awards of investment tribunals.[112]

The ongoing debate as to the perceived legitimacy of the international investment regime highlights the need for some rethinking of the system. Such debate has both evolutionary and revolutionary potential.[113] On the one hand, evolutionary approaches assume that the international investment regime is experiencing growth pains, but many legitimacy concerns 'can be resolved over time'.[114] Evolutionary approaches rely on the traditional tools of treaty interpretation to fine tune international investment law to emerging circumstances. On the other hand, revolutionary approaches assume that the overall structure of the international investment regime is deeply flawed and requires some major reforms.[115] Revolutionary approaches suggest, *inter alia*, returning to state-to-state

[107] L.E. Salles, *Forum Shopping in International Adjudication* (CUP 2014) 46.

[108] See S. Ripinsky, 'Venezuela's Withdrawal from ICSID: What it Does and Does Not Achieve', *ITN*, 13 April 2012 (noting that Bolivia, Ecuador and Venezuela have withdrawn from the ICSID Convention).

[109] T. Voon and A.D. Mitchell, 'Denunciation, Termination and Survival: The Interplay of Treaty Law and International Investment Law' (2016) 31 *ICSID Review* 413–33.

[110] J. Kurtz, 'Australia's Rejection of Investor–State Arbitration: Causation, Omission and Implication' (2012) 27 *ICSID Review* 65–86.

[111] Ryan, 'Meeting Expectations', 761.

[112] Schill, 'Enhancing International Investment Law's Legitimacy', 64.

[113] D. Behn, 'Legitimacy, Evolution, and Growth in Investment Treaty Arbitration: Empirically Evaluating the State of the Art' (2015) 46 *Georgetown JIL* 363–415, 369.

[114] Ibid.

[115] Ibid.

dispute resolution, the introduction of an appeals body to review arbitral awards, and the institution of a permanent World Investment Court.[116]

The use of concepts such as proportionality, reasonableness and standards of review in international investment law and arbitration can simultaneously belong to both evolutionary and revolutionary scenarios. On the one hand, *de lege lata*, proportionality, reasonableness and standards of review can be seen as jurisprudential techniques to interpret vague investment treaty provisions and balance private and public interests in investor–state arbitration. Some even argue that proportionality and reasonableness are general principles of international law, and therefore can be applied as sources of law within investment arbitration.[117] On the other hand, *de lege ferenda*, proportionality, reasonableness and standards of review can be inserted in the text of IIAs.[118]

In both evolutionary and revolutionary scenarios, legitimacy concerns do not play only a negative role indicating dissatisfaction with how the system works. They can also have a positive function in that they can be perceived as tools to strengthen the system's perceived legitimacy by raising important issues, stimulating debate and spurring novel approaches.[119] They should be taken into account to allow the investment treaty system to develop properly. Whether states will opt for evolutionary or revolutionary approaches to the system remains to be seen.

1.5 THE DIFFERENT CONCEPTUALIZATIONS OF INVESTMENT TREATY ARBITRATION

International investment law and arbitration oscillates between national and international law, and private and public law, historically 'borrowing elements from different legal structures'.[120] Given its hybrid features, international investment law and arbitration has been considered to be a system of its own kind and has been analogized to different legal systems, including international commercial arbitration, public law and international law (and within the latter, principally, albeit not exclusively,

---

[116] Schill, 'Enhancing International Investment Law's Legitimacy', 168 (listing the various institutional reform proposals but endorsing evolutionary approaches).

[117] See Chapter 3 and 4 below.

[118] For instance, different parts of the CETA refer to proportionality. See e.g. Article 8.39.5 of CETA (on the adjustment of costs).

[119] Ryan, 'Meeting Expectations', 761.

[120] Puig, 'Recasting ICSID's Legitimacy Debate', 479.

WTO law and human rights law).[121] These analogies are heuristic models used to better understand international investment law and arbitration, and to make sense of the related available knowledge. These analogies are descriptive in nature, and reflect and emphasize some aspects of the system rather than others.

However, far from having a purely theoretical character, the selection of the appropriate analogy is a struggle for the soul of international investment law. In this respect, the appropriate analogy does not merely concern the form, methods and procedure, but also the substance, aims and objectives of international investment law. The debate on the appropriate analogy is a struggle for interpretive power, with the resulting ability to impose a predominant discourse and tame divergent narratives. As Schill aptly points out, 'a culture clash of different epistemic communities' is taking place, 'because private commercial and public international lawyers often have different perspectives on, and different philosophies about, the role of law, the state, and the function of dispute resolution'.[122]

The outcome of this debate is important because it will likely influence the evolution of the field. Not only can analogies explain the past and present of international investment law and arbitration, but they can also shape its future. While different analogies compete for describing and explaining international investment law and arbitration, they can (and have) facilitate(d) the transplantation of concepts from given legal fields to the investment regime.[123]

This section illuminates the way international investment law and arbitration has been compared to other systems such as international commercial arbitration, public law adjudication and international law. Within international law, it also examines how international investment law has been analogized to human rights law and WTO law. After highlighting the promises and pitfalls of such comparisons, the section briefly concludes that comparisons are not neutral, and that the selection of the comparator often depends on the perspective of who draws the

---

121 See generally V. Vadi, *Analogies in International Investment Law and Arbitration* (CUP 2016); A. Roberts, 'Clash of Paradigms: Actors and Analogies Shaping the Investment Treaty System' (2013) 107 AJIL 45–94; V. Vadi, 'Critical Comparisons: the Role of Comparative Law in Investment Treaty Arbitration' (2010) 39 *Denver JIL & Policy* 67–100.

122 Schill, 'Enhancing International Investment Law's Legitimacy', 72.

123 For an analogous argument in relation to other legal fields, see S. Roy, 'Privileging (Some Forms of) Interdisciplinarity and Interpretation: Methods in Comparative Law' (2014) 12 IJCL 786–807, 787.

analogy. At the same time, analogies are useful epistemic tools to study the international investment regime and identify trajectories of the field. They also enable scholars and practitioners to better contextualize the debate on the use of criteria such as proportionality, reasonableness and standards of review in international investment law and arbitration.

1.5.1 The Commercial Law Paradigm

Because of the procedural rules that govern it, investor–state arbitration has been analogized to commercial arbitration.[124] Arbitrators are appointed by the parties and/or an appointing institution; most hearings are held behind closed doors. The parties select the applicable law, and there is no appeal mechanism. Awards rendered against host states are, in theory, readily enforceable against host state property worldwide, due to the widespread adoption of the New York[125] and Washington Conventions,[126] which provide for the prompt enforceability of foreign arbitral awards and ICSID awards respectively. The awards have only limited avenues for revision and cannot be amended by the domestic courts.[127] Furthermore, ICSID arbitrations are wholly exempted from the supervision of local courts, with awards being subject only to an internal annulment process.[128] The grounds for annulment are narrow and concern due process issues: i.e. the tribunal was not properly constituted; it manifestly exceeded its powers; there was corruption on the part of a member; there was a fundamental serious departure from a procedural rule; or the award did not state the reasons on which it was based.

The procedural features of investor–arbitration can be explained in light of the origins of the system.[129] For a long time, most investment disputes had a commercial nature; and both home and host states

---

124 N. Blackaby, 'Investment Arbitration and Commercial Arbitration (or the Tale of the Dolphin and the Shark)', in J.D.M. Lew and L. Mistelis (eds), *Pervasive Problems in International Arbitration* (Kluwer Law International 2006) 217–33.

125 Convention on the Recognition and Enforcement of Foreign Arbitral Awards (New York Convention) 10 June 1958, 330 UNTS 38.

126 Convention on the Settlement of Investment Disputes between States and Nationals of Other States, Washington DC, 18 March 1965, in force 14 October 1966, 575 UNTS 159.

127 New York Convention, Article V.

128 ICSID Convention, Article 53.

129 Pauwelyn, 'At the Edge of Chaos?', 408.

preferred to keep the dispute behind closed doors.[130] Nowadays, investment disputes include not only contract but treaty claims and relate to a wide variety of state conduct, ranging from its commercial behaviour to regulation.[131] Yet, 'as much as the types of claims and disputes changed, the method of settling these disputes remained the same'.[132] The commercial arbitration perspective emphasizes the private law aspects of investor–state arbitration, such as party autonomy and party equality.[133]

However, 'investment treaty arbitration differs from international commercial arbitration in several regards, namely the subject matter of the disputes [and] the relationship of the parties'.[134] While commercial arbitration generally involves private parties and concerns disputes of a commercial nature, investor–state arbitration involves states and private actors and may concern disputes of a public law nature.[135] As investment treaty arbitrations are often regulatory disputes, the resulting awards 'may directly affect the social fabric of the host state'.[136] Moreover, 'investment treaty arbitration affects third parties and their behavior intensely, as the outcome of arbitrations … not only affect future interpretations of similar standards and shape the expectations of investors and states about the decision-making of tribunals, but also affect investment treaty making'.[137]

1.5.2 The Public Law Paradigm

International investment law has been conceptualized as being akin to domestic public law, because of functional analogy.[138] Like domestic public law, international investment law governs 'the relation of private

---

130 Ibid.

131 Ibid.

132 Ibid.

133 Schill, 'Enhancing International Investment Law's Legitimacy', 72.

134 Ibid. 75.

135 See J. Paulsson, 'International Arbitration is not Arbitration' (2008) 2 *Stockholm International Arbitration Review* 1–20.

136 Schill, 'Enhancing International Investment Law's Legitimacy', 76.

137 Ibid. 85.

138 G. Van Harten, *Investment Treaty Arbitration and Public Law* (OUP 2007); S. Montt, *State Liability in Investment Treaty Arbitration: Global Constitutional Law and Administrative Law in the BIT Generation* (Hart Publishing 2009); A. Kulick, *Global Public Interest in International Investment Law* (CUP 2012); S.W. Schill, 'International Investment Law and Comparative Public Law: An Introduction', in S.W. Schill (ed.), *International Investment Law and Comparative Public Law* (OUP 2010) 3–38.

economic actors and governmental power'.[139] In the same way that domestic public law protects private property, prohibits discrimination and endorses rule of law standards for the treatment of private interests, international investment law provides for the protection of foreign direct investments, prohibits discrimination and 'endorse[s] rule of law standards for the treatment of foreign investors by states'.[140]

While investment treaty arbitration structurally resembles a private model of adjudication, substantively, it gives arbitrators a comprehensive jurisdiction over what are essentially regulatory disputes.[141] Adjudication over a state's *acta jure imperii* implies a significant departure from the conventional use of international commercial arbitration.[142] Arbitral awards ultimately shape the relationship between a state, on the one hand, and private individuals, on the other,[143] determining matters such as the legality of governmental activity, the degree to which individuals should be protected from regulation, and the appropriate role of the state.[144] Many of the recent arbitral awards have concerned the determination of the appropriate boundary between two conflicting values: the legitimate sphere for state regulation in the pursuit of public goods; and the protection of foreign investment from state interference.

The public law perspective views international investment law and arbitration as constraining the exercise of state power vis-à-vis private interests.[145] It considers the international investment regime as governing the *transnational* relationship between foreign investors and the host state, rather than *international* relations among states.[146] It encourages arbitral tribunals to interpret and apply vague investment treaty provisions 'expan[ding] public law thinking within the existing structure of investment treaty arbitration itself'.[147] Proponents of the public law perspective recommend using public law concepts such as proportionality

---

139 Schill, 'Enhancing International Investment Law's Legitimacy', 60.

140 Ibid. 59.

141 G. Van Harten, 'The Public–Private Distinction in the International Arbitration of Individual Claims against the State' (2007) 56 ICLQ 371–94, 371.

142 Z. Douglas, 'The Hybrid Foundations of Investment Treaty Arbitration' (2003) 74 BYIL 151–289, 221–2.

143 Van Harten, *Investment Treaty Arbitration and Public Law*, 70.

144 M. Sornarajah, 'The Clash of Globalizations and the International Law on Foreign Investment' (2003) 12 *Canadian Foreign Policy* 1–32, 17.

145 C.E. Foster, 'A New Stratosphere? Investment Treaty Arbitration as "Internationalized Public Law"' (2015) 64 ICLQ 461–85, 463.

146 Ibid.

147 Schill, 'Enhancing International Investment Law's Legitimacy', 57.

in investor–state arbitration[148] 'to guide the interpretation of investment treaties, to understand the role and powers of investment treaty tribunals, and to develop suggestions for legal reform'.[149] Moreover, comparative public analysis can be used to identify general principles of law, which are a source of international (investment) law according to Article 38(1)(c) of the Statute of the International Court of Justice.[150]

The literature advancing a public law approach to international investment law and arbitration 'has been invaluable in generating an awareness ... that investment disputes are public in character'.[151] It has also highlighted the important linkage between comparative law and international law in the genesis of general principles of international law. It has contributed to bringing international investment law to the forefront of international legal debate.

However, 'international investment law remains an international discipline that is detached from the domestic public law of any one state'.[152] Public law approaches risk 'confusing resemblance with equivalence'.[153] The fact that investor–state arbitration is analogous to judicial review does not mean that it is judicial review.[154] Arbitral tribunals have narrower remedies than constitutional courts.[155] Arbitral tribunals rarely award restitution; rather, they award compensation and damages.[156] While public law approaches emphasize the role of states as trustees of their population's well-being, they risk neglecting the fact that states 'have certain basic obligations toward the rest of humanity' under public international law,[157] thus overlooking 'the power of international law to advance international public policy in economic and non-economic

---

[148] B. Kingsbury and S. Schill, 'Public Law Concepts to Balance Investors' Rights with State Regulatory Actions in the Public Interest: The Concept of Proportionality', in S. Schill (ed.), *International Investment Law and Comparative Public Law* (OUP 2010) 75–105.

[149] Schill, 'Enhancing International Investment Law's Legitimacy', 60.

[150] Ibid. 89.

[151] Foster, 'A New Stratosphere?', 462.

[152] Schill, 'Enhancing International Investment Law's Legitimacy', 86.

[153] J.E. Alvarez, 'Is Investor–State Arbitration Public?' (2016) 7 JIDS 534–76, 545.

[154] Ibid.

[155] Ibid.

[156] B. Sabahi, *Compensation and Restitution in Investor–State Arbitration* (OUP 2011) 91.

[157] E. Benvenisti, 'Sovereigns as Trustees of Humanity: On the Accountability of States to Foreign Stakeholders' (2013) 107 AJIL 295–333, 308.

spheres in an integrated and coordinated way'.[158] The public law approach risks increasing the fragmentation of international law and diluting its universality.[159] Finally, by mandating the adoption of public law analogies and the migration of constitutional ideas from the domestic sphere to the international realm, there is a risk of neglecting the cultural background of such concepts and their suitability to public international law in general and international investment law in particular.[160] Therefore, international law scholars have argued that while investor–state arbitration has public law features, it remains 'a creature of public international law'.[161]

1.5.3 The International Law Paradigm

International investment law and arbitration is a subfield of public international law.[162] International investment agreements are international law treaties. Not only do investment treaty obligations 'apply irrespective of internal law',[163] but, as Crawford suggests, '[i]nvestment law ... is about the way in which we bring the state under some measure of control, which is the main aspiration of general international law'.[164] The limited powers available to states to review arbitral awards confirm the primacy of international law obligations over national law.

International investment law 'borrows important legal infrastructure from international law'.[165] International law governs the interpretation and application of investment treaties, including the jurisdiction, competence and powers of arbitral tribunals.[166] Like other international courts and tribunals, arbitral tribunals have to settle disputes in conformity with

---

158 Foster, 'Investment Treaty Arbitration as Internationalized Public Law', 481.

159 Ibid.

160 Vadi, *Analogies in International Investment Law and Arbitration*, 195–207.

161 Alvarez, 'Is Investor–State Arbitration Public?', 540.

162 Schill, 'Enhancing International Investment Law's Legitimacy', 73.

163 Alvarez, 'Is Investor–State Arbitration Public?', 566.

164 J. Crawford, 'International Protection of Foreign Direct Investment: between Clinical Isolation and Systematic Integration', in R. Hofmann and C.J. Tams (eds), *International Investment Law and General International Law: From Clinical Isolation to Systemic Integration?* (Nomos 2011) 17–28, 22.

165 Puig, 'Recasting ICSID's Legitimacy Debate', 480.

166 Ibid.

international law.[167] Customary rules of treaty interpretation, as restated by the Vienna Convention on the Law of Treaties, and in particular Article 31(3)(c), enable ICSID arbitrators to take into account other international law regimes when interpreting an IIA.[168]

Considering international investment law and arbitration as a subfield of international law means that IIAs are viewed as contributing to the governance of international relations between states.[169] In parallel, such an approach 'brings with it the expectation that legal relations between states will serve as vehicles for carrying forward ... international public policies for economic, social, cultural, health, environmental and vital related purposes'.[170] Within public international law, economic aims and objectives 'are pursued as only one dimension of an integrated set of public policies'.[171]

In order to clarify and operationalize vague investment treaty provisions, public international lawyers propose comparative reasoning, drawing parallels between international investment law and other fields of public international law that fulfill analogous functions in restraining the exercise of state power vis-à-vis non-state actors. They propose 'crossregime analysis, drawing, for example, on WTO or human rights law'.[172] For instance, private enforcement of international investment law has been analogized to the private enforcement of human rights law; the limited influence of states on the arbitral process has been analogized to the limited influence that WTO member states have on the WTO dispute-settlement proceedings. Not only can such an approach 'ensure cross regime consistency' and defragment the fragmentation of international law 'by stressing commonalities and openness of international investment law towards other international regimes', but it can also reinforce the perceived legitimacy of the international investment regime.[173]

---

[167] C. McLachlan, 'Investment Treaties and General International Law' (2008) 57 ICLQ 361–401; S.W. Schill, 'System-Building in Investment Treaty Arbitration and Lawmaking' (2011) 12 *German LJ*, 1083–1110, 1088.

[168] Alvarez, 'A New Stratosphere? Is Investor–State Arbitration Public?', 548, 560.

[169] Foster, 'Investment Treaty Arbitration as Internationalized Public Law', 463.

[170] Ibid.

[171] Ibid. 473.

[172] Schill, 'Enhancing International Investment Law's Legitimacy', 88.

[173] Ibid. 88.

Even accepting the theoretical merit of comparative reasoning in a developing field such as international investment law and arbitration, in practice, international lawyers must be mindful that analogies are not neutral, and the selection of the given comparator can have significant implications on the field.[174] Within the matrix of international law, some specific analogies are drawn between international investment law and human rights law, on the one hand, and between international investment law and international trade law, on the other.

1.5.3.1 Human rights law

Human rights law and international investment law are often juxtaposed for both substantive and procedural reasons.[175] At the substantive level, human rights law and international investment law provide for analogous standards of protection.[176] Suffice it to mention that the following binary standards are available under international investment law and human rights law respectively: denial of justice and the right to a fair trial; full protection and certain aspects of the rights to privacy, liberty and life; expropriation and the right to property; fair and equitable treatment and due process; national treatment and non-discrimination.[177]

At the procedural level, access to investor–state arbitration shares many characteristics of the direct right of action before human rights courts.[178] While states are the traditional subjects of international law, both human rights law and international investment law empower individuals to bring claims against states before international courts and tribunals. Both branches of international law are characterized by a

---

174 Vadi, 'Critical Comparisons', 100 ('comparisons are not a neutral or objective phenomenon').

175 See generally U. Kriebaum and C. Schreuer, 'The Concept of Property in Human Rights Law and International Investment Law', in S. Breitenmoser (ed.), *Liber Amicorum Luzius Wildhaber: Human Rights Democracy and the Rule of Law* (Nomos 2007) 743–62. See also C. Tomuschat, 'The European Court of Human Rights and Investment Protection', in C. Binder, U. Kriebaum, A. Reinisch and S. Wittich (eds), *International Investment Law for the 21st Century: Essays in Honour of Christoph Schreuer* (OUP 2009) Ch. 34.

176 See M. Paparinskis, 'Analogies and Other Regimes of International Law', in Z. Douglas, J. Pauwelyn and J.E. Viñuales (eds), *The Foundations of International Investment Law: Bringing Theory into Practice* (OUP 2014) Ch. 3.

177 Ibid.

178 C. Reiner and C. Schreuer, 'Human Rights and International Investment Arbitration', in P.-M. Dupuy, F. Francioni and E.-U. Petersmann (eds), *Human Rights in International Investment Law and Arbitration* (OUP 2008) 82–96.

bottom-up approach to dispute settlement, which make them very dynamic fields of study.

However, international investment law and human rights law have different aims and objectives, as well as different substantive and procedural features.[179] Such differences discourage making any broad analogies. While international investment law aims at promoting (sustainable) development, international human rights law aims at protecting, promoting and fulfilling human rights. While international investment law primarily pursues economic objectives, international human rights law pursues other values. Obligations under international investment law are bilateral and reciprocal; obligations under human rights law are *erga omnes* and do not rely on reciprocity.[180] This does not mean that there may not be some forms of meaningful overlap, as economic development can be a factor in human well-being.

The procedural requirements for having access to investment treaty arbitration differ considerably from those for having access to human rights courts. For instance, in human rights law, the exhaustion of local remedies is a procedural requirement for the admissibility of a claim. By contrast, in international investment law, the exhaustion of local remedies is required only with regard to denial of justice claims – i.e. the claimant cannot invoke denial of justice without prior exhaustion of local remedies. However, the exhaustion of local remedies may not be necessary for other investment treaty claims; rather, it may be precluded by the fork-in-the-road provision. This provision allows the investor to select the desired venue for filing his/her claim, but precludes subsequent recourse to other dispute-settlement mechanisms. Therefore, arbitral tribunals do not merely constitute an additional forum with respect to state courts (as is the case for all international human rights courts), but they are also an alternative to the latter.

While human rights instruments have advocated a human-rights-sensitive interpretation of international investment agreements,[181] it is worth mentioning that such an approach can have a dual effect. On the

---

[179] M. Hirsch, 'Investment Tribunals and Human Rights: Divergent Paths', in P.-M. Dupuy, F. Francioni and E.-U. Petersmann (eds), *Human Rights in International Investment Law and Arbitration* (OUP 2008) 97–114.

[180] E. de Wet and J. Vidmar (eds), *Hierarchy in International Law: The Place of Human Rights* (OUP 2012).

[181] See e.g. Economic and Social Council, Commission on Human Rights, Sub-commission on the Promotion and Protection of Human Rights, Report of the High Commissioner for Human Rights, Trade and Investment, E/CN.4 /Sub.2/2003/9, 2 July 2003.

one hand, it can enhance the state's right to regulate in the public interest, thus restricting investors' property rights. On the other hand, it can also reinforce the protection of investors' rights. For instance, a number of regional human rights instruments protect property rights, and there is a growing body of human rights jurisprudence involving the protection of property rights. However, some scholars wonder whether arbitrators would be able to apply human rights law in a way that is consistent with the interpretation provided by human rights courts.[182]

1.5.3.2 WTO law

International investment law and international trade law are often viewed as similar due to perceived substantive, sociological and procedural commonalities.[183] From a substantive perspective, the case for drawing such an analogy is evident. Both regimes govern global economic integration, promote transnational business, and aim to foster (sustainable) development.[184] Both seek to overcome protectionism and limit discrimination.[185] Both are 'branches of international economic law'.[186] Moreover, certain international trade treaties present an articulated regime that the investment treaties presuppose. For instance, the TRIMS, the TRIPS and the GATS bring FDI into the trade fold.[187] If international investment law and international trade law are not yet merging,[188] they

---

[182] J.E. Alvarez, 'Beware: Boundary Crossings – A Critical Appraisal of Public Law Approaches to International Investment Law' (2016) 17 JWIT 171–228, 214.

[183] Vadi, *Analogies in International Investment Law and Arbitration*, 209.

[184] Ibid.

[185] But see N. DiMascio and J. Pauwelyn, 'Non-Discrimination in Trade and Investment Treaties: Worlds Apart or Two Sides of the Same Coin?' (2008) 102 AJIL 48–89 (suggesting that while international investment law is about protecting foreign investors and individual rights, international trade law is about liberalization and state-to-state exchange of market opportunities).

[186] D. McRae, 'The World Trade Organization and International Investment Law: Converging Systems – Can the Case for Convergence be Made?' (2014) 9 *Jerusalem Review of Legal Studies* 13–23, 14.

[187] Agreement on Trade-Related Investment Measures (TRIMS), 15 April 1994, Marrakesh Agreement Establishing the World Trade Organization, Annex 1A, 1868 UNTS 186; Agreement on Trade-Related Aspects of Intellectual Property Rights (TRIPS), 15 April 1994, Marrakesh Agreement Establishing the World Trade Organization, Annex 1C, 1869 UNTS 299; General Agreement on Trade in Services (GATS), 15 April 1994, Marrakesh Agreement Establishing the World Trade Organization, Annex 1B, 1869 UNTS 183.

[188] S. Puig, 'The Merging of International Trade and Investment Law' (2015) 33 *Berkeley JIL* 1–59, 1.

certainly converge to a certain extent.[189] From a sociological perspective, Members of the WTO Appellate Body often sit on investor–state arbitration.[190]

From a procedural perspective, arbitral tribunals and the WTO dispute-settlement organs essentially share the same functions by settling international disputes in accordance with international economic law. WTO panels, the Appellate Body, and arbitral tribunals are often asked to strike a balance between economic and non-economic concerns. Disputes that cross the boundary between the two regimes are increasing.[191] Moreover, analogizing international investment law to international trade law can facilitate the cross-pollination of concepts and provide predictability.[192] Given 'the almost universal participation in the WTO' of states that are parties to IIAs, WTO law would be relevant in investor–state arbitration under Article 31(3)(c) of the VCLT, which requires adjudicators to 'tak[e] into account, together with context ... any relevant rules of international law applicable in the relations between the parties'.[193]

However, there are significant institutional differences between the two systems. While the WTO is an international organization administering a 'cohesive multilateral system', IIAs have a bilateral or regional scope and almost never set up an organization.[194] The very concept of 'international investment law is an academic systematization' based on 'a comparative analysis'.[195]

The respective dispute-settlement mechanisms also differ. While only states can file claims before the WTO panels and the Appellate Body, foreign investors can pursue investor–state arbitration without any intervention from the home state. After bringing trade disputes before ad hoc panels, states can file appeals on matters of law before a permanent Appellate Body. The WTO Appellate Body only reviews legal errors and ensures consistency in interpretation. Instead, only rarely have appeals mechanisms been included in IIAs. Annulment proceedings are limited to

---

189 J. Kurtz, *The World Trade Organization and International Investment Law: Converging Systems* (CUP 2016).

190 Puig, 'The Merging of International Trade and Investment Law', 14.

191 Vadi, *Analogies in International Investment Law and Arbitration.*

192 L. Hsu, 'Applicability of WTO Law in Regional Trade Agreements: Identifying the Links', in L. Bartels and F. Ortino (eds), *Regional Trade Agreements and the WTO Legal System* (OUP 2006) 525–52, 551.

193 G. Sacerdoti, 'Trade and Investment Law: Institutional Differences and Substantive Similarities' (2014) 9 *Jerusalem Review of Legal Studies* 1–12, 11.

194 Ibid. 6–7.

195 Ibid. 7.

ascertaining grave breaches of due process.[196] In case of breach, while the WTO dispute-settlement mechanism usually provides for re-establishing the status quo ante, arbitral tribunals usually award the payment of compensation.[197] Furthermore, while remedies at the WTO only have prospective character, arbitral tribunals can authorize damages to the foreign investors.

Finally, while economic analysis has always played an important role in international trade law and the settlement of international trade disputes, legal analysis has predominated in investment disputes. In international trade law, 'economists and trade policy experts wrote and administered the General Agreement on Tariffs and Trade (GATT). The lawyers came along later'.[198] Instead, international investment law 'has always been the concern of lawyers'.[199] Lawyers draft IIAs; lawyers have adjudicated investment disputes.[200]

1.5.4 Preliminary Conclusions

These paradigms for categorizing investment treaty arbitrations all have merits and weaknesses and may diverge and converge on specific aspects. Most notably, none of them – except perhaps the international law and public law paradigms due to their comprehensive nature – fully captures the complex phenomenon of investor–state arbitration.

These paradigms are not normative; rather they are descriptive in nature and emphasize some aspects of investment treaty arbitration over others. They are useful theoretical tools to better configure and understand investment treaty arbitration. While investor–state arbitration is a relatively recent phenomenon and remains under-theorized, awareness of the existence of different paradigms promotes a better understanding and functioning of the same.

FINAL REMARKS

In an effort to make their regulatory framework for FDI more attractive to foreign investors, states ratify IIAs. Such adhesion necessarily involves

---

[196] Ibid. 9.

[197] Ibid. 8–9.

[198] McRae, 'The World Trade Organization and International Investment Law', 16.

[199] Ibid.

[200] Ibid.

the surrender of a part of, or limitation of, their sovereignty in exchange for certain benefits.[201] In this regard, however, IIAs are more intrusive than trade agreements as foreign investment takes place within the borders of a state. As one author puts it, 'they may condition … measures taken by governments … in the realm of regulation'.[202] In addition, investment treaties provide foreign investors with direct access to investor–state arbitration.

However, the right to regulate is a basic attribute of sovereignty under international law.[203] In certain cases, not only do states have a right to regulate, but they also have a duty to do so because of international obligations. In these cases, regulation has the function of safeguarding internationally recognized values, and state compliance with its international obligations 'actually serve[s] as a means to reassert sovereignty'.[204]

Therefore, according to some scholars, investment treaty law and arbitration is facing a 'legitimacy crisis', as arbitral awards can affect public policy, but there is uncertainty over the relevance or irrelevance of norms protecting non-economic values within investment treaty arbitration. Furthermore, while developing countries have deemed investment treaty arbitration politically biased against them, even industrialized countries have expressed some concerns about this mechanism. The criticisms on the functioning of investment treaty arbitration in relation to public goods should be taken into account to allow the investment treaty system to develop in accordance with public international law.

Against this background, this study now explores the migration of constitutional ideas from constitutional law to international investment law and arbitration. It then addresses the fundamental question as to whether proportionality, reasonableness and standards of review can facilitate the achievement of a better balance between the public and private interests within international investment law and arbitration or whether they risk fostering expansive interpretations of investment treaty provisions that can further jeopardize the legitimate pursuit of public interests by the host states.

---

201 See generally W. Shan, P. Simons and D. Singh (eds), *Redefining Sovereignty in International Economic Law* (Hart Publishing 2008).

202 L.E. Peterson, *The Global Governance of Foreign Direct Investment: Madly Off in All Directions* (Friedrich Ebert Stiftung Publisher 2005) 4.

203 M. Sornarajah, 'Right to Regulate and Safeguards', in UNCTAD, *The Development Dimension of FDI: Policy and Rule Making Perspectives* (UN 2003) 205.

204 K. Raustiala, 'Rethinking the Sovereignty Debate in International Economic Law' (2003) 6 JIEL 841–78.

2. The migration of constitutional ideas to international investment law and arbitration

INTRODUCTION

The adjudication of investment disputes has become the last frontier of the migration of constitutional ideas. This migration across different branches of law has become a common practice, building bridges between different legal systems, furthering judicial dialogue and borrowing among courts and tribunals. Scholars, adjudicators and practitioners participate in a transnational legal discourse, importing legal ideas from the outside into a given legal system.[1]

The migration of domestic concepts to the international plane and the parallel infusion of international law concepts in the domestic sphere are not new phenomena; rather, under specific circumstances, such migrations can become constituent features of public international law and domestic law respectively. While in theory international law and domestic law comprise separate disciplines, in practice the boundaries among these two fields have become porous.

With regard to the migration of domestic concepts to the international plane, theoretically, no less than two sources of public international law may derive from national law – namely, customary law and general principles of law. In ascertaining the state practice, which is an element of customary international law, adjudicators do consider domestic conduct. In ascertaining general principles of law, adjudicators compare different national experiences.[2] Principles from domestic legal systems often find their way into international law or inform the decisions of international tribunals. Even with regard to the interpretation of vague

---

[1] S. Cassese, 'Beyond Legal Comparison' (2012) *Annuario di diritto comparato e di studi legislativi* 387–95, 388.

[2] M. Hirsch, 'Sources of International Investment Law', in A.K. Bjorklund and A. Reinisch (eds), *International Investment Law and Soft Law* (Edward Elgar 2012) 9–38, 23.

treaty provisions, adjudicators may consider domestic notions in order to clarify treaty terms, albeit of course, there is a theoretically distinguishable divide between the two spheres; the national meaning does not necessarily correspond to the international one, and vice versa.

With regard to the top-down infusion of international law in the domestic sphere, whether a state is governed by a monist system or a dualist system, it is clear that states must comply with public international law because of its binding nature. Given the pervasiveness of international law, very few, if any, areas of domestic law remain impermeable to international law. The growing reach of international law into matters that used to be of domestic jurisdiction means that the boundary of legal orders has changed from a territorial to a functional basis.

While both private and public law concepts have migrated to the international plane, this chapter focuses on the migration of constitutional concepts from the domestic to the international level due to the distinct questions they raise.[3] Can constitutional benchmarks, such as proportionality or reasonableness, help arbitrators in interpreting and applying broad and open-ended investment treaty provisions? Can these constitutional ideas help facilitate the consideration of the commonweal in investment treaty arbitration and/or contribute to the humanization of international (investment) law? Can the use of constitutional analogies contribute to the current debate over the legitimacy of investor–state arbitration? Although the use of constitutional ideas in international investment law and arbitration can offer concrete solutions to emerging conceptual dilemmas, and is forcefully presented by reputed scholars, this chapter contends that a more critical approach to the use of such concepts should be adopted. As argued elsewhere, the migration of

---

[3] For a seminal investigation of private law analogies in international law, see H. Lauterpacht, *Private Law Sources and Analogies of International Law: With Special Reference to International Arbitration* (Longmans, Green & Co Ltd 1927). For seminal investigations of public law analogies in international investment law, see G. Van Harten, *Investment Treaty Arbitration and Public Law* (OUP 2007); S. Montt, *State Liability in Investment Treaty Arbitration – Global Constitutional and Administrative Law in the BIT Generation* (Hart Publishing 2009); and S. Schill (ed.), *International Investment Law and Comparative Public Law* (OUP 2010). For a comprehensive treatment, see V. Vadi, *Analogies in International Investment Law and Arbitration* (CUP 2016).

constitutional ideas is often considered to be a neutral process, but this is not always the case.[4]

Considering international investment law and arbitration as analogous to a public law system emphasizes the relationship between the foreign investors and the host state. However, international investment law and arbitration does not merely govern the relationship between the foreign investors and the host states. It also governs the relationship between the host and home states. It aims to foster peaceful and prosperous relations among nations by spurring private investment in given sectors and facilitating the economic growth of the host state. Moreover, while public law expresses the fundamental political, social and cultural choices of a given polity, international investment law has a more limited focus, requiring the protection of foreign investors and their investments. Thus, international investment law remains a creature of public international law.

Therefore, further reflection on the methodology of constitutional analogies in international investment law and arbitration is needed in light of the public international law nature of this body of law. This is not to say that there is a necessary incompatibility between public law and international law approaches; rather, their interplay needs to be scrutinized and critically assessed.

Public law thinking presents both opportunities and dangers. Public law thinking can contribute to the progress of international law. It provides international law scholars and practitioners with new methods of inquiry for examining their field. In international investment law, public law analysis has spurred a path-breaking debate on the nature of international investment law and arbitration. It certainly contributes to the mosaic of existing methods in investigating international law. However, constitutional ideas vary from jurisdiction to jurisdiction, reflecting the preferences of society. Given the international law setting of investment treaty arbitration, it would be problematic to automatically transpose the experience of any particular jurisdiction to the international level. Only insofar as a discrete number of constitutional experiences constitute evidence of state practice or general principles of law can they assume relevance in the context of supranational adjudication.

Transplanting constitutional ideas into international investment law and arbitration would be legitimate if such concepts were general principles of law or reflected customary international law. If constitutional ideas,

---

[4] V. Vadi, 'Critical Comparisons: The Role of Comparative Law in Investment Treaty Arbitration' (2010) 39 *Denver JIL & Policy* 67–100.

such as proportionality and reasonableness, were general principles of law, or reflected customary law, eventually they could be used in international investment law and arbitration as part of the applicable law or as a matter of treaty interpretation. However, recourse to general principles of law, which characterized early arbitral awards, is increasingly rare.[5] On the one hand, general principles of law 'have a residual nature[,] and international tribunals tend to use them to fill remaining gaps in treaty and customary law'.[6] Therefore, the use of general principles of law is inversely proportional to the proliferation of investment treaties. On the other hand, the identification of general principles of law is perceived to be 'accompanied by a high degree of subjectivity'.[7] Moreover, 'some legal rules, even when shared by numerous domestic statutes, cannot be mechanically imported into the international legal realm'; rather, their transposability must be ascertained.[8]

In the uncertainty as to the legal status of given constitutional ideas in international law, the legal grounds for considering such concepts in investment treaty arbitration become more problematic. This chapter shows that while constitutional ideas have analytical merits, they also present a number of challenges when applied to the context of investment disputes. Therefore – this chapter concludes – more comparative and international law studies are needed to ascertain the legal status of given constitutional ideas in international law.

The chapter proceeds as follows. First, the notion of the migration of constitutional ideas is defined and examined. Second, the chapter discusses the migration of constitutional ideas through legal transplants. Third, the migration of constitutional ideas through cross-judging is examined. Fourth, the chapter highlights the methodological challenges posed by the migration of constitutional ideas and the identification of general principles of law. Fifth, theories and methods of comparative constitutional law are examined, and functional approaches are contrasted with cultural ones. Finally, the conclusions sum up the key arguments of the chapter.

---

5 Hirsch, 'Sources of International Investment Law', 22–3.

6 Ibid. 27.

7 Ibid.

8 Ibid. 23.

2.1 THE MIGRATION OF CONSTITUTIONAL IDEAS

The migration of constitutional ideas refers to the legislative and interpretative act of borrowing concepts belonging to given constitutional traditions and importing them into a different legal system.[9] Constitutional law indicates a body of national law setting up fundamental norms and procedures of state governance and expressing the fundamental political, social and cultural choices of a given polity. Not only does it govern the relationships between the judiciary, the legislature and the executive, but it also regulates the relationship between the state and the individual. In doing so, constitutional law includes mechanisms of checks and balances for delimiting public powers and protecting private rights.[10] The basic idea underpinning constitutional law is that the constitution constitutes 'a higher or supreme law'.[11] Whether codified or uncodified,[12] the gist of constitutional law is to govern the exercise of public powers and subject them to a higher law – the constitutional compact.[13]

The migration of constitutional ideas is related to, but differs from, constitutionalism. The term 'migration' implies a distance and/or an invisible boundary between the source of given concepts (i.e. constitutional law), and their destination (*in casu*, international investment law). It presupposes the existence of theoretical and practical boundaries between public international law and constitutional law.

Rather, constitutionalism is a conceptual movement or doctrinal project – some contend a phenomenon – which affirms that the authority of states derives from, and is limited by, a higher law[14] and conceives public law as a field of knowledge that transcends the dichotomy between the national and the international. The constitutionalists propose the 'constitutionalization' of a number of different areas of law, aiming at 'subjecting the exercise of all types of public power ... to the discipline of

---

[9] See S. Choudry (ed.), *The Migration of Constitutional Ideas* (CUP 2006).

[10] S. Gordon, *Controlling the State: Constitutionalism from Ancient Athens to Today* (Harvard UP 1999) 4.

[11] G. Frankenberg, 'Comparative Constitutional Law', in M. Bussani and U. Mattei (eds), *Cambridge Companion to Comparative Law* (CUP 2012) 171–90.

[12] E.A. Young, 'The Constitution Outside the Constitution' (2007) 117 *Yale LJ* 408–473.

[13] Gordon, *Controlling the State*, 4.

[14] D. Fellman, 'Constitutionalism', in P.P. Wiener (ed.), *Dictionary of the History of Ideas: Studies of Selected Pivotal Ideas* vol. 1 (Charles Scribner's Sons 1973) 485, 491–2.

constitutional procedures and norms'.[15] The constitutionalization of different areas of law, ranging from public international law[16] to international economic law[17] and EU law[18] – scholars argue – promotes their humanization, suggests the idea of a scale of higher values, and thus potentially contributes to the legitimacy of these systems.[19]

Whether international law in general, and international investment law in particular, have undergone processes of constitutionalization remains an open question, albeit it seems that they both lack constitutional

---

[15] M. Loughlin, 'What is Constitutionalization?', in P. Dobner and M. Loughlin (eds), *The Twilight of Constitutionalism?* (OUP 2010) 47–69, 47.

[16] J. Klabbers, A. Peters and G. Ulfstein, *The Constitutionalization of International Law* (OUP 2009) (examining the questions as to whether and, if so, to what extent the international legal system has constitutional features comparable to what we find in national law); B. Fassbender, 'The Meaning of International Constitutional Law', in N. Tsagourias (ed.), *Transnational Constitutionalism: International and European Models* (CUP 2007) 837–51 (suggesting that the Charter of the United Nations can be considered the constitution of the international community); R. St. John MacDonald and D.M. Johnston (eds), *Towards World Constitutionalism: Issues in the Legal Ordering of the World Community* (Martinus Nijhoff 2005) (arguing that constitutional perspectives in international legal discourse would contribute to protecting human welfare).

[17] P.-T. Stoll, 'Constitutional Perspectives on International Economic Law', in M. Cremona et al (eds), *Reflections on the Constitutionalisation of International Economic Law* (Brill 2014) 201–213, 212 (suggesting that 'a constitutionalist view is essential in the era of globalization where the growing interdependence and the emergence of effective international regimes put into question the sovereign powers of states'). See also D.Z. Cass, *The Constitutionalization of the World Trade Organization: Legitimacy, Democracy, and Community in the International Trading System* (OUP 2005).

[18] See J.H.H. Weiler, '*Fin-de-siecle* Europe: Do the New Clothes have an Emperor?', in J.H.H. Weiler, *The Constitution of Europe: 'Do the New Clothes Have an Emperor?' and Other Essays on European Integration* (CUP 1999) 238–63 (elaborating the notion of European constitutionalism as a process restraining the power of nation states and promoting peaceful and prosperous relations through human rights and the rule of law); C. Timmermans, 'The Constitutionalization of the European Union' (2002) 21 *Yearbook of European Law* 1–11, 2 (considering the development of the EU legal order as 'a striking example of … constitutionalization'); T. Christiansen and C. Reh, *Constitutionalizing the European Union* (Palgrave Macmillan 2009) 2 (suggesting that 'the EU has been constitutionalized by way of informal incrementalism').

[19] See M. Kumm, 'The Legitimacy of International Law: A Constitutionalist Framework of Analysis' (2004) 15 EJIL 907–931, 909 (suggesting that 'the legitimacy of international law ought to be assessed using a richer constitutionalist framework').

density.[20] With regard to international investment law, scholars have argued that there are elements for its constitutionalization:[21] 'Like constitutions, [IIAs] restrict state action'.[22] They grant foreign investors the possibility of settling disputes with the host state via binding arbitration.[23] Investor–state arbitrations review state conduct in light of treaty rules. Such scrutiny of the exercise of public authority 'exhibits constitutional features'.[24]

However, the interplay between economic globalization and constitutionalism is more ambiguous than it may seem at first glance. For instance, Schneiderman has questioned whether foreign investors are 'the privileged citizens of a new constitutional order',[25] cautioning that while the use of constitutional principles in investment arbitration can symbolically suggest that investment tribunals are similar to national high courts,[26] not only can IIAs jeopardize the 'constitutional' right of sovereign states to regulate, but investment arbitration risks invoking constitutional principles 'for purposes that are at odds with the doctrine[s]' rationale'.[27]

Moreover, constitutionalism risks blurring the distinction between international and constitutional law, thus interpreting the former through the lens of the latter, while a traditional tenet of international law requires states to comply with international law even if this is in conflict with national law, including constitutional law.[28] One may question whether

---

[20] This does not mean that constitutionalization is not taking place in some regional areas, such as in EU law, where constitutional rhetoric is common. However, the constitutionalization of EU law hardly constitutes a model for international law as a whole, given the different aims, objectives and structures as well as geographical scopes of the two fields.

[21] See P. Behrens, 'Towards the Constitutionalization of International Investment Protection' (2007) 45 *Archiv des Völkerrechts* 153–79, 154 (suggesting that there are elements for the constitutionalization of international investment law).

[22] S.W. Schill, *The Multilateralization of International Investment Law* (CUP 2009) 373.

[23] Ibid.

[24] A. Kulick, *Global Public Interest in International Investment Law* (CUP 2012) 93.

[25] D. Schneiderman, *Constitutionalizing Economic Globalization: Investment Rules and Democracy's Premise* (OUP 2008) 5.

[26] D. Schneiderman, 'Investing in Democracy? Political Process and International Investment Law' (2010) 60 *University of Toronto LJ* 909–940, 914.

[27] Ibid. 927.

[28] PCIJ, *Treatment of Polish Nationals and other Persons of Polish Origin or Speech in the Danzig Territory*, Advisory Opinion, 4 February 1932, 6 ILR (1931–1932) 209.

international law in general and international investment law in particular display instruments and organs truly comparable to domestic ones. IIAs often have concurring objectives including those of promoting peaceful and prosperous relations among nations, protecting foreign investments and promoting the (sustainable) development of the host state. However, international investment law is also part and parcel of international law and cannot undermine the aims and objectives of the latter, which are much broader. Instead of looking primarily *within* the investment regime for the relevant foundational principles, one should take into account the importance of international law when interpreting IIAs.[29] Finally, whether or not the constitutionalization of these areas of law has taken place is subject to debate.[30] This is not to say, however, that a dialogue between constitutional law and international (investment) law is not feasible, useful or desirable.

Constitutional law principles can (and have) influence(d) other areas of the law. This has taken place in three different ways. First, the migration of constitutional ideas can take the form of a legal transplant when the law makers deliberately borrow given legal tools from constitutional systems. Second, the migration of constitutional ideas can take place at the judicial level through cross-judging. Third, constitutional principles can become general principles of international law or even customary international law under certain circumstances. The next sections will explore these modes of migration of constitutional ideas.

2.2 THE MIGRATION OF CONSTITUTIONAL IDEAS THROUGH LEGAL TRANSPLANTS

The migration of constitutional ideas can take the form of a legal transplant from one legal system to another. The concept of legal transplant has been introduced by Alan Watson, who contended that there is no inherent relationship between law and society.[31] According to Watson, being autonomous from any social structure, law develops by

---

29 For an analogous argument with regard to WTO law, see R. Howse and K. Nicolaidis, 'Legitimacy Through "'Higher Law'"? Why Constitutionalizing the WTO is a Step Too Far', in T. Cottier and P.C. Mavroidis (eds), *The Role of the Judge in International Trade Regulation: Experience and Lessons for the WTO* (University of Michigan Press 2003) 307–348, 311.

30 Ibid. 307.

31 A. Watson, 'Comparative Law and Legal Change' (1978) 37 *Cambridge LJ* (1978) 313–36, 314–15.

transplanting.[32] For Watson, a legal concept can be moved from a context and applied elsewhere.[33] Inevitably, the concept will adapt to the new context; rather than implying the failure of the transplant, such adaptation is a natural evolutive process.[34]

In the constitutional realm, legal transplants have been common; constitutional ideas have migrated from one constitutional system to another since ancient times.[35] At the regional and international levels, the migration of constitutional ideas plays a central role in treaty-making.[36] For instance, at the regional level, the treaty drafters structuring the relationship between the courts of the EU and those of the Member States opted for a structure that echoes national systems delineating the interplay between their ordinary and constitutional courts.[37] Constitutional law has played a pivotal role in the making of international (investment) law too. For instance, the provisions against indirect expropriation in a number of IIAs – most notably the US Model BIT – derive from US constitutional law, specifically, the *Penn Central* test, articulated by the US Supreme Court.[38] In parallel, as the 2012 US Model BIT is often used as a template by a number of countries in their investment for treaty negotiations, the *lex Americana* has become the gold standard in the area.[39]

This process has not been uncontroversial or uncontested. Some commentators have argued that the extensive protection granted to investors' rights amounts to an extraterritorial application of the Fifth

---

[32] Ibid.

[33] Ibid.

[34] A. Watson, *Legal Transplants: An Approach to Comparative Law* (University of Georgia Press 1994) 19–20.

[35] M. Andenas and D. Fairgrieve, 'Intent on Making Mischief: Seven Ways of Using Comparative Law', in P.G. Monateri (ed.), *Methods of Comparative Law* (Edward Elgar 2012) 25–60 (noting that Plato's famous conception of the Republic 'built on all the known constitutions of the time').

[36] G.A. Bermann, 'Comparative Law and International Organizations', in M. Bussani and U. Mattei (eds), *The Cambridge Companion to Comparative Law* (CUP 2012) 241–54, 249 (stating that treaty making is one scenario 'to which comparative law has the most obvious contribution to make').

[37] Ibid. 251.

[38] *Penn Central Transportation Co. v New York City*, 438 US 104, 124 (1978).

[39] J.E. Alvarez, 'The Evolving BIT', in I.A. Laird and T. Weiler (eds), *Investment Treaty Arbitration and International Law* (Juris 2010) Ch. 1, 12–13.

Amendment of the US Constitution.[40] The interplay between constitutional law and international investment law in the form of legal transplant has been investigated by a number of authors.[41]

2.3 THE MIGRATION OF CONSTITUTIONAL IDEAS THROUGH CROSS-JUDGING

The migration of constitutional ideas can also take place through cross-judging. Cross-judging – that is, referring to the jurisprudence of other courts and tribunals pertaining to other legal orders – reflects the current spirit of the time (*Zeitgeist*) due to the coexistence of different, at times converging at times diverging, legal systems. Law has become a polycentric phenomenon; multiple regulatory entities compete in its making at national, regional and international levels.[42] Globalization has also eroded traditional boundaries, increasing the availability of information, access to the same and interaction among different legal systems.

Far from being a mere rhetorical device, with no appreciable impact on the resulting jurisprudence, cross-judging by arbitral tribunals can and has shaped the resulting awards. Arbitral tribunals have borrowed various types of 'external' legal materials such as judicial decisions, legal provisions, doctrinal opinions etc. Cross-judging is mainly driven by functional reasons. Arbitral tribunals can refer to the jurisprudence of other courts and tribunals to understand the meaning of treaty provisions, to identify general principles of law and to fill a gap in a particular law. Resort to other cases may provide adjudicators with useful examples, facilitate their reasoning and strengthen their perceived legitimacy.[43] Looking outside one's own system can be a tool for reassessing it, and adjusting it to evolving circumstances. Whether this is done within the

---

[40] D. Schneiderman, 'NAFTA's Takings Rule: American Constitutionalism Comes to Canada' (1996) 46 *University of Toronto LJ* 499–538; G.M. Starner, 'Taking a Constitutional Look: NAFTA Chapter 11 as an Extension of Member States' Constitutional Protection of Property' (2002) 33 *Law & Policy International Business* 405–36.

[41] See generally V. Bean and J.C. Beauvais, 'The Global Fifth Amendment? NAFTA's Investment Protection and the Misguided Quest for an International Regulatory Takings Doctrine' (2003) 78 NYULR 30–143.

[42] See e.g. G. Teubner, 'Global Bukovina: Legal Pluralism in the World Society', in G. Teubner (ed.), *Global Law without a State* (Dartmouth 1997) 3–30, 3 passim.

[43] E.M. Leonhardsen, 'Looking for Legitimacy: Exploring Proportionality Analysis in Investment Treaty Arbitration' (2012) 3 JIDS 95–136, 116.

scope of imitation, or because of convergence in a given policy domain, the influence of borrowing goes beyond the specific case, influencing the culture of the importing system,[44] and determining gravitation towards certain models that exert dominant influence.

Reverse borrowing – i.e. borrowing constitutional concepts and lending them back to the original system – is also possible. For instance, in EU law reverse borrowing is taking place increasingly due to the influential role played by the CJEU. In other words, while the CJEU relies and borrows from the constitutional traditions of the member states of the EU, it also lends concepts to those traditions because of the influential character of its rulings and the primacy of EU law over the domestic law of the member states. Reverse constitutional borrowing has also taken place at the international level. For instance, while international law borrows from constitutional traditions, it also requires countries to change their constitutions to make domestic law compatible with their international investment obligations.

The migration of constitutional ideas through cross-judging[45] has contributed to the phenomenon of 'judicial globalization'[46] and the cross-pollination of different legal cultures. International courts and tribunals as well as constitutional courts around the world have increasingly 'cross-judged' – that is, cited and/or relied upon each other's opinions – with varied success, determining a judicial dialogue at both horizontal and vertical levels.

At the horizontal international level, the migration of constitutional ideas from one international tribunal to another allows these tribunals to de-fragment the alleged fragmentation of international law across its various regimes. The proliferation of different treaty regimes and international courts has raised the question as to whether international law is a fragmented system. There is no institutional hierarchy among these different courts and tribunals, no clear-cut rule to establish priority, and no binding precedent in international law. As international courts and tribunals are not structured in a hierarchical fashion, they are not bound by the decisions of peers. By 'importing' concepts from other international courts and tribunals, international adjudicators counteract the

---

[44] See C.B. Picker, 'International Investment Law: Some Legal Cultural Insights', in L. Trakman and N. Ranieri (eds), *Regionalism in International Investment Law* (OUP 2013) 27–58.

[45] S. Choudry, 'Migration as a New Metaphor in Comparative Constitutional Law', in S. Choudry (ed.), *The Migration of Constitutional Ideas* (CUP 2006) 1–25.

[46] A.-M. Slaughter, 'Judicial Globalization' (2000) 40 *Virginia JIL* 1103–24.

risk of fragmentation and reinforce the perceived unity of international law. In parallel, at the horizontal domestic level, a number of national courts do consider the rulings of analogous foreign courts in addressing analogous issues.[47]

At the vertical domestic level, national courts and tribunals in common law jurisdictions follow the rule of *stare decisis*. Analogously, in civil law jurisdictions, courts do regard the previous decisions of superior courts, albeit they are not formally bound by them. At the vertical transnational level, the migration of constitutional ideas from constitutional law to the regional and international sphere allows a dialogue between national constitutional courts, on the one hand, and supranational courts and tribunals, on the other. Such dialogue has also given rise to a common lexicon, which nourishes the emergence of commonalities[48] and fosters the circular migration of constitutional ideas from constitutional courts to regional and international fora and then back to constitutional courts.[49]

2.4 THE MIGRATION OF CONSTITUTIONAL IDEAS AND THE COALESCENCE OF GENERAL PRINCIPLES OF LAW

In certain cases, the migration of constitutional ideas can also give rise to the coalescence of general principles of international law and/or customary law (as evidence of state practice or *opinio juris*), thus contributing to the development of international law. Therefore, the migration of constitutional ideas can contribute to build up a systematic body of legal principles common to all jurisdictions.

Defined as 'a core of legal ideas which are common to all legal systems',[50] general principles of law are a primary source of international law.[51] The Statute of the ICJ empowers the court, if occasion should arise, to apply the 'general principles of law recognised by civilised

---

47 R. Teitel, 'Comparative Constitutional Law in a Global Age' (2004) 117 *Harvard LR* 2570–96.

48 See e.g. D. Feldman, 'Modalities of Internationalisation in Constitutional Law' (2006) 18 *European Review of Public Law* 131–58.

49 E. Benvenisti, 'Reclaiming Democracy: The Strategic Uses of Foreign and International Law by National Courts' (2008) 102 AJIL 241–74.

50 R.B. Schlesinger, 'Research on the General Principles of Law Recognized by Civilized Nations' (1957) 51 AJIL 734–53, 739.

51 B. Cheng, *General Principles of Law as Applied by International Courts and Tribunals* (CUP 1953).

nations'.[52] Although the statute applies to the court, Article 38 has been deemed to reflect customary international law.[53] Therefore, other international law courts and tribunals consider general principles of law as a source of international law.

General principles express a 'belief in a "common heritage" of international law',[54] or common law of mankind,[55] and contribute to the construction of international law as a unitary legal system. Often considered as a dormant source of international law, general principles of law can revive and govern a certain issue if such issue is not regulated by treaty law and customary law. General principles of law have a flexible, subsidiary and dynamic nature. They help adjudicators to settle a given dispute, filling in the gaps in the applicable law, and responding to new challenges.[56] They also play a role in the legal reasoning of international courts and tribunals to reinforce certain legal arguments.

As international courts and tribunals can refer to general principles of law even in the absence of general practice (which is an element of customary law)[57] or an express consent of the parties in the form of treaty law, arguments have been made that general principles of law amount to an external constraint on state behaviour and in fact 'go beyond legal positivism, according to which states are bound by their will only'.[58] Yet, if one conceives general principles as expressing a common legal heritage of mankind, then, rather than representing a delimitation of state autonomy, general principles of law constitute its highest expression.[59] Certainly, the identification and application of general principles of law give significant discretion to international adjudicators.[60]

---

52 Statute of the International Court of Justice, annexed to the Charter of the United Nations, 26 June 1945, in force 24 October 1946, 1 UNTS XVI, Article 38.

53 J.L. Brierly, *The Law of Nations: An Introduction to the International Law of Peace*, 6th edn (H. Waldock, ed.) (OUP 1963) 56.

54 G. Del Vecchio, *Sui principi generali del diritto* (Giuffré 1958) 11.

55 J. Waldron, 'Foreign Law and the Modern Jus Gentium' (2005) 119 *Harvard LR* 129–45, 132.

56 C. Voigt, 'The Role of General Principles in International Law and Their Relationship to Treaty Law' (2008) 31 *Retfærd Årgang* 3–25, 5.

57 Cheng, *General Principles of Law*, 24.

58 Dissenting Opinion, Judge Tanaka, *South West African Cases* (Second Phase) ICJ Reports 1966, 298.

59 Del Vecchio, *Sui principi generali del diritto*, 69.

60 But see J. Ellis, 'General Principles and Comparative Law' (2011) 22 EJIL 949–71, 949 (arguing that recourse to general principles does not amount to judicial law-making).

What is the *gestalt* of general principles of law? General principles of law can indicate (1) principles that are common to diverse legal systems (thus 'having their roots in a local or national *Volkgeist*');[61] or (2) principles recognized by the international community (transcending national law).[62] An example of a general principle of municipal origin is that of requiring reparation as a consequence of a wrongful act. Examples of general principles of international foundation include, for instance, the principle of non-intervention in national affairs.[63] Both types of principles – irrespective of their legal origin – are acknowledged as binding by the international community.[64]

The identification of the first type of general principles, those that are common to diverse legal systems, entails two processes: (1) the abstraction of the norm from national constitutions, legislations and judicial decisions – a vertical process; (2) the comparison of the national legal systems – a horizontal process – to distil the essence of the legal concept.[65] In ascertaining general principles of law, what legal systems should be considered and how? As Raimondo put it, 'if a legal principle derived from national legal systems is going to be part of international law, then that legal principle should arguably be more universally recognized'.[66] By its name, international law indicates law among nations: reference to a couple of countries can be sufficient to detect the existence of common principles between those two countries; reference to a given region can be sufficient to identify the existence of regional principles of law.[67] However, reference to 'a couple of' or 'a few' jurisdictions is not sufficient for ascertaining the content of general principles of international law.[68]

The international judge should avoid a mechanical transposition of concepts from national law into international proceedings.[69] For instance, in *Klöckner v. Cameroon*, although the applicable law was Cameroonian, the Arbitral Tribunal based its decision on the 'basic principle' of

---

[61] Schlesinger, 'Research on the General Principles of Law Recognized by Civilized Nations', 742.

[62] Voigt, 'The Role of General Principles in International Law', 3, 7.

[63] Ibid. 8.

[64] Ibid.

[65] F. Raimondo, *General Principles of Law in the Decisions of International Criminal Courts and Tribunals* (OUP 2008) 1.

[66] Ibid. 4.

[67] *Odièvre v. France*, 13 February 2003, ECHR 2003–III, ECtHR.

[68] M. Cherif Bassiouni, 'A Functional Approach to "General Principles of International Law"' (1990) 11 *Michigan JIL* 768–818, 789.

[69] *Furundzija*, Judgment, 10 December 1998, para. 178, ICTY.

'frankness and loyalty', borrowing it from French civil law and noting (without reference) that it also belonged to both English law and international law.[70] The Annulment Committee annulled the award, holding that the Arbitral Tribunal had failed to apply the proper law and had based its decision 'more on a sort of general equity than on positive law'.[71]

The adoption of 'a narrow inquiry, which at best attaches special weight and at worst confines the scope of the review to a single, specific legal system'[72] for the determination of general principles of law, can lead to the perception that international adjudicators 'interpret legal norms through the lexicons of their respective traditions, rather than through a truly sui generis prism',[73] elevating municipal concepts with which they are familiar to the level of 'universal truths'.[74]

At the same time, it may not be feasible to consider all of the existing jurisdictions. A comprehensive survey of all of the national legal systems on a given issue is beyond the capacity of international courts and tribunals. International adjudicators are often multilingual, but they are not (nor should they be) expected to master the rich diversity of languages in which legal systems are formulated. In this regard, comparative surveys of the various systems are useful to cope with these unavoidable linguistic hurdles.[75]

The comparative legal analysis to detect general principles of law must be extensive and representative, albeit not necessarily uniform or universal.[76] The criterion of representativeness helps to ensure a level of abstraction and objectivity in the process of elucidating general principles of law. The idea of representativeness is based on three different but related grounds.[77] First, the presence of a concept in many legal systems

---

70 *Klöckner v. Cameroon*, Award, 21 October 1983, 2 *ICSID Reports* 59–61.

71 *Klöckner v. Cameroon*, Decision on Annulment, 16 May 1986, 1 *ICSID Reports* 515 (noting that '[The Tribunal's] reasoning [is] limited to postulating and not demonstrating the existence of a principle ...').

72 A. Zammit Borda, 'Comparative Law and Ad Hoc Tribunals: The Dangers of a Narrow Inquiry' (2012) 40 *International Journal of Legal Information* 22–38, 36.

73 Ibid. (internal citation omitted).

74 Ellis, 'General Principles and Comparative Law', 965.

75 For a seminal study, see P. Allott, 'Language, Method and the Nature of International Law' (1971) 45 *British YIL* 79–135, 120.

76 Zammit Borda, 'Comparative Law and Ad Hoc Tribunals', 28.

77 Ellis, 'General Principles and Comparative Law', 970–71 (criticizing the concept of representativeness in favour of the concept of persuasiveness of legal argumentation).

shows its legal objectivity. Second, that presence is evidence of state consent. Third, the fact that democratic processes have adopted a given concept in their legal systems indirectly legitimizes the use of the concept in international law.

Which legal families should be considered? Should a qualitative search be preferred to a quantitative one? Although Article 38(1)(c) of the ICJ Statute still formally refers to general principles of law recognised by *civilised nations*, this qualification is now commonly understood as indicating the community of nations.[78] Law scholars have developed several taxonomies of legal systems based on diverse criteria such as substance, style, method and ideology among others. Such classifications fail to reflect the complexities and overlapping of the various systems – but they are still relied upon as they are deemed 'necessary for comparative analysis to proceed'.[79]

The common/civil law divide maintains some value in identifying general principles of law. Reportedly:

> Common Law … whether in 'pure' or 'mixed' form, is utilized by some fifty-one nations, or 26.7 percent of all nations of the world. These nations account for 34.81 percent of the world's population. On the other hand, Civil Law … , whether in 'pure' or 'mixed' form, is utilized by some 115 nations, or 60.21 percent of all nations of the world. These nations account for 59.01 percent of the world's population.[80]

Therefore, a discrete and representative number of common law, civil law and mixed systems will have to be taken into account to determine general principles of law. In conclusion, comparative reasoning 'is not a mechanical process; rather, it is a tool which assists the adjudicator in applying (and developing) rules of international law'.[81]

---

[78] J. Alvarez, 'Contemporary Foreign Investment Law: An Empire of Law or the Law of Empire?' (2009) 60 *Alabama LR* 943–75, 950 (noting that '[a]ll states, large or small, enjoy sovereign equality under the UN Charter').

[79] C.B. Picker, 'International Law's Mixed Heritage: A Common/Civil Law Jurisdiction' (2008) 41 *Vanderbilt Journal of Transnational Law* 1083–140, 1094.

[80] W.R. Barnes, 'Contemplating a Civil Law Paradigm for a Future International Commercial Code' (2004–2005) 65 *Louisiana LR* 677–774, 769.

[81] H.C. Gutteridge, 'Comparative Law and the Law of Nations' (1944) 21 *British YIL* 1–10, 10.

2.5 METHODOLOGICAL CHALLENGES

Can constitutional theory can be generalized and transposed from the national terrain to the international sphere?[82] The migration of constitutional ideas to international investment law and arbitration can (and has) be(en) criticized on several grounds. First, by adopting exogenous elements, arbitrators risk making or transforming the law rather than interpreting or applying it. Often arbitrators rely on national cases without explaining why. If arbitrators rely on domestic cases, there is a risk that they 'cherry-pick' the cases they are more familiar with, namely those of the legal systems with which they are acquainted. Personal expertise – the fact that arbitrators lived, studied and worked in given jurisdictions – may cause a selection bias. This possible selection bias increases the risks of importing not necessarily the best qualitative models, but those that are more familiar to the arbitrators.[83]

Second, sovereignty concerns – critics contend – also matter; arbitrators should not impose 'foreign moods, fads, or fashions' on their audiences, as this would go beyond their mandate, transform them into law makers and undermine their legitimacy.[84] In investment treaty arbitration, reference to the constitutional experience of a country different from the host state might seem out of place.[85] Moreover, such judicial borrowing may be perceived as altering the text of the applicable international investment agreement.

Third, some scholars question whether constitutional ideas can migrate successfully from a given constitutional experience to the international plane,[86] contending that constitutional ideas cannot be separated from the

---

[82] G. Teubner, 'Fragmented Foundations: Societal Constitutionalism beyond the Nation State', in P. Dobner and M. Loughlin (eds), *The Twilight of Constitutionalism?* (OUP 2010) 327–41, 328.

[83] R. Hirschl, 'The Question of Case Selection in Comparative Constitutional Law' (2005) 53 AJCL 125–56.

[84] *Lawrence v. Texas*, 123 S.Ct. 2472, 2495 (2003) (Scalia J, dissenting); *Foster v. Florida*, 123 S.Ct. 470, 470–71 (2002) (Thomas J, concurring).

[85] An important instance in which a given constitutional practice may be relevant is when the applicable law is a national law. In fact, some arbitral tribunals have referred to proportionality because proportionality was embedded in the national law that was applicable to the given dispute.

[86] P. Zumbansen, 'Transnational Comparisons: Theory and Practice of Comparative Law as a Critique of Global Governance' (2012) *Osgoode Hall Law School, Research Paper* No. 1/2012, 16 (considering whether constitutional ideas can be 'conceived in near to complete isolation of the historical-intellectual contexts in which the very concepts … ha[d] their origin' and pinpointing the

constitutional culture in which they are rooted. Can constitutional ideas be isolated from the historical, political and cultural context of the country of origin? Zumbansen suggests that 'a closer look' should be given to methodology and the historical, political and cultural background of the item to borrow. In fact, a close reading of each constitutional tradition 'reveals particular connotations of regulatory power and of the relationship between different institutions (legislature, executive, [and] judiciary)'.[87] Constitutional ideas vary from jurisdiction to jurisdiction, reflecting the preferences of society – for example, regarding the allocation of power between the different branches of government. Given the international law setting of investment treaty arbitration, it would be problematic to automatically transpose the experience of any particular jurisdiction to the international level.

Fourth, the question of whether some legal systems are comparable lies at the very heart of any comparative endeavour. At the macro-level, as mentioned in Chapter 1, some scholars suggest that investor–state arbitration is analogous to public law adjudication.[88] Like domestic courts, arbitral tribunals review the exercise of public powers.[89] Arbitrators determine matters such as the legality of governmental activity, the degree to which individuals should be protected from regulation, and the appropriate role of the state.[90]

Nevertheless, other analogies are also proposed,[91] and international law scholars prefer to analogize investment treaty arbitration to other forms of international dispute settlement. Arbitral tribunals review state action in the light of international investment treaty provisions. Like other international courts and tribunals, arbitral tribunals interpret and apply international law. Given the supranational law setting of investment treaty arbitration, it would be inappropriate automatically to transpose the experience of any national jurisdiction to such setting. Only insofar as a

---

need to 'understand the potential of bringing the hidden histories of a particular legal field to light as they feed into the conceptualization on a world scale').

87 Ibid.

88 See generally G. Van Harten, *Investment Treaty Arbitration and Public Law* (OUP 2007); S. Montt, *State Liability in Investment Treaty Arbitration: Global Constitutional Law and Administrative Law in the BIT Generation* (Hart Publishing 2009).

89 See G. Van Harten and M. Loughlin, 'Investment Treaty Arbitration as a Species of Global Administrative Law' (2006) 17 EJIL 121–50, 123.

90 M. Sornarajah, 'The Clash of Globalizations and the International Law on Foreign Investment' (2003) 12 *Canadian Foreign Policy* 1–32, 17.

91 A. Roberts, 'Clash of Paradigms: Actors and Analogies Shaping the Investment Treaty System' (2013) 107 AJIL 45–94, 46.

discrete number of constitutional experiences constitute evidence of state practice or general principles of law can they assume relevance in the context of supranational adjudication. Another instance in which a given constitutional practice may be relevant is when the applicable law is national law.

In conclusion, with regard to the migration of constitutional ideas to international investment law and arbitration, the key question is whether constitutional theory can be generalized and transposed from the national terrain to the international sphere. After having highlighted some key methodological challenges in this section, the next section will examine how to address such challenges.

2.6 THEORIES AND METHODS OF COMPARATIVE REASONING: FUNCTION VERSUS CULTURE?

Methodological concerns have long been a common feature of comparative reasoning.[92] Although there is no single methodological model in comparative law,[93] two fundamental approaches to the field have emerged: the functional approach and the cultural approach. The functional approach relies on the assumption that law addresses social problems and that all societies essentially confront the same challenges.[94] The functional approach thus presupposes similarity among legal systems (*praesumptio similitudinis*),[95] potentially reflecting 'epistemological

---

[92] M. Tushnet, 'Some Reflections on Method in Comparative Constitutional Law', in S. Choudry (ed.), *The Migration of Constitutional Ideas* (CUP 2006) 67–83; P. Zumbansen, 'Comparative Law's Coming of Age: Twenty Years after *Critical Comparisons*?' (2005) 6 *German LJ* 1073–84; G. Frankenberg, 'Critical Comparisons: Re-thinking Comparative Law' (1985) 26 *Harvard ILJ* 411–45.

[93] See, among others, J. Bell, 'Comparing Public Law', in A. Harding and E. Orücü (eds), *Comparative Law in the 21st Century* (Kluwer Law International 2002) 235–48; V.C. Jackson and M. Tushnet (eds), *Defining the Field of Comparative Constitutional Law* (Praeger 2002); G. Frankenberg, 'Comparing Constitutions: Ideas, Ideals, and Ideology – Toward a Layered Narrative' (2006) 4 IJCL 439–59.

[94] See e.g. R. Michaels, 'The Functional Method of Comparative Law', in M. Reimann and R. Zimmermann (eds), *The Oxford Handbook of Comparative Law* (OUP 2006) 339–82; K. Zweigert, 'Méthodologie du droit comparé', in *Mélanges J. Maury* (Dalloz-Sirey 1960) 579–96.

[95] J. Husa, 'Methodology of Comparative Law Today: From Paradoxes to Flexibility?' (2006) 58 *Revue internationale de droit comparé* 1095–117, 1107.

optimism', that is, the belief that legal systems are comparable.[96] Concepts and institutions are compared because of their analogous function. For the functionalists, law is autonomous from any social structure and develops by transplanting.[97] A legal concept can be moved from a context and applied elsewhere.[98] Inevitably, the concept will adapt to the new context.[99] This approach allows a great – yet arguably loose – methodological freedom.[100]

By contrast, cultural approaches reject a purely functional vision of law and contend that law expresses and develops the cultural features of a society. For the proponents of the cultural approaches, law cannot be separated from its context.[101] For instance, Otto Kahn-Freund noted the 'far reaching free trade in legal ideas',[102] and that legal systems develop to address analogous issues. Yet, he pinpointed that legal systems are also embedded in given cultures. Therefore, not only do comparativists need to consider the functions of legal concepts, they also have to contextualize such concepts in their legal, political and cultural matrix.[103] Meaningful comparisons require understanding the cultural context of legal rules.[104] According to Kahn-Freund, not only should one verify whether the item that would be borrowed has proven satisfactory in its system of origin, but one should also consider whether it would be suitable to the potentially recipient system.[105] Cultural approaches oppose legal unification as an undesirable outcome. In fact, the idea of a global uniform law is seen as pursuing the predominance of one particular legal culture over others. Instead, cultural approaches presume cultural differences and consider cultural diversity to be worthy of protection.

---

96 M. Van Hoecke, 'Deep Level Comparative Law', in M. Van Hoecke (ed.), *Epistemology and Methodology of Comparative Law* (Hart Publishing 2004) 165–74, 172–4.

97 See generally A. Watson, *Legal Transplants: An Approach to Comparative Law* (University of Georgia Press 1974).

98 A. Watson, 'Comparative Law and Legal Change' (1978) 37 *Cambridge LJ* 313–36, 314–15.

99 Watson, *Legal Transplants*, 19–20.

100 Michaels, 'The Functional Method of Comparative Law'.

101 Otto Kahn-Freund, 'On Uses and Misuses of Comparative Law' (1974) 37 MLR 1–27.

102 Ibid. 10.

103 J.C. Reitz, 'How to do Comparative Law' (1998) 46 AJCL 617–36, 626.

104 P. Legrand, 'How to Compare Now?' (1996) 16 *Legal Studies* 232–42.

105 Kahn-Freund, 'On Uses and Misuses of Comparative Law', 6.

The cultural turn of comparative reasoning contextualizes law,[106] and can be particularly suitable to the international law context, which is characterized by valuable cultural diversity. Yet, a too broad understanding of the cultural approach makes comparative reasoning impossible. For instance, Legrand has argued that law is a cultural phenomenon, and each legal system is unique.[107] Therefore, for Legrand, comparing legal systems means comparing different worldviews, and legal transplants are impossible.[108] As the entire context of law can never be perfectly understood, legal systems become incommensurable.[109] Such extreme understanding of the cultural approach is valuable as it reminds interpreters and policy makers of the cultural diversity underpinning different legal systems. However, it fails to consider the existence of common values and a common legal heritage, as expressed by international law.

Despite their differences, both cultural and functional approaches share a number of caveats as a common denominator. For instance, borrowing based on inadequately verified information should be avoided. Analogously, the selection of the comparators should be justified. If comparisons are made, these should be explicit rather than implicit. The understanding of the borrowed items should be proper, accurate and contextual. More fundamentally, one should consider whether the migration of given ideas serves outcomes in compliance with the culture of both exporting and importing systems.

Finally, comparative reasoning cannot be a mechanical process because, until recently, both comparative law and international law had a Westphalian[110] – if not Eurocentric – character.[111] For a long time, comparative law (has) focused on European legal systems; the law of former colonies – with the exception of US law – was largely overlooked. Comparative lawyers tended to focus on Western legal systems

---

[106] R. Banakar, 'Power, Culture and Method in Comparative Law' (2009) 5 *International Journal of Law in Context* 69–85, 78, 93.

[107] P. Legrand, 'On the Singularity of Law' (2006) 47 *Harvard ILJ* 517–30, 517.

[108] P. Legrand, 'The Impossibility of Legal Transplants' (1997) 4 *Maastricht Journal of European and Comparative Law* 111–24, 111.

[109] M. Siems, 'The End of Comparative Law' (2007) 2 *Journal of Comparative Law* 133–50, 140–41.

[110] Treaty of Westphalia: Peace Treaty between the Holy Roman Empire and the King of France and Their Respective Allies, 24 October 1648, available at <http://avalon.law.yale.edu/17th_century/westphal.asp>, accessed 4 November 2017.

[111] W. Twining, 'Globalization and Comparative Law' (1999) 6 *Maastricht Journal of European and Comparative Law* 217–43, 233.

rather than adopting a broader focus, and studied non-European systems. This has led to legal principles common to Western countries being used as the legal paradigm, ignoring possible contributions by other countries.[112] Comparative law scholars (have) assumed that law is almost completely of European making, unfolded through nearly the entire world via colonialism, imperialism and trade.

In parallel, the making of international law used to have a predominantly Western character.[113] Some authors have raised the question of just how international it is,[114] highlighting that it draws its categories from Roman law. The founders of international law – such as Gentili, Grotius, and others – borrowed concepts from Roman law for shaping the law of nations.[115] Furthermore, international law mainly governed relations among states, despite some treaties regulating the interaction between states and indigenous peoples.[116]

In the post-colonial era, however, there is an emergent awareness that diffusion of law does not necessarily lead to convergence, harmonization or unification of laws. On the one hand, scholars have pointed out the multicultural genealogy of the Western legal tradition.[117] On the other hand, the imported law did not remain the same; legal transplants are 'transformed by the new context'.[118] Nowadays economic globalization has spurred the constant interaction among legal cultures, facilitating

---

112 J. González Jácome, 'El uso del derecho comparado como forma de escape de la subordinación colonial' (2006) 7 *International Law: Revista Colombiana de Derecho Internacional* 295–338, 301 (affirming that 'se está contribuyendo a la legitimación de un orden geopolítico en donde a los países periféricos se les atribuye poca posibilidad creativa en el mercado de las ideas jurídicas').

113 See generally A. Anghie, *Imperialism, Sovereignty and the Making of International Law* (CUP 2005).

114 K.T. Gaubatz and M. MacArthur, 'How International is International Law?' (2001) 22 *Michigan JIL* 239–82, 239.

115 See generally B. Kingsbury and B. Straumann (eds), *The Roman Foundations of the Law of Nations* (OUP 2010).

116 A notable example is the Treaty of Waitangi, signed on 6 February 1840 by representatives of the British Crown and various Māori chiefs from New Zealand.

117 P.G. Monateri, 'Black Gaius – A Quest for the Multicultural Origins of the "Western Legal Tradition"' (1999–2000) 51 *Hastings LJ* 479–56, 484 (highlighting that Roman law is a multicultural product due to the interaction of different civilizations).

118 Banakar, 'Power, Culture and Method in Comparative Law', 82.

their cross-fertilization and mutual learning.[119] Therefore, many characteristics that define and shape legal families 'are fading or spreading into other systems'.[120] Finally, 'all legal systems are to different degrees hybrids, i.e. cultural and legal mixtures consisting of various elements borrowed from different legal traditions and customs.'[121]

CONCLUSIONS

The migration of legal concepts from the constitutional realm to other fields of law has become an increasingly common phenomenon, highlighting a cosmopolitan if not nomadic character of law. Although the migration of constitutional ideas in other fields of law can offer concrete solutions to emerging conceptual dilemmas, and is forcefully presented by reputed scholars, one may question whether a more critical approach to the use of such concepts should be adopted. This chapter has contributed to the ongoing debate on the migration of constitutional ideas into international investment law and arbitration, highlighting the pros and cons, and the methodological issues raised by the migration of constitutional ideas from one field to another. Borrowing based on inadequately verified information should be avoided. Analogously, the selection of the use of certain countries as examples should be justified. If comparisons are made, these should be explicit rather than implicit. The understanding of the borrowed items should be proper, accurate and contextual. The migration of constitutional ideas is not a neutral process as it may have important consequences. In certain cases, constitutional ideas can acquire the status of general principles of law or customary international law. As such, they become part of the applicable law and also need to be taken into account in the interpretive process.

119 Ellis, 'General Principles and Comparative Law', 966.
120 Picker, 'International Law's Mixed Heritage', 1094.
121 Banakar, 'Power, Culture and Method in Comparative Law', 74.

3. A history of success? Proportionality in international investment law and arbitration

Is proportionality, like beauty, purely in the eye of the beholder?[1]
Thomas M. Franck

INTRODUCTION

Depending on context, proportionality can be defined as 'a goal of government, and a particular structured approach to judicial review'.[2] Proportionality requires that policy makers and adjudicators strike an appropriate balance between the public and private interests and give reasons for the restriction of individual autonomy.[3] A 'doctrinal tool for the resolution of conflicts' between competing interests,[4] proportionality seems to have a mathematical precision.[5] By assuming the existence of a common scale on which conflicting private and public interests can be measured, proportionality is often perceived as offering an 'arithmetic' balance of competing interests and values.[6] It offers an analytical framework to guide policy makers and adjudicators to assess whether or

[1] T.M. Franck, 'Proportionality in International Law' (2010) 4 LEHR 230–42, 242.

[2] V.C. Jackson, 'Constitutional Law in an Age of Proportionality' (2015) 124 *Yale LJ* 3094–3193, 3098.

[3] See generally M. Cohen-Eliya and I. Porat, *Proportionality and Constitutional Culture* (CUP 2012).

[4] K. Möller, 'Proportionality: Challenging the Critics' (2012) 10 IJCL 709–731, 710.

[5] Ibid. 724.

[6] N.J. Calamita, 'The Principle of Proportionality and the Problem of Indeterminacy in International Investment Treaties', in A. Bjorklund (ed.), *Yearbook of International Investment Law and Policy* (2013–2014) 157–200, 174.

not a policy respects rights.[7] In this manner, proponents argue, policy makers and adjudicators 'do not have to reinvent the wheel (that is, the adequate structure of the ... argument) in each case'.[8] Rather, they use a common grammar to engage in a conversation about matters of public concern.[9]

The proportionality test has three parts. The first part articulates the state's interest, asking whether the measure adopted by a state was a suitable means of achieving a legitimate aim.[10] The second part articulates the individual's interest, asking whether there was 'a means of achieving that aim which would be less restrictive of the applicant's interest'.[11] The third part of the test requires a balancing of public and private interest, investigating whether the measure had a disproportionate impact on the individual's interest.[12] If a tribunal finds the measure to be disproportionate to achieve its purported aim, the tribunal may suspect that 'that was not in fact the primary aim of the [measure] at all'.[13]

However, critics contend that proportionality is 'a chimera'.[14] While formally appealing, the concept remains substantively indeterminate. Therefore, it contributes little to restraining the legislative, executive and adjudicative powers of states.[15] In particular, critics contend, the lack of commensurability of certain values means that 'proportionality is a scale without weights'.[16] It can lead its users to irrational results unless it is grounded in a 'constitutional system'.[17] In the absence of a constitutional

---

7 Möller, 'Proportionality: Challenging the Critics', 726.

8 Ibid.

9 S.W. Schill, 'Cross-regime Harmonization through Proportionality Analysis: The Case of International Investment Law, the Law of State Immunity and Human Rights' (2012) 27 *ICSID Review* 87–119.

10 G. De Búrca, 'The Principle of Proportionality and its Application in EC Law' (1993) 13 *Yearbook of European Law* 105–150, 113.

11 Ibid.

12 Ibid.

13 Ibid. 131.

14 N. Lacey and H. Pickard, 'The Chimera of Proportionality' (2015) 78 MLR 216–40.

15 J. Bomhoff, 'Beyond Proportionality: Thinking Comparatively About Constitutional Review and Punitiveness' (2016) 12 *LSE Law, Society and Economy Working Papers* 1–22, 6 (noting that 'even if scholars agree that proportionality is a good thing', 'they do not agree on what it requires').

16 Calamita, 'The Principle of Proportionality and the Problem of Indeterminacy', 174–5.

17 Ibid.

value set, proportionality remains indeterminate. On the contrary, 'sometimes the most proportionate results may be achieved by doctrinal means other than a structured proportionality test'.[18] Moreover, the proportionality test risks empowering the adjudicators to second guess legislators, unless some institutional deference delimits such test.[19]

Can a constitutional benchmark such as proportionality help arbitrators in interpreting and applying broad and open-ended treaty provisions? Can proportionality help facilitate the consideration of the commonweal in international investment law and arbitration? Can the use of proportionality contribute to the current debate over the legitimacy of international investment law and arbitration? Can this concept successfully migrate from constitutional law to international investment law and arbitration?

This chapter aims to address these questions, and proceeds as follows. First, the chapter defines the notion of proportionality and briefly outlines its historical origins. Second, it examines several key promises of the concept. Third, it examines the pitfalls of proportionality analysis. Fourth, it illustrates the migration of the notion of proportionality from its constitutional matrix to the regional sphere, focusing on European Union (EU) law as a case study of successful legal migration. Fifth, it examines the use of the proportionality analysis in international trade law. Sixth, it investigates the use of proportionality analysis in international investment law and arbitration. Seventh, it critically assesses whether proportionality has migrated to international investment law, and if not yet, why. Eighth, the chapter investigates whether proportionality can be considered to be a general principle of international investment law. The chapter concludes that while proportionality may be suitable to those regimes that have a certain constitutional density, it may not be suitable to investor–state arbitration due to the latter's current lack of constitutional density. That being said, this does not mean that proportionality might not be useful in the future, if an agreement on a multilateral investment court or further institutionalization was achieved.

---

18 Bomhoff, 'Beyond Proportionality', 9.

19 G. Sartor, 'Doing Justice to Rights and Values: Teleological Reasoning and Proportionality' (2010) 18 *Artificial Intelligence and Law* 175–215, 204–205.

3.1 NOTION, ORIGINS AND STRUCTURE OF PROPORTIONALITY

What does 'proportionality' mean? The notion of proportionality takes on different meanings depending on the context to which it applies. As a geometrical concept, proportion indicates the comparative relationship between elements with respect to different criteria including size, amount and degree. As a mathematical concept, proportion indicates a type of equation between variables whose ratio is constant.[20] In art history, Renaissance architects, such as Leon Battista Alberti,[21] used 'a proportion of extraordinary beauty and perfection'[22] – the so-called golden section – to erect buildings of unique harmony and beauty.[23] Such proportion expressed the 'right measure' for 'capturing the harmonious order of the cosmos' and positioning humankind in the 'ideal city'.[24] In the long search for an elusive canon of perfect beauty, human beings seem to prefer forms possessing certain proportions or 'obey[ing] certain geometrical rules'.[25]

As a legal concept, 'the element of proportion … is virtually present in all legal systems of the world'.[26] It lies at the core of justice.[27] Proportionality expresses the idea that there should be a balance between competing objectives or values. As mentioned, within constitutional systems, proportionality constitutes 'a goal of government and … a

---

[20] M. Livio, *The Golden Ratio: The Story of Phi, The World's Most Astonishing Number* (Broadway Books 2002) 3.

[21] L.B. Alberti, *On the Art of Building in Ten Books* (J. Rykwert, N. Leach and R Tavernor, trans) [*De Re Aedificatoria*, 1450] (MIT Press 1988) (developing an arithmetical theory of proportion).

[22] R. Wittkower, 'The Changing Concept of Proportion' (1960) 89 *Daedalus* 199–215, 204.

[23] Livio, *The Golden Ratio*, 10 (noting that 'The history of art shows … the long search for an elusive canon of perfect proportion'). See also R. Wittkower, *Architectural Principles in the Age of Humanism* (Warburg Institute 1949) (applying a proportional reading to Renaissance architecture).

[24] T. Poole, 'Proportionality in Perspective' (2010) NZLR 369–91, 387.

[25] Livio, *The Golden Ratio*, 178. But see M.A. Cohen, *Beyond Beauty: Re-examining Architectural Proportion* (Marsilio 2013) 19 (reframing the subject of architectural proportion 'as part of the rhetorical, rather than visual, structure of architecture').

[26] A. Portuese, 'Principle of Proportionality as Principle of Economic Efficiency' (2013) 19 *European LJ* 612–35, 612.

[27] Ibid.

particularly structured approach to judicial review'.[28] As a goal of government, it is a 'precept of justice'.[29] It is a 'model of optimization of values in conflict'.[30] As an approach to judicial review, it helps adjudicators review measures limiting recognized rights.[31] Courts assess whether a challenged measure limits a recognized right.[32] If it does, they then verify whether the limitation can be justified.[33] In particular, proportionality is 'used to establish whether a limitation of rights is justifiable'.[34] While 'proportionate limitations of rights are justifiable; disproportionate ones are not'.[35]

What are the historical origins of proportionality as a legal concept? Historically, the concept of proportionality has played a key role in the quest for justice.[36] The notion of proportionality 'can be found in various shapes and forms throughout the history of law'.[37] A brief overview of the historical trajectories of this concept can help understand its historical importance, current relevance and future path.

The concept that there should be a proportion between the committed offence and a given penalty dates back to antiquity. The Babylonian code of Hammurabi, enacted in 1772 BC, already scaled punishments depending on the magnitude of the crime.[38] The idea of proportion as an archetype of justice also appeared in Plato's *Republic* and Aristotle's *Nicomachean Ethics*.[39] While Plato defined justice as 'rendering to each according to his or her merits',[40] Aristotle viewed it as 'an arithmetical

---

[28] Jackson, 'Constitutional Law in an Age of Proportionality', 3098.

[29] Ibid.

[30] L.B. Tremblay, 'An Egalitarian Defence of Proportionality-based Balancing' (2014) 12 IJCL 864–90, 864.

[31] Ibid. 865.

[32] Ibid.

[33] Ibid.

[34] J. Rivers, 'Proportionality and Variable Intensity of Review' (2006) 65 *Cambridge LJ* 174–207, 174.

[35] Ibid.

[36] B. Schlink, 'Proportionality', in M. Rosenfeld and A. Sajó (eds), *The Oxford Handbook of Comparative Constitutional Law* (OUP 2012) 719–36, 728.

[37] J. Christoffersen, *Fair Balance: A Study of Proportionality, Subsidiarity and Primarity in the European Convention on Human Rights* (Martinus Nijhoff 2009) 33.

[38] M.J. Fish, 'An Eye for an Eye: Proportionality as a Moral Principle of Punishment' (2008) 28 OJLS 57–71, 57.

[39] Aristotle, *Nicomachean Ethics* (S. Broadie and C. Rowe, eds) (OUP 2002) Book V, 158–75.

[40] Plato, *The Republic*, Book I, 332b (J. Adam, trans) (CUP 1902).

proportion', that is, an average between two extremes.[41] For Aristotle, 'the just is the proportional, the unjust is what violates the proportion'.[42] In commercial relations, he explained, justice requires proportionate consideration.[43] Notions of proportionality also appeared in Greek law, Roman law and even medieval law.[44]

Since the nineteenth century, proportionality has become 'an element of a globalised, common constitutional grammar'.[45] Several constitutional traditions have adopted the concept of proportionality as a methodological framework for balancing conflicting values and delimiting the legitimate exercise of state authority. In the last decades of the nineteenth century, the Prussian High Administrative Court developed a 'jurisprudence of proportionality' to delimitate the task of the police.[46] In the second half of the twentieth century, the German Constitutional Court (*Bundesverfassungsgericht*) similarly developed a jurisprudence of proportionality, balancing individuals' rights and freedoms with the regulatory power of the state.[47] Proportionality is now 'part of a deep structure of constitutional grammar that forms the basis of ... different constitutional languages and cultures'.[48]

How does proportionality work in practice? Proportionality is a tool for reviewing the conduct of states (and thus is closely connected with the aim of ensuring good governance). It is a 'structured form of inquiry',[49] 'a model for judicial analysis',[50] which involves 'a determination that the enjoyment of a protected right has been limited, *i.e.*, an

---

41 L. Judson, 'Aristotle on Fair Exchange' (1997) 15 *Oxford Studies in Ancient Philosophy* 147–75, 151.

42 Schlink, 'Proportionality', 719.

43 Aristotle, *Nicomachean Ethics*, Book V, 1131a (C. Rowe, trans) (OUP 2002).

44 Christoffersen, *Fair Balance*, 33.

45 I.M. Rautenbach, 'Proportionality and the Limitation Clauses of the South African Bill of Rights' (2014) 17 *Potchefstroom Elec. LJ* 2228–67, 2229.

46 B. Schlink, 'Proportionality in Constitutional Law: Why Everywhere but Here?' (2012) 22 *Duke J of Comparative & International Law* 291–302, 294.

47 Ibid. 295 (referring to the seminal case in which the German Constitutional Court held that a law limiting the number of pharmacies within a district to avoid the harmful effects of competition constituted a disproportionate restriction on the freedom to choose one's profession).

48 Ibid. 302.

49 P. Craig, *Administrative Law*, 6th edn (Sweet and Maxwell 2008).

50 E.M. Leonhardsen, 'Looking for Legitimacy: Exploring Proportionality Analysis in Investment Treaty Arbitration' (2012) 3 JIDS 95–136, 112.

infringement or *prima facie* violation'.[51] Then, the proportionality review is usually articulated in four main phases: (1) legitimate ends; (2) suitability; (3) necessity; and (4) proportionality in a strict sense.[52]

First, adjudicators check whether the state authorities pursued a legitimate objective.[53] Not every purpose can justify the limitation of individual entitlements. Rather, the measure interfering with private interests must have a proper purpose.[54] For constitutional law scholars, the legitimacy of legislative, administrative or judicial measures depends on the constitution.[55] Questions arise with regard to the transposability of this point of reference at the international level. Arguably, for international lawyers, the legitimacy of given state measures depends on international law. In fact, compliance with a national constitution does not necessarily indicate compliance with the state international law obligations.

Second, the suitability test requires that the adopted measure be appropriate to achieve a legitimate public aim. The adjudicator checks whether there is a suitable connection between the means chosen and the given policy goal. There must be a rational, logical and causal relationship between the measure and its objective.

Third, adjudicators verify whether a limitation of rights is necessary. The necessity test aims at verifying that the measure was the least restrictive available alternative.[56] This test 'expresses the idea of efficiency' and requires 'a comparison with alternative hypothetical acts ...

---

[51] J. Rivers, 'The Presumption of Proportionality' (2014) 77 MLR 409–433, 412.

[52] M. Klatt and M. Meister, *The Constitutional Structure of Proportionality* (OUP 2012) 8–9; Cohen-Eliya and Porat, *Proportionality and Constitutional Culture*, 2. Other scholars consolidate the first and second stages of proportionality analysis (legitimacy and suitability) into one, requiring that state measures use means appropriate to the achievement of a legitimate goal. Craig, *Administrative Law*, 637.

[53] W.W. Burke White and A. von Staden, 'Private Litigation in a Public Law Sphere: The Standard of Review in Investor–State Arbitrations' (2010) 35 *Yale JIL* 283–346, 334; A. Barak, *Proportionality: Constitutional Rights and their Limitations* (CUP 2012) 251 (noting that 'a purpose conflicting with ... constitutional provisions could not be considered proper for purposes of constitutional review').

[54] F.J. Urbina, *A Critique of Proportionality and Balancing* (CUP 2017) 5.

[55] Schlink, 'Proportionality', 722–3.

[56] Some constitutional and international systems adopt the 'less restrictive means analysis' rather than the 'least restrictive means analysis'. Barak, *Proportionality: Constitutional Rights and their Limitations*, 317–18 (supporting the

which may achieve the same aim to the same degree but with less cost to rights'.[57] Arguably, 'the more alternatives [a state] has considered and rejected, the more confident [the state] can be that a measure is necessary'.[58] If there is 'an alternative course of action equally capable of achieving the aim, but at less cost to rights', then the measure is not necessary, and the measure is disproportionate.[59] If there is no such alternative, then the measure is necessary.

Fourth, adjudicators assess whether the damage caused by the adopted measure does not exceed the benefit obtained from realizing the objective. As Ahron Barak, a prominent scholar of constitutional law and former Justice of the Supreme Court of Israel, puts it, 'there must be a proportionate balance between the social benefit of realizing the appropriate goal, and the harm caused to the right'.[60] Such balancing 'is the most delicate and controversial aspect' of the proportionality analysis.[61] It is a form of 'cost-benefit analysis' that 'requires the court to quantify the gain and the loss respectively'.[62] The proportionality in the strict sense test is 'strongly evaluative'.[63]

If the measure satisfies all four stages of the proportionality analysis, 'the infringement [of rights] is justified and the prima facie violation turns out not to be a violation after all'.[64] If the measure 'fails at any hurdle, the violation is confirmed'.[65]

---

less restrictive test). If properly formulated, the less restrictive means analysis can offer significant leeway for state regulation and avoid the risk of the adjudicator passing judgment on the relative importance of the goal chosen by the invoking state. Arguably, the adjudicator would focus on (1) whether there is an alternative measure available to the state that achieves the same level of protection as the chosen measure; where (2) the alternative measure results in less restrictive effects on foreign investment. An alternative measure would only be assessed under this test if it achieves the same level of protection as the chosen measure and the adjudicator could not substitute his/her own judgment to that of the state in the appropriate level of protection of the relevant public interest. This more nuanced version of necessity has in fact been adopted in some WTO cases and investment arbitrations.

[57] Rivers, 'Proportionality and Variable Intensity of Review', 198.

[58] Rivers, 'The Presumption of Proportionality', 425.

[59] Ibid. 412.

[60] A. Barak, 'Proportionality and Principled Balancing' (2010) 4 LEHR 1–18, 6.

[61] Sartor, 'Doing Justice to Rights and Values', 208, 199.

[62] Rivers, 'Proportionality and Variable Intensity of Review', 200.

[63] Ibid.

[64] Rivers, 'The Presumption of Proportionality', 412–13.

[65] Ibid. 413.

While these steps are analytically distinct, some scholars argue that they overlap to a large extent, and constitute 'a legal version of the Russian matryoshka doll, with each stage of the constitutional analysis containing all the preceding ones'.[66] Arguably, 'the necessity test encompasses the rationality test', while the proportionality test in the strict sense includes both the necessity and rationality requirement. Although the hypothesis is visually attractive, there may be disproportionate measures with legitimate aims, and proportionate measure with illegitimate aims; therefore, considering the various steps as distinct rather than overlapping remains a preferable analytical approach. After having illustrated the concept of proportionality, its origins and its structure, we now move on to examine the promises and pitfalls of the proportionality test.

3.2 THE MERITS AND FUNCTIONS OF PROPORTIONALITY ANALYSIS

The reasons for proportionality's success in the marketplace of ideas are multifold. Proportionality expresses the perennial quest for perfection, precision and order. Proportionality has 'aesthetic' qualities, because 'there is something good – certainly something beautiful – in the very idea of things being properly aligned'.[67] It responds to the human need for symmetry, balance and proportion.[68] Several scholars and practitioners perceive it as a neutral, clear and objective framework of analysis that can restrain the exercise of public authority, shape judicial review, and manage private actors' expectations.

Proportionality is deemed to express objectivity, harmony and justice in legal reasoning.[69] It can foster analytical clarity, rendering more transparent the legal reasoning of policy makers and adjudicators.[70] Proportionality is seen as a useful 'heuristic device', providing 'a simple, structured and manageable method' to adjudicate conflicting values.[71] By

---

[66] A.L. Bendor and T. Sela, 'How Proportional is Proportionality?' (2015) 13 IJCL 530–44, 538.

[67] Poole, 'Proportionality in Perspective', 387.

[68] Ibid. 390.

[69] S. Tsakyrakis, 'Proportionality: An Assault on Human Rights?' (2009) 7 IJCL 468–93, 469.

[70] C. Henckels, *Proportionality and Deference in Investor–State Arbitration: Balancing Investment Protection and Regulatory Autonomy* (CUP 2015) 27.

[71] Tsakyrakis, 'Proportionality: An Assault on Human Rights?', 490 (reporting but criticizing this view).

encompassing balancing that constitutes a 'powerful metaphor', 'a basic way of practical reasoning' and 'suggests precision', proportionality 'claims to capture, as a whole, the best method of decision making'.[72]

Proportionality has three main functions: (1) restraining the exercise of public authority; (2) shaping judicial review; and (3) managing private actors' expectations. Let us examine these roles. First, proportionality is based on 'a culture of justification' which 'requires that governments should provide substantive justification for all their actions'.[73] In order to be legitimate, a governmental action must be 'justified in terms of its "cogency" and its capacity for "persuasion," that is, in terms of its rationality[,] reasonableness', and efficiency.[74] Proportionality is a 'deliberative methodology',[75] which requires that all of the relevant factors be considered; therefore, it can insert 'Socratic contestation' in the deliberative process of governmental action,[76] and establish 'a proper dialogue between the political branches and the judiciary'.[77] When adjudicators sanction the non-conformity of a given state action with the law, they have the capacity to inform future state conduct.[78] Not only does proportionality push the state organs to provide coherent reasons for their conduct, but it also requires adjudicators to strike a balance between competing interests according to a structured set of criteria, thus enhancing the accountability of policy makers and adjudicators.[79]

Second, proportionality constitutes a limit to the subjectivity of the adjudicator, providing a structured, formalized and seemingly objective method. Proportionality also allows adjudicators to adopt nuanced decisions rather than 'all-or-nothing' approaches,[80] and to structure their

---

[72] Ibid. 469 (reporting but criticizing this view).

[73] M. Cohen-Eliya and I. Porat, 'Proportionality and the Culture of Justification' (2011) 59 AJCL 463–90, 467.

[74] Ibid. 467, 475.

[75] I. Porat, 'Some Critical Thoughts on Proportionality', in G. Bongiovanni, G. Sartor and C. Valentini (eds), *Reasonableness and Law* (Springer 2009) 234–50, 244.

[76] M. Kumm, 'The Idea of Socratic Contestation and the Right to Justification: The Point of Rights Based Proportionality Review' (2010) 4 LEHR 141–75, 141.

[77] Barak, *Proportionality. Constitutional Rights and their Limitations*, 465.

[78] Ibid. 460–67.

[79] W. Sadurski, 'Reasonableness and Value Pluralism in Law and Politics', in Bongiovanni, Sartor and Valentini (eds), *Reasonableness and Law*, 129–46, 145.

[80] B. Kingsbury and S. Schill, 'Public Law Concepts to Balance Investors' Rights with State Regulatory Actions in the Public Interest: The Concept of

analysis in a framework that 'may produce better and more convincing reasoning', thus enhancing predictability[81] and bringing order and coherence into legal systems. Proportionality can provide 'a common language that transcends national borders and that allows for dialogue and exchange of information' between courts and tribunals.[82] It can also 'constitute a gateway for non-investment law principles to enter into the argumentative framework of investment treaty arbitration and thereby help to overcome the fragmentation of international law'.[83]

Third, proportionality can also delimit the legitimate expectations of private actors vis-à-vis state regulation. Proportionality analysis can 'reduc[e] the sense of defeat for the losing party. As such, it is consensus-oriented because it acknowledges explicitly that there are valid constitutional arguments on both sides, and that the arguments outweighed by the opposing ones do not lose thereby their constitutional weight'.[84]

In conclusion, this section has reviewed the leading arguments in favour of proportionality and its functions. Proportionality is seen as a neutral, clear and objective framework of analysis. It can restrain the exercise of public authority, shape judicial review, and manage private actors' expectations. The next section will present arguments against proportionality.

3.3 THE PERILS OF SUCCESS

The widespread diffusion of the proportionality analysis does not necessarily establish proportionality as 'a superior mode of analysis' exclusive of 'other frequently used forms of interpretive reasoning'.[85] The very notion that 'beauty resides in certain fundamental and universally valid proportions', that 'mathematical ratios as such can be beautiful' has been contested. In particular, scholars have contended that beauty has nothing

---

Proportionality', in S. Schill (ed.), *International Investment Law and Comparative Public Law* (OUP 2010) 75–105, 79.

[81] Ibid. 103.

[82] Cohen-Eliya and Porat, 'Proportionality and the Culture of Justification', 472.

[83] Kingsbury and Schill, 'Public Law Concepts to Balance Investors' Rights', 104.

[84] Sadurski, 'Reasonableness and Value Pluralism in Law and Politics', 129, 145.

[85] V.C. Jackson, 'Being Proportional About Proportionality' (2004) 21 *Constitutional Commentary* 803–859, 818.

to do with calculation[86] and even supporters of the notion admit that 'it [is not] possible to prove that one system of proportion is better than another'.[87] While proportionality analysis should not necessarily be seen as 'a kind of dogma' to be challenged,[88] certainly its migration from constitutional law to the international sphere poses a range of challenges. In particular, the viability of proportionality as the main tool for balancing different interests and values has been challenged on five grounds: (1) institutional competences; (2) scale of values; (3) cultural arguments; (4) incommensurability; and (5) overprotection of economic interests.

First, proportionality can be perceived as running against the traditional allocation of institutional competences among the legislative, executive and judiciary powers because it empowers courts and tribunals to review state conduct in a significant fashion. Arguments run against using balancing to review the host state's decision, because adjudicators would second-guess the decision of the host state by replicating the original decision-making process.[89] The rise of proportionality analysis as a 'juristic method' for settling disputes, rather than as 'a method restricted to legislation', 'threatens the sharp distinction between legislation and legal interpretation'.[90] As Stone Sweet and Mathews put it, 'balancing can never be dissociated from lawmaking: it requires judges to behave as legislators'.[91] However, this may not be the outcome the

---

[86] E. Burke, *Enquiry into the Origin of Our Ideas of the Sublime and the Beautiful* (1757); cited by Wittkower, 'The Changing Concept of Proportion', 202.

[87] Wittkower, 'The Changing Concept of Proportion', 210 (reporting these criticisms, but concluding, at 213, that 'the search for systems of proportion in the arts will continue as long as art remains a [human endeavour]').

[88] R. Gordon, 'Two Dogmas of Proportionality' (2011) *Judicial Review* 182–91, 182.

[89] I. Porat, 'Why All Attempts to Make Judicial Review Balancing Principled Fail?', paper presented at the VII World Congress of the International Association of Constitutional Law, Athens, 11–15 June 2007, 7.

[90] D. Kennedy, 'Political Ideology and Comparative Law', in M. Bussani and U. Mattei (eds), *The Cambridge Companion to Comparative Law* (CUP 2012) 35–56, 36.

[91] A. Stone Sweet and J. Mathews, 'Proportionality Balancing and Global Constitutionalism' (2008) 47 *Columbia Journal of Transnational Law* 72–164, 88.

parties to an IIA intended, when they signed such agreement. Then the question is: how far can the adjudicators second-guess state authorities?[92]

By considering different alternatives to given legislative or executive measures under the necessity test, and by balancing competing interests under the proportionality test (in the narrow sense), the adjudicator interferes with the regulatory autonomy of states, supplanting the role of legitimately deputed decision-makers.[93] On the one hand, the necessity test would – almost without exception – invalidate the given measure since the arbitral tribunal can always envisage alternatives retrospectively with the benefit of hindsight.[94] On the other hand, the proportionality in the strict sense test requires a normative judgment concerning the competing public and private interests. Decisions about how to pursue the common good are 'unavoidably subjective'[95] and 'intrinsically political'.[96]

Although the syntax of proportionality analysis looks determinate, 'the formulation gives no clues as to how the process is to be undertaken'.[97] While procedurally, proportionality constrains the adjudicators, requiring them to follow specific tests, substantively it expands their power.[98] Although proportionality analysis might seem simple and clear, it brings with it 'complexities and obscurities'.[99] In fact, it has 'a darker side – both in what it may permit governments to do and what it may permit courts to prohibit or require of governments'.[100] Because of the 'creative aspect' of proportionality,[101] the outcomes of such balancing are 'likely

---

92 G. Nolte, 'Thin or Thick? The Principle of Proportionality in International Humanitarian Law' (2010) 4 LEHR 245–55, 246.

93 A. Kulick, *Global Public Interest in International Investment Law* (CUP 2012) 172.

94 Schlink, 'Proportionality in Constitutional Law: Why Everywhere but Here?', 299.

95 Ibid.

96 Schlink, 'Proportionality', 736 (stating that 'the legal expertise [of judges] cannot legitimize their rendering political decisions').

97 Gordon, 'Two Dogmas of Proportionality', 183–4.

98 X. Contiades and A. Fotiadou, 'Social Rights in the Age of Proportionality: Global Economic Crisis and Constitutional Litigation' (2012) 10 IJCL 660–86, 667.

99 T. Hickman, 'Problems for Proportionality' (2010) NZLR 303–326, 324.

100 Jackson, 'Being Proportional about Proportionality', 809–810 (considering proportionality's complexity, and urging a 'more proportionate use of proportionality' in response).

101 Contiades and Fotiadou, 'Social Rights in the Age of Proportionality', 665.

to be highly controversial'.[102] Especially when complex data is involved, legislators may be better equipped than adjudicators in balancing private and public interests.[103] There is a risk that adjudicators impose values that are not those of the host states involved let alone required by the relevant international investment treaty. In sum, proportionality analysis risks enabling arbitral activism, that is, letting arbitrators play outside the boundaries within which they operate.

Second, proportionality analysis tells us nothing about the scale of values to be used in order to evaluate competing objectives. Webber has pointed out that proportionality 'brings with it a vocabulary all of its own', which includes the notions of 'cost, benefit, weight', but eludes 'concepts of good (and bad), right (and wrong), correct (and incorrect)'.[104] In other words, it purports to transform legal issues into 'technical questions of weight and balance', as if the former could be subject to mathematical measurement.[105]

However, not only do 'alternative structures' exist, but by 'avoid[ing] the language of interest, cost, weight, and balance' they may better reconcile conflicting interests and values.[106] The proportionality test has a demanding nature; it can halt progressive regulation; it assumes that everything can be balanced, and nothing deserves heightened protection. By contrast, what appears to be a less than perfect standard may nonetheless produce the right results.[107]

Moreover, under the proportionality in the strict sense test, a measure is assessed in the light of competing norms and objectives. In this context, '[t]he central question [i]s what must be proportionate to what'.[108] As Tsakyrakis aptly puts it, 'it is not clear what is weighted (interests, rights, considerations); how it is weighted (with what metric); and who is doing – or should [be] do[ing] – the balancing (judges or legislators)'.[109] Proportionality analysis tells us nothing about the scale of values that will determine the final outcome.

---

[102] Sartor, 'Doing Justice to Rights and Values', 208

[103] Ibid. 204.

[104] G.C.N. Webber, 'Proportionality, Balancing, and the Cult of Constitutional Rights Scholarship' (2010) 23 *Canadian Journal of Law and Jurisprudence* 179–202, 180.

[105] Ibid. 191.

[106] Ibid. 193.

[107] R. Levi Montalcini, *In Praise of Imperfection* (Basic Books 1989).

[108] J.H. Jans, 'Proportionality Revisited' (2000) 27 *Legal Issues of Economic Integration* 239–65, 239.

[109] Tsakyrakis, 'Proportionality: An Assault on Human Rights?', 470.

Does proportionality analysis give 'a false impression of accuracy', while remaining substantively empty?[110] Can proportionality lead to 'irrational' decisions by placing only formal constraints but not substantive ones on adjudicators?[111] Does it leave the adjudicator free to select his/her own value system?[112] Critics of the proportionality analysis contend that proportionality is substantively empty, and thus risks 'obscur[ing] the moral considerations' that are central to adjudication,[113] and transforming legal discourses into technical ones.[114] They view the proportionality analysis as 'irrational' because it requires the weighting of incommensurable options.[115] Critics contend that 'proponents of the principle of proportionality rarely identify a common criterion for evaluating the weight of ... conflicting ... interests',[116] therefore leaving the adjudicator free to select his/her own value system.

Proponents of the proportionality analysis argue that interests and values are commensurable and that the importance of competing interests can be assessed in light of the constitution, which provides 'a common point of view', and a single metric.[117] Yet, questions arise with regard to the transposability of this point of reference at the international level. As is known, international law prevails over domestic law and even constitutional law. The duty to bring national law into conformity with international law is a well-settled part of customary law and this is confirmed by consistent jurisprudence. In turn, reliance on national constitutional provisions does not justify a violation of international law.

Proponents of the proportionality analysis argue that proportionality analysis is not only 'technically and politically possible' but also desirable in 'integrated systems' such as constitutional systems or systems with a constitutional density (e.g. the European Convention of Human

---

[110] Y. Arai-Takahashi, 'Proportionality', in D. Sheldon (ed.), *Oxford Handbook of International Human Rights Law* (OUP 2013) 446–68, 467 (reporting these critiques).

[111] N. Petersen, *Proportionality and Judicial Activism* (CUP 2017) 9.

[112] Stone Sweet and Mathews, 'Proportionality Balancing and Global Constitutionalism', 89; see also Kennedy, 'Political Ideology and Comparative Law', 35, 38 (stressing that there is a risk that proportionality analysis 'operates in the shadow of ideology').

[113] Tsakyrakis, 'Proportionality: An Assault on Human Rights?', 493.

[114] Arai-Takahashi, 'Proportionality', 467 (reporting these criticisms).

[115] Jackson, 'Constitutional Law in an Age of Proportionality', 3156.

[116] Webber, 'Proportionality, Balancing and the Cult of Constitutional Rights Scholarship', 194.

[117] Ibid. (reporting this approach).

Rights or the European Union).[118] Yet, even admitting that systems with a constitutional density provide the adjudicator with a useful value system, one may question whether international investment law has such constitutional density.

While 'constitutional systems ... paradigmatically govern and unite all aspects of the common good within their territories and for all persons subject to their authority',[119] international investment law has a 'very monothematic nature', because it focuses mainly 'on affording protection to foreign investments' and promoting the development of the host state.[120] International investment law is a specialized regime of international law. While constitutional courts have functional authority over almost any kind of human activity and have 'the formal or effective power to coordinate various sectors into a single coherent fabric of law',[121] arbitral tribunals have jurisdiction over investment disputes only. Therefore, the lack of constitutional density of the investment regime 'does not allow for an accurate and thus legitimate balancing of a variety of different interests'.[122]

Given that no special regime is self-contained – rather, it remains part of international law – questions arise as to whether international law itself is analogous to a constitutional system. Is there an international constitution? For some scholars, international law and its subsystems are undergoing a process of 'constitutionalization', i.e. they are gradually developing into that which resembles a constitutional order.[123] The UN

---

[118] F. Ortino, 'Investment Treaties, Sustainable Development and Reasonableness Review: A Case against Strict Proportionality Balancing' (2017) 30 *Leiden JIL* 71–91, 91 (cautioning that proportionality is 'technically and politically possible but only in ... integrated systems (such as within the European Convention of Human Rights or the European Union)').

[119] P.G. Carozza, 'The Problematic Applicability of Subsidiarity to International Law and Institutions' (2016) 61 *American Journal of Jurisprudence* 51–67, 59.

[120] Ortino, 'Investment Treaties, Sustainable Development and Reasonableness Review, 91.

[121] Carozza, 'The Problematic Applicability of Subsidiarity to International Law and Institutions', 59.

[122] Ibid.

[123] J. Klabbers, A. Peters and G. Ulfstein (eds), *The Constitutionalization of International Law* (OUP 2009) (discussing the extent to which the international system is developing constitutional features).

Charter has been seen as the 'Constitution of the international community'.[124] Other scholars have also examined the question as to whether *jus cogens* norms constitute the constitutional law of the international community. However, the concept of constitution is vague and its meaning varies across different legal cultures. Therefore, it seems premature to affirm that international law is a constitutional system of its own kind.

Third, proportionality analysis has been criticized on cultural grounds. Not only can proportionality analysis run the risk of not taking into account the cultural context of a given measure, it also risks importing the specific cultural baggage of other legal systems into the adjudicative process. On the one hand, supranational adjudicators may not be familiar with the context of a given domestic measure. As Burke White and von Staden point out, consideration of the values chosen by a given community 'requires both familiarity with those values and a degree of embeddedness within that polity'.[125] However, supranational adjudicators are far removed from the polities over which they exercise control.

On the other hand, proportionality comes from a certain historical setting,[126] reflecting distrust toward the public administration in the aftermath of World War II.[127] Since its beginnings, it has endorsed a particular 'individualistic conception of rights'.[128] In a number of European countries, including Germany, constitutional law has gained an increasing primacy since the end of the war and the democratic transitions that followed.[129] The use of proportionality analysis marked a shift

---

[124] B. Fassbender, *The United Nations Charter as the Constitution of the International Community* (Brill 2009) (considering the fundamental values expressed in the Charter as supreme law of the international community). But see J. Alvarez, 'Constitutional Interpretation in International Organizations', in J.M. Coicaud and V. Heiskanen (eds), *The Legitimacy of International Organizations* (UN University Press 2001) 104–120 (arguing that 'neither logic, function, text or history support constitutional analogies as applied to the UN Charter').

[125] W.W. Burke-White and A. von Staden, 'Private Litigation in a Public Law Sphere: The Standard of Review in Investor–State Arbitrations' (2010) 35 *Yale JIL* 283–346, 336.

[126] Cohen-Elya and Porat, *Proportionality and Constitutional Culture*, 8.

[127] M. Bobek, 'Reasonableness in Administrative Law: A Comparative Reflection on Functional Equivalence', in G. Bongiovanni, G. Sartor and C. Valentini (eds), *Reasonableness and Law* (Springer 2009) 311–26, 323.

[128] C. Bernal Pulido, 'The Migration of Proportionality across Europe' (2013) NZJPIL 483–515, 485.

[129] M. Schor, 'Mapping Comparative Judicial Review' (2008) 7 *Washington University Global Studies LR* 257–87, 271.

from a 'culture of authority' to a 'culture of justification'.[130] Constitutional courts have played a key role in making constitutional law effective,[131] aiming to be an 'impenetrable bulwark against any infringement of the rights of the people'.[132] At the same time, lawyers elaborated the respective constitutions on the basis of 'their understanding of state and society' with 'distinct starting points and trajectories'.[133]

Can proportionality be conceived in almost complete isolation from the cultural context in which it originated? Critical legal theorists contend that 'hegemonic elites' might use balancing to entrench their values and shift power from the democratic process to the courts,[134] and that proportionality might have an 'imperialistic effect', in that it might set aside local constitutional values.[135]

Fourth, proportionality analysis has also been criticized on the ground of incommensurability.[136] While proportionality assumes measurability – to be balanced, two competing principles should be based on a common scale of value – arguments are made that cost-benefit analysis is flawed with respect to public sector decisions due to the incommensurability of values. There are interests that cannot be measured against each other.[137] Justice Scalia once stated that balancing constitutional values is like ascertaining whether 'a particular line is longer than a particular rock is heavy'.[138] In this regard, critics contend that 'if courts are balancing things that cannot be balanced, then their decision seems to represent a departure from the rule of law, in favour of arbitrary rule by judges'.[139]

---

130 See generally Cohen-Eliya and Porat, *Proportionality and Constitutional Culture*.

131 M. Cappelletti, 'Repudiating Montesquieu? The Expansion and Legitimacy of "Constitutional Justice' (1985) 35 *Catholic University LR* 1–32.

132 Ibid.

133 P. Zumbansen, 'Transnational Comparisons: Theory and Practice of Comparative Law as a Critique of Global Governance', (2012) *Osgoode Hall Law School, Research Paper* No. 1/2012, 19.

134 R. Hirschl, *Towards Juristocracy: The Origins and Consequences of the New Constitutionalism* (Harvard UP 2004).

135 Cohen-Elya and Porat, *Proportionality and Constitutional Culture*, 8–9.

136 P.-E. Veel, 'Incommensurability, Proportionality, and Rational Legal Decision-Making' (2010) 4 LEHR 178–230.

137 T. Endicott, 'Proportionality and Incommensurability', *Oxford Legal Research Paper* 40 (2012) 9.

138 *Bendix Autolite Corp v. Midwesco Enter Inc*, 486 U.S. 888, 897 (1988) (Scalia J. concurring).

139 Endicott, 'Proportionality and Incommensurability', 13 (also arguing, at 20, that 'incommensurabilities result in a dramatically creative judicial role').

For them, proportionality is 'a chimera',[140] formally expressing 'mathematical precision', but substantively remaining subjective, indeterminate and irrational.[141]

Regulatory choices limiting given economic freedoms are often based on an array of considerations, 'not a single metric'.[142] By overlooking the polycentric nature of given regulations, the proportionality analysis risks 'undermining any alternative modes of reasoning' that can better integrate the multiple interests involved in a given dispute.[143] Proportionality analysis also 'risks putting second-order considerations ... into the balance', potentially leading to the exclusion of some first order considerations.[144] Proportionality risks being 'not proportional'[145] and 'neglecting the complexity of moral evaluation'.[146]

Yet, some incommensurability can be an unavoidable aspect of the judicial role.[147] After all, 'legal systems ... necessarily authorize judges to reconcile incommensurable considerations'.[148] Barak argues that a common denominator exists in the form of the marginal social importance of each value.[149] For Barak, social importance 'is derived, *inter alia*, from ... the unique history of each country, from the structure of the political system, and from the different social values'.[150] He argues that constitutional adjudicators should assess the social importance of each value taking into account 'the normative structure of each legal system'.[151] Robert Alexy suggests that a common denominator exists in the form of the constitution. From this point of view, Alexy argues, 'incommensurability is nothing other than disagreement'.[152]

---

140 Tsakyrakis, 'Proportionality: An Assault on Human Rights?', 472.

141 Bendor and Sela, 'How Proportional is Proportionality?', 542.

142 F.J. Urbina, 'A Critique of Proportionality' (2012) 57 *American Journal of Jurisprudence* 49–80, 55.

143 Arai-Takahashi, 'Proportionality', 467 (reporting this criticism).

144 Endicott, 'Proportionality and Incommensurability', 20 (internal quotation omitted).

145 Bendor and Sela, 'How Proportional is Proportionality?', 534.

146 Tsakyrakis, 'Proportionality: An Assault on Human Rights?', 475.

147 Endicott, 'Proportionality and Incommensurability', 14.

148 Ibid.

149 Barak, *Proportionality: Constitutional Rights and their Limitations*, 482–4.

150 Ibid. 56.

151 Ibid.

152 R. Alexy, 'Constitutional Rights and Proportionality' (2014) 22 *Revus* 51–65, 64.

The very criterion of social relevance, however, may prove to be incommensurable.[153] Moreover, even admitting that one can reach measurability by looking at the 'framework of society's fundamental conceptions',[154] how can we transfer such criterion from constitutional law to international investment law? One can question whether international law is adequately 'constitutionalized' to allow the migration of proportionality analysis from the constitutional to the international realm. Admittedly, under international law, of which international investment law is a subfield, a number of fundamental interests and values are more important than others. Such interests have a special normative status, and include *jus cogens* norms prohibiting torture, racial discrimination, slavery and those requiring the protection of human dignity and fundamental human rights.[155] Yet, there are ongoing disagreements about the role of non-economic considerations in international investment law and arbitration. Most IIAs do not mention human rights. It is true that Article 31(3)(c) can be a tool for the constitutionalization of international law and that international investment law is not a self-contained system.[156] However, arbitral tribunals are of limited jurisdiction. Enforcement of human rights through investment arbitration is debatable as it can constitute a form of 'epistemological appropriation'.[157] Any rational comparison of the weight of the competing interests must presuppose the existence of a common scale. Constitutional systems provide such measure, i.e. the importance of the interests as expressed in the unique history of each country and reflected in the domestic constitution. However, the proportionality test per se does not provide a common scale or common denominator between competing interests. Therefore, proportionality is a sophisticated test for framing problems in constitutional systems, yet it may not work well in those systems that do not have a constitutional density yet, such as international investment law and arbitration, and where balancing would enable arbitral activism.

---

153 Urbina, 'A Critique of Proportionality', 56; Endicott, 'Proportionality and Incommensurability', 8.

154 Barak, 'Proportionality and Principled Balancing', 9.

155 V. Vadi, 'Jus Cogens in International Investment Law and Arbitration' (2015) 46 *Netherlands YIL* 357–88.

156 G. Bücheler, *Proportionality in Investor–State Arbitration* (OUP 2015) 86, 120.

157 P. Alston, 'Resisting the Merger and Acquisition of Human Rights by Trade Law: A Reply to Petersmann' (2002) 13 EJIL 815–44, 815.

Fifth, the use of proportionality analysis can lead to the overprotection of economic interests if it is used in a very exacting fashion.[158] In fact, the proportionality analysis can restrict the regulatory power of the state to a large extent if arbitral tribunals do not adopt deferential standards of review. This argument is indirectly supported by parallel developments in the international trade law context, where the concept of proportionality has translated economic considerations in legal terms[159] and 'tipped the balance in favour of trade liberalization'.[160] Proportionality in the WTO jurisprudence mainly relates to the balancing of trade versus non-trade values and interests – namely the protection of human, animal, or plant life or health, and the conservation of exhaustible natural resources. The Appellate Body (AB) of the WTO held that:

> determination of whether a measure, which is not 'indispensable', may nevertheless be 'necessary' [under Article XX(d)] … involves in every case a process of weighing and balancing a series of factors which prominently include the contribution made by the compliance measure to the enforcement of the law or regulation at issue, the importance of the common interests or values protected by that law or regulation, and the accompanying impact of the law or regulation on imports or exports.[161]

Yet, rarely have state measures to protect public health passed scrutiny.[162]

In conclusion, although proportionality seems to endorse 'elegant formal structures' of analysis and 'mathematical precision',[163] some argue that 'it fails to deliver … what it promises'.[164] Rather than enhancing clarity and coherence, it risks providing an 'opaque' and

---

158 H. Xiuli, 'The Application of the Principle of Proportionality in *Tecmed v. Mexico*' (2007) 6 *Chinese JIL* 635–52.

159 Portuese, 'Principle of Proportionality as Principle of Economic Efficiency', 622.

160 G. Kapterian, 'A Critique of the WTO Jurisprudence on Necessity' (2010) 59 ICLQ 89–127, 91.

161 *Korea–Measures Affecting Imports of Fresh, Chilled and Frozen Beef*, AB Report, WT/DS161/AB/R, WT/DS169/AB/R, 11 December 2000, para. 163.

162 L. Gruszczynski and V. Vadi, 'Standard of Review and Scientific Evidence in WTO Law and International Investment Arbitration: Converging Parallels?', in L. Gruszczynski and W. Werner (eds), *Deference in International Courts and Tribunals: Standard of Review and Margin of Appreciation* (OUP 2014) 152–72.

163 W. Sauter, 'Proportionality in EU Law: A Balancing Act?', TILEC Discussion Paper (2013) 2.

164 Tsakyrakis, 'Proportionality: An Assault on Human Rights?', 482.

'impressionistic assessment of the relevant weights of competing considerations'.[165] Rather than asking 'what is right and wrong', adjudicators investigate whether something is proportionate.[166] Proportionality – like any conceptual framework – is not a neutral process; rather, it is based on the primacy and priority of individual entitlements over the exercise of public powers.[167] The spread of proportionality analysis highlights 'a shift from a culture of authority to a culture of justification', which is connected, *inter alia*, to the rise of the human rights movement that developed after World War II. Whether this entails a neglect of a polity's choices toward a judicial dictatorship or the achievement of a higher rule of law – the ultimate rule of law[168] – is open to debate. Nonetheless, scholars caution for 'a more proportional approach to the benefits of proportionality analysis'.[169]

3.4 PROPORTIONALITY IN EU LAW

The migration of the proportionality analysis from constitutional law to EU law is a paradigm of successful legal transplant. Proportionality is a general principle of EU law and can be used for reviewing EU action and member state action that falls within the sphere of EU law.[170] Largely fashioned by the EU courts, proportionality has subsequently assumed treaty status since the inception of the Maastricht Treaty.[171] The criteria for its application are set out in the Protocol No. 2 on the Application of

---

165 Ibid.

166 Ibid. 487.

167 M. Sakellaridou, 'La généalogie de la proportionalité', paper presented at the VII World Congress of the International Association of Constitutional Law, held in Athens, 11–15 June 2007, 20.

168 See generally D.M. Beatty, *The Ultimate Rule of Law* (OUP 2003).

169 Jackson, 'Being Proportional About Proportionality', 859; Bendor and Sela, 'How Proportional is Proportionality?', 544.

170 P. Craig and G. De Búrca, *EU Law*, 5th edn (OUP 2011) 526. See generally E. Ellis (ed.), *The Principle of Proportionality in the Laws of Europe* (Hart Publishing 1999); N. Emiliou, *The Principle of Proportionality in European Law: A Comparative Study* (Kluwer Law International 1996).

171 Treaty on European Union (TEU), signed on 7 February 1992, in force 1 November 1993. Consolidated Version of the Treaty on European Union [2010] OJ C83/01, Article 5(4) (stating that 'Under the principle of proportionality, the content and form of Union action shall not exceed what is necessary to achieve the objectives of the Treaties').

the Principles of Subsidiarity and Proportionality annexed to the treaties.[172] Proportionality is also present in a number of treaty articles.[173]

The success of proportionality in EU law is due to several reasons. Let us consider how the EU courts have transformed the various challenges posed by the proportionality concept into opportunities. First, with regard to institutional competences, the courts have interpreted the concept of proportionality in a flexible manner,[174] conferring it a relative character and showing varying degrees of deference. In some cases, the Court of Justice of the European Union (CJEU) has adopted 'a very deferential approach'; in others, it has conducted 'quite a rigorous and searching examination of the justification for a measure which has been challenged'.[175] In a seminal article, De Búrca noted that 'in reaching decisions, the Court of Justice is influenced not only by what it considers to be the nature and the importance of the interest or right claimed by the applicant, and the nature and importance of the objective alleged to be served by the measure, but by the relative expertise, position, and overall competence of the Court as against the decision-making authority in assessing those factors'.[176] The varied intensity of review reflects some subsidiarity: 'where the measure is seen to be primarily within the competence of the state, the Court is likely to be reluctant, unless a very important community interest is adversely affected, to examine the proportionality of the national measure too closely'.[177]

Some authors contend that the Court has adopted a stricter proportionality test when assessing national regulations (vertical dimension), and a more lenient approach when assessing EU regulations (horizontal dimension).[178] Therefore, according to these authors, the court will adopt a more demanding proportionality test in the former case, requiring the

---

[172] Protocol (No. 2) on the application of the principles of subsidiarity and proportionality, annexed to the Treaty on European Union and the Treaty on the Functioning of the European Union by the Treaty of Lisbon of 13 December 2007 [2010] OJ C83/01.

[173] See e.g. TEU, Article 12.

[174] T.I. Harbo, 'The Function of the Proportionality Principle in EU Law' (2010) 16 *European LJ* 158–85.

[175] G. De Búrca, 'The Principle of Proportionality and its Application in EC Law' (1993) 13 *Yearbook of European Law* 105–150, 111–12.

[176] Ibid.

[177] Ibid. 112.

[178] See generally T. Tridimas, *The General Principles of EU Law*, 2nd edn (OUP 2006) Chs 3, 5; Portuese, 'Principle of Proportionality as Principle of Economic Efficiency', 630.

national legislation to choose the least trade restrictive alternative.[179] In such case, the Court tends to undertake a strict test of proportionality and considers only the less trade restrictive measures to be proportionate to the stated objective.[180] For instance, in the seminal *Cassis de Dijon* case, the ECJ used the proportionality analysis to strike down a German regulation that produced an effect equivalent to a quantitative restriction on the free movement of goods. The case concerned the sale of *Cassis de Dijon*, a blackcurrant liqueur, produced in France containing 15 to 20 per cent alcohol. A German law requiring fruit liqueurs to contain at least 25 per cent alcohol did not allow the marketing of *Cassis de Dijon* in Germany. The ECJ held that the measure requiring minimum alcohol content for a beverage was unnecessary to protect consumers and thus disproportionate. In fact, state authorities could use less trade restrictive tools for informing consumers, such as labelling.[181]

Instead, when reviewing EU action, the Court will show a deferential approach, deeming the regulatory measure to be disproportionate only if it finds it manifestly inappropriate to achieve the stated objective.[182] For instance, in *Hauer*, the Court found that a Community regulation to control wine production was proportionate and thus not infringing the right to property. The claimant argued that the regulation prohibiting the planting of new vines on certain lands for three years violated her property rights. The Court dismissed the claim emphasizing that the regulation pursued objectives of general interest and did not constitute a disproportionate interference with the property rights of the owner. The temporary prohibition was justified by the objectives of general interest pursued by the Community, namely the reduction of wine production surpluses and the restructuring of the European wine industry.[183] The judicial self-restraint of the ECJ when it reviews Union action 'does not

[179] Harbo, 'The Function of the Proportionality Principle in EU Law', 172; T.I. Harbo, *The Function of the Proportionality Analysis in European Law* (Brill 2015) 17.

[180] See e.g. Case 104/75, *de Peijper* [1976] ECR 613 (deeming a national measure conditioning the importation of medical products to the obtainment of certain documents to be disproportionate as a means to protect public health).

[181] Case 120/78, *Rewe-Zentral AG v. Bundesmonopolverwaltung für Branntwein (Cassis de Dijon)* [1979] ECR 649, paras 13–14. See also Case 178/84, *Commission v. Germany (Beer Purity)* [1987] ECR 1227; Case 302/86, *Commission v. Denmark (Danish Bottles)* [1988] ECR 4607 (also finding the state measure to be disproportionate to the environmental objective pursued).

[182] Harbo, 'The Function of Proportionality Principle in EU Law', 172; Harbo, *The Function of the Proportionality Analysis in European Law*, 17.

[183] Case 44/79, *Liselotte Hauer v. Land Rheinland-Phalz* [1979] ECR 3727.

necessarily mean that the judicial review of proportionality of EU measures is absent'.[184] Rather, in a number of cases, the ECJ struck down EU measures on the grounds of their disproportion.[185]

Certainly, the CJEU has interpreted the proportionality analysis differently according to the various areas of EU law, such as national security, and agricultural, environmental and social policy among others.[186] In this respect, the Court has shown a more deferential approach in the adjudication of cultural diversity,[187] public morals[188] or public health-related disputes.[189] For instance, in *Omega*, a case concerning the German ban on laser games for reasons of human dignity, the Court formally adopted the three-prong proportionality test, but de facto left aside the demanding necessity test, thus upholding the ban.[190] By contrast, the Court has adopted the complete proportionality analysis even for Union measures, for instance, 'where an individual argues

---

184 Portuese, 'Principle of Proportionality as Principle of Economic Efficiency', 632.

185 Joined Cases C-402/05 P and C-415/05 P, *Yassin Abdullah Kadi and Al Barakaat International Foundation v. Council and Commission* [2008] ECR I-6351 (finding a Commission Regulation freezing assets of persons associated with the Al-Qaeda network to be a disproportionate restriction of the right to property because they lacked procedural safeguards); Joined Cases C-453/03, C-11/04, C-12/04 and C-194/04, *ABNA Ltd and others v. Secretary of State for Health and others* [2005] ECR I-10423, paras 80–84 (declaring a EU measure requiring the precise composition of animal feedstuff to be manifestly disproportionate).

186 Harbo, 'The Function of the Proportionality Principle in EU Law', 172; Portuese, 'Principle of Proportionality as Principle of Economic Efficiency', 634; De Búrca, 'The Principle of Proportionality and its Application in EC Law', 132–45.

187 Case C-250/06, *United Pan-Europe Communications Belgium and others* [2007] ECR I-11135.

188 Case C-36/02, *Omega* [2004] ECR I-9609; Case 34/79, *R v. Henn and Derby* [1979] ECR 3795.

189 Case C-376/98, *Germany v. Parliament and Council* [2000] ECR I-08419; Case C-377/98, *Netherlands v. Parliament and Council* [2001] ECR I-7079; Case C-419/01, *The Queen v. Secretary of State for Health ex p British American Tobacco Ltd* [2002] ECR I-11453; Case C-210/03, *Swedish Match AB and Swedish Match UK Ltd* [2004] ECR I-11893; Case C-372/04, *Watts* [2006] ECR I-4325; Joined Cases C-171/07 and C-172/07, *Apothekerkammer des Saarlandes et al v. Deutscher Apothekerverband* and *Helga Neumann-Siewert v. Saarland* [2009] ECR I-4171; Case C-89/09, *Commission v. France* (*Medical Laboratories*) [2010] ECR I-12941.

190 Case C-36/2002, *Omega Spielhallen und Automatenaufstellungs GmbH v. Oberbürgermeisterin der Bundesstadt Bonn* [2004] ECR I-9609, para. 39.

that her rights have been unduly restricted by Union action'.[191] There are a number of examples where such measures were deemed to be disproportionate.[192]

The varying intensity of the proportionality test in EU adjudication is certainly not neutral. Rather, it is value-laden, expressing the Court's function – that of adjudicating disputes and promoting European integration. If the CJEU seems to show some deference in adjudicating some disputes, it is because it presumes that European institutions pursue European integration.[193] In this regard, proportionality has been a tool of judicial 'activism',[194] promoting legal and economic integration.[195] As De Búrca aptly pointed out, 'the more severe the impact on the Community interest or aim, the lower the degree of deference to the national measure the Court will display'.[196]

Second, with regard to the scale of values, the case of the CJEU is unique, as the Court has recently acquired a mandate to adjudicate on human rights violations. In fact, the Lisbon Treaty[197] conferred binding nature to the Charter of Fundamental Human Rights.[198] Not only has the EU integrated the consideration of human rights in its treaty texts, it is also negotiating its accession to the European Convention on Human Rights (ECHR).[199] Even before these notable institutional developments, since the early 1970s, the Court has considered fundamental rights to be

---

191 Craig and De Búrca, *EU Law*, 529.

192 See e.g. Case 114/76, *Bela-Muhle v. Grows Farm* (*Skimmed Milk*) [1977] ECR 1211 (holding that a regulation requiring animal foodstuff producers to buy skimmed milk powder at a price three times more expensive than its current value was disproportionate).

193 Portuese, 'Principle of Proportionality as Principle of Economic Efficiency', 631.

194 See generally M. Dawson, B. De Witte and E. Muir (eds), *Judicial Activism at the European Court of Justice* (Edward Elgar 2013).

195 M. Blauberger and S.K. Schmidt, 'The European Court of Justice and its Political Impact' (2017) *West European Politics* 1–12, 3.

196 De Búrca, 'The Principle of Proportionality and its Application in EC Law', 126.

197 Treaty of Lisbon Amending the Treaty on European Union and the Treaty Establishing the European Community, 13 December 2007 [2007] OJ C306/1.

198 Charter of Fundamental Rights of the European Union [2000] OJ C364/1.

199 Convention for the Protection of Human Rights and Fundamental Freedoms, 4 November 1950, in force 3 September 1953, 213 UNTS 222. On the ongoing accession process, see A. Brabcová, 'Accession of the European Union to the European Convention on Human Rights Examining the CJEU's Approach in the Opinion 2/13 the Future of the EU-ECHR Accession Process', Charles University in Prague Faculty of Law Research Paper No. 2016/I/4.

general principles of European law, and has referred to the ECHR as 'a source of inspiration underpinning these general principles'.[200] Therefore, favouring the objective of European integration does not necessarily entail a predominance of economic interests vis-à-vis other non-economic values, as the latter constitute part of the European project.

Third, with regard to the cultural arguments, the proportionality principle is 'endogenous to the EU legal order'.[201] The Court has distilled the proportionality concept from the common European legal heritage.[202] The application of the proportionality analysis has at times converged[203] and at times diverged from that of national courts.[204] The CJEU has made consistent use of comparisons, referring to the constitutional experiences of the member states to elaborate general principles of EU law,[205] but it 'has deliberately refrained from citing the rulings of national courts in order to avoid allegations of cherry-picking or of the privileging of the rulings of one or more Member State courts over others'.[206] Moreover, when reviewing state measures, the CJEU has acknowledged the possibility of different approaches by member states to similar issues,[207] and has been 'willing to interpret proportionality in the light of the Member State's particular values, notwithstanding that those values differ from those of other Member States'.[208] In a few cases, the court accepted constitutional history and identity as a ground for relaxing the proportionality test.[209]

---

[200] G. De Búrca, 'After the EU Charter of Fundamental Rights: The Court of Justice as a Human Rights Adjudicator?' (2013) 14 *Maastricht Journal of European and Comparative Law* 168–84, 170.

[201] Portuese, 'Principle of Proportionality as Principle of Economic Efficiency', 618.

[202] Harbo, 'The Function of the Proportionality Principle in EU Law', 172.

[203] See e.g. Case 44/79, *Liselotte Hauer v. Land Rheinland-Phalz* [1979] ECR 3727 (in which both the national court and the ECJ held that the relevant Community regulation was proportionate to the stated objective).

[204] See e.g. Case 11/70, *Internationale Handelsgesellschaft v. Einfuhr und Vorratstelle für Getreide und Futtermittel* [1970] ECR 1125 (in which the national court had found that the Community measure was disproportionate, while the Court deemed it proportionate to the stated objective).

[205] G. Repetto, *Argomenti comparativi e diritti fondamentali in Europa. Teorie dell'interpretazione e giurisprudenza sovranazionale* (Iovene 2011) 192.

[206] De Búrca, 'After the EU Charter of Fundamental Rights', 178.

[207] Case C-108/96, *Criminal Proceedings against Dennis Mac Quen and others* [2001] ECR I-837, para. 34.

[208] Craig and De Búrca, *EU Law*, 532.

[209] Case C-208/09, *Sayn Wittgenstein* [2010] ECR I-13693, paras 83, 92.

The Court has also contributed to the formation of a European legal heritage through 'the *erga omnes* relevance' of its jurisprudence. While the decisions of most international courts and tribunals are only relevant *inter partes*, 'the relevance of an ECJ ruling … is not restricted to the dispute at hand, since it has *erga omnes* effect. Once the Court clarifies a legal matter, this ruling is valid throughout the EU'.[210]

Fourth, with regard to incommensurability, the Court has found a common denominator of the various interests at stake in their social function and the gradual constitutionalization of the European project. Finally, with regard to the eventual overprotection of property rights, relying on the jurisprudence of the ECtHR, the ECJ has pointed out that such rights are not absolute; rather, there may be cases in which private interests may be limited for the commonweal.[211] While this does not mean that the CJEU has reached an optimal balance between the competing interests in all cases,[212] at least there is an indication that the court has taken the interplay between economic interests and other values into account.

In conclusion, proportionality has migrated successfully from the legal systems of the EU member states to the EU legal system. On the one hand, the EU courts have relied on the legal heritage of the member states to establish proportionality as a general principle of EU law. On the other hand, they have interpreted the concept of proportionality in a flexible manner – so flexible as to transcend the classical understanding

---

210 Blauberger and Schmidt, 'The European Court of Justice and its Political Impact', 5.

211 See e.g. Case C-331/88, *R v. Minister for Agriculture, Fisheries and Food ex p Fedesa* [1990] ECR I-4023 (upholding a Community regulation prohibiting the use of hormones in meat production); Case C-112/00, *Schmidberger, Eugen Schmidberger, Internationale Transporte und Planzüge v. Austria* [2003] ECR I-5659 (involving a clash between free movement and freedom of expression and assembly); Case C-210/03, *Swedish Match AB and Swedish Match UK Ltd* [2004] ECR I-11893, paras 56–8 (upholding the ban on tobacco for oral use deeming it to be proportionate to the stated objective, namely the protection of public health, and acknowledging that other measures, such as labelling, could not achieve the same preventive effect).

212 See e.g. Case C-438/05, *International Transport Workers' Federation and Finnish Seamen's Union v. Viking Line* [2007] ECR I-10779, para. 46 (holding that 'the exercise of … freedom of expression and freedom of assembly and respect for human dignity, respectively, … must be reconciled with the requirements relating to rights protected under the Treaty and in accordance with the principle of proportionality); Case C-341/05, *Laval Un Partneri Ltd v. Svenska Byggnadsarbetareförbundet* (holding that the right to strike must be exercised proportionately).

of proportionality – shaping and adapting it to the various needs of European integration and the parallel protection of human rights and fundamental freedoms. The CJEU has coupled proportionality analysis with varying standards of review, 'ranging from a very deferential approach to quite a rigorous and searching examination of the justification for a measure which has been challenged'.[213]

Ultimately, the migration of proportionality from the national realm to the regional level may constitute a case of 'overfitting legal transplant', i.e. a legal transplant that works even better in the destination system than in that of origin.[214] The concept of proportionality fits particularly well in the peculiar multi-level structure of the EU. It is used in 'different contexts', at 'different levels' and for multiple purposes.[215] Proportionality is used to calibrate public and private interests, to allocate powers between the EU and the member states, as well as to promote European integration while respecting state sovereignty. Finally, the accordion-like interpretation of proportionality as broad or narrow in a particular case allows the EU courts to accommodate the converging divergences of the member states and acknowledge their unity in diversity.

3.5 PROPORTIONALITY IN INTERNATIONAL TRADE LAW

The question as to whether the concept of proportionality has migrated to international trade law remains debated. On the one hand, the World Trade Organization (WTO) Agreements do not refer to proportionality in explicit terms.[216] In addition, only some elements of the proportionality analysis appear in the jurisprudence of the WTO panels and the AB.[217]

---

[213] De Búrca, 'The Principle of Proportionality and its Application in EU Law', 111.

[214] M.M. Siems, 'The Curious Case of Overfitting Legal Transplants', in M. Adams and D. Heirbaut (eds), *The Method and Culture of Comparative Law: Essays in Honour of Mark Van Hoecke* (Hart Publishing 2014) 133–45, 134.

[215] Sauter, 'Proportionality in EU Law', 30.

[216] There are only minimal references to proportionality under the covered agreements, which will be mentioned below.

[217] A. Desmedt, 'Proportionality in WTO Law' (2001) 4 JIEL 441–80.

On the other hand, some scholars contend that 'the principle of proportionality is one of the more basic principles underlying the multilateral trading system'.[218]

As this section shows, while the WTO Agreements do not expressly refer to proportionality, the WTO adjudicative bodies have used some elements of the proportionality analysis. This is not to say that there exists a principle of proportionality embedded in WTO law; rather, some elements of proportionality are built into the system for reconciling trade and non-trade issues. WTO provisions that reflect elements of the proportionality analysis comprise terms such as 'necessary', 'proportionate', 'less trade restrictive', and 'commensurate'.[219] In particular, elements of proportionality analysis play a role in three major areas of international trade law: (1) the General Agreement on Tariffs and Trade (GATT);[220] (2) the Agreement on Technical Barriers to Trade (TBT Agreement)[221] and the Agreement on the Application of Sanitary and Phytosanitary Measures (SPS Agreement);[222] and (3) in the determination of countermeasures.[223]

With regard to the first area,[224] GATT Article XX provides a list of general exceptions. WTO members can adopt measures that would at first sight (*prima facie*) be in breach of the relevant GATT obligations if they comply with the conditions set out in this provision. GATT Article XX is divided into two parts. The first part of the provision – that is, the introductory paragraph generally known as the *chapeau* – relates to the way a given policy is implemented. The second part of the provision includes a detailed list of policy aims. Some such objectives require that a measure be necessary to protect a specific public policy goal (e.g.

---

218 M. Hilf, 'Power, Rules and Principles – Which Orientation for WTO/GATT Law?' (2001) 4 JIEL 111–20, 120.

219 A.D. Mitchell, 'Proportionality and Remedies in WTO Disputes' (2007) 17 EJIL 985–1008, 987.

220 General Agreement on Tariffs and Trade 1994, 15 April 1994, Marrakesh Agreement Establishing the World Trade Organization, Annex 1A, 1867 UNTS 187.

221 Agreement on Technical Barriers to Trade, 15 April 1994, Marrakesh Agreement Establishing the World Trade Organization, Annex 1A, 1868 UNTS 120.

222 Agreement on the Application of Sanitary and Phytosanitary Measures, 15 April 1994, Marrakesh Agreement Establishing the World Trade Organization, Annex 1A, 1867 UNTS 493.

223 Mitchell, 'Proportionality and Remedies in WTO Disputes'.

224 M. Andenas and S. Zleptnig, 'Proportionality: WTO Law: in Comparative Perspective' (2007) 42 *Texas ILJ* 371–423.

public morals; human, animal or plant life or health). Other objectives require that a given measure be related to goals such as the conservation of exhaustible natural resources.

The assessment of the necessity of a given measure to reach the particular objectives mentioned in paragraphs (a), (b), (d) and (i) of Article XX – including the protection of public morals and of human, animal or plant life or health – requires some elements of the proportionality analysis, namely the suitability and necessity tests. As Shoenbaum points out, there has been a semantic change in the interpretation of necessary, as 'necessary no longer relates to the protection of living things, but to whether or not the measure is a "necessary" departure from the trade agreement'.[225]

In the *Thai – Cigarettes* case, a case concerning Thailand's import restrictions on cigarettes and other tobacco products, the panel stated that trade restrictions were necessary 'only if there were no alternative measures consistent with the GATT or less inconsistent with it, which Thailand could reasonably be expected to employ to achieve its health policy objectives'.[226] The Panel held that the import restrictions were inconsistent with Article XI:1 and were unnecessary under Article XX(b). In *Korea – Beef*, a case concerning a Korean regulation that allegedly discriminated against imported beef, by *inter alia*, confining sales of imported beef to separate stores, the AB stated that the necessity of a measure should be ascertained taking into account, first, 'the extent to which the measure contributes to the realization of the end pursued', and, second, 'the extent to which the compliance measure produces restrictive effects on international commerce'.[227] The AB added that 'determination of whether a measure … may … be "necessary" … involves in every case a process of weighting and balancing a series of factors which … include the importance of the … interests or values protected by that law or regulation at issue, and the accompanying impact of the law or regulation on imports or exports'.[228] The AB upheld the panel's conclusion that the Korean measure was in violation of Article III:4 of the GATT 1994, and that such violation could not be justified under Article XX(d) of the GATT 1994.

---

225 T.J. Shoenbaum, 'International Trade and Protection of the Environment: The Continuing Search for Reconciliation' (1997) 91 AJIL 269–76, 276.

226 Panel Report, *Thailand – Restrictions on Importation of and Internal Taxes on Cigarettes*, 7 November 1990, DS10/R – 37 S/200, para. 75.

227 Appellate Body Report, *Korea – Measures Affecting Imports of Fresh, Chilled and Frozen Beef*, 11 December 2000, WT/DS161/AB/R, para. 163.

228 Ibid. para. 164.

The jurisprudence of panels and the AB has treated certain values more deferentially than others. For instance, in the *EC – Asbestos* case, concerning a French ban on imports of asbestos and products containing asbestos, the AB noted that health is 'vital and important to the highest degree',[229] and held that the adopted measures were indispensable. Once the adjudicative body reaches a preliminary conclusion that the measure is necessary, 'this result must be confirmed by comparing the measure with its possible alternatives, which may be less trade restrictive while providing an equivalent contribution to the achievement of the objective pursued'.[230] The necessity test helps in identifying 'whether a less WTO-inconsistent measure is reasonably available'.[231] This judicial development marked an evolution 'from the least trade restrictive approach to the less trade restrictive one'.[232]

The necessity test has been criticized as 'overbroad and under-inclusive' at the same time.[233] On the one hand, 'it seems to elevate trade values to a pre-eminent status'.[234] On the other hand, as noted by Trachtman, 'by keeping the regulatory benefit constant and working on the trade detriment side', the necessity test, as it is used at the WTO, 'evaluates a much more limited range of options, ignoring other groups of options that may be superior'.[235] However, the fact that the necessity test does not address the chosen level of protection that a member wants to achieve but the design of the instrument it has chosen to use restricts the discretion of the adjudicators and indicates that a full-fledged proportionality analysis or balancing is still missing from this sector of WTO adjudication.

The assessment of the relation between a given measure and one of the particular objectives mentioned in the specific paragraphs of GATT Article XX includes some elements of the proportionality analysis, namely the suitability and proportionality (in the strict sense) tests. For instance, in *US – Shrimp*, concerning a ban on importation of shrimp and

---

229 Appellate Body Report, *European Communities – Measures Affecting Asbestos and Asbestos Containing Products*, 12 March 2001, WT/DS135/AB/R, para. 172.

230 Appellate Body Report, *Brazil – Measures Affecting Imports of Retreaded Tyres*, 17 December 2007, WT/DS332/AB/R, para. 156.

231 *Korea – Beef*, para. 166.

232 Andenas and Zleptnig, 'Proportionality: WTO Law: in Comparative Perspective', 408.

233 J.P. Trachtman, 'Trade and ... Problems, Cost-Benefit Analysis and Subsidiarity' (1998) 9 EJIL 32–85, 72.

234 Ibid.

235 Ibid.

shrimp products adopted by the US for the conservation of sea turtles, the AB clarified that the requirement 'relating to' is about a 'close and genuine relationship of ends and means'.[236] It added that the design of the measure was 'not disproportionately wide in its scope and reach in relation to the policy objective of protection and conservation of sea turtle species'.[237] The AB nonetheless concluded that the measure, while qualifying for provisional justification under Article XX(g), failed to meet the requirements of the *chapeau* of Article XX.

After a measure is found to be provisionally justified under any of the specific paragraphs of Article XX, the adjudicators turn to the *chapeau* of the same provision to assess whether the application of the measure does not constitute an 'arbitrary or unjustifiable discrimination between countries where the same conditions prevail' or 'a disguised restriction on trade'.[238] Although the *chapeau* does not in and of itself contain a proportionality requirement, some scholars consider that it is an expression of, or at least 'resembles, a proportionality analysis'.[239] First, proportionality can help in ascertaining the lack of arbitrariness of given regulatory measures.[240] Second, the AB held that the *chapeau* 'embodies the recognition on the part of the WTO Members of the need to maintain a balance of rights and obligations[;] between the right of a member to invoke … the exceptions of Article XX … , and the substantive rights of the other Members under the GATT 1994'.[241]

Other elements of the proportionality analysis surface in the interpretation of certain provisions of the SPS and TBT Agreements. For instance, Article 2.2 of the SPS Agreement requires that 'Members shall ensure that any sanitary or phytosanitary measure is applied only to the extent necessary to protect human, animal or plant life or health, is based on scientific principles and is not maintained without sufficient scientific evidence'. On the one hand, 'sufficient scientific evidence' has been deemed to embody elements of the suitability test. For instance, in *Japan – Apples*, concerning the adoption by Japan of quarantine restrictions on apples imported into the country, to prevent the spread of fire blight, a disease affecting apple trees, the AB held that the sufficient scientific

---

236 Appellate Body Report, *United States – Import Prohibition of Certain Shrimp and Shrimp Products*, 12 October 1998, WT/DS58/AB/R, para. 136.

237 Ibid., para. 141.

238 GATT, Article XX.

239 Andenas and Zleptnig, 'Proportionality: WTO Law: in Comparative Perspective', 411.

240 Desmedt, 'Proportionality in WTO Law', 478.

241 *US – Shrimp*, para. 156.

evidence criterion required 'a rational and objective relationship' between the measure and the relevant scientific evidence.[242] The Appellate Body upheld the panel's findings that the measure was inconsistent, *inter alia*, with Japan's obligations under Articles 2.2 of the SPS Agreement. On the other hand, Article 5.6 of the SPS Agreement clarifies that measures necessary to protect human, animal or plant life and health should not be 'more trade restrictive than required to achieve their appropriate level of ... protection, taking into account technical and economic feasibility'.[243]

Finally, elements of the proportionality analysis appear in the determination of countermeasures and in enforcement provisions. For instance, Article 46 of the Agreement on Trade-Related Aspects of Intellectual Property Rights (TRIPS)[244] refers to the 'need of proportionality' in the context of enforcement provisions.[245] In parallel, footnote 9 of Article 4.10 of the Agreement on Subsidies and Countervailing Measures (SCM Agreement)[246] clarifies that 'appropriate countermeasures' do not include 'countermeasures that are disproportionate'.[247] In *EC – Bananas*, concerning the European Communities' regime for the importation, distribution and sale of bananas, the arbitrators refused to 'double-count' nullification of benefits, as this would be contrary to 'the general international law principle of proportionality of countermeasures'.[248] In *US – Line Pipe*, concerning the imposition of a safeguard measure by the US, the AB held that the idea that 'countermeasures in response to breaches by States of their international obligations' should 'be proportionate to such breaches' is 'a recognized

---

242 Appellate Body Report, *Japan – Affecting the Importation of Apples*, 26 November 2003, WT/DS245/AB/R, para. 147.

243 SPS Agreement, Article 5.6.

244 Agreement on Trade-Related Aspects of Intellectual Property Rights (TRIPS), 15 April 1994, Marrakesh Agreement Establishing the World Trade Organization, Annex 1C, 1869 UNTS 299, 33 ILM 1197 (1994).

245 TRIPS Agreement, Article 46.

246 Agreement on Subsidies and Countervailing Measures (SCM Agreement), 15 April 1994, Marrakesh Agreement Establishing the World Trade Organization, Annex 1A, 1869 UNTS 14.

247 SCM Agreement, footnote 9 of Article 4.10.

248 Decision by the Arbitrators, *European Communities – Regime for the Importation, Sale and Distribution of Bananas* – Recourse to Arbitration by the European Communities Under Art 22.6 of the DSU, 9 April 1999, WT/DS27/ARB, para. 6.16.

principle of customary international law', which is fully applicable in the WTO system.[249]

In conclusion, while there is no explicit reference to proportionality in the WTO Agreement, some elements of the proportionality analysis appear in the interpretation and application of certain of its provisions.

3.6 PROPORTIONALITY IN INTERNATIONAL INVESTMENT LAW AND ARBITRATION?

Has proportionality successfully migrated to international investment law and arbitration? Given the successful migration of the concept of proportionality from a few constitutional traditions to various areas of international law, some scholars contend that arbitral tribunals should adopt proportionality analysis, arguing that it 'offers the best available doctrinal framework with which to meet the present challenges' to international investment law.[250]

However, arbitral tribunals have not relied extensively on proportionality analysis.[251] Several international law scholars have pointed out that the legal basis for the application of the proportionality analysis does not seem strong in the cases where it has been applied and that the conceptual foundations for using proportionality analysis in investment arbitration are shaky.[252] Moreover, scholars pinpoint that 'proportionality is not the only method to promote [a culture of] justification or even the best one'.[253] Rather, other concepts, such as reasonableness, 'can be used to control the extent to which interferences of host states with foreign investments are permitted'.[254]

---

[249] Appellate Body Report, *United States – Definitive Safeguard Measures on Imports of Circular Welded Carbon Quality Line Pipe from Korea*, 15 February 2002, WT/DS202/AB/R, para. 259.

[250] A. Stone Sweet, 'Investor–State Arbitration: Proportionality's New Frontier' (2010) 4 LEHR 46–76, 48.

[251] B. Kingsbury and S. Schill, 'Investor–State Arbitration as Governance: Fair and Equitable Treatment, Proportionality and the Emerging Global Administrative Law', in A.J. van den Berg (ed.), *50 Years of the New York Convention* (Kluwer Law International 2009) 5–68, 12 (noting that 'in investor–state arbitration only a few tribunals have taken [the proportionality] approach').

[252] See generally B. Pirker, *Proportionality Analysis and Models of Judicial Review* (Europa Law Publishing 2013).

[253] Cohen-Eliya and Porat, 'Proportionality and Justification', 477.

[254] Kingsbury and Schill, 'Investor–State Arbitration as Governance', 23.

Most investment treaties do not refer to proportionality.[255] However, this does not necessarily mean that proportionality is not part of the investment regime. For instance, in EU law, proportionality did not initially appear in the relevant treaties; rather, it gradually emerged as a jurisprudential concept elaborated by the European Court of Justice (now the CJEU) before becoming a general principle of EU law. Only after its jurisprudential elaboration by the Court, and its consolidation as a general principle of EU law, was the concept of proportionality inserted in various provisions of the relevant treaties.[256] Analogously, the fact that proportionality does not appear in most investment treaties does not necessarily mean that it cannot enter into the system. In fact, if arbitral tribunals consistently used such concept, considering it binding, it could crystallize as a general principle of international law or even become a customary norm. Against the background of a lively doctrinal debate on the migration of proportionality to investment treaty arbitration, an examination of the arbitral practice is of critical relevance for ascertaining whether, and if so how, proportionality has migrated to investment treaty arbitration.

While reference to proportionality used to be rare in investment arbitration, in the past decade arbitral tribunals have increasingly relied on some form of proportionality analysis.[257] This section explores how some arbitral tribunals have used the concept to define standards of protection, including the protection against unlawful expropriation, fair and equitable treatment, and non-discrimination. It also discusses some cases that referred to proportionality as required under the applicable national law[258] and other cases in which proportionality was used to

---

[255] See, however, Annex 11-B(3)b of the Free Trade Agreement (FTA) between the Republic of Korea and the United States of America and Annex 2 of the 2009 ASEAN Comprehensive Investment Agreement.

[256] See section 3.4 above.

[257] This section does not purport to be exhaustive, as some arbitral tribunals may not be disclosed to the public and other awards may have referred to proportionality only implicitly. This section only discusses selected awards that have used the concept of proportionality *expressis verbis*. The argument is that the use of some elements of the proportionality test, like suitability, does not necessarily imply the use of the whole proportionality test; rather, it is a common judicial endeavour and therefore should not be reconnected to proportionality as such. The implicit use of all of the various elements of proportionality without identifying or naming it would give rise to a number of distinct hermeneutical concerns.

[258] *Autopista Concesionada de Venezuela CA v. Bolivarian Republic of Venezuela*, ICSID Case No. ARB/00/5, Award, 23 September 2003, para. 338.

define the ambit of application of given exceptions. Finally, the section concludes by discussing how several tribunals have used proportionality with regard to procedural matters.

3.6.1 Expropriation

Expropriation can take different forms: essentially, it can be (1) direct or (2) indirect. Direct expropriation takes place 'where an investment is nationalised or otherwise … expropriated through formal transfer of title or outright physical seizure'.[259] Indirect expropriation can 'occur through interference by a state in the use of that property or with the enjoyment of the benefits even where the property is not seized and the legal title to the property is not affected'.[260]

Direct expropriations are 'easy cases': 'the act of expropriation is clear, the legal obligation to compensate is clear, and typically the only difficult legal question is how to calculate compensation'.[261] Instead, indirect expropriations are not so easy to detect and to deal with.[262] They require contextual determinations to ascertain whether there is an indirect expropriation in the first place, or whether the host state legitimately exercised its police powers. While direct expropriation is increasingly rare, most expropriation claims are primarily about 'whether governmental action has crossed some line' from legitimate regulation that requires no compensation to indirect expropriation that requires it.[263]

The concept of proportionality has been used to assess the adequacy of compensation, or even to ascertain the lawfulness of an expropriation, or existence of an indirect expropriation. While the role of proportionality with regard to compensation will be discussed below,[264] this section will explore the role proportionality can (and has) play(ed) in the assessment of lawful or indirect expropriations. Some arbitral tribunals have used the concept of proportionality to ascertain whether given measures could be

---

See also *Occidental Petroleum Co and Occidental Exploration and Production Co v. Republic of Ecuador*, ICSID Case No. ARB/06/11, Award, 16 December 2011, paras 396–401 (on the principle of proportionality in Ecuadorian law).

259 OECD, 'Indirect Expropriation and the Right to Regulate in International Investment Law', Working Paper on International Investment 4/2004, 1–22, 3.

260 Ibid. 3–4.

261 M.R. Poirier, 'The NAFTA Chapter 11 Expropriation Debate through the Eyes of a Property Theorist' (2003) 33 *Environmental Law* 851–928, 859.

262 Ibid.

263 S.R. Ratner, 'Regulatory Takings in Institutional Context: Beyond the Fear of Fragmented International Law' (2008) 102 AJIL 475–528, 477–8.

264 See section 3.6.5 below.

characterized as a form of expropriation, endorsing the claimants' argument that '[r]egulatory measures ... that are disproportional ([that is,] lack [a] fair balance between the aim sought and means employed) qualify as expropriation'.[265] From this perspective, when state measures disproportionally affect foreign investments, a compensable indirect expropriation occurs. In turn, other tribunals have held that '[p]roportionality is a condition that renders expropriation lawful, although it does not exclude compensation for the damage caused'.[266]

For instance, in *El Paso Energy International Company v. Argentina*,[267] a case arising out of a series of measures adopted by Argentina during an economic crisis, the Tribunal considered that 'disproportionate general regulations have the potential to be considered as expropriatory if there is a sufficient interference with the investor's rights'.[268] Other tribunals have similarly held that proportionality may play a role in assessing whether the host state exercised regulatory power properly or whether its conduct amounted to indirect expropriation.[269]

While arbitral tribunals have not developed 'bright-line tests' for 'determining the point at which governmental regulation becomes an indirect expropriation', they have generally considered the purpose of the governmental measure, its impact on the investment, and in some cases, 'the proportionality between the harm to the investor and the benefit to the public'.[270] For instance, in *Tecnicas Medioambientales Tecmed SA v. the United Mexican States*,[271] which concerned the replacement of an unlimited licence by a concession of limited duration for the operation of a landfill, the Arbitral Tribunal used the concept of proportionality to

---

265 For an articulation of this argument, see *Telenor Mobile Communications AS v. Republic of Hungary*, Case No. ARB/04/15, Award, 22 June 2006, para. 40. However, the Tribunal rejected the claimant's claims on jurisdictional grounds. Ibid. para. 108.1.

266 *Urbaser SA and Consorcio de Aguas Bilbao Bizkaia, Bilbao Biskaia Ur Partzuergoa v. The Argentine Republic*, ICSID Case No. ARB/07/26, Award, 8 December 2016, para. 969.

267 *El Paso Energy International Co v. Argentina*, ICSID Case No. ARB/03/15, Award, 31 October 2011.

268 Ibid. para. 243.

269 *Siemens AG v. the Argentine Republic*, ICSID Case No. ARB/02/8, Award, 6 February 2007, para. 354 (holding that 'considering the purpose and proportionality of the measures taken ... w[as] part of th[e] tribunal's determination of whether an expropriation had occurred').

270 Ratner, 'Regulatory Takings in Institutional Context', 482.

271 *Tecnicas Medioambientales Tecmed SA v. the United Mexican States*, ICSID Case No. ARB (AF)/00/, Award, 29 May 2003, para. 122.

ascertain whether such measures amounted to an expropriation. The Tribunal assessed whether the measures adopted by Mexico were 'proportional to the public interest presumably protected thereby and to the protection legally granted to investments, taking into account that the significance of such impact has a key role upon deciding the proportionality'.[272] The Tribunal held that the host country had destroyed the economic value of the investment and that the means were disproportionate to the end.

Analogously, in *Fireman's Fund v. Mexico*, concerning an expropriation claim brought by a US insurance company that owned debentures issued by a Mexican financial services company, the Tribunal considered a series of factors as relevant for determining whether an indirect expropriation had taken place. First, it checked 'whether the measure is within the recognized police powers of the host state'. Second, it scrutinized 'the public purpose and effect of the measure'. Third, it examined 'whether the measure is discriminatory'. Fourth, it investigated 'the proportionality between the means employed and the aim sought to be realized'. Finally, it ascertained 'the bona fide nature of the measure'.[273]

In *Philip Morris v. Uruguay*,[274] concerning a regulation requiring health warnings to take up 80 per cent of cigarette packaging, and corporations to adopt one single variant of their brand, the Tribunal used the notion of proportionality to distinguish legitimate regulation from compensable expropriation. It held that 'in order for a State's action in exercise of regulatory powers not to constitute indirect expropriation, the action … must be taken bona fide for the purpose of protecting the public welfare, must be non-discriminatory and proportionate'.[275] The Tribunal concluded that the single presentation requirement and the 80 per cent regulation 'satisf[ied] these conditions'.[276] In particular, it deemed such requirements to be 'proportionate' to the public health objective that they intended to achieve.[277]

In *Azurix*, which involved a water concession contract, Argentina had enacted measures for the protection of public health after an algae

---

272 Ibid. para. 122.

273 *Fireman's Fund Insurance Co v. Mexico*, ICSID Case No. ARB(AF)/02/1, Award, 17 July 2006, para. 176 (referring to *Tecmed*).

274 *Philip Morris Brands Sàrl, Philip Morris Products SA and Abal Hermanos SA v. Oriental Republic of Uruguay*, ICSID Case No. ARB/10/7, Award, 8 July 2016.

275 Ibid. para. 305.

276 Ibid.

277 Ibid. para. 306.

outbreak contaminated a water supply.[278] Warnings not to drink the water were enacted and customers were dissuaded from paying their water bills.[279] In order to ascertain whether there was a (compensable) expropriation or a (non-compensable) legitimate exercise of police powers, the Tribunal relied on *Tecmed*, and its analysis of the ECtHR's jurisprudence, stating that an expropriatory measure must pursue a 'legitimate aim in the public interest' and the means employed must be (reasonably) proportional to the stated objective.[280] After concluding that the effect of the state measure on the claimant's investment did not reach the threshold to constitute an expropriation, the Tribunal dismissed the claim of expropriation.

In *Burlington Resources Inc v. Ecuador*, which concerned an investment in the hydrocarbon industry, Ecuador contended that '[its] intervention in Blocks 7 and 21 did not constitute an expropriation of Burlington's investment'; rather, it 'aimed at preventing significant harm to the Blocks' and, in Ecuador's view, it 'was necessary, adequate, proportionate under the circumstances'.[281] The Arbitral Tribunal confirmed that Ecuador's intervention in the Blocks 'was necessary to avoid significant economic loss and the risk of permanent damage to the Blocks. It was also appropriate because Ecuador entered the Blocks without using force. It was equally proportionate as the means employed were suited to the ends of protecting the Blocks'.[282]

In *LG&E v. Argentina*,[283] a case arising out of emergency measures adopted by Argentina during its economic crisis in 2001–2002, the Tribunal rejected the claim of indirect expropriation on the ground that the effects of the state measure on the foreign investment were not sufficiently critical to amount to an indirect expropriation. The Tribunal also added an *obiter dictum*:

> With respect to the power of the State to adopt its policies, it can generally be said that the State has the right to adopt measures having a social or general welfare purpose. In such a case, the measure must be accepted without any

---

[278] *Azurix v. Argentine Republic*, ICSID Case No. ARB/01/12, Award, 23 June 2006.

[279] Ibid. para. 283.

[280] Ibid. para. 311.

[281] *Burlington Resources Inc v. Ecuador*, ICSID Case No. ARB/08/5, Decision on Liability, 14 December 2012, para. 164.

[282] Ibid. para. 504.

[283] *LG&E Energy Corp and Others v. The Argentine Republic*, ICSID Case No. ARB/02/1, Decision on Liability, 3 October 2006.

> imposition of liability, except in cases where the State's action is obviously disproportionate to the need being addressed.[284]

Analogously, in *Total v. Argentine Republic*,[285] relating to several investments in different areas including the power generation industry, the Arbitral Tribunal stated that:

> When foreign investors complain of State regulatory actions under a BIT, in order to decide whether the measures also amount to an indirect expropriation (a so-called regulatory taking), a tribunal must take into account their features and object so as to assess their proportionality and reasonableness in respect of the purpose which is legitimately pursued by the host State. These regulatory measures, when judged as legitimate, proportionate, reasonable and non-discriminatory, do not give rise to compensation in favour of foreign investors.[286]

However, other tribunals have declined to adopt the proportionality concept. For instance, in *Bernhard von Pezold and others v. Republic of Zimbabwe*,[287] the Claimants alleged, *inter alia*, unlawful expropriation of their farms in Zimbabwe, compulsorily acquired by the government of Zimbabwe as part of its land reform programme in the 2000s.[288] The Respondent 'invoke[d] the principle of proportionality in connection with a State's legitimate exercise of its police powers.'[289] The claimants noted that 'there has been limited adoption of the principle of proportionality by investment treaty tribunals'[290] and that, in any case, 'even where adopted, proportionality does not generally shield a State from claims'.[291] In addition, the claimants contended that the land reform lacked proportionality.[292] They also emphasized that '[r]acial discrimination will always be disproportional because it breaches a peremptory norm.'[293]

---

[284] Ibid. para. 195.
[285] *Total SA v. Argentine Republic*, ICSID Case No. ARB/04/1, Decision on Liability, 27 December 2010.
[286] Ibid. para. 197, footnote 232.
[287] *Bernhard von Pezold and Others v. Republic of Zimbabwe*, ICSID Case No. ARB/10/15, Award, 28 July 2015.
[288] Ibid. para. 469.
[289] Ibid. para. 454.
[290] Ibid. para. 455.
[291] Ibid.
[292] Ibid. para. 456.
[293] Ibid. para. 455.

The Tribunal found that the state action amounted, *inter alia*, to unlawful expropriation.[294] For the Tribunal, failure to pay compensation, the lack of due process and of public purpose, and discrimination made the expropriation unlawful.[295] The Tribunal warned that 'due caution should be exercised in importing concepts from other legal regimes (in this case European human rights law) without a solid basis for doing so'.[296] The Tribunal was 'not persuaded by the Respondent's argument that the doctrine of proportionality should be employed here to balance the competing interests of the State and the individual in the present case'.[297] The Tribunal highlighted that if 'proportionality has featured in some investment treaty cases', tribunals have used it to ascertain 'whether a termination (for example of licence or contract) by the State has been a proportionate response to an alleged breach of obligations by the investor'.[298] Instead, the Tribunal noted that the respondent advocated 'a rather different application of the doctrine of proportionality ... whereby proportionality is being used as a defence to what would otherwise be a violation of the BIT (i.e., expropriation without compensation).'[299] Therefore, the Tribunal 'dismisse[d] the Respondent's proportionality argument'.[300] 'In any case', the Tribunal added, 'neither the "margin of appreciation" nor the proportionality doctrine can be used to justify illegal conduct, such as a breach of an obligation *erga omnes*', such as 'engaging in racial discrimination'.[301] The Tribunal then noted the 'ample evidence' that the claimants were discriminated against because of their ethnicity.[302]

In conclusion, while there is no 'magical formula' for deciding claims of indirect expropriation,[303] elements of proportionality analysis have gradually emerged in the arbitral jurisprudence. However, far from using the three-prong proportionality test, those tribunals that have referred to 'proportionality' seem to have adopted only the third prong of the test,

---

294 Ibid. para. 492.
295 Ibid. paras 497; 499; 501 and 502.
296 Ibid. para. 465.
297 Ibid. para. 460.
298 Ibid.
299 Ibid.
300 Ibid. para. 463.
301 Ibid. para. 467.
302 Ibid.
303 J. Paulsson, 'Indirect Expropriation: Is the Right to Regulate a Risk?' (2006) TDM 1–9, 9 (arguing that '[t]he magical formula for deciding claims of indirect expropriation is the international lawyer's equivalent of proving Fermat's Last Theorem').

the proportionality in the strict sense test. Some tribunals have only mentioned proportionality together with reasonableness *ad abundantiam*, providing an additional argument to an already sufficient collection, while other tribunals have mentioned it passim, here and there, without a detailed or orderly analysis. Finally, other tribunals have declined to use this concept to distinguish legitimate regulation from unlawful expropriation or as a circumstance precluding wrongfulness.

3.6.2 Fair and Equitable Treatment and Full Protection

The fair and equitable treatment standard includes a variety of requirements, generally associated with good governance, such as the provision of a stable and predictable legal framework, the protection of legitimate expectations, procedural due process and the prohibition of denial of justice. In parallel, the full protection standard requires states to protect the safety of the investment. Some arbitral tribunals have interpreted the fair and equitable treatment and full protection standards to require that states must act in a proportionate manner towards investors.[304]

For instance, in *MTD Equity SDN BHD and MTD Chile SA v. Republic of Chile*,[305] which concerned the failure of a construction project deemed to be inconsistent with zoning regulations, the Arbitral Tribunal held that the fair and equitable treatment provision included the notion of proportionality. For the Tribunal, the fair and equitable treatment standard 'encompass[es] … good faith, due process, nondiscrimination and proportionality'.[306] Analogously, in *Total SA v. Argentine Republic*, the Tribunal referred to a standard of reasonableness and proportionality in assessing compliance with the requirement of fair and equitable treatment.[307]

---

[304] See Henckels, *Proportionality and Deference in Investor–State Arbitration*, 125 (contending that 'proportionality analysis can be a workable methodology in regulatory disputes', but cautioning that 'tribunals have been more inclined to rely on the concept of reasonableness as the applicable method of substantive review in relation to fair and equitable treatment claims').

[305] *MTD Equity SDN BHD and MTD Chile SA v. Republic of Chile*, ICSID Case No. ARB/01/7, Award, 25 May 2004.

[306] Ibid. para. 109.

[307] *Total SA v. Argentine Republic*, ICSID Case No. ARB/04/1, Decision on Liability, 27 December 2010, para. 123 (noting that '[t]he circumstances and reasons … for carrying out a [regulatory] change impacting negatively on a foreign investor's operations on the one hand, and the seriousness of the prejudice caused on the other hand, compared in the light of a standard of reasonableness and proportionality are relevant').

Proportionality was 'one of the cornerstones' of the *Occidental* award.[308] In *Occidental Petroleum Corporation and Occidental Exploration and Production Company v. Republic of Ecuador*, which concerned an investment in the oil sector, the Arbitral Tribunal stated that 'numerous investment treaty tribunals have found that the principle of proportionality is part and parcel of the overarching duty to accord fair and equitable treatment to investors'.[309] The Tribunal noted that proportionality is a general principle of administrative law under Ecuadorian law.[310] It also added that proportionality analysis is applied 'in a variety of international settings', including the WTO Panel reports, decisions of the ECJ, and of the European Court of Human Rights.[311]

The claimant contended that a given sanction imposed by Ecuador was disproportionate and therefore violated the legitimate expectations of the investor under the relevant BIT.[312] The Tribunal concluded that while the claimant had breached the contract it had with Ecuador, the government's measure 'was not a proportionate response ... in the particular circumstances of this case'[313] and was 'in breach of Ecuadorian law, in breach of customary international law, and in violation of the Treaty'.[314] In fact, the Tribunal unanimously concluded that Ecuador had other legal options,[315] but notwithstanding these alternatives, chose a radical sanction, determining the loss of the claimants' investment. In conclusion, the concept of proportionality was the pivot of the Tribunal's finding that Ecuador had expropriated Occidental's investment.[316]

Ecuador requested annulment of the award, contending, *inter alia*, that the Tribunal 'appl[ied] a principle of proportionality that is not encompassed in the Participation Contract, Ecuadorian law, the Treaty or customary international law', thus allegedly 'manifestly exceed[ing] its

[308] *Occidental Petroleum Corporation Occidental Exploration and Production Co v. Republic of Ecuador*, ICSID Case No. ARB/06/11, Decision on Annulment of the Award, 2 November 2015, para. 311.

[309] *Occidental Petroleum Corporation and Occidental Exploration and Production Co v. Republic of Ecuador*, ICSID Case No. ARB/06/11, Award, 5 October 2012, footnote 7, p. 70.

[310] Ibid. para. 398.

[311] Ibid. para. 324.

[312] Ibid. para. 277.

[313] Ibid. para. 338.

[314] Ibid. para. 452.

[315] Ibid. para. 434.

[316] Ibid. paras 453–5.

powers'.[317] The claimants counter-argued that 'the [a]ward clearly stated the Tribunal's reasons for its decision',[318] and that 'the Tribunal applied the proper law when it concluded that the Caducidad Decree was a disproportionate sanction'.[319] For the Annulment Committee:

> [t]he Tribunal has convincingly reasoned and explained its decision. But even if the reasoning had been less convincing, the weighing of evidence and the eminently factual evaluation of whether an administrative decision is or is not proportional, form part of the Tribunal's prerogatives, which under Article 52 of the [ICSID] Convention, as a general rule, fall outside the remit of an ad hoc committee.[320]

For the Annulment Committee, the Tribunal 'convincingly explained that the principle of proportionality between intensity and scope of the illicit activity, and severity of the sanction is a general principle of punitive and tort law, both under Ecuadorian and under international law'.[321]

Instead, in *Spyridon Roussalis v. Romania*, the Tribunal considered that '[the] Respondent's conduct did not infringe the principles of legal certainty and proportionality in violation of the full protection and safety clause contained in Article 2(2) of the BIT'.[322] The claimant argued that 'instead of freezing only the cash equivalent to the claimed tax amount, Romania chose, through its fiscal authorities, to sequester all [the claimant's] assets, … and bank accounts … This decision impaired the Claimant's right to dispose of its investment and was taken in breach of the principles of due process, proportionality and reasonableness'.[323] However, the Tribunal held that the 'Claimant has not proved that this sequestration was discriminatory, disproportionate or otherwise improper under Romanian law'.[324]

Yet, in *Glamis Gold v. United States of America*, concerning a gold mining project in California, the claimant's attempt to impose upon the respondent the burden of justifying the appropriateness of the regulatory measures and proving that they were 'the least restrictive measures

---

317 *Occidental Petroleum Corporation Occidental Exploration and Production Co v. Republic of Ecuador*, Decision on Annulment, para. 315.
318 Ibid. para. 319.
319 Ibid. para. 320.
320 Ibid. para. 346.
321 Ibid. para. 350.
322 *Spyridon Roussalis v. Romania*, ICSID Case ARB/06/1, Award, 7 December 2011, para. 358.
323 Ibid. para. 394.
324 Ibid. para. 515.

available' and 'necessary, suitable and proportionate' failed.[325] The Tribunal noted that 'it is not for an international tribunal to delve into the details of and justifications of domestic law'.[326] It also stated that '[i]t is not the role of this Tribunal, or any international tribunal, to supplant its own judgment of underlying factual material and support for that of a qualified domestic agency'.[327] To deem it otherwise – in the words of the respondent – would amount to the transformation of arbitrators into 'archeologists and ethnographers'.[328]

In conclusion, references to proportionality in arbitral jurisprudence on fair and equitable treatment and full protection remain uncommon.[329] Some tribunals refer to it, but do not really engage in the proportionality analysis.[330] Rather, they refer to proportionality *ad abundantiam*, to complement, rather than supplant, more traditional types of analysis. One notable exception is the *Occidental v. Ecuador* award. It remains to be seen whether other arbitral tribunals will follow such approach in a consistent manner.

3.6.3 Non-discrimination

Non-discrimination is a key obligation in international investment law and covers both direct and indirect discrimination. Some arbitral tribunals have used elements of proportionality analysis to detect indirect or de facto discrimination, that is, measures that apply generally, but have a more negative impact on some groups as opposed to others. In this context, some elements of the proportionality test such as necessity are used to identify whether a given regulatory measure is affecting foreign investors, or a group of investors, to a greater extent than national investors or other groups.

For instance, in *Myers v. Canada*,[331] a dispute arising out of Canada's ban on the export of polychlorinated biphenol (PCB) wastes from Canada to the United States, the claimant, a US company, specializing in the

---

325 *Glamis Gold Ltd v. United States of America*, ICSID/UNCITRAL, Award, 8 June 2009, para. 590.

326 Ibid. para. 762.

327 Ibid. para. 779.

328 Ibid. para. 779.

329 Bücheler, *Proportionality in Investor–State Arbitration*, 193.

330 Ibid. 193 (referring to the *MTD* award).

331 *SD Myers Inc v. Canada*, UNCITRAL/NAFTA, Partial Award, 13 November 2000.

remediation of PCB waste, argued that the ban applied in a discriminatory manner, in effect favouring Canadian operators who were not involved in transborder activities.[332] The Tribunal used the concept of proportionality to assess whether Canada had breached the national treatment provision of the North American Free Trade Agreement (NAFTA).[333] It investigated whether the ban on the export of PCBs had a legitimate aim, and whether it disproportionately benefitted nationals over foreign investors.[334] The Tribunal considered the ability to process PCBs within Canada to be a legitimate objective in light of the Basel Convention on the Control of Transboundary Movements of Hazardous Wastes and their Disposal (Basel Convention).[335] However, the Tribunal found that the ban infringed the national treatment provisions because there were other less restrictive ways to achieve the same objective.[336] While the Tribunal did not explain why it used the proportionality analysis, it paid very little attention to the Basel Convention. However, one may wonder whether, by being a signatory to the Basel Convention, the host state was legitimately entitled, and in fact required, to ensure the availability of adequate in-country disposal facilities for PCB.[337]

Analogously, in *Parkerings v. Lithuania*,[338] which concerned the planned construction of a parking area, the Tribunal stated that 'to violate international law, discrimination must be unreasonable or lacking proportionality, for instance, it must be inapposite or excessive to achieve an otherwise legitimate objective of the State'.[339] The Tribunal dismissed all the claims in their entirety.

Yet, in *Pope & Talbot v. Canada*,[340] concerning an investment in the softwood lumber trade, the Tribunal correctly dismissed Canada's argument that the foreign investor should prove that it was 'disproportionately

---

332 For a discussion of the case, see V. Vadi, *Public Health in International Investment Law and Arbitration* (Routledge 2012) 145.

333 North American Free Trade Agreement (NAFTA), signed on 17 December 1992, in force 1 January 1994, 32 ILM 289 and 605 (1993).

334 *SD Myers Inc v. Canada*, Partial Award, para. 252.

335 Basel Convention on the Control of Transboundary Movements of Hazardous Wastes and their Disposal (Basel Convention), 22 March 1989, 28 ILM 656 (1989).

336 Ibid. para. 255.

337 Vadi, *Public Health in International Investment Law and Arbitration*, 145.

338 *Parkerings v. Lithuania*, ICSID Case No. ARB/05/8, Award, 11 September 2007, para. 368.

339 Ibid. para. 368.

340 *Pope & Talbot v. Canada*, NAFTA/UNCITRAL, Award on the Merits of Phase 2, 11 April 2001, 40 ILM 258.

disadvantaged' by the measure.[341] The Tribunal considered that the disproportionate disadvantage test would weaken the ability of NAFTA Chapter 11 to protect foreign investors.[342]

In conclusion, if several arbitral tribunals have used elements of proportionality analysis to detect indirect discrimination – or to check whether a given regulatory measure is affecting foreign investors, or a group of investors, to a greater extent than national investors or other groups – this approach remains interesting, but relatively isolated, and has not been confirmed by consistent jurisprudential patterns yet.

3.6.4 Non-Precluded Measures and Exception Clauses

A growing number of IIAs contain non-precluded measures (NPMs) or exception clauses. Such clauses aim to safeguard a variety of public interests – such as security interest, public order, public health, environmental concerns, and financial stability – and preclude liability for state actions taken in response to exceptional circumstances. Various ICSID tribunals are interpreting and applying these NPM clauses in relation to Argentina's response to the economic crisis in 2001–2002. The interpretation and application of such clauses will be critical to both host states and foreign investors in determining government power to respond to exceptional circumstances, and to determine the scope of investment protections available under BITs.

In some cases, arbitral tribunals used the proportionality concept to define the ambit of application of given exceptions. For instance, in *Continental Casualty v. Argentine Republic*,[343] concerning an insurance business, the Tribunal imported the 'weighting and balancing' formula from international trade law.[344] Both parties referred to the concept of proportionality. Continental, the claimant, pointed out to Argentina's Supreme Court decisions that declared a given decree 'to be unconstitutional on the grounds that it was an unreasonable measure, lacking in

[341] Ibid. paras 43–5.

[342] Ibid. para. 79.

[343] *Continental Casualty Company v. Argentine Republic*, ICSID Case No. ARB/03/9, Award, 5 September 2008. See also *Continental Casualty Company v. Argentine Republic*, ICSID Case No. ARB/03/9, Decision on the Application for Partial Annulment of Continental Casualty Company and the Application for Partial Annulment of the Argentine Republic, 16 September 2011 (dismissing in its entirety the application for annulment of Continental Casualty Company; and dismissing in its entirety the application for partial annulment of the Argentine Republic).

[344] *Continental Casualty Company v. Argentine Republic*, Award, para. 192.

proportionality between the deprivation of property rights and the objective of averting the crisis'.[345] In turn, Argentina, the respondent, argued that '[t]he fair and equitable treatment … means reasonability, proportionality and no discrimination' and that the adopted measures were 'proportional to the situation in which they were passed, and they [we]re reasonable'.[346]

The Tribunal applied the concept of proportionality to determine whether the state measures fell under the scope of the necessity defence under Article XI of the US–Argentina BIT.[347] The Tribunal did not question the aim and objectives of the state measures,[348] that is, to prevent 'the complete break-down of the financial system, the implosion of the economy and the growing threat to the fabric of Argentinean society and generally to assist in overcoming the crisis'.[349] Rather, it assessed the suitability of such measures, holding that there was 'a genuine relationship of ends and means between the objective pursued and the measure at issue'.[350] It then assessed their necessity; considering that they were 'in part, inevitable, or unavoidable, in part indispensable and in any case material or decisive in order to react positively to the crisis'.[351] Finally, the Tribunal examined their proportionality in the strict sense, concluding that the measures were proportional. For the Tribunal, 'the Government's efforts struck an appropriate balance between that aim and the responsibility of any government towards the country's population'.[352] The Tribunal added that: 'it is self-evident that not every sacrifice can properly be imposed on a country's people in order to safeguard a certain policy that would ensure full respect towards international obligations in the financial sphere, before a breach of those obligations can be considered justified as being necessary under this BIT. The standard of reasonableness and proportionality do not require as much'.[353]

---

345 Ibid. para. 67.

346 Ibid. para. 56.

347 Treaty Between United States of America and the Argentine Republic Concerning the Reciprocal Encouragement and Protection of Investment, 14 November 1991, 31 ILM (1992) 124.

348 *Continental Casualty Co v. Argentine Republic*, Award, para. 199.

349 Ibid. para. 197.

350 Ibid.

351 Ibid.

352 Ibid. para. 227.

353 Ibid.

The Tribunal completed the proportionality analysis in the context of NPM provisions with some arbitral self-restraint. Although the award has been criticized and was subject to annulment proceedings, its reasoning remains plausible and, in fact, the Annulment Committee did not annul the award. Therefore, one may conclude that this approach, albeit uncommon, is not perceived as radically 'unorthodox' within the arbitral community in particular, and among international lawyers more generally.

3.6.5 Compensation

If arbitral tribunals find one or more breaches of investment treaty provisions, they are called to award the appropriate monetary compensation to the foreign investor. Arbitral tribunals have used different tools to strike a balance between the interests of the parties in the quantum phase, such as equity,[354] fairness, reasonableness,[355] and proportionality.

In *Lemire v. Ukraine*,[356] concerning an investment in the radio broadcasting sector, the Arbitral Tribunal explicitly used the proportionality analysis.[357] In particular, the Tribunal calculated the amount of damages applying a discounted cash flow (DCF) method of evaluation. It then adjusted the model in light of Ukraine's situation and the conduct of the investor.[358] On the one hand, the Tribunal noted that Ukraine was a transitional economy, changing from a centrally planned economy to a market economy. On the other hand, it noted that the investor 'devoted a significant proportion of his career to the Gala Radio Project in Ukraine'.[359] For the Tribunal, Mr. Lemire 'was not a passive investor in a mature market'.[360] Rather, '[h]e had the courage to venture into a transitional state and to create … a completely new business [from scratch]'.[361] The Tribunal concluded that there was an adequate

---

[354] F. Francioni, 'Compensation for Nationalisation of Foreign Property: The Borderland between Law and Equity' (1975) 24 ICLQ 255–83.

[355] See Ch. 4, section 4.4.7.

[356] *Joseph Charles Lemire v. Ukraine*, ICSID Case No. ARB/06/18, Award, 28 March 2011.

[357] Ibid. paras 298–306.

[358] Ibid. para. 304 (asking: '[i]s this amount [calculated with the DCF method] a fair reflection of the actual loss, reasonably proportional to the investment?').

[359] Ibid. para. 305.

[360] Ibid. para. 303.

[361] Ibid.

proportion between the compensation awarded to Mr Lemire and his investment.[362]

3.6.6 Procedural Matters

Arbitral tribunals have also used notions of proportionality in relation to procedural matters. In *Libananco Holdings Co Ltd v. Republic of Turkey*,[363] concerning the alleged seizure of two electric utility companies, the Tribunal stated that 'there needs to be some proportionality in the award (as opposed to the expenditure) of legal costs and expenses. A party with a deep pocket may have its own justification for heavy spending, but it cannot expect to be reimbursed for all its expenditures as a matter of course simply because it is ultimately the prevailing party'.[364] Therefore, the Tribunal opted for adopting 'a "broad-brush" approach to the task of determining a reasonable figure to award for such legal costs and expenses',[365] and ordered the losing claimant to pay the respondent 'a proportion of the [r]espondent's legal fees and out of pocket expenses'.[366]

In *Liman Caspian Oil BV and NCL Dutch Investment BV v. Republic of Kazakhstan*,[367] concerning a licence to explore and extract hydrocarbons, the Tribunal acknowledged that:

> on [the] one hand, ordering the production of documents can be helpful for a party to present its case and in the Tribunal's task of establishing the facts of the case relevant for the issues to be decided, but, on the other hand, (1) the process of discovery and disclosure may be time consuming, excessively burdensome and even oppressive, and that unless carefully limited, the burden may be disproportionate to the value of the result, and (2) Parties may have a legitimate interest of confidentiality.[368]

---

[362] Ibid. para. 306.

[363] *Libananco Holdings Co Ltd v. Republic of Turkey*, ICSID Case No. ARB/06/8, Award, 2 September 2011.

[364] Ibid. para. 565(c).

[365] Ibid. para. 566.

[366] Ibid. para. 569.

[367] *Liman Caspian Oil BV and NCL Dutch Investment BV v. Republic of Kazakhstan*, ICSID Case No. ARB/07/14, Award, 22 June 2010.

[368] Ibid. para. 26.

The Tribunal also noted that while 'requests and orders regarding the production of documents are today a regular feature of international arbitration … the present arbitration … involv[es] parties of a Civil Law country where production of documents is used far less than in Common Law countries'.[369] It concluded that 'insofar as a Party [had] the burden of proof, it [was] sufficient for the other Party to deny what the respective Party [had] alleged and then respond to and rebut the evidence provided by that respective Party to comply with its burden of proof'.[370]

3.6.7 Preliminary Conclusions

These arbitrations took place in a variety of different locations, were conducted by different arbitral tribunals under different IIAs, and concerned different subject matters and causes of action. One may legitimately wonder whether there is any commonality between these awards. One may also legitimately wonder about the relevance of discussing such awards, given the fact that there is no binding precedent in international (investment) law, and that a number of awards remain unpublished. Yet, the study of such awards is useful because awards, and patterns of consistent use of proportionality analysis within the same, can and do influence subsequent awards. In the short term, such patterns highlight a judicial dialogue between arbitral tribunals and other international, regional and domestic courts and tribunals, showing once more that international investment law and arbitration is not a self-contained regime. In the long term, such patterns can become more consistent and indicate the emergence of general principles of international law and/or the formation of customary law.

These awards show an increasingly frequent pattern in the use of some form of proportionality analysis in investment treaty arbitration. While reference to proportionality used to be rare in investment arbitration, since the past decade arbitral tribunals have increasingly relied on some form of proportionality analysis. Although most investment treaties do not refer to proportionality, in several cases arbitral tribunals have used the concept to define substantive standards of protection, including the protection against unlawful expropriation, fair and equitable treatment, and non-discrimination. Other tribunals referred to proportionality as required under the applicable national law. Other tribunals used proportionality to define the ambit of application of given exceptions. They

---

369 Ibid.

370 Ibid.

have clarified that states cannot invoke proportionality to justify breaches of investment treaty provisions. Finally, arbitral tribunals have used proportionality also in relation to compensation and procedural matters.

Yet, the examined awards show that those arbitral tribunals that used proportionality analysis did not use it consistently according to a predetermined analytical framework. As mentioned, arbitral tribunals have used the proportionality concept in different contexts. Proportionality is often mentioned in passing together with other concepts such as reasonableness and rationality. Proportionality is sometimes regarded as an element of reasonableness, a criterion that is often used in investment arbitration. Most tribunals have not used proportionality at all. More importantly, arbitral tribunals seem to have elaborated notions of proportionality only for particular purposes depending on circumstances. No single unified notion of proportionality has emerged in investment treaty arbitration. In this context, the proportionality analysis lacks the clearly articulated structure it has in other fields of national, regional and international law. Finally, most arbitral tribunals have not explained why they used the proportionality analysis. For instance, the *Tecmed* Tribunal did not clarify 'whether it was conducting regular interpretation' as well as some form of systemic integration through Article 31(3)(c) of the Vienna Convention on the Law of Treaties (VCLT)[371] 'or appl[ying] some kind of general legal principle'.[372]

In conclusion, while reference to proportionality has increased in the awards rendered in the past decade, a critical mass of awards relying on this test is still missing. In addition, and beyond purely quantitative analysis, at a qualitative and analytical level, one may legitimately wonder whether proportionality is useful or desirable in international investment law and arbitration, given the specific features of the field. The next section will address this question, showing that while proportionality is useful and desirable in legal systems with constitutional density, it may not be so in legal systems that lack constitutional features.

---

[371] Vienna Convention on the Law of Treaties (VCLT), adopted 23 May 1969, in force 27 January 1980, 1155 UNTS 331.

[372] Leonhardsen, 'Looking for Legitimacy', 123.

3.7 CRITICAL ASSESSMENT

Proportionality has been described as 'the most successful legal transplant of the twentieth century'.[373] It has moved across boundaries and successfully migrated to a number of domestic and supranational systems. While EU adjudicators, WTO panels and the AB have used elements of the proportionality analysis albeit to different extents, arbitral tribunals have only recently started using the concept.[374] Why is this the case?

The answer is multifold. In general, legal tools, such as proportionality, can migrate from one legal field to another. In order for such legal transplants to flourish, 'there must certainly be a connection' between the intrinsic qualities of the legal concept, and the features of the legal field in which it is being transplanted.[375] Neither the abstract merits of the proportionality concept nor its success in its original context sufficiently justify its migration to another legal field.[376] In fact, given constitutional ideas that falter in certain contexts, flourish in others. Rather, the key question is: does proportionality fit with international investment law? Is the migration of proportionality to international investment law useful and/or desirable?

Several factors can explain the success of proportionality in EU law and its limited relevance in international investment law. These relate to: (1) different institutional settings; (2) different aims and objectives; and (3) textual differences among EU law, WTO law and international investment law. This section examines these three factors, which can help explain why proportionality analysis has not yet become a general feature of international investment law and arbitration. The section then examines what reasons might justify the migration of proportionality analysis to international investment law and arbitration. The section concludes showing that proportionality is useful and desirable in legal systems with constitutional density. However, it may not be so desirable and/or useful in legal systems that lack constitutional or quasi-constitutional features. Having said that, any such assessment is necessarily provisional. Because

---

373 M. Kumm, 'Constitutional Rights as Principles: On the Structure and Domain of Constitutional Justice' (2004) 3 IJCL 574–96, 595.

374 Leonhardsen, 'Looking for Legitimacy', 98 (noting that arbitral tribunals have started 'conducting some forms of proportionality analysis … with mixed success').

375 Bernal Pulido, 'The Migration of Proportionality across Europe', 487.

376 Ibid. 487–8.

international investment law and arbitration is a vibrant field of international law, its current evolution and eventual constitutionalization may lead arbitral tribunals to adopt the proportionality analysis in a more consistent fashion in the future.

First, the different institutional frameworks characterizing the EU, the WTO and the investment treaty system respectively can help to explain why proportionality analysis has successfully migrated to EU law, and, to a more limited extent, to WTO law, but has received limited acceptance by arbitral tribunals.

EU law constitutes a system of its own kind lying somewhere between a fully fledged constitutional order and an international organization.[377] Joseph Weiler has argued that 'one of the great perceived truisms, or myths, of the European Union legal order is its alleged rupture with, or mutation from, public international law, and its transformation into a constitutional legal order'.[378] Certainly, the Union is not a federal system, and the failure to ratify an explicit EU Constitution in 2005 signaled some reticence in that regard, at least in some member states.

Yet, undeniably, EU law has a 'constitutional dimension'.[379] Over time, the EU treaties have gradually assumed some constitutional features.[380] Although the Treaty of Rome has the form of an international treaty, it has become the constitutional charter of the EU.[381] The pre-existence of a common European legal heritage, the jurisprudence of

---

[377] See generally M. Poiares Maduro, 'How Constitutional Can the EU Be? The Tension between Intergovernamentalism and Constitutionalism in the EU', in J.H.H. Weiler and C.L. Eisgruber (eds), *Altneuland: The EU Constitution in a Contextual Perspective* (Jean Monnet Working Paper No. 5/04, 2004); T. Moorhead, 'European Union Law as International Law' (2012) 5 EJLS 125–44, 126.

[378] J.H.H. Weiler, *The Constitution of Europe* (CUP 1999) 295.

[379] W. Sauter, 'Proportionality in EU Law: A Balancing Act?' TILEC Discussion Paper (2013) 1–31, 4–5.

[380] See e.g. Advocate General Poiares Maduro's Opinion, Joined Cases C–402/05 P and C–415/05 P, *Kadi and Al Barakaat International Foundation v. Council and Commission* [2008] ECR I-6351, para. 285 (holding that 'obligations imposed by an international agreement cannot have the effect of prejudicing the constitutional principles of the EC Treaty').

[381] Case 249/83, *Partiécologiste 'Les Verts' v. European Parliament* [1986] ECR 1357, para. 23 (stating that '[T]he European Economic Community is a Community based on the rule of law, inasmuch as neither its Member States nor its institutions can avoid a review of the question whether the measures adopted by them are in conformity with the basic constitutional charter, the Treaty').

the CJEU, and constitutional dialogue in Europe have facilitated the constitutionalization process of EU law.

The CJEU has played a pivotal role in the 'constitutionalization' of the regime,[382] construing the founding treaties 'in a constitutional mode rather than employing the traditional international law methodology'.[383] The CJEU has not interpreted such treaties as treaties between states, but rather, as if they amounted to a supranational constitution. For instance, the Court has held that such treaties established 'a new legal order of international law' whose subjects do not comprise member states only but also their nationals.[384] Far from constituting a 'simple agent' of member states, the CJEU has become 'trustee' of its regime, 'discharging various fiduciary duties in the service of the overarching objectives of the regime'.[385] By interpreting the founding treaties in an overtly teleological manner, the Court has made such treaties function like an 'implicit constitution'.[386]

In parallel, since the inception of the WTO in 1995, international trade law has gone through parallel processes of juridification and judicialization to an extent unknown before.[387] Some authors have argued that the WTO presents some constitutional features already, albeit this remains contested.[388] Certainly, since the establishment of the WTO, there have been both a juridification and a judicialization of the regime. The covered agreements expand the scope and intensity of international trade law. The WTO Dispute Settlement System includes an appeal mechanism, a rare feature in international adjudication, whereby ad hoc panel decisions may be reviewed by a permanent body, the AB. Described as the 'jewel in the

---

382 E. Stein, 'Lawyers, Judges, and the Making of a Transnational Constitution' (1981) 75 AJIL 1–27, 1.

383 Ibid. 27.

384 Opinion 1/91 of the Court pursuant to Article 228 of the EEC Treaty on the Draft Treaty on the Establishment of the European Union Economic Area [1991] ECR I-6079.

385 A. Stone Sweet and T.L. Brunell, 'Trustee Courts and the Judicialization of International Regimes' (2013) *Journal of Law and Courts* 61–88, 62.

386 Sauter, 'Proportionality in EU Law', 5.

387 J.H.H. Weiler, 'The Rule of Lawyers and the Ethos of Diplomats: Reflections on the Internal and External Legitimacy of WTO Dispute Settlement' (2001) 35 JWT 191–207, 192; A. Reich, 'From Diplomacy to Law: The Juridicization of International Trade Relations' (1996–97) 17 *Northwestern JIL & Business* 775–849, 776.

388 J.P. Trachtman, 'The Constitutions of the WTO' (2006) 17 EJIL 623–46.

crown' of the WTO,[389] 'the AB is a court in all but name'.[390] Both panels and the Appellate Body have accrued influence over the treaty system's dynamics.[391] The negative consensus rule ensures an almost automatic adoption of their reports.[392] This has enabled the AB to pursue the values enshrined in treaty instruments such as trade liberalization while interpreting and applying WTO law. The AB has also 'embed[ed] the interest of free trade in a broader context of societal values', incorporating 'a balancing discourse into the reading of particular WTO provisions, juxtaposing the objective of trade liberalization and states' right to regulate for non-trade social values'.[393]

The 'courts' of the EU and the WTO 'exercise compulsory jurisdiction over questions concerning state noncompliance; states are under a legal obligation to comply with their rulings'.[394] In both legal systems, each dispute is not a simple disagreement among the parties (*lis inter partes*), but may involve the consideration of multiple factors and interests of relevance to other member states. Both 'courts' have a steady caseload, and some path dependence has emerged in the respective jurisprudence.[395]

---

389 L. Bartels, 'The Separation of Powers within the WTO: How to Avoid Judicial Activism' (2004) 53 ICLQ 861–95, 861.

390 Weiler, 'The Rule of Lawyers and the Ethos of Diplomats', 201.

391 Stone Sweet and Brunell, 'Trustee Courts and the Judicialization of International Regimes', 62.

392 Ibid. 81.

393 S. Shlomo-Agon, 'Clearing the Smoke: The Legitimation of Judicial Power at the WTO' (2015) 49 JWT 539–89, 542.

394 Stone Sweet and Brunell, 'Trustee Courts and the Judicialization of International Regimes', 66.

395 See e.g. G. Sacerdoti, 'Precedent in the Settlement of International Economic Disputes: The WTO and Investment Arbitration Models', in A. Rovine (ed.), *Contemporary Issues in International Arbitration and Mediation* (Martinus Nijhoff 2010) 225–46 (noting that the Appellate Body has referred to, and relied extensively on, its own previous reports and occasionally also on previous panel reports); M. Jacob, *Precedents and Case-based Reasoning in the European Court of Justice* (CUP 2014) (noting that the CJEU privileges general references to 'established case-law' and stringing citations over employing more substantive reasoning when dealing with precedents); T. Tridimas, 'Precedent and the Court of Justice: A Jurisprudence of Doubt?', in J. Dickson and P. Eleftheriadis (eds), *The Philosophical Foundations of EU Law* (OUP 2012) 307–330, 308 (arguing that judicial behaviour of the ECJ 'is close in result, albeit not in methodology, to that of Ango-Saxon supreme courts which adhere to the doctrine of *stare decisis*').

By contrast, international investment law differs from the EU and WTO regimes in many respects. International investment law is a fluid, complex and dynamic system, with 'minimal structure and continuity'.[396] Constantly in search of equilibrium and 'on the edge of chaos', it lacks the centralization, organization and structure of WTO and EU law.[397] On the one hand, it lacks a single multilateral substantive treaty that could function as a 'constitutional charter' of investors' rights and obligations. While international trade law and EU law have been characterized by distinctive constitutive phases, international investment law has 'emerged through evolution', 'partly designed by states … , partly constructed by arbitrators … , partly molded by academics and commentators … and heavily influenced by historical events'.[398] EU law, WTO law and investment law are at different stages of development[399] and this makes their comparison necessarily approximate. On the other hand, the institutions associated with IIAs 'are so freestanding that, at first glance, one might call into question whether [IIAs] belong to a distinct regime at all'.[400] International investment law lacks a central organization that could supervise the implementation of the 'charter' and provide a forum for ongoing negotiations. There is no world investment court that could act as the trustee of international investment agreements. Rather, different one-off arbitral tribunals interpret different treaties.

Second, despite some commonalities, EU law, WTO law and international investment law have different aims and objectives. All of these systems presuppose a triangular relationship between: (1) the individual (the EU citizen, the trader and the investor respectively); (2) the state (the member state, the trading nation and the host state respectively) imposing certain burdens on that individual that may preclude the exercise of his/her rights (under EU law, WTO law and investment law respectively); and (3) the supranational court (the CJEU, the WTO 'courts' and the

---

[396] J. Pauwelyn, 'At the Edge of Chaos? Foreign Investment Law as a Complex Adaptive System' (2014) 29 *ICSID Review* 372–418, 376.

[397] Ratner, 'Regulatory Takings in Institutional Context', 518; Pauwelyn, 'At the Edge of Chaos?', 376.

[398] Pauwelyn, 'At the Edge of Chaos?', 379.

[399] The CJEU has adjudicated thousands of cases. In the past two decades, over 525 disputes have been brought to the WTO. This jurisprudence adds to 132 cases brought to the GATT. As of 31 December 2016, ICSID has registered 597 cases under the ICSID Convention and the Additional Facility Rules. See ICSID, *The ICSID Caseload – Statistics*, Issue 1 (2017) 7.

[400] Ratner, 'Regulatory Takings in Institutional Context', 517.

relevant arbitral tribunal respectively).[401] Despite this common tripartite framework, different assumptions underlie the three systems.

On the one hand, the early market-based 'economic constitution' of the once European Economic Community (EEC), which focused on economic freedoms, has expanded into a more complex 'constitution based on broader individual rights'.[402] The once EEC 'market citizen' (*Marktbürger*) – entitled to market freedoms under the EEC Treaty[403] – has become a 'European Union citizen'[404] entitled to a number of rights, not only of an economic nature.[405] While most legal scholars argue that within the EU, sovereignty is shared among the member states and the EU, legal theorists have even suggested that European sovereignty lies with the citizens in their double capacity as national and European citizens.[406]

Adopting a constitutional perspective on the EU 'may help to explain the development of proportionality as 'a master technique of judicial governance' and European integration.[407] Even if the constitutionalization thesis is not accepted, and the EU is considered to be an international organization, it remains a legal and political entity unprecedented in history. In the EU context, not only does proportionality serve to balance private and public interests but it also plays a role in the allocation of rights and responsibilities between the different levels of government,[408] and the promotion of European integration.[409] The use of proportionality

---

[401] For analogous reasoning with regard to EU law, see N. Reich, 'How Proportionate is the Proportionality Principle? Some Critical Remarks on the Use and Methodology of the Proportionality Principle in the Internal Market Case Law of the ECJ', Working Paper, presented at the Oslo conference on 'The Reach of Free Movement', 2011.

[402] Sauter, 'Proportionality in EU Law', 5.

[403] Reich, 'How Proportionate is the Proportionality Principle?', 11.

[404] E. Guild, C. Gortázar Rotaeche and D. Kostakopoulou (eds), *The Reconceptualization of European Union Citizenship* (Brill 2014) (examining how EU citizenship has developed and contributed to the development of a common European identity).

[405] See W. Weiß, 'Human Rights in the EU: Rethinking the Role of the European Convention on Human Rights after Lisbon' (2011) 7 *European Constitutional LR* 64–95.

[406] J. Habermas, *The Crisis of the European Union. A Response* (C. Cronin, trans) (Polity Press 2012).

[407] Stone Sweet and Matthews, 'Proportionality Balancing and Global Constitutionalism', 140–141.

[408] Sauter, 'Proportionality in EU Law', 6.

[409] G. Nolte, 'General Principles of German and European Administrative Law – A Comparison in Historical Perspective' (1994) 57 MLR 191–212, 206.

has been a 'conscious decisio[n] about fundamental aspects of legal policy'.[410] Therefore, the concept of proportionality is a general principle of EU law. It has helped to foster economic, social and political cohesion, as well as balance economic freedoms and the public interest within a well-developed, sophisticated and integrated legal framework. Over time, multiple versions of the proportionality test have emerged to achieve various degrees of deference.[411]

On the other hand, international trade law and international investment law aim at fostering peaceful and prosperous relations among nations by facilitating free trade and foreign direct investment respectively and promoting growth.[412] Neither the WTO dispute-settlement mechanism nor arbitral tribunals have the comprehensive jurisdiction of the CJEU; rather, they have a more limited mandate. For instance, WTO panels and arbitral tribunals have no mandate to adjudicate the correctness of state measures under human rights law; their mandate is to adjudicate on the eventual breach of relevant trade obligations.

Third, textual differences also explain why arbitral tribunals have referred to proportionality analysis only to a limited extent. The CJEU has borrowed the proportionality principle from the legal systems of its member states. The WTO-covered agreements include some elements of proportionality analysis. Most IIAs do not refer to proportionality. Unless the concept of proportionality is a principle of international law, or is part of the applicable domestic law, its application might seem shaky in the context of investment treaty arbitration.[413] Moreover, arbitral tribunals have not used proportionality in a consistent fashion; rarely have they articulated the distinct suitability, necessity and proportionality in the strict sense tests.[414] Often, they have referred to proportionality in a generic manner, as if it was an afterthought, or in conjunction with other criteria such as rationality and reasonableness. Finally, most arbitral tribunals have not explained why they have referred to proportionality.[415]

---

410 Ibid. 212.

411 Sauter, 'Proportionality in EU Law', 2 (noting that in the EU context, 'a proliferation of different proportionality tests appears to have occurred').

412 See e.g. J. Bhagwati, 'Why Multinationals Help Reduce Poverty' (2007) 30 *World Economy* 211–28, 211.

413 Leonhardsen, 'Looking for Legitimacy', 123.

414 Ibid. 124 (highlighting that the *Tecmed* tribunal 'skipped the suitability and necessity stages' and undertook the proportionality (in the strict sense) test only).

415 Calamita, 'The Principle of Proportionality and the Problem of Indeterminacy', 194.

In conclusion, the migration of proportionality from constitutional law to EU law has been a relatively straightforward process because such principles already belonged to the legal heritage of a few member states. The legal transplant was subject to some adaptation; in fact, the European courts have fashioned the proportionality to meet their own needs. In the 'naturalization' process, the CJEU has applied the proportionality analysis with varied degrees of deference, or interpreted it in a lenient way, transforming it into a reasonableness test.[416] Critics suggest that despite its success, proportionality remains unpredictable, an *enfant terrible* of the Court.[417] Yet, the migration of proportionality from constitutional law to EU law has been successful precisely because the European courts have adapted it to the needs of European integration, relying on the common European legal heritage. Drawing on a common past, they have adapted the concept of proportionality to present needs to shape a common future.

One may question whether the same preconditions for success also exist in investment arbitration. Arbitrators should be aware of the methodological risks and opportunities offered by the migration of constitutional ideas. Such migrations work well in quasi-constitutional legal systems, sharing a common legal tradition, or sharing common values. However, such migrations may prove problematic in systems lacking such constitutional density, such as international investment law, which is a fragmented legal system without a central court. Therefore, for the time being, it may seem premature to engage in the proportionality test, without explicit reference to the same in investment treaties, and in the absence of a quasi-constitutional framework. Whether proportionality analysis will become the predominant mode of analysis in investor–state arbitration in the future remains uncertain.

What factors might favour the migration of the proportionality concept to international investment law and arbitration? While 'existing literature seems to justify the migration of proportionality as a matter of conceptual necessity',[418] this section considers such migration dependent on different legal factors specular to the three challenges examined above, namely: (1) institutional consolidation; (2) growing consideration of

---

[416] T.I. Harbo, 'The Function of the Proportionality Principle in EU Law' (2010) 16 *European LJ* 158–85, 185.

[417] T.T. Tridimas, *The General Principles of EC Law* (OUP 1998) 4 (stating that general principles of EU law were 'children of national law, but as brought in front of the Court, they became *enfants terribles*').

[418] Bernal Pulido, 'The Migration of Proportionality across Europe', 488.

non-economic values within international investment law; and (3) jurisprudential developments.

First, international investment law is in flux.[419] If a multilateral agreement on investment was ever achieved and a permanent World Investment Court and/or an appellate mechanism established, such institutionalization could make the field a more suitable framework for the application of proportionality concepts in the adjudication of investment disputes. Some incremental reform is already underway. States routinely renegotiate treaties, and increasingly detail the rights and obligations of foreign investors.[420] Moreover, a Working Group of the United Nations Commission on International Trade Law (UNCITRAL) that has a broad mandate to work on the possible reform of investor–state arbitration is considering the creation of an international investment court.[421] In parallel, the European Commission recently issued a Recommendation for a Council Decision authorising the same Commission to open negotiations on behalf of the EU for an international convention establishing a multilateral court for the settlement of investment disputes.[422]

Second, developmental objectives and non-economic concerns have increasingly appeared in the preamble and other provisions of IIAs. Reference to fundamental concerns such as environmental goods, public health and cultural heritage protection in the text of IIAs can gradually make such instruments more similar to quasi-constitutional instruments than they are now. Moreover, even in the absence of such reference to

---

[419] See e.g. A. Roberts, 'The Shifting Landscape of Investor–State Arbitration: Loyalists, Reformists, Revolutionaries and Undecideds', *International Economic Law and Policy Blog*, 15 June 2017 ('the investor–state arbitration landscape is shifting under our feet').

[420] The EU can play a facilitating role in this regard. By referring to human rights concerns in the agreements it negotiates, and pressing for the introduction of standing investment court(s), the EU can lead to some paradigm shift in the system. It has also (albeit indirectly) influenced the evolution of the arbitral jurisprudence, since arbitral tribunals have referred to the decisions of the CJEU on several occasions.

[421] UNCITRAL, Possible Future Work in the Field of Dispute Settlement: Reforms of Investor–State Dispute Settlement (ISDS) Note by the Secretariat, 20 April 2017, A/CN.9/917, 8 (discussing the setting up of an international investment court).

[422] European Commission, Recommendation for a Council Decision authorising the opening of negotiations for a Convention establishing a multilateral court for the settlement of investment disputes, 13 September 2017, COM (2017) 493 final.

non-economic concerns, international investment law is not a self-contained regime; rather, customary norms of treaty interpretation as restated in the VCLT require adjudicators to take into account 'any relevant rules of international law applicable in the relations between the parties'.[423] In fact, international investment treaties are creatures of public international law and must be read not only in their own contexts, but in the wider context of public international law.[424]

Third, arbitrators can gradually become more and more familiar with the proportionality analysis given the number of scholarly contributions advocating its use in investor–state arbitration. In turn, arbitral awards can influence the development of the subsequent jurisprudence. While these jurisprudential developments should ideally complement the above-mentioned factors, they can contribute to the realization of proportionality as a truly general principle of international law and/or a customary norm of international law.

In conclusion, the migration of proportionality from constitutional law to EU law has been a straightforward process because such principles already belonged to the legal heritage of a few member states. European courts have borrowed the concept of proportionality and adapted it to their own needs. In some areas, the CJEU interprets proportionality in a way that is closer to the reasonableness test than the classical proportionality analysis.[425] While European courts have used the proportionality analysis in an avant-garde, albeit unpredictable, manner, the migration has been successful precisely because the European courts have adapted it to the dynamics of European integration. In parallel, some elements of proportionality analysis appear in the treaty text of some WTO covered agreements. One may question whether the same preconditions for success also exist in investment arbitration.

This chapter identified three main reasons that can help explain why proportionality analysis has not yet become a general feature of international investment law and arbitration. These relate to the institutional features of the field; its aims and objectives; and textual characteristics of international investment treaties. The chapter also examined what reasons might justify the migration of proportionality analysis to international investment law and arbitration. The section concludes showing that proportionality is useful and desirable in legal systems with constitutional

423 VCLT, Article 31(3)(c).

424 V. Vadi, *Analogies in International Investment Law and Arbitration* (CUP 2016) 119.

425 Harbo, 'The Function of the Proportionality Principle in EU Law', 185.

density. However, it may not be so desirable and/or useful in legal systems that lack constitutional or quasi-constitutional features. Having said that, any such assessment is necessarily provisional. In the meanwhile, arbitrators should be aware of the methodological risks and opportunities offered by the migration of constitutional ideas.

3.8 PROPORTIONALITY AS A GENERAL PRINCIPLE OF LAW?

What are the legal foundations for using proportionality analysis in investment arbitration? Given that the concept of proportionality does not appear in most IIAs, an inquiry into the legal foundations for using it seems to be in order. This section will briefly examine the question as to whether proportionality is a general principle of international law.

General principles of law are considered to be a residual source of international law that may fill gaps 'where no applicable treaty provision or international customary rule exists'.[426] General principles constitute 'a core of legal ideas which are common to all legal systems'[427] and express 'a common juridical heritage of mankind'.[428] While early arbitral tribunals often referred to general principles of law to avoid a finding of *non liquet*,[429] and adjust the law dynamically to changing circumstances, modern tribunals rarely use them.[430] On the one hand, the rising juridification of the field, led by the proliferation of investment treaties and growing arbitral jurisprudence, has marginalized general principles of law.[431] On the other hand, 'there is concern that this source of law lends itself 'too readily to abuse'.[432] In fact, 'when international judges

[426] M. Hirsch, 'Sources of International Investment Law', in A.K. Bjorklund and A. Reinisch (eds), *International Investment Law and Soft Law* (Edward Elgar 2012) 9–38, 22.

[427] R.B. Schlesinger, 'Research on the General Principles of Law Recognized by Civilized Nations' (1957) 51 AJIL 734–53, 739.

[428] Vadi, *Analogies in International Investment Law and Arbitration*, 121.

[429] *Eastern Extension, Australasia and China Telegraph Co Ltd (Great Britain) v. United States*, 9 November 1923, (1923) 6 RIIA, 112–18.

[430] Vadi, *Analogies in International Investment Law and Arbitration*, 122–3.

[431] Hirsch, 'Sources of International Investment Law', 27.

[432] Ibid.

develop general principles of law, they become architects of their own legal systems'.[433]

General principles of law can have a municipal origin or international foundation.[434] Certainly, the comparative legal analysis to detect general principles of law must be extensive and representative, albeit not necessarily uniform or universal.[435] Nevertheless, 'even if all municipal systems include a particular legal rule, this rule is not automatically recognised as a general principle of law'.[436] In fact, the 'transposability to international law' is a critical matter to assess; and the way international law borrows concepts from domestic sources cannot be 'lock, stock and barrel'.[437] In fact, in any legal system, there is a clear link between law and context.

As mentioned, the mobility of proportionality across a wide range of national, regional and international legal systems constitutes a paradigmatic example of the migration of constitutional ideas.[438] In the past decades, proportionality analysis has spread over different fields of law:[439] from constitutional law[440] to intellectual property law,[441] and other areas of domestic law. It has also crossed boundaries, successfully migrating to Canada, Latin America, South Africa, Israel, India, South Korea, Singapore and New Zealand.[442] Similarly, it has become a general principle of EU law.[443]

---

433 A. Stone Sweet and G. Della Cananea, 'Proportionality, General Principles of Law, and Investor–State Arbitration: A Response to José Alvarez' (2014) *NYU JIL and Politics* 911–54, 913.

434 Vadi, *Analogies in International Investment Law and Arbitration*, 122.

435 Ibid. 123.

436 Hirsch, 'Sources of International Investment Law', 23.

437 Ibid. 23–4.

438 Cohen-Elya and Porat, *Proportionality and Constitutional Culture*, 2.

439 Ibid.

440 J. Bomhoff, 'Balancing, the Global and the Local: Judicial Balancing as a Problematic Topic in Comparative (Constitutional) Law' (2008) 31 *Hastings International and Comparative LR* 555–86.

441 See e.g. J. Pila, 'Pluralism, Principles and Proportionality in Intellectual Property' (2014) 34 OJLS 181–200.

442 Hirsch, 'Sources of International Investment Law', 23–4.

443 See generally E. Ellis (ed.), *The Principle of Proportionality in the Laws of Europe* (Hart Publishing 1999).

Furthermore, proportionality has also appeared in different areas of international law: from the law of the sea[444] to the law of countermeasures;[445] from human rights law[446] to international trade law;[447] and from international criminal law[448] to the law of war.[449] Given the presence of the concept of proportionality in various areas of international law, some authors contend that it represents an emerging general principle of international law,[450] or even an already established one.[451] For Cannizzaro, proportionality acquires a special meaning in each field of international law, but preserves a common core constituting a method or technique to fill legal

---

444 D. McRae, 'Proportionality and the Gulf of Maine Maritime Boundary Dispute' (1981) 19 *Canadian YIL* 287–302, 290.

445 See e.g. *Case Concerning the Air Service Agreement of 27 March 1946 Between the United States of America and France*, 9 December 1978, 18 RIAA 417–93, para. 83; *Case Concerning Military and Paramilitary Activities in and Against Nicaragua (Nicaragua v. United States of America)* Merits, 27 June 1986 [1986] ICJ Reports 14, para. 176; *Case Concerning the Gabčíkovo–Nagymaros Project*, 25 September 1997 [1997] ICJ Reports 7, para. 85; *Oil Platforms (Iran v. US)*, Judgment, 6 November 2003, [2003] ICJ Reports 161, para. 43; *Legal Consequences of the Construction of a Wall in the Occupied Palestinian Territory*, Advisory Opinion, 9 July 2004 [2004] ICJ Reports, para. 136; *Case Concerning Armed Activities in the Territory of the Democratic Republic of Congo (CRC v. Uganda)*, Judgment, 19 December 2005 [2005] ICJ Reports 168, para. 147; *Naulilaa Arbitration Award (Portugal v. Germany)*, 31 July 1928 [1949] 2 RIAA 1011 ff. See R. O'Keefe, 'Proportionality', in J. Crawford, A. Pellet and S. Olleson (eds), *The Law of International Responsibility* (OUP 2010) 1157–68; T.M. Franck, 'On Proportionality of Countermeasures in International Law' (2008) 102 AJIL 715–67; E. Cannizzaro, 'The Role of Proportionality in the Law of International Countermeasures' (2001) 12 EJIL 889–916; J.G. Gardam, 'Proportionality and Force in International Law' (1993) 87 AJIL 391–413.

446 F. De Vittor and E. Cannizzaro, 'Proportionality in the European Convention on Human Rights', in R. Kolb and G. Gaggioli (eds), *Research Handbook on Human Rights and Humanitarian Law* (Edward Elgar 2013) 125–45.

447 See section 3.5 above.

448 Rome Statute of the International Criminal Court, adopted 17 July 1998, in force 1 July 2002, 37 ILM 999 (1998), Article 81.2.

449 See M. Newton and L. May, *Proportionality in International Law* (OUP 2014).

450 Kulick, *Global Public Interest in International Investment Law*, 169.

451 See E. Cannizzaro, *Il principio della proporzionalità nell'ordinamento internazionale* (Giuffré 2000) 429–57; S.W. Schill, 'General Principles of Law and International Investment Law', in T. Gazzini and E. de Brabandere (eds), *International Investment Law: The Sources of Rights and Obligations* (Martinus Nijhoff 2012) 133–81, 178; Stone Sweet and Della Cananea, 'Proportionality, General Principles of Law, and Investor–State Arbitration', 937.

gaps and to reconcile private and public interests.[452] In other words, it would be 'an inherent feature in the structure of the international legal order'.[453]

While a number of domestic systems have adopted the notion of proportionality, most legal systems, including Australia, China and the United States, have remained out of reach.[454] To date, no major scholarly work has investigated the diffusion of the proportionality concept across the globe; rather, studies have focused on a selected range of constitutional cultures. Yet, the examination of a few case studies does not support the claim that proportionality is a *general* principle of *international* law. Even among the countries that adopt it, proportionality analysis is not uniformly applied.[455] Cultural factors shape judicial review in different legal systems.[456] Such 'cultural filters' explain why several constitutional traditions have shown some caution in approaching proportionality. Moreover, international courts and tribunals rarely rely on domestic experience to reconstruct general principles of law, rather relying on international law considerations.[457]

No consensus seems to have arisen yet with regard to the legal status of proportionality in general international law.[458] While proportionality belongs to certain areas of international law, it remains a relative newcomer in other fields. Analogously, proportionality does not seem to be a rule of customary international law.[459] Certainly, more comparative

---

452 Cannizzaro, *Il principio della proporzionalità nell'ordinamento internazionale*, 429–32.

453 Ibid. 483.

454 Calamita, 'The Principle of Proportionality and the Problem of Determinacy', 168; Cannizzaro, *Il principio della proporzionalità nell'ordinamento internazionale*, 452.

455 Kulick, *Global Public Interest in International Investment Law*, 169 (noting that '[w]hile the basic structure of proportionality analysis is similar across systems', its conceptualization and application remains 'context specific').

456 Bomhoff, 'Beyond Proportionality', 12.

457 G. Gaja, 'Principi generali del diritto (Diritto internazionale)' (1986) 36 *Enciclopedia diritto* 533–8, 538.

458 See J. Alvarez, 'Beware: Boundary Crossings – A Critical Appraisal of Public Law Approaches to International Investment Law' (2016) 17 JWIT 171–228 (denying that proportionality is a general principle of international law); R. Higgins, *Problems and Process: International Law and How We Use It* (OUP 1994) 236.

459 Calamita, 'The Principle of Proportionality and the Problem of Determinacy', 168; Cannizzaro, *Il principio della proporzionalità nell'ordinamento internazionale*, 450; J. Kilcup, 'Proportionality in Customary International Law: An Argument Against Aspirational Laws of War' (2016) 17 *Chicago JIL* 244–72,

and international law studies are needed to address the question as to whether proportionality has migrated from the domestic realm to the international one, or whether it already belongs to the international realm, and if so, whether it has become a general principle of international law.

If one admits that proportionality is a general principle of international law,[460] then such a contention would constitute a formidable entry point for proportionality analysis in investment treaty arbitration, as arbitrators could refer to proportionality in their awards as part of the applicable law or as a matter of treaty interpretation. Proportionality would be either part of the applicable law, under Article 42 of the Convention on the Settlement of Investment Disputes between States and Nationals of Other States (ICSID Convention),[461] or a rule of international law applicable in the relations between the parties under Article 31(3)(c) of the VCLT.[462]

In the uncertainty as to the legal status of proportionality in international law, the legal grounds for considering proportionality in investment treaty arbitration can be problematic. Certainly, if the applicable law is the law of the host state and this law refers to proportionality, such concept becomes relevant in the context of investment treaty arbitration.[463] Arbitral tribunals that have used the concept often refer to previous awards.[464]

247 (noting that 'proportionality as a matter of [customary international law] is in need of clarification').

460 See e.g. G. Bücheler, *Proportionality in Investor–State Arbitration* (OUP 2015) 29.

461 Convention on the Settlement of Investment Disputes between States and Nationals of Other States (ICSID Convention or Washington Convention), Washington, adopted 18 March 1965, in force 14 October 1966, 575 UNTS 159, Article 42.

462 B. Kingsbury and S. Schill, 'Investor–State Arbitration as Governance: Fair and Equitable Treatment, Proportionality and the Emerging Global Administrative Law' (2009) NYU School of Law, Public Law & Legal Research Theory Research Paper Series, Working Paper 09-46, 1–56, 23.

463 *Occidental Petroleum Corporation and Occidental Exploration and Production Company v. Republic of Ecuador*, ICSID Case No. ARB/06/11, Award, 16 December 2011, para. 427 (noting that the principle of proportionality was 'established in [Ecuador's] Constitution and reiterated in subsequent legislation').

464 Ibid. para. 427 (adding that proportionality was also 'applicable as a matter of general international law, [being] … applied in many ICSID arbitrations in the past') and para. 403 (noting that the principle of proportionality 'has

Regardless of whether proportionality qualifies as a general principle of international law, some argue that, as a conceptual tool, it can help calibrate the scope and effect of investment treaty arbitration.[465] By providing a well-structured set of tests requiring the state to give reasons for its conduct,[466] and a template for the settlement of conflicts between competing interests,[467] proportionality constitutes a judicial technique for balancing competing values. Scholars suggest that it is not necessary to identify a positive legal basis for using proportionality in international investment law. Following this line of argument, proportionality would be delocalised because of its alleged intrinsic merits and functional considerations.

However, subjecting the lawfulness of state conduct to the additional condition that it be proportionate restricts the autonomy of host states to a greater extent than do IIAs.[468] As Xiuli points out, proportionality can pose 'a tremendous threat' to the regulatory power of the host state 'since the measures adopted [by the state] may lose their legitimacy for not conforming to the principle of proportionality'.[469] Therefore, such approach does not explain why arbitral tribunals should go beyond the limits of state consent and exceed their mandate. It also fails to explain why states should accept the analogical extension of the grounds for their liability.

Even accepting that proportionality can be used as a mere methodology, without any need for further investigating its legal status, questions

---

been adopted and applied countless times by the European Court of Justice in Luxembourg, and by the European Court of Human Rights in Strasbourg'). For a criticism of these statements, see Calamita, 'The Principle of Proportionality and the Problem of Indeterminacy', 193 (arguing that 'international tribunals such as investor–state arbitral tribunals … [have to] apply international law … and not to fashion it from a mix of policy preferences, unsupported incorporation from other legal systems, and rote repetition of the decisions of other tribunals').

465 Henckels, *Proportionality and Deference in Investor–State Arbitration*; S. Schill, 'Public Law Concepts to Balance Investors' Rights with State Regulatory Actions in the Public Interest – The Concept of Proportionality', in S. Schill (ed.), *International Investment Law and Comparative Public Law* (OUP 2010) 75–105, 79 (considering proportionality 'a method of legal interpretation and decision making in situations of collisions or conflict of different values').

466 Cohen-Eliya and Porat, 'Proportionality and Justification' 458.

467 Ibid. 459.

468 Contiades and Fotiadou, 'Social Rights in the Age of Proportionality', 685.

469 H. Xiuli, 'On the Application of the Principle of Proportionality in ICSID Arbitration and Proposals to Government of the People's Republic of China' (2006) 13 *James Cook University LR* 233–58, 244.

remain as to whether it is suitable for transposition in international investment law and arbitration. Even if there were an emerging world consensus about its merits, the concept would have to be appropriate for application in international investment law.[470]

Proposals to use only some parts of the proportionality test do not seem persuasive. Even if one narrowed the proportionality test, that is, examined only some of its steps, rather than examining all of them, questions arise as to which tests should be retained. Confining review to the examination of suitability would exclude from judicial review the greatest number of treaty breaches.[471] Some scholars suggest that only two prongs of the proportionality test – suitability and necessity – should be accepted.[472] For these scholars, proportionality in a strict sense test is either unnecessary or unjustified in almost all cases.[473]

However, one may wonder whether it would be appropriate to continue referring to proportionality review, or whether narrowing the scope of proportionality review in this manner would lead to an entirely different type of review. By altering the proportionality analysis to such a significant extent, we are no longer talking about proportionality but something different. Some international courts, such as the CJEU, have used different versions of the proportionality test. However, the investment treaty system is multi-layered, with no permanent World Investment Court to settle investment disputes; rather, a variety of arbitral tribunals interpreting and applying a myriad of investment treaties. In this fragmented context, the use of different versions of proportionality can lead to 'doctrinal confusion rather than the hoped-for simplicity'.[474]

More fundamentally, proposals to use only some parts of the proportionality test indirectly confirm that, at least in some circumstances, proportionality can be 'an inadequate heuristic device' to settle certain disputes.[475] For Jackson, '[b]eing proportional about proportionality

---

470 Hirsch, 'Sources of International Investment Law', 23.

471 Contiades and Fotiadou, 'Social Rights in the Age of Proportionality', 668.

472 Nolte, 'Thin or Thick?', 248.

473 Ibid.

474 E. Bjorge and J.R. Williams, 'The Protean Principle of Proportionality: How Different is Proportionality in EU Contexts?' (2016) *Cambridge LJ* 186–9, 188.

475 F. Fontanelli, 'The Mythology of Proportionality in Judgments of the Court of Justice of the European Union on Internet and Fundamental Rights' (2016) 36 OJLS 630–60, 631 (claiming that, with regard to internet disputes, the ECJ 'is less engaged in actual proportionality than in a pragmatic moderation of conflicting interests').

means that proportionality as a principle is not always served by proportionality as a doctrine'.[476] Its 'high level of proceduralization and its operation reminiscent of a mathematical formula' can 'facilitate the thankless task of second-guessing ... state preferences'.[477] There can be, and indeed there are, other methods of review that may be appropriate to investor–state arbitrations. Proportionality is not the only doctrinal tool for calibrating different interests and values in investor–state arbitration. One could counterargue that the use of such alternative doctrinal tools 'hide[s] or disguise[s] the requirements of proportionality'.[478] However, if proportionality is everywhere, as certain scholars assume it to be, why are arbitral tribunals so wary of using it explicitly? In conclusion, proportionality is certainly transposable to the international level.[479] However, questions remain as to whether it has migrated to international investment law and arbitration, or whether it should do so.

CONCLUSIONS

Conceived as an analytical tool to assist adjudicators in determining the interaction between public and private interests, the concept of proportionality has attracted increasing attention by scholars and policy makers alike and has migrated from constitutional law to a number of other legal fields. It offers a structured method of reasoning that can delimit the exercise of public powers, shape adjudication and manage private actors' expectations. Often depicted as an ideal mechanism for balancing opposing interests and thus creating equilibrium between private and public interests, it is 'a manifestation of the perennial quest to invest adjudication with precision and objectivity'.[480]

This chapter investigated the question as to whether, and if so, to what extent, proportionality has migrated from constitutional law to EU law, WTO law and international investment law respectively. Undoubtedly, the migration of proportionality to EU law is a paradigmatic case of successful legal transplant. Not only is proportionality analysis part of EU law, but it has become a general principle of it. While the migration of proportionality to WTO law remains a work in progress, some of its

---

476 Jackson, 'Constitutional Law in an Age of Proportionality', 3104.

477 Fontanelli, 'The Mythology of Proportionality', 641.

478 Bernal Pulido, 'The Migration of Proportionality across Europe', 508 (reporting this argument).

479 Bücheler, *Proportionality in Investor–State Arbitration*, Ch. 3.

480 Tsakyrakis, 'Proportionality: An Assault on Human Rights?', 469.

elements belong to the international trade regime. Instead, no consensus seems to have arisen with regard to the legal status of proportionality in international investment law.

Recent arbitrations signal an increasing openness of arbitral tribunals to rely on some elements of the proportionality analysis. However, it remains to be seen whether the growing frequency of reference to proportionality is evidence of a proper migration rather than an ephemeral phenomenon.

A corollary question is whether proportionality *should* migrate to international investment law. The doctrine is divided. A number of prominent scholars argue that proportionality is, and/or should be, part of the international investment law regime. Adopting a functionalist approach, proponents of proportionality argue that, like other legal tools, proportionality is a response to, and aims to address, universal legal problems and that therefore it can be transplanted from one field to another. In their view, proportionality analysis can be a useful tool of judicial governance to calibrate private and public interests in international investment law, contribute to its humanization and promote its perceived legitimacy.[481]

Yet, the use of proportionality analysis for ascertaining whether or not the value pursued by a host state should prevail over the burden imposed on the foreign investment can (and has) be(en) contested on a number of grounds. First, the legal systems in which proportionality has flourished present more cohesion, integration and uniformity than international investment law and arbitration. Constitutional law systems are integrated expressions of a given constituency. In parallel, EU law has a constitutional dimension, being a system of its own kind, going beyond pure market integration, and including the protection of human rights and fundamental freedoms. Proportionality has acquired the status of general principle of EU law, expressing the common European legal past, responding to current needs of balancing economic and non-economic values, and shaping the common future of the EU. The CJEU uses proportionality in conjunction with varying degrees of deference, adapting it to the complex needs of the European integration. Instead, international investment law is composed of different IIAs; it governs the relations among states concerning foreign investments and lacks a centralized dispute-settlement mechanism. Therefore, the desirability of

---

481 See e.g. Kingsbury and Schill, 'Public Law Concepts to Balance Investors' Rights', 75.

the migration of proportionality to international investment law remains questionable, at least for the time being.

Second, the legal basis for introducing proportionality analysis in international investment arbitration appears shaky. Certainly, if the applicable law is the law of the host state and this law includes the proportionality principle, such principle becomes relevant in the context of investment treaty arbitration. Generally, international investment treaties do not provide a textual hook for proportionality. If proportionality were a general principle of law, or an element of customary law, it could eventually be used in international investment law and arbitration as part of the applicable law or as a matter of treaty interpretation. Proportionality is a general principle of EU law; it has acquired customary status in certain areas of international law. For instance, it is undisputed that countermeasures must be proportionate under customary international law.[482] That said, is proportionality a general principle of international law? Is it a customary norm of international law? More comparative and international law studies are needed to ascertain the legal status of proportionality in international law. In the uncertainty as to the legal status of proportionality in international law, the legal grounds for considering proportionality in investor–state arbitration can be problematic.

Even in accepting that proportionality can be used as a mere methodology, without any need of further investigating its legal status, questions remain as to whether it is suitable for transposition. Having the capacity to restrict state sovereignty, one may wonder whether states should be subject to it, without having given their consent. Proposals to use only some parts of the proportionality test do not seem persuasive as they do not seem to be referring to proportionality but something different.

Third, critics argue that the use of the proportionality concept permits arbitrators to second-guess the decisions of the host state by replicating the original decision-making process. Proportionality can be an invasive tool for reviewing state conduct. A separate, albeit related concern relates to the fear of arbitral activism – meant as a philosophy of decision-making whereby arbitrators allow their personal views rather than the law to guide their decisions. This criticism stresses the 'monothematic' nature of international investment law, as a field of international law governing

---

[482] *Archer Daniels Midland Co and Tate & Lyle Ingredients Americas, Inc v. the United Mexican States*, ICSID Case No. ARB(AF)/04/05, Award, 21 November 2007, para. 160 (acknowledging the 'customary international law' nature of the proportionality requirement for the validity of countermeasures and finding that a given tax did not meet 'the proportionality requirement for the validity of countermeasures under customary international law').

foreign direct investments. The fact that arbitrators can take other instruments of international law into account when interpreting investment treaties under Article 31(3)(c) of the VCLT does not expand their jurisdiction.

Fourth, cultural arguments suggest that law is an emanation of culture, that context matters, and that therefore, there cannot be purely mechanical transplants from one legal field to another. Cultural arguments conceive legal transplants as cultural transplants, thus calling for the development of context-sensitive methodologies. While proportionality analysis can work perfectly well in given domestic constitutional contexts and in EU law, this does not necessarily mean that it can do so in the international investment regime. Proportionality analysis is value-laden,[483] reflecting given historical developments and institutional contexts. Therefore, one may wonder whether international investment law is a suitable terrain for transplantation. This is not to say that there is no room for improvement in arbitral reasoning; rather, if proportionality is one of the available tools, it is not the only means, as will be illustrated in Chapter 4.

Thus, this chapter shows that while the concept of proportionality has analytical merits, it also presents a number of pitfalls when applied to the context of investment disputes. If arbitral tribunals are to use proportionality to form their interpretation of particular provisions, they must ensure that they master the relevant methodological risks and opportunities.

Having said that, the fact that international investment law lacks constitutional density does not mean that it cannot acquire this in the future through treaty making – through the insertion of non-economic considerations in the preambles and in the text of international investment agreements. Moreover, proportionality can become a general principle or even customary law in the future. Future reforms of the international investment regime in general and the eventual creation of a World Investment Court in particular may also lead to some appreciation of the proportionality analysis.

Consequently, this chapter shows that the debate as to whether proportionality analysis should migrate (and be part of) international investment law remains open, and in fact, is currently far from being settled. Certainly, from a legal/doctrinal perspective, more comparative constitutional and international law studies are needed to address the

483 Arai-Takahashi, 'Proportionality', 467.

question as to whether proportionality is a general principle of international law and/or reflects customary international law.

4. Reasonableness in investment treaty arbitration

One man's 'reason' is the other man's insanity.[1]

Paul K. Feyerabend

INTRODUCTION

Under most investment treaties, states have agreed to give arbitrators a comprehensive jurisdiction over what are essentially regulatory disputes. Many of the recent arbitral awards have determined the boundary between two conflicting values: the legitimate sphere for state regulation in the pursuit of public goods, on the one hand; and the protection of foreign investment from state interference, on the other. Is investor–state arbitration a suitable forum to protect public interests? Are there appropriate tools for reconciling conflicting interests within investment treaty arbitration? This chapter addresses these questions by examining the analytical merits and pitfalls of the concept of reasonableness and its use in investment treaty arbitration. This scrutiny can contribute some theoretical and practical legal insights into the ongoing search for legal tools to reconcile opposing interests in international investment law and arbitration.

If one considers international adjudication as a form of continual dialogue between international courts, states and the international community about how best to protect given interests and values, reasonableness offers a valuable dialogic tool. In broad strokes, reasonableness requires states to adopt measures that logically relate to their aims.[2] Reasonableness is a standard of good governance that guides states in adopting measures, calibrating public and private interests and giving reasons for their action. It also requires adjudicators to interpret the

[1] P.K. Feyerabend, *Against Method: Outline of an Anarchistic Theory of Knowledge* (Verso 1978) 217.

[2] J. Wouters and S. Duquet, 'The Principle of Reasonableness in Global Administrative Law' (2013) 12 *Jean Monnet Working Paper* 1–42, 5.

applicable law reasonably and to provide reasons for their decisions. Finally, it enables private actors to have legitimate and reasonable expectations only. In summary, reasonableness 'ensur[es] that different actors … have been given the opportunity to have their voices heard (dialogical reasonableness) and reflected in the [relevant] deliberations'.[3]

As well as certain national legal systems, several international law instruments also require that state action be reasonable. International courts and tribunals have also used reasonableness to review state action. Despite its pervasiveness, scholars have analyzed the concept only to a limited extent.[4] The concept of reasonableness remains underexplored in international law in general,[5] and international investment law in particular.[6] A few studies have focused on reasonableness as an element of good faith and the rule of law under the fair and equitable treatment standard,[7] but have not addressed the growing pervasiveness of reasonableness in international investment law and arbitration and its nexus with other treaty standards, including expropriation, non-discrimination and others.

This chapter contends that while the concept of reasonableness has analytical merits, it also presents a number of flaws when applied to the context of investment disputes. The joint use of reasonableness and proportionality may (but does not necessarily) constitute an alternative approach to address the specificities of investment treaty law and arbitration. Rather, of critical importance is the interplay between proportionality and reasonableness, on the one hand, and standards of review, on the other. Arbitral jurisprudence reveals that these disparate elements do interact in a variety of different ways.

The chapter unfolds as follows. Section 4.1 defines the notion of reasonableness engaging with literature on international law, constitutional law, and legal theory. Section 4.2 identifies the analytical merits of

---

[3] Ibid. 40.

[4] P. Craig, 'The Nature of Reasonableness Review' (2013) 66 *Current Legal Problems* 131–67 (noting that '[w]hile there is voluminous literature on proportionality, there is considerably less on reasonableness as a test for judicial review of discretionary determinations').

[5] For a seminal study, see O. Corten, *L'utilisation du raisonnable par le juge international* (Bruylant 1997). See also J. Salmon, 'Le concept de raisonnable en droit international public', in P. Reuter (ed.), *Mélanges offerts à Paul Reuter. Le droit international: unité et diversité* (Pedone 1982) 447–78.

[6] But see V. Vadi, 'Proportionality, Reasonableness and Standards of Review in Investment Treaty Arbitration', in A. Bjorklund (ed.), *Yearbook of International Investment Law and Policy* (2013–2014) 201–228.

[7] K.J. Vandevelde, 'A Unified Theory of Fair and Equitable Treatment' (2010) 43 *NYU JIL & Politics* 43–106.

reasonableness, that is, the reasons why it has been adopted by a number of constitutional traditions and has migrated to other legal fields. Section 4.3 explores the practical and theoretical pitfalls of reasonableness. Section 4.4 illuminates whether, and if so to what extent, reasonableness has migrated to international investment law and arbitration and/or whether it belongs to the field. Section 4.5 pushes the analysis further, understanding and evaluating whether the use of reasonableness in investment arbitration can be desirable and, if so, under what circumstances. The conclusions then sum up the key arguments of the chapter.

4.1 REASONABLENESS

Reasonableness is an 'essentially contested concept': while there is no single definition of reasonableness, the concept includes diverse, and at times competing, notions,[8] serving a range of functions, and assuming different meanings depending on context.[9] There is no abstract notion of reasonableness; rather, it is a context-specific notion.[10] As the International Court of Justice (ICJ) put it, '[w]hat is reasonable and equitable in any given case must depend on its particular circumstances'.[11] In broad strokes, reasonable regulatory measures surely include logical, rational, consequential and well-founded measures reflecting good governance. A given measure can be deemed logical when it does not contradict itself and/or it does not clash with other parts of the legal

[8] S.P. Young, 'Introduction', in S.P. Young (ed.), *Reasonableness in Liberal Political Philosophy* (Routledge 2014) 1–6, 2 (noting that 'reasonableness is an essentially contested concept, a quality the specifics of which have been understood in a number of different and, at times, competing ways'); Craig, 'The Nature of Reasonableness Review', 131 (noting that 'the very nature of reasonableness review … remains contested').

[9] C. Perelman, *Le raisonnable et le déraisonnable en droit* (Libraire Générale de Droit et de Jurisprudence 1984); C. Perelman, 'Le raisonnable et le déraisonnable en droit' (1978) 23 *Archives de Philosophie du droit* 35–42.

[10] O. Corten, 'Reasonableness in International Law', in R. Wolfrum (ed.), *Max Planck Encyclopedia of Public International Law* (OUP 2013) 16.

[11] *Interpretation of the Agreement of 25 March 1951 between the WHO and Egypt*, Advisory Opinion [1980] ICJ Reports, para. 49; *Continental Shelf (Tunisia/Libyan Arab Jamahiriya)* [1982] ICJ Reports, para. 72.

system (logicality *intra legem* or *intra jus*, respectively).[12] A given measure is rational if it is at least compatible with its own aim.[13]

By contrast, 'unreasonableness' is very close to 'arbitrariness' which, under international law, involves a breach beyond the ordinary meaning of reason, an act that shocks, or at least surprises, a sense of juridical propriety. The ICJ has equated reasonableness with lack of arbitrariness,[14] absurdity and contradiction.[15] In the *ELSI* case,[16] a dispute arising out of the requisition by the Government of Italy of the plant owned by two US corporations, the Court held that if an act of a public authority is unreasonable or arbitrary under municipal law, this does not necessarily mean that such act is also arbitrary under international law. Certainly, reasonableness cannot be based on mere compliance with domestic law, 'though the qualification given to the impugned act by a municipal authority may be a valuable indication'.[17] The Court also stated that 'arbitrariness is not so much something opposed to a rule of law, as something opposed to the rule of law … It is a willful disregard of due process of law, an act which shocks, or at least surprises, a sense of judicial propriety'.[18]

Reasonableness constitutes a practical guide for state behaviour, requiring states to behave reasonably. It 'applies both to the conception of the measures as well as their implementation'.[19] It also requires states to give reasons for their selected course of action. For instance, in the *Case Concerning Rights of Nationals of the United States of America in Morocco*,[20] arising in connection with a Moroccan decree that restricted

---

[12] A. Morrone, 'Constitutional Adjudication and the Principle of Reasonableness', in G. Bongiovanni, G. Sartor and C. Valentini (eds), *Reasonableness and Law* (Springer 2009) 215–22, 222.

[13] Ibid. 223.

[14] *Case Concerning Elettronica Sicula SpA (ELSI) (United States v. Italy)* Judgment, 20 July 1989 [Merits] [1989] ICJ Reports 76, para. 124.

[15] *Case Concerning the Temple of Preah Vihear (Cambodia v. Thailand)* Judgment, 26 May 1961 [Preliminary Objections] [1961] ICJ Reports 32, 33.

[16] *Case Concerning Elettronica Sicula SpA (ELSI) (United States v. Italy)* Judgment, 20 July 1989 [1989] ICJ Reports 15, 28 ILM 1109.

[17] Ibid. para. 29.

[18] Ibid. para. 128.

[19] X. Contiades and A. Fotiadou, 'Social Rights in the Age of Proportionality: Global Economic Crisis and Constitutional Litigation' (2012) 10 IJCL 660–86, 678.

[20] *Case Concerning Rights of Nationals of the United States of America in Morocco (France v. United States of America)*, Judgment, 27 August 1952 [1952] ICJ Reports 176.

imports into Morocco from countries other than France, the ICJ held that '[t]he power of making the valuation rests with the customs authorities, but it is a power which must be exercised reasonably and in good faith'.[21] In the seminal *Barcelona Traction* case, as is known, Belgium sought compensation for the damage caused to its nationals – shareholders in the Barcelona Traction, Light and Power Company – by acts committed by organs of the Spanish State. The ICJ held that 'in the field of diplomatic protection as in all other fields of international law, it is necessary that the law be applied reasonably'.[22]

At the same time, reasonableness allows the state 'a wide discretion'.[23] Adjudicators applying the reasonableness criterion do not enquire whether other, more desirable, more effective or more economical measures could have been adopted.[24] Even if according to the adjudicator, given state choices 'fail to achieve the best outcome, [they] can still stand when they remain within the domain of the reasonable'.[25] Therefore, the application of the reasonableness criterion in adjudication prevents adjudicators from excessively interfering in state choices.[26] Moreover, adjudicators assess the reasonableness of given measures 'in accordance [with] the social, economic and historical context'.[27] For instance, in *James v. United Kingdom*, a case concerning the right to buy a home from one's landlord, the European Court of Human Rights (ECtHR) held that it will 'respect a national legislature's judgment as to what is in the public interest ... unless that judgment is manifestly without reasonable foundation'.[28]

---

21 Ibid. 212.

22 ICJ, *Barcelona Traction, Light and Power Company, Ltd (Belgium v. Spain)*, Judgment, 5 February 1970 [1970] ICJ Reports 3, 48, para. 93.

23 Contiades and Fotiadou, 'Social Rights in the Age of Proportionality', 679.

24 Ibid. 678.

25 G. Sartor, 'Doing Justice to Rights and Values: Teleological Reasoning and Proportionality' (2010) 18 *Artificial Intelligence and Law* 175–215, 177.

26 Ibid.

27 Contiades and Fotiadou, 'Social Rights in the Age of Proportionality', 678.

28 *James and others v. United Kingdom*, ECtHR, Judgment, 21 February 1986, [1986] ECHR 2, para. 46.

Reasonableness constitutes a conceptual tool to reconcile competing interests.[29] In the *Dispute Regarding Navigational and Related Rights*,[30] and the *Whaling in the Antarctic* case,[31] the ICJ used reasonableness as a tool for calibrating diverging interests. In the *Dispute Regarding Navigational and Related Rights*, a case concerning riparian states' rights on the lower course of Nicaragua's San Juan river, the ICJ stated that state regulation should not be 'unreasonable', that is, 'its negative impact ... must not be manifestly excessive when measured against the protection afforded to the purpose invoked'.[32] In the *Whaling in the Antarctic* case, a dispute in which the ICJ assessed the legality of a whaling programme allegedly designed to pursue purposes of scientific research, the Court used reasonableness in evaluating the state's conduct.[33] The Court held that the respondent had not complied in a reasonable manner with its international obligations. In particular, the Court examined whether the design and implementation of a Japanese whaling programme were reasonable in relation to achieving the programme's stated research objectives.[34] Analogously, in *Sporrong and Lonnroth v. Sweden*, a case in which the claimants challenged orders expropriating their properties for redevelopment, the ECtHR emphasized that 'a fair balance [must be struck] between the demands of the general interest of the community and the requirements of the protection of the individual's fundamental rights'.[35] The Court concluded that a fair balance does not exist where an individual bears an unreasonably large burden.[36]

After having defined the concept of reasonableness and examined its functions as (1) a practical guide for state behavior; (2) a judicial criterion in reviewing state's conduct; and (3) a conceptual tool to reconcile competing interests; this section now investigates the similarity and difference between reasonableness and other competing notions. This

---

29 A. Garrido-Muñoz, 'Managing Uncertainty: The International Court of Justice, "Objective Reasonableness" and the Judicial Function' (2017) 30 *Leiden JIL* 1–18, 4.

30 ICJ, *Dispute Regarding Navigational and Related Rights* (*Costa Rica v. Nicaragua*), Judgment, 13 July 2009 [2009] ICJ Reports 249.

31 ICJ, *Whaling in the Antarctic Case* (*Australia v. Japan*), Judgment, 31 March 2014 [2014] ICJ Reports 226.

32 ICJ, *Dispute Regarding Navigational and Related Rights*, para. 87.

33 ICJ, *Whaling in the Antarctic Case*, paras 67, 212.

34 Ibid. para. 67.

35 *Sporrong and Lonnroth v. Sweden*, ECtHR, Judgment, 23 September 1982, A 52, 26.

36 Ibid.

scrutiny helps us illuminate the significance of reasonableness by juxtaposing, comparing it with, and distinguishing it from competing notions. Let us now examine the commonalities and differences between reasonableness and rationality, on the one hand, and reasonableness and proportionality, on the other.

Although both rationality and reasonableness designate conformity with reason, generally the two terms are not interchangeable.[37] Defined as the efficient pursuit of one's objectives, rationality indicates the adoption of logical measures appropriate to their ends. Derived from a mathematical model, rationality requires compelling reasoning.[38] It is analogous to the 'suitability' element that constitutes the first part of the proportionality analysis. It also evokes the idea of a type of decision-making that maximizes the utility of an individual, without necessarily taking into account the interests of others.[39]

Instead, reasonableness constitutes a more comprehensive standard than rationality. Reasonableness does not merely include rationality but transcends it. While rationality requires reasons, reasonableness requires 'satisfactory reasons'.[40] Reasonableness includes a sense of justice, the idea of taking into account not only one's own interests but also the legitimate interests of others.[41] Reasonableness implies that 'different reasonable assessments of the importance of values and of the appropriateness of means are possible'.[42] Such reasonable assessments also cover non-optimal determinations, which may nonetheless remain appropriate or adequate.[43] Therefore, reasonableness leaves latitude for differences of opinion, for rival views of what is needed in given circumstances.

---

37 C. Perelman, 'The Rational and the Reasonable', in C. Perelman (ed.), *The New Rhetoric and the Humanities: Essays on Rhetoric and Its Applications* (Reidel 1979) 117–23.

38 Ibid. 117.

39 G. Sartor, G. Bongiovanni and C. Valentini, 'Reasonableness in International Law', *Oxford Bibliographies* (OUP 2016) 1–20, 2.

40 Wouters and Duquet, 'The Principle of Reasonableness in Global Administrative Law', 12 (noting that 'irrationality means devoid of reasons', unreasonableness means 'devoid of satisfactory reasons').

41 A. Barak, *Purposive Interpretation in Law* (Princeton UP 2005) 199 (noting that 'a decision is reasonable if it is reached after giving the proper weight to the different values that need to be taken into account').

42 Sartor, Bongiovanni and Valentini, 'Reasonableness in International Law', 3.

43 Ibid. 1.

Influenced by common sense, reasonableness seeks, in all domains, what is adequate and may vary over time and across different communities.[44]

Reasonableness seems a more appropriate standard than pure rationality in the context of investor–state arbitration. On the one hand, a pure rationality analysis 'may not always offer sufficient protection of investor rights'.[45] As an Arbitral Tribunal put it, 'for a state conduct to be reasonable, it is not sufficient that it be related to a rational policy; it is also necessary that, in the implementation of that policy, the state's acts have been appropriately tailored to the pursuit of that rational policy with due regard for the consequences imposed on investors'.[46] On the other hand, a pure rationality analysis does not show sufficient consideration of all the interests and values pertaining to a given dispute. By contrast, reasonableness enables the interpretation and application of international law, taking into account the local context.[47]

This is particularly appropriate in international (investment) law, given that 'reasonable disagreement among states is widespread and persistent' in the field.[48] Adjudicators should evaluate state conduct not only in the light of its effects on investment protection, but also in light of the aims, objectives and design of the given measure. The purpose of international investment agreements is not merely to protect foreign investors and their investments, but also to contribute to the developments of the host state;[49] and development has been interpreted as inclusive not only of mere economic growth, but also of human flourishing and well-being.

Moving now to examine the link between reasonableness and proportionality, the relationship between the two concepts remains ambiguous and asymmetrical, and yet potentially complementary. The link between reasonableness and proportionality is ambiguous because of the uncertainty as to whether one concept implies, partially overlaps with, or expands the other. If there is an obligation of reasonableness, is there also

---

[44] Perelman, 'The Rational and the Reasonable', 118–19.

[45] W.W. Burke-White and A. von Staden, 'Private Litigation in a Public Law Sphere: The Standard of Review in Investor–State Arbitrations' (2010) 35 *Yale JIL* 283–346, 339.

[46] *Ioan Micula, Viorel Micula, S.C. European Food S.A, S.C. Starmill S.R.L. and S.C. Multipack S.R.L. v. Romania*, ICSID Case No. ARB/05/20, Award, 11 December 2013, para. 525.

[47] J. Crawford (ed.) *Brownlie's Principles of Public International Law*, 8th edn (OUP 2012) 46–7.

[48] S. Besson, 'State Consent and Disagreement in International Law-Making: Dissolving the Paradox' (2016) 29 *Leiden JIL* 289–316, 307.

[49] *Amco Asia Corp v. Republic of Indonesia*, ICSID Case No. ARB/81/01, Award on Jurisdiction, 24 September 1985, para. 23.

an (implied) obligation of proportionality? If there is an obligation of proportionality, is there also an (implied) obligation of reasonableness? What does one add to the other? The two notions remain distinct in theory; yet, they may partially overlap in practice.

Reasonableness and proportionality are asymmetrical. For instance, given measures can be reasonable but may in fact be disproportionate.[50] In turn, what is proportionate can be unreasonable.[51] In other cases, however, proportionality and reasonableness 'can yield the same result' and partially overlap.[52] Moreover, in some cases, proportion can be considered as evidence of reasonableness, while lack of proportion 'is a strong indicator of unreasonableness'.[53]

Reasonableness and proportionality at times overlap, despite their conceptual differences. Both proportionality and reasonableness require that the state measure under review pursue a legitimate objective. Both proportionality and reasonableness require that the state measure under review be suitable to contribute to, or achieve, its purported objective. If one were to accept the proposals – endorsed by a number of scholars – to avoid a review based on proportionality in the strict sense,[54] and use an abbreviated form of proportionality analysis, then reasonableness and proportionality would converge to such an extent as to be virtually indistinguishable. By depriving the proportionality analysis of its proportionality in the strict sense test, proportionality would become close, if

---

[50] F. Batlan, 'Law in the Time of Cholera: Disease, State Power, and Quarantines Past and Future' (2007) 80 *Temple LR* 53–122, 53 (examining two cases of threatened epidemics, and the excessive reaction of local authorities vis-à-vis foreigners).

[51] Sartor, Bongiovanni, and Valentini, 'Reasonableness in International Law', 9 (noting that while proportionality 'provid[es] an instantiation and enrichment of the idea of reasonableness, [it] fails to cover all aspects of reasonableness').

[52] P. Daly, *A Theory of Deference in Administrative Law – Basis, Application and Scope* (CUP 2012) 212; Wouters and Duquet, 'The Principle of Reasonableness in Global Administrative Law', 28.

[53] Id.

[54] P. Ranjan, 'Using the Public Law Concept of Proportionality to Balance Investment Protection with Regulation in International Investment Law: A Critical Appraisal' (2014) 3 CJICL 853–83, 862 (arguing that cost-benefit analysis should be excluded because investor–state arbitration lacks constitutional features); C. Henckels, *Proportionality and Deference in Investor–State Arbitration: Balancing Investment Protection and Regulatory Autonomy* (CUP 2015) 164–8.

not equivalent, to reasonableness.[55] And one may wonder why one should adopt the proportionality analysis to deprive it of one or two of its essential features that are the necessity and the proportionality in the strict sense test, when reasonableness analysis is ready for use, and in fact international courts such as the ICJ and arbitral tribunals have massively used it.

However, reasonableness and proportionality maintain notable differences. While proportionality adopts a more disciplined, structured and methodical test than reasonableness, reasonableness involves an element of free style. The reasonableness analysis does not necessarily entail the necessity and proportionality tests in the strict sense. The reasonableness review does not assess whether the action taken is optimal, or the most effective or efficient measure available; it does not question whether the adverse economic impact of a given measure on the foreign investment is disproportionate vis-à-vis its purported benefits. Rather, it assesses whether a given measure is logically, rationally related to its objectives and adequate to achieve them. It also assesses whether such measure does not unreasonably prejudice the legitimate interests of the foreign investors. Therefore, it avoids the most intrusive prongs of review of the proportionality test.

The difference between proportionality and reasonableness is not only in their procedure, but also in their substance. As well as remaining distinct in theory, they 'often produc[e] different outcomes when applied' in practice.[56] In fact, the adoption of one test or another does not seem to make the other criterion redundant; as mentioned, what can be perfectly proportionate may be unreasonable and what is reasonable may be disproportionate. Moreover, this assessment depends on circumstances.[57]

Proportionality and reasonableness can be complementary as adjudicators often consider reasonableness and proportionality together,

---

55 F. Ortino, 'Investment Treaties, Sustainable Development and Reasonableness Review: A Case Against Strict Proportionality Balancing' (2017) 30 *Leiden JIL* 71–91, 74 (arguing that 'when reviewing host state conduct on the basis of reasonableness-type standards, investment tribunals should avoid a review based on strict balancing or proportionality in the strict sense').

56 T. Hickman, 'Problems for Proportionality' (2010) NZLR 303–326, 315.

57 Y. Shany, 'Towards a General Margin of Appreciation Doctrine in International Law' (2005) EJIL 907–940, 923 (noting that 'the same conduct which was "reasonable" or "proportional" in one set of circumstances, might be deemed "unreasonable" or "disproportional" in different circumstances').

approaching the 'reasonable proportionality' or 'proportionate reasonableness' of given measures.[58] In fact, the two tests could coexist side by side, requiring that state action be both reasonable and proportionate.[59] While the ICJ has often used reasonableness on its own, it has also used reasonableness in conjunction with proportionality. For instance, the Court used the criterion of the 'reasonable degree of proportionality' for setting maritime boundaries.[60] Human rights courts and arbitral tribunals have used the same criterion in the adjudication of human rights and investment disputes respectively.[61] Analogously, the International Criminal Tribunal for the former Yugoslavia has also used reasonableness in conjunction with proportionality.[62]

However, there are arguments that, all things being equal, among competing hypotheses, the one with fewest assumptions should be selected; that simpler theories seem preferable to more complex ones – the so-called 'Ockham's razor'.[63] While the proportionality analysis seems to offer greater analytical clarity, its components – suitability, necessity and proportionality in the strict sense – are not necessarily clearer than reasonableness. Moreover, while the concept of necessity suggests that the least restrictive option is the only acceptable choice or that there are few other viable alternatives, the concept of reasonableness admits more than one answer to a question. While proportionality is a

---

[58] See e.g. *Tecmed v. Mexico*, ICSID Case No. ARB (AF)/00/2, Award, 29 May 2003, para. 122 (holding that '[t]here must be a reasonable relation of proportionality between the charge or weight imposed to the foreign investor and the aim sought to be realized by any expropriatory measure').

[59] Hickman, 'Problems for Proportionality', 306

[60] *North Sea Continental Shelf* (*Federal Republic of Germany v. Denmark; Federal Republic of Germany v. Netherlands*), Judgment, 20 February 1969 [Merits] [1969] ICJ Reports 3, para. 98.

[61] See for example, ECtHR, *Case of Hadjianastassiou v. Greece*, Judgment, 16 December 1992, Ser. A, No. 252, 16 December 1992, para. 47; *Chorherr v. Austria*, Judgment, 25 August 1993, para. 33; *Continental Causalty Co. v. Argentine Republic*, Award, para. 227.

[62] *Prosecutor v. Zoran Kupreskic*, Judgment, 14 January 2000, Case No.: IT-95-16-T, para. 524.

[63] B. Pirker, *Proportionality Analysis and Models of Judicial Review* (Europa Law Publishing 2013) 4 (reporting that 'Ockham famously suggested: *[F]rustra fit per plura quod potest fieri per pauciora*. It is futile to do with more things that which can be done with fewer').

demanding standard of review,[64] reasonableness accords states more latitude in the implementation of their international obligations.

The concept of reasonableness has roots in classical thought. Roman sources defined law as 'the highest reason, inherent in nature'[65] and considered reason (*ratio naturalis*) to underpin the law of nations (*ius gentium*),[66] which was considered to be 'the rational order *par excellence*'.[67] This vision of the law served to promote the diffusion of Roman law as an expression of natural law.[68] Roman law influenced a number of domestic legal systems and the early modern law of nations.

The concept of reasonableness is relatively common in both domestic and international legal systems. At the domestic level, the concept of reasonableness is present in common law jurisdictions, such as Australia, Canada, India, New Zealand, the United Kingdom and the United States.[69] It is also present in a number of mixed[70] and civil law jurisdictions, such as Belgium, the Netherlands and Italy,[71] as well as other legal systems.[72] Comparative surveys show that the concept of reasonableness is not a uniform standard. Rather, those jurisdictions applying reasonableness have done so with varied outcomes and different levels of deference.[73]

---

64 Henckels, *Proportionality and Deference in Investor–State Arbitration*, 28 (noting that '[p]roportionality analysis can be a very far-reaching method of review in terms of its intrusiveness into governmental policy-making because the method permits adjudicators to substitute their judgment with respect to each stage of review').

65 Cicero, *Laws*, Book I, 18–19.

66 Justinian, *Digest*, 1:1.1.9 ('*Quod vero naturalis ratio inter omnes homines constituit, id apud omnes peraeque custoditur vocaturque ius gentium*') ('The law that natural reason has established among all persons, that law is observed uniformly among all, and is called the law of nations').

67 Garrido-Muñoz, 'Managing Uncertainty', 6.

68 T. Poole, 'Proportionality in Perspective' (2010) NZLR 369–91, 385.

69 Wouters and Duquet, 'The Principle of Reasonableness in Global Administrative Law', 9.

70 F. Coomans, 'Reviewing Implementation of Social and Economic Rights: An Assessment of the"Reasonableness" Test as Developed by the South African Constitutional Court' (2005) 65 *Heidelberg JIL* 167–96.

71 Wouters and Duquet, 'The Principle of Reasonableness in Global Administrative Law', 10.

72 A.L. Epstein, 'The Reasonable Man Revisited: Some Problems in the Anthropology of Law' (1972–1973) 7 *Law & Society R.* 643–64.

73 Wouters and Duquet, 'The Principle of Reasonableness in Global Administrative Law', 17.

At present, reasonableness is 'ubiquitous in the domain of international law, in which it plays a fundamental role' for three different, albeit related reasons.[74] First, reasonableness is a positive public international law concept in many areas of the same, including international criminal law,[75] human rights law,[76] the law of the sea,[77] international environmental law,[78] international disability law,[79] EU law,[80] private international

---

[74] Sartor, Bongiovanni and Valentini, 'Reasonableness in International Law', 5.

[75] Rome Statute of the International Criminal Court, adopted 17 July 1998, in force 1 July 2002, 37 ILM 999 (1998), Article 66(3) (reasonable doubt).

[76] See e.g. International Covenant on Civil and Political Rights, 16 December 1966, in force 23 March 1976, 999 UNTS 171, Article 9 (reasonable time to exercise judicial power); Article 25 (prohibiting unreasonable restrictions to civil, social and political rights); European Convention for the Protection of Human Rights and Fundamental Freedoms, 4 November 1950, 213 UNTS 222, Article 6 (reasonable time) and Article 5 (reasonable suspicion).

[77] United Nations Convention on the Law of the Sea, adopted 10 December 1982, in force 16 November 1994, 21 ILM 1261 (1982), Articles 74, 83 and 246 ('reasonable time'); Articles 79 and 115 ('reasonable measures'); Articles 108, 110 and 206 ('reasonable grounds'); and Article 292 ('reasonable bond'). For commentary, see e.g. C. Brown, 'Reasonableness and the Law of the Sea: The Prompt Release of the Volga' (2003) 16 *Leiden JIL* 621–30; J. Gao, 'Reasonableness of the Bond Under Article 292 of the LOS Convention: Practice of the ITLOS' (2008) 7 *Chinese JIL* 115–42.

[78] Convention on the Protection and Use of Transboundary Watercourses and International Lakes, adopted 17 March 1992, in force 6 October 1996, 1936 UNTS 269, Article 2.2.c (on the principle of equitable and reasonable utilization of water resources). For commentary, see e.g. O. McIntyre, 'The Principle of Equitable and Reasonable Utilisation', in A. Tanzi, O. McIntyre, A. Kolliopoulos, A. Rieu-Clarke and R. Kinna (eds), *The UNECE Convention on the Protection and Use of Transboundary Watercourses and International Lakes* (Brill 2015) 146–59. See also the United Nations Convention on the Law of the Non-Navigational Uses of International Watercourses, adopted 21 May 1997, in force 17 August 2014, 36 ILM 700 (1997), Articles 5 and 6 (equitable and reasonable utilization).

[79] United Nations Convention on the Rights of Persons with Disabilities (CRPD), adopted 13 December 2006, in force 3 May 2008, 2515 UNTS 3, Article 2 (defining 'discrimination on the basis of disability' as, *inter alia*, 'denial of reasonable accommodation'); World Intellectual Property Organization, Marrakesh Treaty to Facilitate Access to Published Works for Persons Who Are Blind, Visually Impaired or Otherwise Print Disabled, 27 June 2013, in force 30 September 2016, Article 11.

[80] See G. Tesauro, 'Reasonableness in the European Court of Justice Case Law', in A Rosas, E. Levits and Y. Bots (eds), *The Court of Justice and the Construction of Europe* (Springer 2013) 307–327, 316 (noting that the ECJ has

law[81] and WTO law[82] to mention a few. Second, given its diffusion and the fact that 'international legal practice uses reasonableness as an implicit legal requirement' to ascertain the lawfulness of state action, it has been considered as a general principle of international law.[83] Third, international courts and tribunals often refer to reasonableness in a variety of contexts, ranging from procedural matters[84] to treaty interpretation[85] and compensation issues.[86] More interestingly, for our purposes, international courts and tribunals have used the concept of reasonableness

mainly absorbed reasonableness in its proportionality test even when the applicants refer to reasonableness); A. Adinolfi, 'The Principle of Reasonableness in European Union Law', in G. Bongiovanni, G. Sartor and C. Valentini (eds), *Reasonableness and Law* (Springer 2009) 381–404, 383 (noting that although explicit reference to reasonableness is uncommon in the jurisprudence of the CJEU, the concept is often implicit in legal reasoning); Wouters and Duquet, 'The Principle of Reasonableness in Global Administrative Law', 30 (noting that in the CJEU's jurisprudence, reasonableness can justify limitations of proportionality or specify how the proportionality test should be applied).

[81] A.F. Lowenfeld, *International Litigation and the Quest for Reasonableness – Essays in Private International Law* (OUP 1996).

[82] See e.g. Article X:3(a) of the General Agreement on Tariffs and Trade (GATT) (requiring member states to 'administer in a uniform, impartial and reasonable manner all [their] laws, regulations, decisions and rulings'); Article 21.3(c) of the Understanding on Rules and Procedures Governing the Settlement of Disputes ('reasonable period of time' to implement the dispute-settlement body's rulings). For commentary, see S. Peng, 'How Much Time is Reasonable – The Arbitral Decisions under Article 21.3(c) of the DSU' (2008) 26 *Berkeley JIL* 323–51.

[83] R. Domingo, *The New Global Law* (CUP 2010) (considering reasonableness as a general principle of international law); K. Nadavukaren Schefer, *International Investment Law* (Edward Elgar 2013) 273; C. Foster, 'A New Stratosphere? Investment Treaty Arbitration as "Internationalized Public Law"' (2015) 64 ICLQ 461–85, 470 (noting that reasonableness can be advanced as a general principle of law).

[84] ICJ, *Armed Activities in the Territory of the Congo (Democratic Republic of the Congo v. Uganda)*, Order of 29 November 2001 [2001] ICJ Reports 660, paras 48–9 (reasonableness of time limits).

[85] Vienna Convention on the Law of Treaties, adopted 23 May 1969, in force 27 January 1980, 1155 UNTS 331, 8 ILM 679, Article 32 (requiring interpreters to reject any 'result which is manifestly absurd or unreasonable').

[86] ICJ, *Reparations for Injuries Suffered in the Service of the United Nations*, Advisory Opinion, 11 April 1949 [1949] ICJ Reports 174, 181; *Republic of Guinea v. Democratic Republic of the Congo*, Compensation, Judgment, 19 June 2012 [2012] ICJ Reports 324, para. 24.

to review the exercise of state powers.[87] In this sense, reasonableness indicates a scrutiny aimed at assessing the rationality, congruence and logicality of state measures, thus limiting the amount of state discretion.[88] As an arbitral tribunal aptly put it, 'like the exercise of any authority, the exercise of regulatory authority is always subject to the rule of reasonableness'.[89]

4.2 THE MERITS OF REASONABLENESS

Reasonableness has become an increasingly common interpretive tool in investment treaty arbitration, being used in a variety of different contexts. A concept of variable geometry (*à géométrie variable*),[90] reasonableness allows the constant adaptation of law to changing circumstances.[91] It expresses the search for an internal equilibrium between the text and the aim of a given norm (*l'équilibre entre la lettre et l'esprit*).[92] It also bridges the divide between 'the essentially static character of legal texts and the dynamic character of the reality to which they apply'.[93] It gives 'a justifiable degree of discretion to judges, enabling them to make difficult adjudicatory choices without departing from the legal framework under consideration'.[94] In other words, reasonableness can constitute the link or *trait d'union* between the treaty-makers and the adjudicators. It also expresses the search for a fair balance between individual and public interests.

In the context of investment treaty arbitration, the concept of reasonableness can delimit and define the role of the three relevant actors: the host state and the investor, on the one hand, and the adjudicators, on the other. The concept of reasonableness has a tripartite structure. The first pillar of reasonableness requires states to adopt reasonable regulatory measures. The second pillar acknowledges the need to protect the

---

87 S. Jovanović, *Restriction de compétences discrétionnaires des Etats en droit international* (Pédone 1988).

88 See Craig, 'The Nature of Reasonableness Review', 131.

89 *Dispute Concerning Filleting within the Gulf of St Lawrence* (*Canada v. France*), Decision, 17 July 1986 (1986) 19 RIIA 225–96, para. 54.

90 N. MacCormick, 'On Reasonableness', in C. Perelman and R. Van der Elst (eds), *Les notions à contenu variable en droit* (Bruylant 1984) 131–56.

91 Corten, *L'utilisation du raisonnable par le juge international*, 150–51.

92 Ibid. 56.

93 O. Corten, 'The Notion of Reasonable in International Law: Legal Discourse, Reason and Contradictions' (1999) 48 ICLQ 613–25, 615.

94 Garrido-Muñoz, 'Managing Uncertainty', 3.

legitimate/reasonable expectations of the investor. The third pillar requires arbitrators to provide reasons for their awards.

First, reasonableness is based on 'a culture of justification', which requires that states 'provide substantive justification for all their actions'.[95] In order to be legitimate, a governmental action must be 'justified in terms of its … capacity for "persuasion", that is, in terms of its rationality and reasonableness'.[96] As the argument goes, it is an implied condition on the grant of every power that the power will be exercised reasonably.[97] Reasonableness requires that all of the relevant factors be considered and, then, that an equilibrium be struck according to their relative importance depending on the contextual circumstances.[98] In this field, 'reasonableness functions as a normative yardstick to control the exercise of discretionary powers by [s]tates' that may have an adverse impact on investment flows across states.[99] As Ortino points out, 'the concept of reasonableness may be used to protect … investors vis-à-vis unjust or irrational treatment afforded to them by the … host country through internal measures'.[100] While state regulatory autonomy is 'not in itself called into question[,] [t]he exercise of this power … must be accompanied by a justificatory discourse'.[101]

The issue consists precisely in identifying 'what regulatory action is to be considered reasonable and what is not'.[102] While there are many different notions of what is reasonable, the concept of reasonableness can take a concrete form by reference to international standards.[103] Arbitrators can evaluate the reasonableness of state action in the light of international treaties, customs and/or general principles of international

---

95 M. Cohen-Eliya and I. Porat, 'Proportionality and the Culture of Justification' (2011) 59 AJCL 463–90, 467.

96 Ibid. 475.

97 See e.g. *Minister v. Li* (2013) 297 *Australian Law Reports* 225.

98 R. Alexy, 'The Reasonableness of Law', in G. Bongiovanni, G. Sartor and C. Valentini (eds), *Reasonableness and Law* (Springer 2009) 3–15, 8.

99 F. Ortino, 'From "Non-discrimination" to "Reasonableness": A Paradigm Shift in International Economic Law?' (2005) *NYU Jean Monnet Working Paper* 01/05, 33.

100 Ibid.

101 Corten, 'The Notion of Reasonable in International Law', 624.

102 G. Verhoosel, 'Foreign Direct Investment and Legal Constraints on Domestic Environmental Policies: Striking a "Reasonable" Balance between Stability and Change' (1997–1998) 29 *Law & Policy in International Business* 451–78, 478.

103 Ibid. 460.

law.[104] If regulatory measures were in conformity with international practice, international treaties and/or specialized agency guidelines, they should be presumed to be reasonable. In this context, reasonableness can contribute to the consistency, unity and coherence of international law.[105]

Second, the reasonableness test can be used in the context of investment treaty arbitration to evaluate the legitimacy of investors' expectations. In this regard, reasonableness can constitute 'the essence of investors' legitimate expectations'.[106] This particular conception of reasonableness is rooted in most legal systems and in the field of comparative jurisprudence. It relates to the concept of the reasonable person, that is, the hypothetical person who exercises average care, skill and judgment in conduct and who serves as a comparative standard that a real person must live up to in order to avoid negligence.[107] The concept belongs to 'an intellectual tradition of defining a legal standard by reference to a hypothetical person, which stretches back to the creation by Roman jurists of the figure of the *bonus paterfamilias*'.[108]

The reasonable investor standard holds that each investor owes a duty to behave as a reasonable investor would under the same circumstances. Arbitral tribunals have found that 'the reasonableness or legitimacy of the investor's expectations had to be measured against the background of the situation prevailing in the host State'.[109] Accordingly, 'tribunals should consider whether the alleged expectation is that of a diligent or prudent investor, that is, an investor that has taken into account all circumstances surrounding the investment', including the political, social and economic

---

[104] M. Atienza, 'On Reasonableness in Law' (1990) 3 *Ratio Juris* 148–58, 158.

[105] Corten, *L'utilisation du raisonnable par le juge international*, 220.

[106] F. Mutis Tellez, 'Conditions and Criteria for the Protection of Legitimate Expectations under International Investment Law' (2012) 28 *ICSID Review*–FILJ 432–42, 432–5.

[107] This language is already part of positive international law. See e.g. the United Nation Convention on Contracts for the International Sale of Goods, adopted 11 April 1980, entered into force 1 January 1988, 1489 UNTS 3, Articles 8 and 25 (referring to 'the reasonable person'). Although sales are not investments, and therefore the Convention does not seem relevant to the investment context, it nonetheless shows the analytical merits of reasonableness and the application of such concept in a different area of international law.

[108] UK Supreme Court, *Healthcare at Home Ltd v. The Common Services Agency* [2014] UKSC 49 at [1]–[4] (Lord Reed).

[109] U. Kriebaum, 'The Relevance of Economic and Political Conditions for Protection under Investment Treaties' (2011) 10 *The Law and Practice of International Courts and Tribunals* 383–404, 403.

conditions of the host state.[110] An expectation will be objectively unreasonable if it conflicts with laws, policies or practices that were in place at the time of the investment, and which were, or ought to have been, known to the investor before making the investment.[111] Reasonable regulatory changes to further important policy objectives such as public health, environmental protection and others during the lifespan of the investment 'should not be seen as a violation of legitimate expectations'.[112] Not only is it unreasonable to expect that any form of regulation be frozen in time, but it is also unreasonable to expect that states do not align their regulation with international standards. As Kriebaum points out, '[o]nly in case of explicit assurances to the contrary, should there be legitimate expectations that no such changes would occur'.[113] To sum up, only legitimate and reasonable expectations of foreign investors would be protected;[114] and international investment treaties would not constitute a blanket protection against any business risk.

Third, reasonableness can constitute a limit to the subjectivity of the adjudicator. In fact, as adjudicators must provide reasons for their decisions, arbitrators must provide reasons for their awards. All awards must be supported by reasons.[115] Failure to state the reasons on which a given award is based is a ground for annulment of the award.[116] According to traditional canons of treaty interpretation, as restated in the Vienna Convention on the Law of Treaties (VCLT), interpretation must

---

110 Tellez, 'Conditions and Criteria', 3.

111 *Thunderbird Gaming Corporation v. The United Mexican States*, NAFTA/UNCITRAL, Award, 26 January 2006, paras 148, 164.

112 Kriebaum, 'The Relevance of Economic and Political Conditions', 403 (convincingly arguing that 'States should not be punished for striving to better implement environmental protection, the protection of cultural heritage or human rights norms').

113 Ibid.

114 *Thunderbird Gaming Corporation v. The United Mexican States*, Award, paras 147–8 (observing that 'the concept of "legitimate expectations" relates, within the context of the NAFTA framework, to a situation where a Contracting Party's conduct creates reasonable and justifiable expectations on the part of an investor (or investment) to act in reliance on said conduct, such that a failure by the NAFTA Party to honour those expectations could cause the investor (or investment) to suffer damages').

115 See generally P. Lalive, 'On the Reasoning of International Arbitral Awards' (2010) 1 JIDS 55–65, 55; T. Landau, 'Reasons for Reasons: The Tribunal's Duty in Investor–State Arbitration', in A.J. Van den Berg (ed.), *50 Years of the New York Convention* (Kluwer 2009) 187–205.

116 ICSID Convention, Article 52(1).

be reasonable.[117] In general terms, international adjudicators will have to reach a reasonable interpretation;[118] customary rules on treaty interpretation enable the adjudicators to recur to supplementary means of treaty interpretation when the ordinary ones 'lead to a result which is manifestly absurd or unreasonable'.[119] International courts and tribunals also rely on reasonableness as a general principle of law to avoid declaring *non liquet*, thus filling legal gaps and contributing to the perceived coherence of international law.[120] In conclusion, reasonableness belongs to the lexicon of treaty interpretation. It constitutes a sort of 'safety valve'; it aims to 'prevent consequences which are manifestly undesirable, and yet which would be likely to occur if a state used the standard, conventional methods of legal interpretation'.[121]

4.3 ARGUMENTS AGAINST REASONABLENESS

Three principal criticisms can (and have) be(en) raised against the reasonableness criterion: (1) vagueness; (2) complexity; and (3) ambivalence. This section briefly discusses each of these criticisms, offering some counterarguments.

---

[117] VCLT, Article 32. See also *ICJ Anglo-Iranian Oil Co Case* (*United Kingdom v. Iran*) (Jurisdiction), Judgment [1952] ICJ Reports 93, 104 (holding that 'the Court cannot base itself on a purely grammatical interpretation of the text. It must seek the interpretation which is in harmony with a natural and reasonable way of reading the text').

[118] See *ex multis*, *Impregilo SpA v. Argentine Republic*, ICSID Case No. ARB/07/17, Award, 21 June 2011, para. 86.

[119] VCLT, Article 32.

[120] Corten, 'The Notion of Reasonable in International Law', 617; C. Ryngaert, *Jurisdiction in International Law* (OUP 2008) (arguing that reasonableness should be considered to be a general principle of international law); Wouters and Duquet, 'The Principle of Reasonableness in Global Administrative Law', 3 (examining whether 'at the European and international level a principle of reasonableness is used as a standard against which (quasi-) judicial bodies scrutinize administrative acts' and arguing that 'the common understanding exists that reasonableness serves as an important guiding principle'). But see C. Focarelli, *International Law as Social Construct: The Global Struggle for Justice* (OUP 2012) 241–355 (arguing the reasonableness is not an independent source of international law).

[121] W. Sadurski, 'Reasonableness and Value Pluralism in Law and Politics', in G. Bongiovanni, G. Sartor and C. Valentini (eds), *Reasonableness and Law* (Springer 2009) 129–46, 130.

First, some scholars and adjudicators criticize reasonableness as a vague, indeterminate[122] and even self-contradictory[123] conceptual tool. Because of its intrinsic vagueness, it is impossible to apply reasonableness 'in a general way'.[124] Rather, reasonableness remains 'vulnerable to misunderstandings' and 'conflicting interpretations'.[125] Because of the indeterminacy of the concept of reasonableness, the distinction between the reasonable and the unreasonable is subjective, arbitrary and ultimately indefensible.[126] Without given parameters – critics contend – reasonableness leaves state authority (and adjudicators) unbound, as this criterion does not articulate a clear-cut methodology, nor does it provide a well-structured analytical framework.[127] Rather, it 'carries a tendency for circular reasoning'.[128]

The indeterminacy of reasonableness leads to two separate, albeit related, paradoxes. The first paradox of reasonableness lies in the fact that 'the notion of reasonable is both definable and undefinable, both within and outside the law'.[129] Reasonableness is 'generally perceived as opening the door to several ethical or moral, rather than legal, considerations', and 'even to conceptions of natural law'.[130] For some, reasonableness requires 'an assessment which goes beyond law'.[131] Rather than excluding value judgments, reasonableness 'formalizes them in legal

[122] *The Government of Sudan/The Sudan People's Liberation Movement Army (Abyei Arbitration)*, Award, 22 July 2009, Dissenting Opinion of Judge Al-Khasawneh, para. 182 (arguing that reasonableness 'is often a false friend that gives the impression of an objective threshold where none exists').

[123] *Whaling in the Antarctic (Australia v. Japan)*, Dissenting Opinion of Judge Bennouna, 342.

[124] *Whaling in the Antarctic (Australia v. Japan)* Judgment, 31 March 2014 [Merits] [2014] ICJ Reports 226, para. 39 (Judge Owada, Dissenting Opinion).

[125] S.P. Young, 'Preface', in S. Young (ed.), *Reasonableness in Liberal Political Philosophy* (Routledge 2009) vii.

[126] Henckels, *Proportionality and Deference in Investor–State Arbitration*, 123.

[127] A. Barak, *Proportionality: Constitutional Rights and their Limitations* (CUP 2012) 375.

[128] G. Nolte, 'Thin or Thick? The Principle of Proportionality in International Humanitarian Law' (2010) 4 LEHR 245–55, 247.

[129] Corten, 'The Notion of Reasonable in International Law', 614.

[130] Corten, 'Reasonableness in International Law', 1, 25.

[131] Corten, 'The Notion of Reasonable in International Law', 614 (reporting these criticisms).

terms'.[132] Therefore, scholars highlight the risk of 'judicial subjectivity',[133] and the fact that by adopting a 'discourse which – formally – appears to be value-neutral', reasonableness 'masks the ideological dimension of judgment'.[134] In other words, by invoking reasonableness, the arbitrators might not reveal to the public all of the components of their reasoning.[135]

The second 'paradox of reasonableness' – that is, the unreasonableness of reasonableness – allegedly lies in the fact that 'making reasonableness the final court of appeal with respect to public matters facilitates the emergence of unreasonableness (i.e. abusive behaviour)'.[136] The fluidity of reasonableness would prevent transparency, consistency and predictability.[137]

Yet, reasonableness 'may be necessary in complex cases in which … judges are called to balance competing values that are simply impossible to quantify'.[138] While international adjudicators must interpret and apply the applicable law, relying on customary norms of treaty interpretation as restated by Articles 31 and 32 of the VCLT, they have used the criterion of reasonableness to assess the implementation of a treaty. For instance, in the *Gabcikovo Nagymaros* case, a dispute arising out of the construction of a dam on the Danube, the ICJ stated that '[t]he principle of good faith obliges the parties to apply [a treaty] in a reasonable way and in such a manner that its purpose can be realized'.[139] Because treaties often reflect 'a carefully negotiated equilibrium between competing purposes',

---

132 Ibid. 625.

133 S.R. Tully, 'Objective Reasonableness as a Standard for International Judicial Review' (2015) 6 JIDS 546–67, 546.

134 Corten, 'The Notion of Reasonable in International Law', 625.

135 For an illustrative example see e.g. P. Mavroidis, N. Meagher, T.J. Prusa and T. Yanguas, 'Ask for the Moon, Settle for the Stars. What is a Reasonable Period to Comply with WTO Awards?' *EUI Working Paper* RSCAS 2016/45 (2016) 1–23, 1 (noting that, in calculating the reasonable period that defendants will have to comply with adverse rulings of a WTO panel or the Appellate Body, WTO arbitrators explicitly take into account the particular circumstances of the case; nonetheless, they also implicitly 'take the path of compromise, opting for a reasonable period of time that approximately lies half-way between the time proposed by the complaining Member(s) and that by the defending Member').

136 Young, 'Introduction', 4–5.

137 Nolte, 'Thin or Thick?' 247.

138 Garrido-Muñoz, 'Managing Uncertainty', 6.

139 *Case Concerning the Gabčíkovo/Nagymaros Project (Hungary v. Slovakia)* Judgment, 25 September 1997 [1997] ICJ Reports 7, para. 142.

international adjudicators often have to consider such purposes to assess whether a treaty has been 'implemented reasonably'.[140]

Second, the concept of reasonableness is of only apparent simplicity. As Professor Craig points out, 'insofar as incommensurability is a problem for proportionality, it also poses analogous difficulties for reasonableness review'.[141] The identification of the relevant comparators for assessing whether a given measure is reasonable can be problematic.[142] The fundamental dilemma is: Should reasonableness be measured against the expectations of the parties to the applicable international investment agreement, or the legitimate expectations of the investor, or the number of means available to a state to achieve its goals? If reasonableness had to be measured against the expectations of the parties to the international investment agreement, a careful interpretation of the applicable treaty and the *travaux préparatoires* would be essential. If reasonableness had to be measured against the legitimate expectations of the investor, a comparative survey of the available jurisprudence would be crucial. If reasonableness had to be measured against regulatory practices, the arbitral tribunals would need to rely on comparative surveys of regulatory approaches.[143]

While arbitral tribunals are required to interpret and apply the relevant treaty, comparative surveys of arbitral jurisprudence and of regulatory approaches may be more difficult to obtain. On the one hand, only a fraction of the existing jurisprudence is available to the public. There is no World Investment Court, and arbitral tribunals often interpret and apply different legal instruments. On the other hand, with regard to comparative surveys of regulatory approaches, any analogy must, in each case, take into account the culture of the systems of origin, the transposability of given concepts and the culture of the borrowing system.[144]

Yet, reasonableness enables international adjudicators to overcome the constraining proportionality tests. It goes beyond pure mathematical reasoning.[145] It does not 'enable mechanical adjudicatory choices in

---

[140] Garrido-Muñoz, 'Managing Uncertainty', 8.

[141] Craig, 'The Nature of Reasonableness Review', 132.

[142] V. Vadi, 'Critical Comparisons: The Role of Comparative Law in Investment Treaty Arbitration' (2010) 39 *Denver JIL & Policy* 67–100.

[143] On the need for comparative surveys of best regulatory practices, see P. Eeckhout, 'The Scales of Trade – Reflections on the Growth and Functions of the WTO Adjudicative Branch' (2010) 13 JIEL 3–26.

[144] M. Andenas and S. Zleptnig, 'Proportionality: WTO Law in Comparative Perspective' (2006–2007) 42 *Texas ILJ* 371–423, 382.

[145] Garrido-Muñoz, 'Managing Uncertainty', 18.

accordance with certain pre-established parameters'.[146] Rather, it enables a more nuanced assessment of the applicable law and the circumstances of each case. It permits adjudicators to move from the abstract (applicable law), to the particular (facts of the case).[147]

Third, the notion of reasonableness can be ambivalent. Adopting a restrictive or minimalist interpretation of reasonableness, such criterion consists of a procedural assessment concerning the deliberation process of a given measure. In this respect, reasonableness would promote transparency and accountability by requiring the relevant authorities to give reasons and explain the rationale and structure of given measures. Reasonableness and persuasion would be the two sides of the same coin.[148] Yet, one may wonder whether scrutiny based on argumentative patterns can be sufficient to detect indirect forms of discrimination, expropriation and similar measures. This approach renders the interpretation of the relevant standards of protection less effective, as it would detect only evident forms of misbehaviour by state authorities. Instead, by adopting an expansive or maximalist notion of reasonableness, such criterion would lead to a substantive assessment of the given measure. There is a risk that arbitral tribunals substitute their judgments for that of national parliaments.

However, the pervasiveness of reasonableness in the jurisprudence of the ICJ and arbitral tribunals shows that the flexible character of reasonableness well suits international adjudication. The adoption of reasonableness in international adjudication is a matter of evolution rather than revolution.[149] Moreover, as will be shown in Chapter 6, it is the combination of proportionality and/or reasonableness with the appropriate standards of review that makes the scrutiny of state conduct more or less intense.

4.4 REASONABLENESS IN INVESTMENT TREATY LAW AND ARBITRATION

Now that the meaning of reasonableness, as well as its promises and pitfalls, has been clarified, this section explores the use of reasonableness in investment treaty law and arbitration. Reasonableness appears in the

---

146 Ibid.
147 Ibid.
148 M. Atienza, *El derecho como argumentacion* (Ariel 2006) 203.
149 Garrido-Muñoz, 'Managing Uncertainty', 18.

text of investment treaties under different provisions. Several international investment agreements (IIAs) prohibit 'unreasonable or discriminatory measures', affecting foreign investors and/or their investments.[150] Other IIAs require state parties to grant 'equitable and reasonable treatment' to foreign investors and/or their investments,[151] or link reasonableness to full protection and security.[152] The Harvard Draft Convention on the International Responsibility of States for Injuries to Aliens provides that unlawful expropriation includes 'unreasonable interference with the use, enjoyment or disposal of property'.[153] The same Draft Convention also used the reasonableness criterion to distinguish the legitimate exercise of police powers from indirect expropriation.[154] Although the Draft Convention is not binding, it has influenced the drafting of subsequent IIAs and arbitral practice.

In parallel, arbitral tribunals have used the concept of reasonableness extensively. Such use in investor–state arbitration seems to confirm the triadic structure of reasonableness. On the one hand, arbitrators have used the reasonableness test to evaluate the legitimacy of state conduct and the legitimate expectations of foreign investors.[155] On the other hand, arbitral tribunals have also referred to the need of reasonable interpretation of the relevant investment treaty provisions. Finally, reasonableness also frequently appears with regard to procedural matters. For instance, in *Philip*

---

[150] See e.g. 1991 Netherlands–Czech Republic BIT, Article 3(1); Energy Charter Treaty, Article 10(1).

[151] See e.g. Norway–Lithuania BIT, Article III.

[152] Energy Charter Treaty, signed 17 December 1994, in force 16 April 1998 (1995) 34 ILM 360, 385, Article 10 (stating that 'such Investments shall also enjoy the most constant protection and security and no Contracting Party shall in any way impair by unreasonable or discriminatory measures their management, maintenance, use, enjoyment or disposal').

[153] Harvard Law School, Draft Convention on the International Responsibility of States for Injuries to Aliens, Article 10(3)(a), in L.B. Sohn and R.R. Baxter, 'Responsibility of States for Injuries to the Economic Interests of Aliens' (1961) 55 AJIL 548–84.

[154] Ibid. Article 10(5) (providing that '[a]n uncompensated taking of property … which results from the operation of tax laws; … from the action of competent authorities of the state in the maintenance of public order, health or morality … shall not be considered wrongful provided: [*inter alia*] it is not an unreasonable departure from the principles of justice recognised by the principal legal systems of the world').

[155] See e.g. *Saluka v. Czech Republic*, Award, 17 March 2006, para. 306 (holding that the fair and equitable treatment standard 'requires a weighting of the Claimant's legitimate and reasonable expectations on the one hand and the Respondent's legitimate regulatory interests on the other').

Morris v. Australia,[156] arising out of plain packaging legislation adopted by the respondent, the Tribunal extensively referred to the criterion of reasonableness to determine whether the arbitration claim amounted to an abuse of right. The claimant asserted that the purpose of, or motivation for, a corporate restructuring did not amount to bad faith even if a claimant could reasonably foresee a potential future dispute with the host state at the time of restructuring.[157] The Tribunal, however, concluded that 'the commencement of treaty-based investor–State arbitration constitutes an abuse of right (or abuse of process) when an investor has changed its corporate structure to gain the protection of an investment treaty at a point in time where a dispute was foreseeable. A dispute is foreseeable when there is a reasonable prospect that a measure that may give rise to a treaty claim will materialise'.[158] Because such corporate restructuring 'was carried out for the principal, if not sole, purpose of gaining Treaty protection', the Tribunal declared the claims raised in the arbitration inadmissible and did not exercise jurisdiction over the dispute.[159]

This section proceeds as follows. First, it highlights how arbitrators have used the reasonableness test to evaluate the legitimacy of state conduct and the legitimate expectations of foreign investors in the light of investment treaty standards such as fair and equitable treatment, non-discrimination, expropriation, and full protection and security. Second, it examines how reasonableness can contribute to the interpretation and application of exceptions. Third, it discusses the important role played by reasonableness in treaty interpretation. Because a number of arbitral awards are not public, this overview cannot be exhaustive. Moreover, additional cases may arise in the future. Nonetheless, this section aims to shed light on how arbitral tribunals have used the reasonableness criterion thus far, and highlights the analytical features of such use. The methodological choice is not to burden the reader with too many cases but rather to concentrate on key arbitrations that can exemplify the main trends described in the chapter.

---

156 *Philip Morris Asia Ltd v. The Commonwealth of Australia*, PCA Case No. 2012-12 Award on Jurisdiction and Admissibility, 17 December 2015.

157 Ibid. para. 444.

158 Ibid. para. 585.

159 Ibid. para. 588.

4.4.1 Fair and Equitable Treatment

A number of arbitral awards have referred to the concept of reasonableness in evaluating whether a given measure was in breach of the fair and equitable treatment standard.[160] In particular, some tribunals have equated 'reasonable' with 'fair' and have scrutinized the reasonableness of state measures in the light of the more common fair and equitable treatment standard. Other tribunals have maintained the distinction between reasonableness and fairness, and nonetheless used the former as a criterion to evaluate a state's conduct under the fair and equitable treatment standard. Tribunals assess the reasonableness of state conduct and determine whether a given measure reasonably relates to a legitimate policy.[161]

For instance, in *Marion Unglaube v. Costa Rica*,[162] a dispute arising out of an expropriation for the enlargement of a national park, the Arbitral Tribunal stated that 'to prove a breach of the [fair and equitable treatment] standard, a claimant must show more than mere legal error'.[163] Rather, the Tribunal criticized measures that are 'manifestly inconsistent, non-transparent [or] unreasonable (i.e., unrelated to some rational policy)'.[164] The Tribunal added that governments are required to use due diligence in the protection of foreigners and will not be excused from liability if their action has been arbitrary or discriminatory'[165]

In *Micula v. Romania*,[166] a dispute arising out of the government's introduction of a series of investment incentives for the development of certain disfavoured regions of Romania and from the subsequent partial withdrawal of those incentives, in the context of Romania's accession to the EU, the Tribunal addressed the question as to whether 'Romania acted reasonably'.[167] The Tribunal stated that 'the determination of

---

160 R. Kläger, *Fair and Equitable Treatment in International Investment Law* (CUP 2011) 241–45; K.J. Vandevelde, 'A Unified Theory of Fair and Equitable Treatment' (2010) 43 *NYU JIL and Politics* 43–106.

161 R. Kläger, 'Fair and Equitable Treatment: A Look at the Theoretical Underpinnings of Legitimacy and Fairness' (2010) 11 JWIT 435–42, 442.

162 *Marion Unglaube v. Republic of Costa Rica*, ICSID Case No. ARB/08/1, Award, 16 May 2012.

163 Ibid. para. 246.

164 Ibid.

165 Ibid. para. 247.

166 *Ioan Micula, Viorel Micula, SC European Food SA, SC Starmill Srl and SC Multipack Srl v. Romania*, ICSID Case No. ARB/05/20, Final Award, 11 December 2013.

167 Ibid. para. 755.

whether the state's conduct is reasonable requires the analysis of two elements: the existence of a rational policy; and the reasonableness of the act of the state in relation to the policy'.[168] According to the Tribunal, 'for a state's conduct to be reasonable, it is not sufficient that it be related to a rational policy; it is also necessary that, in the implementation of that policy, the state's acts have been appropriately tailored to the pursuit of that rational policy with due regard for the consequences imposed on investors'.[169] The Tribunal considered whether Romania reasonably tailored its decision to repeal the incentives to harmonize its laws with EU law.[170] It concluded that although Romania could have done more to protect the investor, its actions were not arbitrary and were 'justified under the specific circumstances of the accession negotiations'.[171]

In *Parkerings-Compagniet v. Lithuania*,[172] which concerned the planned construction of a parking area, the Tribunal analogized the notion of fairness, a component of the fair and equitable treatment standard, to reasonableness, holding that 'equitable and reasonable' has the same meaning as 'fair and equitable'.[173] The Tribunal stated that '[a]s a matter of fact, any businessman or investor knows that laws will evolve over time. What is prohibited however is for a State to act unfairly, unreasonably or inequitably in the exercise of its legislative power'.[174] Rather, the fair and equitable treatment standard requires that the host state's conduct 'bears a reasonable relationship to some rational policy'.[175]

---

[168] Ibid. para. 525 (internal citations omitted).

[169] Ibid.

[170] Ibid. para. 825.

[171] Ibid.

[172] *Parkerings-Compagniet AS v. Republic of Lithuania*, ICSID Case No. ARB/05/8, Award, 11 September 2007.

[173] Ibid. para. 278. Compare with *Micula v. Romania*, Final Award, para. 826 (declining to state that 'any conduct that is "reasonable" ... will be "fair and equitable"'. Instead, the Tribunal stated that 'the determination of what is fair and equitable cannot be made in the abstract: it requires the assessment of all the factual and legal circumstances surrounding both the state's conduct and an investor's investments. There are conceivably cases in which reasonable action by a state in pursuit of a rational policy may nonetheless be unfair with respect to certain investors').

[174] *Parkerings v. Lithuania*, Award, para. 332.

[175] Ibid. para. 460.

In *EnCana v. Ecuador*,[176] relating to certain VAT refunds to which the investor claimed it was entitled, the Tribunal noted that under the fair and equitable treatment standard, 'the State must act with reasonable consistency and without arbitrariness in its treatment of investments'.[177] In *Genin v. Estonia*,[178] a dispute arising out of the cancellation by the Central Bank of Estonia of a licence held by a financial institution in which the claimants were shareholders, the Tribunal considered the reasonableness of the state's decision to revoke the licence. It concluded that such revocation did not breach, *inter alia*, the fair and equitable treatment standard.[179] Instead, in *Saluka v. Czech Republic*, another case concerning the banking sector, the Tribunal concluded that the Czech Republic had violated the fair and equitable treatment standard 'by unreasonably frustrating [the bank]'s and its shareholders' good faith efforts to resolve the bank's crisis'.[180] The Tribunal also added that '[t]he [r]espondent ha[d] not offered a reasonable justification for its treatment of Saluka'.[181] In the same vein, in *Impregilo v. Argentine Republic*,[182] a dispute arising out of Argentina's alleged interference with the tariff regime applicable to the claimant's investment during the 2001–2002 economic crisis, the Tribunal also referred to the duty of the host state to adopt reasonable regulation. In particular, it held that 'the legitimate expectations of foreign investors cannot be that the State will never modify the legal framework, especially in times of crisis, but certainly investors must be protected from unreasonable modifications of that legal framework'.[183]

At the same time, tribunals have also acknowledged that investors' expectations must be reasonable.[184] Arbitral tribunals have referred to

---

[176] *EnCana Corp v. Republic of Ecuador*, Award, 3 February 2006, LCIA Case No. UN 3481, 45 ILM 901.

[177] Ibid. para. 158.

[178] *Alex Genin, Eastern Credit Ltd Inc and AS Baltoil v. The Republic of Estonia*, ICSID Case No. ARB/99/2, Award, 25 June 2001.

[179] Ibid. para. 347 (holding that the state conduct 'was not, in the circumstances, unreasonable according to accepted accounting practices').

[180] *Saluka v. Czech Republic*, Partial Award, para. 499.

[181] Ibid.

[182] *Impregilo SpA v. Argentine Republic*, ICSID Case No. ARB/07/17, Award, 21 June 2011.

[183] Ibid. para. 191.

[184] *Saluka Investments BV v. The Czech Republic*, Partial Award, UNCITRAL/PCA, 17 March 2006, para. 305 (stating that '[t]heir expectations, in order for them to be protected, must rise to the level of legitimacy and reasonableness in light of the circumstances').

'the diligence and reasonableness of the investor'.[185] In the context of the North American Free Trade Agreement (NAFTA), arbitral tribunals have elaborated the concept of legitimate expectations to include reasonable ones. For instance, in *Mobil Investments Canada Inc and Murphy Oil Corporation v. Canada*,[186] relating to two petroleum development projects off the Eastern coast of Canada, the Tribunal elaborated the notion of reasonable expectations as expectations engendered by representations by state organs. The Tribunal stated that '[i]n applying th[e] standard [of fair and equitable treatment] it is relevant that the treatment is in breach of representations made by the host State which were reasonably relied on by the claimant'.[187] Analogously, in *Thunderbird v. Mexico*,[188] concerning an investment in gaming activities, the Tribunal explained that legitimate expectations of the investor were protected under NAFTA Chapter 11. In particular, the Tribunal clarified that a breach of the fair and equitable treatment standard occurs 'where a Contracting Party's conduct creates reasonable and justifiable expectations on the part of an investor … to act in reliance on [the] said conduct', and the NAFTA party fails to honour those expectations, causing the investor to suffer damages.[189] In *Waste Management II v. Mexico*,[190] concerning an investment in an enterprise to provide waste management services to the City of Acapulco, the Arbitral Tribunal acknowledged that '[i]n applying [the fair and equitable treatment] standard it is relevant that the treatment is in breach of representations made by the host State which were reasonably relied on by the claimant'.[191] In *Chemtura v. Canada*,[192] a case concerning the ban of lindane, a pesticide used on canola, the Tribunal found that the review of lindane did not infringe the fair and equitable treatment

[185] See J. Viñuales, *Foreign Investment and the Environment in International Law* (CUP 2012) 375 (noting that 'an investor that has lacked diligence and/or reasonableness in doing its investment … should not be allowed to recover (at least not in full) for what is little more than an unsuccessful business venture').

[186] *Mobil Investments Canada Inc and Murphy Oil Corporation v. Canada*, NAFTA Chapter 11, ICSID Case No. ARB(AF)/07/4, Decision on Liability and on Principles of Quantum, 22 May 2012.

[187] Ibid. para. 141.

[188] *International Thunderbird Gaming Corporation v. The United Mexican States*, NAFTA/UNCITRAL, Award, 26 January 2006.

[189] Ibid. para. 147.

[190] *Waste Management Inc v. United Mexican States*, ICSID Case No. ARB(AF)/00/3, Award, 30 April 2004, paras 94 and 98.

[191] Ibid. para. 98.

[192] *Chemtura Corp (formerly Crompton Corp) v. Government of Canada*, Award, 2 August 2010.

standard. Rather, '[a]s a sophisticated registrant experienced in a highly regulated industry, the Claimant could not reasonably ignore' the practices of the federal agency responsible for the regulation of pest control products in Canada.[193]

Even outside NAFTA, arbitral tribunals have required expectations to be reasonable in order to be protected. For instance, in *Saluka v. Czech Republic*,[194] a case arising out of events immediately after the privatisation of the Czech banking sector, the Tribunal concluded that '[t]he determination of a breach of [the fair and equitable treatment] standard by the host state … requires a weighing of the Claimant's legitimate and reasonable expectations on the one hand, and the Respondent's legitimate regulatory interests on the other'.[195] The *Saluka* Tribunal added that:

> no investor may reasonably expect that the circumstances prevailing at the time the investment is made remain totally unchanged. In order to determine whether frustration of the foreign investor's expectations was justified and reasonable, the host State's legitimate right subsequently to regulate domestic matters in the public interest must be taken into consideration as well.[196]

As the Tribunal acknowledged, 'governments must be free to act in the broader public interest … Reasonable governmental regulation of this type cannot be achieved if any business that is adversely affected may seek compensation, and it is safe to say that customary international law recognizes this'.[197]

Other tribunals have similarly referred to legitimate and reasonable expectations. For instance, in *Parkerings v. Lithuania*,[198] concerning the construction of a parking area in the historical centre of Vilnius, the Tribunal stated that '[t]he investor will have a right of protection of its legitimate expectations provided it exercised due diligence and that its legitimate expectations were reasonable in light of the circumstances'.[199] Analogously, in *Spyridon Roussalis v. Romania*, concerning the privatization of a former state enterprise, the Tribunal held that '[t]he case law … confirms that to comply with the FET standard, the State must respect

---

[193] Ibid. para. 149.

[194] *Saluka Investments BV v. The Czech Republic*, Partial Award, UNCITRAL/PCA, 17 March 2006.

[195] Ibid. paras 304–306.

[196] Ibid. para. 305.

[197] Ibid. para. 103.

[198] *Parkerings-Compagniet AS v. Republic of Lithuania*, ICSID Case No. ARB/05/8, Award, 11 September 2007.

[199] Ibid. para. 333.

the investor's reasonable and legitimate expectations'.[200] The Tribunal concluded that 'Romania's conduct was reasonable and adequate and did not breach the fair and equitable treatment requirement'.[201]

In *EDF Services v. Romania*, concerning an investment in duty-free business within airports, the Tribunal further clarified the extent of legitimate and reasonable expectations. In particular, the Tribunal held that: 'except where specific promises or representations are made by the State to the investor, the latter may not rely on a bilateral investment treaty as a kind of insurance policy against the risk of any changes in the host State's [l]egal and economic framework. Such expec[t]ation would be neither legitimate nor reasonable'.[202] Analogously, in *Micula v. Romania*, the case concerning the change of subsidies after Romania's accession to the EU, the Tribunal addressed the question as to whether the investors' expectation that the given subsidies would last at least ten years was reasonable.[203] The Tribunal stated that '[w]hen the alleged legitimate expectation is one of regulatory stability, the reasonableness of the expectation must take into account the underlying presumption that, absent an assurance to the contrary, a state cannot be expected to freeze its laws and regulations'.[204] In light of the circumstances of the case, the Tribunal concluded that 'it was reasonable for the Claimants to believe that the incentives were legal under Romanian law'.[205] Therefore, the majority of the Tribunal found a breach of legitimate expectations.[206] In order to provide a complete ruling on Romania's compliance with its obligation to provide fair and equitable treatment, it then examined the reasonableness of state conduct,[207] and concluded that the state behaved reasonably.

In *El Paso Energy v. Argentina*,[208] a case arising out of a series of measures adopted by Argentina during an economic crisis (including restrictions on transfers, and pesification of US dollar deposits) that allegedly affected the energy company's investments, the Tribunal held

---

200 *Spyridon Roussalis v. Romania*, ICSID Case No. ARB/03/9, Award, 5 September 2008, para. 316.

201 Ibid. para. 337.

202 *EDF Services Ltd v. Romania*, ICSID Case No. ARB/05/13, Award, 8 October 2009, para. 217.

203 *Micula v. Romania*, Award, para. 557.

204 Ibid. para. 673.

205 Ibid. para. 717.

206 Ibid. para. 726.

207 Ibid.

208 *El Paso Energy International Co v. Argentina*, ICSID Case No. ARB/03/15, Award, 31 October 2011.

that 'the basic touchstone of fair and equitable treatment is to be found in the legitimate and reasonable expectations of the parties, which derive from the obligation of good faith'.[209] On the one hand, the investor has reasonable expectations 'that the State should not unreasonably modify the legal framework'.[210] On the other hand, '[t]he State has to be able to make the reasonable changes called for by the circumstances and cannot be considered to have accepted a freeze on the evolution of its legal system'.[211] In fact, 'a reasonable evolution of the host state's law is part of the environment with which investors must contend'.[212] In other words, the Tribunal held that 'a balance should be established between the legitimate expectation of the foreign investor to make a fair return on its investment and the right of the host State to regulate its economy in the public interest'.[213] The Tribunal added that 'if the circumstances change completely, any reasonable investor should expect that the law also would drastically change'.[214] The Tribunal added that '[t]here can be no legitimate expectation for anyone that the legal framework will remain unchanged in the face of an extremely severe economic crisis. No reasonable investor can have such an expectation unless very specific commitments have been made towards it, or unless the alteration of the legal framework is total'.[215] The Tribunal concluded that because of 'their cumulative effect, th[e] state measures amount[ed] to a breach of the fair and equitable treatment standard'.[216]

To ascertain the reasonableness of state measures, arbitral tribunals have considered local circumstances. In *Enron v. Argentine Republic*,[217] a dispute arising out of certain tax assessments allegedly imposed by Argentinean provinces in respect to a gas transportation company, the Arbitral Tribunal took local conditions into account. In particular, it noted that '[t]he economic balance of the license was clearly affected by the crisis situation, and just as it is not reasonable for the licensees to bear the entire burden of such changed reality, neither would it be reasonable for them to believe that nothing happened in Argentina since the [l]icense

209 Ibid. paras 339 and 348.
210 Ibid. para. 363.
211 Ibid. para. 371.
212 Ibid. fn 329.
213 Ibid. para. 358.
214 Ibid. para. 363.
215 Ibid. para. 374.
216 Ibid. para. 519.
217 *Enron Corporation and Ponderosa Assets LP v. Argentine Republic*, ICSID Case No. ARB/01/3, Award, 22 May 2007.

was approved'.[218] In *Total SA v. Argentine Republic*,[219] relating to several investments in different areas including the power generation industry, the Tribunal noted that 'an evaluation of fairness must take into account the evolution of the host economy, the reasonableness of the normative changes challenged, and their appropriateness in the light of a standard of reasonableness and proportionality'.[220] In *Renée Rose Levy de Levi v. Peru*,[221] concerning claims in relation to Peru's handling of a bank crisis, the Tribunal deemed that Peru's treatment of the bank was reasonable under the circumstances of the crisis.[222]

To evaluate the reasonableness of state measures, arbitral tribunals have also used comparative analysis and/or reference to international treaties. For instance, in *Pope & Talbot Inc. v. Canada*, concerning an investment in the softwood lumber trade, the Tribunal deemed that Canada's measures constituted a 'reasonable response' in the implementation of an international agreement and did not amount to a breach of fair and equitable treatment.[223] In *ADF Group v. United States*,[224] the Tribunal found that a domestic content regulation for steel used in highway construction did not breach the fair and equitable treatment standard. The fact that the statute had been modified over time by Congress was not 'grossly unfair or unreasonable' because other countries also included similar domestic content requirements.[225]

Finally, arbitral tribunals have used the concept of reasonableness to identify cases of denial of justice. The customary norm prohibiting denial of justice has been folded into modern investment treaty protection, especially the fair and equitable treatment standard. Denial of justice does not occur if state courts have made a mere error of law. Investment treaty tribunals are not an appeal mechanism for the decisions of domestic courts. Rather, denial of justice implies the failure of a national legal system as a whole to satisfy international minimum standards of treatment. Denial of justice is difficult to prove and such claims have

---

218 Ibid. para. 232.

219 *Total SA v. Argentine Republic*, ICSID Case No. ARB/04/1, Decision on Liability, 27 December 2010.

220 Ibid. para. 309.

221 *Renée Rose Levy de Levi v. The Republic of Peru*, ICSID Case No. ARB/10/17, Award, 26 February 2014.

222 Ibid. para. 338.

223 *Pope & Talbot Inc v. Canada*, NAFTA Chapter 11, Award on the Merits of Phase II, 10 April 2001, paras 123, 125 and 128.

224 *ADF Grp v. United States*, ICSID Case No. ARB(AF)/00/1, Award, 9 January 2003, (2004) 6 ICSID Reports 470.

225 Ibid. paras 188–9.

rarely been successful. Certainly, denial of justice encompasses notions of egregious irrationality, manifest unreasonableness and 'unreasonable delay in administering justice.'[226] Much more uncertain is its applicability to jurisprudential developments and/or misapplication of domestic law.

For instance, in *Eli Lilly and Co v. Canada*,[227] arising in the pharmaceutical sector, the US position seemed to be that, in the words of the Tribunal, 'as long as it is possible to say that a court acted on a reasoned and rational basis, no question of liability could arise, … under either NAFTA Article 1105 or Article 1110'.[228] The Tribunal did not reach a decision on this specific point, exercising judicial economy. However, it noted in passing that '[a]s a matter of principle … , having regard to the content of the customary international law minimum standard of treatment, [it was] unwilling to shut the door to the possibility that judicial conduct characterized other than as a denial of justice may engage a respondent's obligations under NAFTA Article 1105'.[229] The Tribunal concluded that Canadian law 'did in fact undergo a reasonable measure of change and development', and found that the claimant 'ha[d] not met its burden of proving a violation of its legitimate expectations'.[230]

4.4.2 Non-discrimination

The principle of non-discrimination is infringed when identical or reasonably similar factual situations are treated differently. In order to detect whether a state action has been discriminatory, arbitral tribunals first consider the issue of whether two circumstances are analogous; if they are, arbitrators will assume that their similarity requires the same treatment. Therefore, any state conduct that treats similar situations differently is considered to be *prima facie* discriminatory. However, such measures can be legitimate provided there are reasonable grounds to differentiate the treatment of investments.[231] Certain IIAs expressly link

---

[226] Z. Douglas, 'International Responsibility for Domestic Adjudication: Denial of Justice Reconstructed' (2014) ICLQ 1–34, 15.

[227] *Eli Lilly and Co v Canada*, ICSID Case No. UNCT/14/2, Award, 16 March 2017.

[228] Ibid. para. 218.

[229] Ibid. para. 223.

[230] Ibid. paras 384–5.

[231] See e.g. ICJ, *Judgment No. 2867 of the Administrative Tribunal of the International Labour Organization Upon a Complaint Filed Against the International Fund for Agricultural Development*, Advisory Opinion, 1 February

the requirements of reasonableness and non-discrimination,[232] prohibiting the adoption of 'unreasonable or discriminatory measures' that affect foreign investors and their investments.[233] The widely used expression 'unreasonable or discriminatory' requires that guarantees should be provided against unreasonable conduct that may not be discriminatory at the same time.[234] Yet, as mentioned, reasonableness has been conceived as an articulation of (or partially coinciding with) the principle of non-discrimination.[235]

In *Renée Rose Levy de Levi v. Peru*, concerning claims by a French national in relation to Peru's handling of a bank crisis, the Tribunal considered that the investor's bank was not comparable to other national banks.[236] Therefore, given that the banks were not in competition, the

---

2012, [2012] ICJ Reports 27, para. 39 (holding that 'if procedural rights are accorded, they must be provided to all the parties unless distinctions can be justified on objective and reasonable grounds'); *Certain Aspects of the Laws on the Use of Languages in Education in Belgium*, Judgment, 23 July 1968, ECtHR, Series A No. 6, p. 31 ('following the principles which may be extracted from the legal practice of a large number of democratic States, [the Court] holds that the principle of equality of treatment is violated if the distinction has no objective and reasonable justification'); *Observer and Guardian v. United Kingdom*, Judgment, 26 November 1991, ECtHR, Series A No. 216, para. 73 (defining discrimination as 'different treatment, without an objective and reasonable justification, of persons in similar situations'); *Karlheinz Schmidt v. Germany*, Judgment, 18 July 1994, ECtHR, Series A No. 291-B, para. 24 (holding that 'a difference of treatment is discriminatory if it has no objective and reasonable justification').

232 See e.g. Energy Charter Treaty (ECT), Article 10 ('no Contracting Party shall in any way impair by unreasonable or discriminatory measures their management, maintenance, use, enjoyment or disposal'); Georgia – Israel BIT, Article 2 ('Neither Contracting Party shall in any way impair by unreasonable or discriminatory measures the management, maintenance, use, enjoyment or disposal of investments in its territory of investors of the other Contracting Party').

233 See e.g. Agreement between the Government of the United Kingdom of Great Britain and Northern Ireland and the Government of Argentina on the promotion and protection of investments, signed 11 December 1990, Article 2.2; Agreement on Encouragement and Reciprocal Protection of Investments Between the Kingdom of The Netherlands and the Czech and Slovak Federal Republic, signed on 29 April 1991, Article 3.1.

234 Verhoosel, 'Foreign Direct Investment and Legal Constraints on Domestic Environmental Policies', 477.

235 See generally Ortino, 'From "Non-discrimination" to "Reasonableness"'.

236 *Renée Rose Levy de Levi v. The Republic of Peru*, Award, para. 396 (stating that 'as the banking sector is a sensitive area for any country, there are marked differences between the various banks operating in it. For example, there

Tribunal held that their diverse regulation did not amount to discrimination. The Tribunal did not check 'the reasonableness of the State's measure', because it found that there was no discrimination in the first place.[237] In *Parkerings v. Lithuania*, concerning the construction of a parking area in the historical centre of Vilnius, the Tribunal stated that 'to violate international law, discrimination must be unreasonable or lacking proportionality[;] for instance, it must be inapposite or excessive to achieve an otherwise legitimate objective of the State'.[238] In *Ely Lilly v. Canada*, a case concerning the regulation of pharmaceuticals, the Tribunal found no discrimination on various grounds. It also added: 'Even if the Tribunal were to accept Claimant's position … that a measure is discriminatory [*inter alia*] where there is … "any differential treatment of a foreign investor … based on unreasonable distinctions and demands" … Claimant would not succeed in its allegation of discrimination'.[239]

As mentioned, reasonableness can legitimize distinctions between investors. As an Arbitral Tribunal put it, '[o]nce unequal treatment has been proved, the State has to show the existence of reasonable grounds for such treatment; otherwise, it would be a discriminatory measure violating the national treatment standard'.[240] In *Feldman Karpa v. Mexico*, concerning an investment in the tobacco sector, the Tribunal held that '[i]n the investment context, the concept of discrimination has been defined to imply unreasonable distinctions between foreign and domestic investors in like circumstances'.[241] *In casu*, the Tribunal found that there were 'at least some rational bases for treating producers and re-sellers differently', including the protection of intellectual property and the prevention of smuggling. Therefore, it did not consider the distinction between producer and reseller as a discrimination prohibited under international law.[242] In *Saluka v. Czech Republic*, a case concerning the banking sector, the Tribunal held that 'any differential treatment of a foreign investor must not be based on unreasonable distinctions and demands, and must be justified by showing that it bears a reasonable

---

are banks primarily engaged in asset management and investment, others in corporate and consumer banking').

237 Ibid. para. 215.

238 *Parkerings v. Lithuania*, Award, para. 368.

239 *Eli Lilly and Co v. Canada*, ICSID Case No. UNCT/14/2, Award, 16 March 2017, para. 439.

240 *Renée Rose Levy de Levi v. The Republic of Peru*, Award, para. 215.

241 *Marvin Roy Feldman Karpa v. United Mexican States*, ICSID Case No. ARB(AF)/99/1, Award, para. 170.

242 Ibid.

relationship to rational policies not motivated by a preference for other investments over the foreign-owned investment'.[243]

In *El Paso v. Argentina*,[244] a case arising out of a series of measures adopted by Argentina during an economic crisis, the Arbitral Tribunal noted that 'the banking and hydrocarbon sectors were not subject to the same measures', but thought that such distinction was reasonable.[245] For the Tribunal, it was:

> reasonable for the Government to institute a tax on the unexpected profits made by the oil and gas companies to re-balance the situation of the banking sector. Far from being discriminatory, this measure aimed at equalising the playground of the different economic actors, by distributing more equitably the burden of the country's economic crisis among all those affected.[246]

In fact, the Arbitral Tribunal stressed that 'it was common knowledge that at the time of the Argentine crisis the international price of oil increased tremendously, which was all to the benefit of the exporting companies'.[247] In conclusion, the Tribunal 'found no discrimination between the different sectors of the economy, although they were indeed treated differently, as there was no capricious, irrational or absurd differentiation in the treatment accorded to the Claimant as compared to other entities or sectors'.[248]

4.4.3 Expropriation

Arbitral tribunals have also used reasonableness in relation to expropriation claims. They have examined the reasonableness, duration and due process of state measures, as well as their impact on the foreign investors to ascertain the lawfulness of expropriatory measures[249] or distinguish the legitimate exercise of police powers from indirect expropriation.[250]

---

243 *Saluka v. Czech Republic*, Partial Award, para. 307.

244 *El Paso Energy International Co v. Argentina*, ICSID Case No. ARB/03/15, Award, 31 October 2011.

245 Ibid. para. 310.

246 Ibid. para. 314.

247 Ibid.

248 Ibid. para. 315.

249 *Tecnicas Medioambientales Tecmed SA v. United Mexican States*, ICSID Case No. ARB(AF)/00/2, Award, 29 May 2003, para. 122.

250 Iran–United States Claims Tribunal, *Harza Engineering v. Islamic Republic of Iran*, 1 Iran–US Cl. Trib. Rep. 499, 505 (1982) (finding that new banking

Finally, in other cases, they have used the criterion of reasonableness to evaluate the amount of compensation.[251]

In *Kardassopoulos & Fuchs v. Georgia*,[252] a dispute arising out of the cancellation of the concession rights of a company, in which the claimants held interests, devoted to the development of an oil pipeline from Azerbaijan to the Black Sea, the Tribunal considered that:

> due process in the context of expropriation demands an actual and substantive legal procedure for a foreign investor to raise its claims against the depriving actions already taken, or about to be taken against it. … In general, the legal procedure must be of a nature to grant an affected investor a reasonable chance within a reasonable timeframe to claim its legitimate rights and have its claims heard.[253]

Reasonableness can help in distinguishing the legitimate exercise of police powers from indirect expropriation.[254] As early as 1903, in the *Bischoff* case[255] – a dispute based on the taking of a carriage belonging to the claimant at Caracas during an epidemic of smallpox – the German Venezuelan Commission held that 'during an epidemic of an infectious disease there can be no liability for the reasonable exercise of police powers'.[256]

A century later, arbitral tribunals have reached analogous conclusions. In *Philip Morris v. Uruguay*,[257] the dispute arose in relation to a regulation requiring health warnings to comprise 80 per cent of cigarette packaging, and corporations to adopt one single variant of their brand. The Tribunal noted that: '[t]he principle that the State's reasonable bona fide exercise of police powers in such matters as the maintenance of

---

regulations imposing signature authentication requirements were not 'unreasonable or even inconsistent with normal Iranian banking practice').

[251] *Saur International SA v. République Argentine*, ICSID Case No. ARB/04/4, Award, 22 May 2014, para. 395.

[252] *Kardassopoulos & Fuchs v. Georgia*, ICSID Case No. ARB 05/18 and 07/15, Award, 3 March 2010.

[253] Ibid. para. 395.

[254] A. Newcombe and L. Paradell, *Law and Practice of Investment Treaties* (Kluwer Law International 2009) 358 (considering that 'a state does not incur responsibility for the legitimate and bona fide exercise of sovereign police powers' subject, *inter alia*, to an analysis of reasonableness).

[255] *Bischoff* case, RIIA X (1903) 420–21.

[256] Ibid. 420.

[257] *Philip Morris Brands Sàrl, Philip Morris Products SA and Abal Hermanos SA v. Oriental Republic of Uruguay*, ICSID Case No. ARB/10/7, Award, 8 July 2016.

public order, health or morality, excludes compensation even when it causes economic damage to an investor and that the measures taken for that purpose should not be considered as expropriatory did not find immediate recognition in investment treaty decisions'.[258] However, the Tribunal added that 'a consistent trend in favor of differentiating the exercise of police powers from indirect expropriation emerged after 2000'.[259] The Tribunal then used the Framework Convention on Tobacco Control[260] as 'a point of reference on the basis of which to determine the reasonableness of the two measures'.[261] The Tribunal did not investigate whether plain packaging 'actually had the effects that were intended by the State'. Rather, it assessed 'whether it was a "reasonable" measure when it was adopted'.[262] The Tribunal concluded that plain packaging was 'a reasonable measure', adopted 'in good faith' 'to address a real public health concern'.[263]

In *EDF (Services) v. Romania*,[264] concerning the provision of duty-free services at Romanian airports, in evaluating a measure falling within the police power of the state, the Tribunal held that 'in addition to a legitimate aim in the public interest there must be a *reasonable* relationship of proportionality between the means employed and the aim sought to be realized'.[265]

In *El Paso Energy v. Argentina*,[266] a case arising out of a series of measures adopted by Argentina during an economic crisis, the Tribunal held that '[a]s a matter of principle, general regulations do not amount to indirect expropriation. By exception, unreasonable general regulations can amount to indirect expropriation'.[267] The Tribunal added that 'if general regulations are unreasonable, i.e., arbitrary, discriminatory, disproportionate or otherwise unfair, they can … be considered as amounting to indirect expropriation if they result in a neutralisation of the

---

258 Ibid. para. 295.

259 Ibid.

260 Framework Convention on Tobacco Control, adopted 21 May 2003, in force 27 February 2005, 42 ILM 518 (2003).

261 *Philip Morris v. Uruguay*, Award, para. 401.

262 Ibid. para. 409.

263 Ibid. paras 409–410.

264 *EDF Services Ltd v. Romania*, ICSID Case No. ARB/05/13, Award, 8 October 2009.

265 Ibid. para. 293 (emphasis added).

266 *El Paso Energy International Co v. Argentina*, ICSID Case No. ARB/03/15, Award, 31 October 2011.

267 Ibid. para. 233.

foreign investor's property rights'.[268] With regard to the measures adopted by Argentina, the Tribunal considered that 'the creation of export duties on oil and gas [was] a reasonable governmental regulation within the context of the crisis'.[269] It then noted that 'a tax of such a percentage [under 20 per cent] is by no means an unreasonable measure that could be deemed expropriatory: under no circumstances may a tax of under 20% on exports be characterised as expropriation of an investment'.[270] The Tribunal concluded that the different tax measures did not amount to indirect expropriation, 'as they were reasonable and did not result in the neutralisation of the property rights of the Claimant'.[271]

Finally, in *Feldman Karpa v. Mexico*, concerning an investment in the tobacco sector, the Tribunal held that:

> governments must be free to act in the broader public interest through protection of the environment, new or modified tax regimes, the granting or withdrawal of government subsidies, reductions or increases in tariff levels, imposition of zoning restrictions and the like. Reasonable governmental regulation of this type cannot be achieved if any business that is adversely affected may seek compensation, and it is safe to say that customary international law recognizes this.[272]

On the other hand, 'unreasonable interference with an alien's property' determines state responsibility.[273] As the *Feldman Karpa* Tribunal acknowledged, the 'imposition of unreasonable regulatory regimes' can be considered to be 'an expropriatory action'.[274] Analogously, in *Azurix v. Argentina*, which involved a water concession contract, Argentina had enacted measures for the protection of public health after an algae outbreak contaminated the water supply after privatization. Warnings not to drink the water were enacted, and customers were dissuaded from paying their water bills.[275] In order to ascertain whether there was a (compensable) expropriation or a (non-compensable) legitimate exercise of police powers, the Tribunal relied on *Tecmed*, and its analysis of the

---

268 Ibid. para. 241 (also stressing 'the need for reasonableness and proportionality of State measures interfering with private property').

269 Ibid. para. 297.

270 Ibid. para. 298.

271 Ibid. para. 299.

272 Ibid. para. 103.

273 *Marvin Roy Feldman Karpa v. United Mexican States*, Award, para. 106.

274 Ibid.

275 *Azurix v. Argentine Republic*, ICSID Case No. ARB/01/12, Award, 14 July 2006, para. 283.

ECtHR jurisprudence, stating that an expropriatory measure must pursue a 'legitimate aim in the public interest' and the means employed must be (reasonably) proportional to the stated objective.[276] The Tribunal dismissed the claim of expropriation.

Moreover, as Viñuales aptly points out, because the police powers doctrine constitutes an autonomous concept, rather than an exception, 'procedurally, this means that the state does not have the burden of proving ... the reasonableness of its regulatory action'.[277] Rather, a presumption of reasonableness operates, 'unless the claimant can show unreasonableness by pointing inter alia to the lack of public purpose, discrimination, arbitrariness, [and lack of] due process'.

4.4.4 Full Protection and Security

Arbitral tribunals have linked the concept of reasonableness to full protection and security. The standard 'full protection and security' concerns the duty of states to protect foreign investments from damage caused either by state organs or by the actions of others.[278] It establishes a 'due diligence obligation to take measures that prevent the investment from being harmed'.[279] The standard has traditionally referred to the prevention of physical harm to investors and their investments. However, recent interpretive trends have expanded the scope of the full protection and security standard to include the notion of 'legal security'. This expansion may be due to the wording of some treaties, but such interpretation is questionable as it may unnecessarily duplicate the fair and equitable treatment standard.[280]

In *Houben v. Burundi*, a dispute concerning the development of a residential project in Burundi and the occupation of half of the relevant land by squatters, the Tribunal held that 'States should use due diligence (*diligence raisonnable*) to prevent unjustified damage to the person or property of aliens in their territory and, if they cannot prevent such

---

276 Ibid. para. 311.

277 J.E. Viñuales, 'Sovereignty in Foreign Investment Law', in Z. Douglas, J. Pauwelyn and J.E. Viñuales (eds), *The Foundations of International Investment Law* (OUP 2014) 317–62, 344.

278 C. McLachlan, L. Shore and M. Weiniger, *International Investment Arbitration* (OUP 2007) 247.

279 G. Cordero Moss, 'Full Protection and Security', in A. Reinish (ed.), *Standards of Investment Protection* (OUP 2009) 131–50, 150.

280 Ibid.

damage, they should exercise at least due diligence (*diligence raisonnable*) in punishing the perpetrators of such damage'.[281] The Tribunal further explained that 'the obligation to exercise due diligence (*diligence raisonnable*) does not mean that the State has a duty to prevent any damage … On the contrary, the obligation is generally understood as requiring the State to take reasonable measures when it is, or should be, aware of a risk of harm'.[282] Relying on *APPL v. Sri Lanka*, the Tribunal endorsed the former Tribunal's holding that due diligence requires the adoption of 'reasonable measures of prevention', which a well-administered government could be expected to adopt under similar circumstances.[283] The precise degree of what is reasonable, the Tribunal added, depends in part on the circumstances and the capacities of the state.[284] Analogously, in *AAPL v. Sri Lanka*,[285] the Tribunal held that the full protection and security standard in the UK–Sri-Lanka BIT imposed an obligation of due diligence, requiring the adoption of 'all possible measures that could be reasonably expected to prevent the eventual occurrence of killings and property destructions'.[286]

In *El Paso Energy v. Argentina*,[287] a case arising out of a series of measures adopted by Argentina during an economic crisis, the Tribunal held that 'due diligence does not mean that the State has to prevent each and every injury. Rather, the obligation is generally understood as requiring that the state take reasonable actions within its power to avoid injury when it is, or should be, aware that there is a risk of injury. The

---

[281] *Joseph Houben v. Republic of Burundi*, ICSID Case No. ARB/13/7, Award, 12 January 2016, para. 161 (author's translation of the Tribunal's ruling: '*les États doivent utiliser une "diligence raisonnable" pour prévenir les dommages injustifiés à la personne ou aux biens des étrangers sur leur territoire et, s'ils n'y ont pas réussi, exercer au moins une "diligence raisonnable" pour punir les auteurs de tels dommages*').

[282] Ibid. (author's translation of the Tribunal's ruling: '*L'obligation d'exercer une "diligence raisonnable" ne signifie ainsi pas que l'État a le devoir d'empêcher tout dommage … Au contraire, l'obligation est généralement comprise comme exigeant que l'Etat prenne des mesures raisonnables en son pouvoir lorsqu'il est, ou devrait être, au courant d'un risque de dommage*').

[283] Ibid. para. 162 (referring to *Asian Agricultural Products Ltd (AAPL) v. Republic of Sri Lanka*, ICSID Case No. ARB/87/3, Award, 27 June 1990, para. 77).

[284] Ibid. para. 163.

[285] *Asian Agricultural Products Ltd v. Republic of Sri Lanka*, ICSID Case No. ARB/87/3, Award, 27 June 1990.

[286] Ibid. para. 85(b).

[287] *El Paso Energy International Co v. Argentina*, ICSID Case No. ARB/03/15, Award, 31 October 2011.

precise degree of care, of what is "reasonable" or "due", depends in part on the circumstances'.[288]

In *Spyridon Roussalis v. Romania*, concerning the privatization of a former state enterprise, the Tribunal considered that '[the] Respondent's conduct did not infringe the principles of legal certainty and proportionality in violation of the full protection and safety clause contained in Article 2(2) of the BIT'.[289] The claimant argued that 'instead of freezing only the cash equivalent to the claimed tax amount, Romania chose, through its fiscal authorities, to sequester all [the claimant's] assets, ... and bank accounts ... This decision impaired Claimant's right to dispose of its investment and was taken in breach of the principles of due process, proportionality and reasonableness'.[290] However, the Tribunal held that the 'Claimant has not proved that this sequestration was discriminatory, disproportionate or otherwise improper under Romanian law'.[291] In *Emanuel Too v. Greater Modesto*, the Iran–United States Claims Tribunal held that '[o]rdinarily, the standard of police protection for foreign nationals is unreasonable if it is less than what is provided generally for the state's nationals'.[292]

4.4.5 Reasonable Measures

Some IIAs include the prohibition of unreasonable measures. Such provision requires the host state to treat investors 'in accordance with the rule of law'.[293] Usually this prohibition is linked to some other standard of treatment such as non-discrimination or the fair and equitable treatment standard.[294] However, the prohibition of unreasonable measures remains conceptually distinct from other standards, and it is worth examining how arbitral tribunals have interpreted this standard.

In *AES Summit Generation Ltd and AES-Tisza Erömü Kft v. Republic of Hungary*,[295] relating to the imposition of caps on the price charged for

---

[288] Ibid. para. 523.

[289] *Spyridon Roussalis v. Romania*, ICSID Case No. ARB/06/1, Award, 7 December 2011, para. 358.

[290] Ibid. para. 394.

[291] Ibid. para. 515.

[292] *Emanuel Too v. Greater Modesto Insurance Associates and the United States of America*, Iran–US Claims Tribunal, Award, 29 December 1989, 23 Iran–US CTR 378, para. 22.

[293] Nadavukaren Schefer, *International Investment Law*, 281.

[294] See e.g. UK–Argentina BIT, Article 2.2.

[295] *AES Summit Generation Ltd and AES-Tisza Erömü Kft v. Republic of Hungary*, ICSID Case No. ARB/07/22, Award, 23 September 2010.

energy generated by AES in Hungary, the Tribunal ascertained the compliance of Hungary with the Energy Charter Treaty.[296] In so doing, the Tribunal considered 'the question of whether Hungary was, may have been, or may have felt obliged under EC law to act as it did ... when determining the "rationality", "reasonableness", "arbitrariness" and "transparency" of the [state measure]'.[297] The majority of the Tribunal concluded that 'Hungary's reintroduction of administrative pricing ... was motivated principally by widespread concerns relating to ... excessive profits earned by generators and the burden on consumers'.[298] The Tribunal found that reducing luxury profits was 'a perfectly valid and rational policy objective for a government'.[299]

The Tribunal then examined whether there was 'a reasonable correlation between the state's policy objective and the measure adopted to achieve it'.[300] It noted that the Hungarian government had in vain attempted to renegotiate the prices with the generators and that 'in the absence of a specific commitment to the Claimants that administrative pricing was never going to be reintroduced, the Hungarian parliament voted for the reintroduction of administrative pricing'.[301] After finding that the state measures were 'reasonable, proportionate and consistent with the public policy expressed by the parliament',[302] the Tribunal dismissed all of AES's claims on their merits.

In *El Paso Energy International Co v. Argentina*,[303] a case arising out of a series of measures adopted by Argentina during an economic crisis, the Tribunal had to ascertain whether the measures adopted by the state violated the prohibition of arbitrary measures under the US–Argentina BIT.[304] The Tribunal defined 'arbitrary' as 'wilful and unreasonable action without consideration or in disregard of facts or law'.[305] The Tribunal held that 'the measures adopted in the context of the crisis were

---

296 Energy Charter Treaty, opened for signature 17 December 1994, in force 16 April 1998, 34 ILM 360.

297 *AES Summit Generation Ltd and AES-Tisza Erömü Kft v. Republic of Hungary*, Award, para. 7.6.9.

298 Ibid. para. 10.3.31.

299 Ibid. para. 10.3.34.

300 Ibid. para. 10.3.35.

301 Ibid.

302 Ibid. para. 10.3.36.

303 *El Paso Energy International Co v. Argentina*, ICSID Case No. ARB/03/15, Award, 31 October 2011.

304 See US–Argentina BIT, Article 2.2.b (prohibiting 'arbitrary or discriminatory measures').

305 *El Paso Energy International Co v. Argentina*, Award, para. 319.

not arbitrary but reasonable and consistent with the aim pursued. They were intended to face the extremely serious crisis that Argentina was going through and emanated from the police power regularly exercised by governments'.[306]

Instead, in *BG Group plc v. Argentina*,[307] a case also arising out of a series of measures adopted by Argentina during the same economic crisis, the Tribunal 'd[id] not deem it appropriate to equate unreasonableness and arbitrariness'.[308] Rather, it considered that reasonableness should be 'measured against the expectations of the parties to the bilateral investment treaty'.[309] While the Tribunal did not question the reasonableness of the state measures 'as a matter of political economy', it found that the state 'unilaterally withdrew commitments which [had] induced BG to make its investment in Argentina, and this constitutes unreasonable action and a breach of this provision of the Treaty'.[310]

4.4.6 Exceptions

In other cases, arbitral tribunals used the reasonableness criterion to define the ambit of application of given exceptions. For instance, in *Continental Casualty v. Argentine Republic*,[311] concerning an insurance business, the Tribunal applied the concepts of reasonableness and proportionality to the determination of the scope of an exception provided by the treaty, considering that:

> the Government's efforts struck an appropriate balance between that aim and the responsibility of any government towards the country's population: it is self-evident that not every sacrifice can properly be imposed on a country's people in order to safeguard a certain policy that would ensure full respect towards international obligations in the financial sphere, before a breach of those obligations can be considered justified as being necessary under this BIT. The standards of reasonableness and proportionality do not require as much.[312]

---

306 Ibid. para. 323.

307 *BG Group plc v. The Republic of Argentina*, UNCITRAL, Final Award, 24 December 2007.

308 Ibid. para. 341.

309 Ibid. para. 342.

310 Ibid. para. 343.

311 *Continental Casualty Co v. Argentine Republic*, ICSID Case No. ARB/03/9, Award, 5 September 2008.

312 Ibid. para. 227.

While this case is often cited in relation to its adoption of the proportionality analysis,[313] it is worth highlighting the fact that it used the proportionality test in conjunction with reasonableness.

4.4.7 Compensation

Arbitral tribunals have harnessed the concept of reasonableness to set the amount of compensation to be paid in given investment disputes. For instance, in *Houben v. Burundi*,[314] a dispute concerning the development of a residential project in Burundi and the occupation by squatters of half of the relevant land, the Tribunal identified the market value of a given plot by determining the price that a hypothetical reasonable buyer would have expected to pay to acquire the land.[315] The Tribunal also explained that arbitral tribunals have wide discretion in determining the interest rate, provided that 'the interest rate chosen is reasonable in relation to the circumstances of the case and permits full compensation for the harm suffered by the investor'.[316]

Other arbitral tribunals take into account the factual background of the case to assess the reasonableness of the valuation analysis, after having identified the market value of a given investment and the relevant interest rate. For instance, in *Occidental v. Ecuador*,[317] the Arbitral Tribunal found that 'as a result of their material and significant wrongful act, the Claimants have contributed to the extent of 25% to the prejudice which they suffered'. Therefore, it held that it was 'fair and reasonable' to reduce the responsibility of the respondent to 75 per cent.[318]

In *Lemire v. Ukraine*,[319] a case concerning radio broadcasting, the Tribunal 'made an evaluation of the loss suffered' and then asked whether the determined amount was 'a fair reflection of the actual loss, reasonably proportional to the investment'.[320] The Tribunal held that 'it is … important that the overall result [of the valuation analysis] be tested

313 See section 3.6.4 above.

314 *Joseph Houben v. Republic of Burundi*, ICSID Case No. ARB/13/7, Award, 12 January 2016.

315 Ibid. para. 243.

316 Ibid. paras 256–7 (translation of the author).

317 *Occidental Petroleum Corporation and Occidental Exploration and Production Co v. Republic of Ecuador*, ICSID Case No. ARB/06/11, Award, 5 October 2012.

318 Ibid. para. 687.

319 *Joseph Charles Lemire v. Ukraine*, ICSID Case No. ARB/06/18, Award, 18 March 2011.

320 Ibid. para. 304.

against other parameters, in order to confirm the reasonability of the calculation'.[321] It then specified such parameters elaborating several tests of reasonableness including, *inter alia*: (1) 'comparing the compensation to be awarded with the amount invested by Claimant';[322] (2) 'the risk environment';[323] and (3) the 'personal commitment' of the investor.[324] Other tribunals have also stressed the need to take the circumstances of the case into account in assessing the reasonableness of compensation.[325]

4.4.8 Costs

Arbitral tribunals have harnessed the concept of reasonableness to allocate the costs of the proceedings and expenses, as well as to verify the rationality of such expenses incurred by the parties. Article 61 of the ICSID Convention 'does not set forth any presumption concerning allocation of costs among the parties',[326] thus permitting ICSID tribunals to allocate costs in the manner that some arbitral tribunals consider 'fair and reasonable'.[327] Instead, Article 40 of the UNCITRAL Rules endorses the loser pays principle.[328] However, the same provision acknowledges that the 'arbitral tribunal may apportion each of [the] costs [of the proceedings] between the parties if it determines that apportionment is reasonable, taking into account the circumstances of the case'.[329] With respect to the costs of legal representation, the arbitral tribunal can 'determine which party shall bear such costs or may apportion such costs between the parties if it determines that apportionment is reasonable'.[330]

In the apportionment of costs and expenses investment arbitral tribunals, like other international courts and tribunals, have traditionally

---

[321] Ibid. para. 298.

[322] Ibid. para. 299.

[323] Ibid. para. 303.

[324] Ibid. para. 306.

[325] *American Manufacturing & Trading Inc v. Republic v. Zaire*, ICSID Case No. ARB/93/1, Award, 21 February 1997, para. 7.14 (rejecting the method of valuation proposed by the investor and holding that 'it would be neither practical nor reasonable to apply the method of assessment of compensation in a way so far removed from the striking realities of the current situation').

[326] *PNG Sustainable Development Program Ltd v. Independent State of Papua New Guinea*, ICSID Case No. ARB/13/33, Award, 5 May 2015, para. 402.

[327] *Noble Ventures Inc v. Romania*, ICSID Case No. ARB/01/11, Award, 12 October 2005, para. 236.

[328] UNCITRAL Rules, Article 40.1.

[329] Ibid.

[330] UNCITRAL Rules, Article 40.2.

followed 'the practice ... to split the costs evenly, whether the claimant or the respondent prevails'.[331] For instance, in *KT Asia Investment Group BV v. Republic of Kazakhstan*,[332] arising out of the government's alleged forced nationalization of claimant's interest in a bank, 'the Tribunal f[ound] it appropriate that each Party bear one half of the ICSID costs and bear its own legal and other costs'.[333] The Tribunal considered that '[s]uch approach seem[ed] fair and reasonable considering [*inter alia*] that while the Respondent prevailed on jurisdiction, the issues involved were complex and the Claimant's case was certainly not brought lightly'.[334] Splitting the costs evenly is even more 'reasonable' when each party has prevailed on certain aspects of its arguments.[335]

In *PNG v. Papua New Guinea*,[336] a case arising out of an alleged investment in a copper and gold mine, the Tribunal decided that it did not have jurisdiction.[337] It then considered that its decision on costs allocation should generally be guided, *inter alia*, by the reasonableness of the arguments of the parties[338] and 'the reasonableness of the parties' legal costs'.[339] After noting that 'the Claimant advanced serious and reasonable arguments in support of jurisdiction',[340] the Tribunal ultimately applied the 'costs lie where they fall' principle, and found that 'there [was] no need to assess the reasonableness of the costs'.[341]

Analogously, in *Corona Materials LLC v. Dominican Republic*,[342] concerning the denial of the environmental approval of a mining concession, the Arbitral Tribunal rejected the claims on jurisdictional grounds. The Tribunal then considered whether to 'award to the prevailing disputing party reasonable costs and attorney's fees' as permitted

---

331 *EDF (Services) Ltd v. Romania*, ICSID Case No. ARB/05/13, Award, 8 October 2009, para. 322.

332 *KT Asia Investment Group BV v. Republic of Kazakhstan*, ICSID Case No. ARB/09/8, Award, 17 October 2001.

333 Ibid. para. 228.

334 Ibid.

335 *Houben v. Burundi*, Award, para. 259.

336 *PNG Sustainable Development Program Ltd v. Independent State of Papua New Guinea*, ICSID Case No. ARB/13/33, Award, 5 May 2015.

337 Ibid. para. 417.a.

338 Ibid. para. 409 (noting that 'both Parties have submitted reasonable applications and carefully articulated the grounds for those applications').

339 Ibid. para. 406.

340 Ibid. para. 412.

341 Ibid. para. 416.

342 *Corona Materials LLC v. Dominican Republic*, ICSID Case No. ARB(AF)/14/3, Award, 31 May 2016.

under the applicable treaty, but ultimately decided that the claimant's claim was not frivolous and that 'counsel for both Parties worked professionally and efficiently in pursuing their clients' interests'.[343] Therefore, it held that 'Each Party [should] ... bear its own legal fees and expenses'.[344]

However, other arbitral tribunals have applied the loser pays principle, requiring 'that the successful party should have its reasonable costs paid by the unsuccessful party, in accordance with the general position in other forms of transnational commercial arbitration'.[345] For instance, in *Ansung Housing v. People's Republic of China*,[346] a dispute relating to a Korean company's investment in a condominium development project in China, the Arbitral Tribunal rejected the claimant's claims and held that the respondent should be awarded, *inter alia*, its 'reasonable costs'.[347] As the Tribunal determined that 'Ansung's claim manifestly lack[ed] legal merit as time-barred' and held that 'the claim should not have been brought', it concluded that 'China should not bear the reasonable costs for successfully defending the claim'.[348] On the one hand, the Tribunal noted that the 'Claimant's limitations arguments were not reasonable'.[349] On the other, it addressed the question of the reasonableness of the amount of costs claimed by the respondent, and after concluding that such costs were disproportionate, it apportioned only 75 per cent of respondent's costs to claimant.[350] China's request of post-award interest, 'at a commercially reasonable rate to be set by the Tribunal' was granted.[351]

---

343 Ibid. paras 272–9.

344 Ibid. para. 279.

345 *Gemplus SA SLP SA and Gemplus Industrial SA de CV v. United Mexican States*, ICSID Case No. ARB(AF)/04/3 & ARB(AF)/04/4, Award, 16 June 2010, Part XVII, paras 17–22; *Generation Ukraine Inc v. Ukraine*, ICSID Case No. ARB/00/9, Award, 16 September 2003, para. 24.1 (referring to 'the general rule that an unsuccessful litigant in international arbitration should bear the reasonable costs of its opponent').

346 *Ansung Housing Co Ltd v. People's Republic of China*, ICSID Case No. ARB/14/25, Award, 9 March 2017.

347 Ibid. para. 159.

348 Ibid.

349 Ibid. para. 162.

350 Ibid. para. 163.

351 Ibid. para. 164.

Analogously, in *Transglobal Green Energy v. Republic of Panama*,[352] arising out of the government's cancellation of a hydro-electric power plant concession, the Tribunal held that 'in a case of abuse of process ... Claimants should bear the costs of the proceeding and attorneys' fees and expenses of Respondent, provided that the latter are reasonable'.[353] It then assessed 'the proportionality of fees and expenses claimed on both sides'.[354] Other tribunals applied the loser pays principle, and after finding that the parties' expenses were reasonable, they held that the loser should bear the costs of the arbitration.[355]

4.4.9 Interpretation

Arbitral tribunals have held that the interpretation of investment treaties must be reasonable, relying on customary rules of treaty interpretation as restated by Articles 31–33 of the VCLT.[356] Article 31 of the VCLT requires, *inter alia*, that '[a] treaty shall be interpreted in good faith'.[357] Under Article 32 of the VCLT, 'the Tribunal may have recourse to supplementary means of interpretation (i) in order to confirm the meaning resulting from the application of Article 31 of the VCLT, or (ii) when the interpretation according to Article 31 of the VCLT either leaves the meaning ambiguous or obscure, or leads to a result which is manifestly absurd or unreasonable'.[358] Article 33 of the VCLT concerns the interpretation of treaties authenticated in two or more languages.

For instance, in *Amco Asia Corporation and others v. Republic of Indonesia*, a case arising out of an investment in an hotel complex, the Tribunal noted that 'any convention, including conventions to arbitrate,

352 *Transglobal Green Energy LLC and Transglobal Green Panama SA v. Republic of Panama*, ICSID Case No. ARB/13/28, Award, 2 June 2016.

353 Ibid. para. 126.

354 Ibid. para. 126.

355 *Eli Lilly and Co v. Canada*, ICSID Case No. UNCT/14/2, Award, 16 March 2017, paras 455.d and 457; *Phoenix Action Ltd v. Czech Republic*, ICSID Case No. ARB/06/5, Award, 15 April 2009, para. 152.

356 *Menzies Middle East and Africa SA and Aviation Handling Services International Ltd v. Republic of Senegal*, ICSID Case No. ARB/15/21, Award, 5 August 2016, para. 156.

357 VCLT, Article 31.

358 VCLT, Article 32.

should be construed in good faith'.[359] For the Tribunal, such interpretation requires 'taking into account the consequences of their commitments the parties may be considered as having reasonably and legitimately envisaged'.[360] In *Poštová Banka and Istrokapital v. Hellenic Republic*,[361] a dispute arising out of the retroactive and unilateral amendment of sovereign bond terms by the Greek government in the context of its 2012 sovereign debt restructuring, the Tribunal held that 'an interpretation in good faith' does not merely indicate 'the absence of *mala fides*', or 'the rejection of an interpretation that is abusive or that may result in the abuse of rights'.[362] Rather, for the Tribunal, 'an interpretation in good faith' also 'requires elements of reasonableness that go beyond the mere verbal or purely literal analysis'.[363]

Analogously, with regard to the interpretation of domestic legislation, in *PNG v. Papua New Guinea*, a case concerning the claimant's alleged investment in an open pit copper and gold mine, the Tribunal held that '[t]he starting point of interpretation of [domestic] investment legislation is the ordinary or grammatical meaning of the words used in the relevant statutory provisions, objectively construed, as they would be understood by a reasonable investor or other addressee'.[364] With regard to the interpretation of national jurisprudence, a recent Arbitral Tribunal noted that 'reasonable minds may differ in the interpretation of the cases'.[365]

ICSID annulment committees have stated their reluctance to substitute their own views for those of the original tribunal's, if the views of the latter were 'tenable' or 'reasonable'.[366] They have restated that the

---

[359] *Amco Asia Corp and others v. Republic of Indonesia*, ICSID Case No. ARB/81/1, Decision on Jurisdiction, 25 September 1983, 23 ILM 351 (1984) 359.

[360] Ibid.

[361] *Poštová Banka AS and Istrokapital v. Hellenic Republic*, ICSID Case No. ARB/13/8, Award, 9 April 2015.

[362] Ibid. para. 284.

[363] Ibid.

[364] *PNG Sustainable Development Program Ltd v. Independent State of Papua New Guinea*, ICSID Case No. ARB/13/33, Award, 5 May 2015, para. 275.

[365] *Eli Lilly and Co v. Canada*, ICSID Case No. UNCT/14/2, Award, 16 March 2017, para. 333.

[366] *Caratube International Oil Co LLP v. Republic of Kazakhstan*, Decision on the Annulment, Application of Caratube International Oil Company LLP, ICSID Case No. ARB/08/12, 21 February 2014, para. 144 (affirming that '[u]nder normal circumstances errors of law do not permit annulment: applicant must prove a gross or egregious error of law, which can be perceived by any reasonable person. If the tribunal's legal interpretation is reasonable or tenable,

interpretation must be 'reasonable'.[367] As one Committee put it, 'the grounds for annulment set out in Article 52 [of the ICSID Convention] must be examined in a neutral and reasonable manner, that is, neither narrowly nor extensively'.[368] Annulment Committees have also stressed that 'the reasoning presented in the award should be coherent and not contradictory, so as to be understandable by the [p]arties and must reasonably support the solution adopted by the tribunal'.[369] They have held that 'implicit reasons may be read into the award provided they can be reasonably inferred by a reader'.[370]

In *Caratube v. Kazakhstan*,[371] in which the investor applied for the annulment of an arbitral award dismissing jurisdiction, the Annulment Committee held that the mere:

> misinterpretation or misapplication of the proper law, even if serious, does not justify annulment. That being said, in exceptional circumstances, a gross or egregious error of law, acknowledged as such by any reasonable person, could be construed to amount to a failure to apply the proper law, and could give rise to the possibility of annulment. But the threshold for applying this exceptional rule must be set very high – otherwise the annulment mechanism permitted by the Convention would expand into a prohibited appeal system.[372]

Annulment committees have also clarified that 'genuinely contradictory reasons' capable of leading to the annulment of a given award 'must be such as to be incapable of standing together on any reasonable reading of the decision'.[373]

---

even if the committee might have taken a different view on a debatable point of law, the award must stand – otherwise the annulment procedure would expand into an appeal mechanism, in contravention of the clear wording of the Convention').

[367] Ibid. para. 233.

[368] *Poštová Banka AS and Istrokapital SE v. Hellenic Republic*, ICSID Case No. ARB/13/8, Decision on Partial Annulment, 29 September 2016, para. 129.

[369] *Hussein Nuaman Soufraki v. The United Arab Emirates*, ICSID Case No. ARB/02/7, Decision of the ad hoc Committee on the Application for Annulment of Mr. Soufraki, 5 June 2007, para. 23 (referring to Article 52(1)(e) of the ICSID Convention).

[370] *Poštová Banka and Istrokapital v. Hellenic Republic*, Decision on Partial Annulment, para. 141.

[371] *Caratube International Oil Co LLP v. Republic of Kazakhstan*, Decision on the Annulment, para. 81.

[372] Ibid.

[373] *Continental Casualty v. Argentina*, ICSID Case No. ARB/03/9, Decision on the Application for Partial Annulment of Continental Casualty Company and

4.5 CRITICAL ASSESSMENT

The concept of reasonableness has been understudied by international law scholars in general, and investment law scholars in particular, certainly in comparison to the burgeoning literature on proportionality analysis.[374] Yet, the various features of reasonableness make it an interesting topic for examination and a useful tool for international investment governance and the adjudication of investment disputes.

Reasonableness is a deliberative methodology that constrains policy makers to adopt reasonable policies, and a flexible interpretive tool that enables adjudicators to interpret and apply the law to the concrete circumstances of cases. It can also help identify the legitimate expectations of foreign investors. Reasonableness addresses the tension between the 'static nature of a legal system', on the one hand, and the dynamic 'need to integrate facts, and sometimes values, within that system', on the other.[375] It also allows international adjudicators to overcome the utopian vision that 'one, and only one legal solution applies to any particular case'.[376] It enables pluralist approaches, making it possible to identify the points of convergence between the abstract norm of international law and the concrete local circumstances.[377] It can provide an analytical and practical alternative to, or, in some instances complement, the proportionality analysis.[378] By enabling pluralist approaches, reasonableness is better suited than proportionality to acknowledge the cultural diversity characterizing the international community, while contributing to its unity.

The notion of reasonableness has been used extensively in international law. Originally a public law concept, reasonableness is also part and parcel of public international law. Often states include the term 'reasonable' in their treaties to introduce a degree of flexibility. Not only does

---

the Application for Partial Annulment of the Argentine Republic, 16 September 2011, para. 103.

[374] But see Corten, *L'utilisation du raisonnable par le juge international*; and Vadi, 'Proportionality, Reasonableness and Standards of Review in Investment Treaty Arbitration'.

[375] Corten, 'Reasonableness in International Law'.

[376] Ibid.

[377] G. Bongiovanni, G. Sartor and C. Valentini, 'Introduction', in G. Bongiovanni, G. Sartor and C. Valentini (eds), *Reasonableness and Law* (Springer 2009) xi–xiii, xiii.

[378] J. Waldron, 'Some Models of Dialogues between Judges and Legislators' (2004) 23 *Supreme Court LR* 7–37.

reasonableness appear in many of international law's primary rules across a wide range of subject areas, but international courts and tribunals, including the ICJ, have applied reasonableness extensively.[379]

Reasonableness has also become part and parcel of international investment law and arbitration. It appears in both IIAs and arbitral awards. It bridges the gap between treaty law and state practice, helping tribunals to clarify vague treaty provisions, provide reasoned awards, and review state action. Arbitral tribunals almost constantly refer to reasonableness in interpreting and applying the various investment treaty provisions. It is true that jurisprudential patterns must be taken with a grain of salt (*cum grano salis*) because a number of arbitral awards remain unpublished and there is no binding precedent in international law. However, consistent patterns of jurisprudence show that, far from being a purely theoretical tool, reasonableness has acquired practical relevance, helping arbitrators to reach sensible practical outcomes. Therefore, the claim that there is no better alternative to proportionality is overstated,[380] at least with regard to international adjudication in general, and investor–state arbitration in particular.

Through the close analysis of arbitral jurisprudence, this chapter highlighted that arbitral tribunals have applied the concept of reasonableness in a relatively consistent manner. The question of this concept's role and status across the different fields of international law remains open. While there is an abstract understanding and practical application of the notion of reasonableness across the different domains of international law, the question as to whether it has evolved into a self-standing legal notion remains open. While eminent scholars have pointed out that the requirement for states to behave reasonably may not have achieved customary law status yet, others have stressed that reasonableness may be a general principle of international law. Irrespective of its legal status, this chapter has shown that reasonableness certainly plays an important role in international investment law and arbitration. Not only do distinct treaty provisions require that state conduct be reasonable, but arbitral tribunals have applied the notion of reasonableness to a variety of cases under different treaty provisions.

---

379 Corten, 'Reasonableness in International Law', 2–3.

380 D.M. Beatty, 'Law's Golden Rule', in G. Palombella and N. Walker (eds), *Relocating the Rule of Law* (Hart Publishing 2009) 99–115, 103 (defining proportionality as 'law's golden rule'); Barak, *Proportionality: Constitutional Rights and their Limitations*, 3 (claiming that there is no better alternative to proportionality analysis in the context of constitutional adjudication).

Quintessentially, reasonableness serves three different, albeit complementary, functions: (1) constraining state behaviour; (2) requiring a reasoned analysis from the decision-makers; and (3) delimiting the legitimate expectations of investors. Reasonableness is slightly more deferential than the proportionality test. In fact, it can provide states and adjudicators with more flexibility than proportionality. While proportionality includes efficiency and optimization concerns, reasonableness is more concerned with quality rather than quantity.

CONCLUSIONS

Reasonableness is a dialogical instrument that, like proportionality, expresses a culture of justification. It requires states to offer reasons for their actions and to adopt measures that are reasonable, calibrating public and private interests. It requires adjudicators to clarify vague treaty provisions, to review state action and to give reasons for their decisions and awards, helping them to bridge the gap between treaty law and the concrete circumstances of each case. Finally, it asks investors to behave reasonably and have only legitimate and reasonable expectations. While the concept of reasonableness remains vague, its open-endedness makes it particularly fit for use in evolving legal systems because it enables such systems to adapt to emerging circumstances. Reasonableness is a flexible, pragmatic and contextual standard that has a distinct evaluative character and can deliver 'just results in individual cases'.[381]

Reasonableness and proportionality at times overlap, despite their conceptual differences. Both proportionality and reasonableness require that the state measure under review pursue a legitimate objective and be suitable to contribute to, or achieve, its purported objective. If one were to accept the proposals – endorsed by a number of scholars – to avoid a review based on proportionality in the strict sense, and use an abbreviated form of proportionality analysis, then reasonableness and proportionality would converge to such an extent as to be virtually indistinguishable. By depriving the proportionality analysis of its proportionality in the strict sense test, proportionality would become close, if not equivalent, to reasonableness.

However, reasonableness and proportionality maintain notable differences. While proportionality adopts a more disciplined, structured and methodical test than reasonableness, reasonableness involves an element

[381] Wouters and Duquet, 'The Principle of Reasonableness in Global Administrative Law', 42.

of free style. As mentioned, the reasonableness analysis does not include the necessity and proportionality tests in the strict sense. The reasonableness review does not assess whether the state measure is the most effective or efficient; it does not question whether the adverse economic impact of a given measure on the foreign investment is disproportionate vis-à-vis its purported benefits. Rather, it assesses whether a given measure is logically, rationally related to its objectives and adequate to achieve them. It also assesses whether such measure does not unreasonably prejudice the legitimate interests of the foreign investors. Therefore, it avoids the most intrusive prongs of review of the proportionality test. While proportionality is a demanding standard of review, reasonableness accords states more latitude in the implementation of their international obligations and accommodates some pluralism.

The principal merit of reasonableness lies in its flexibility. Reasonableness allows the constant adaptation of law to changing circumstances; it looks for the equilibrium between the text and the aim of a given norm; it bridges the divide between the static character of international investment law provisions and the dynamic character of social contexts. Reasonableness can constitute the link between the treaty-makers and the arbitrators. It also expresses the search for a fair balance between individual and public interests.

At the same time, reasonableness has been criticized for its vagueness. Yet, it is because of its inherent vagueness and flexibility that reasonableness enables international adjudicators to overcome the constraining proportionality tests. In fact, reasonableness goes beyond pure mathematical reasoning, enabling a more nuanced assessment of the applicable law and the circumstances of each case.

Reasonableness is part and parcel of international law in general, and international investment law and arbitration in particular. Not only does reasonableness belong to positive law, being present in a number of public international law instruments, but international legal practice uses it as an implicit legal requirement to ascertain the lawfulness of state action. In addition, international courts and tribunals often refer to reasonableness in a variety of contexts, to review the exercise of state powers.

While the role of reasonableness varies across the different fields of international law and the question of its status remains open, this chapter has shown that reasonableness certainly plays an important role in international investment law and arbitration. It appears in both IIAs and arbitral awards. Reasonableness has both theoretical and practical relevance, which can help international adjudicators to reach sensible practical outcomes. Therefore, it can constitute a valuable alternative to proportionality, at least in some circumstances. In conclusion, in the absence of explicit provisions about which ground of review is applicable, the choice of which parameter to apply is left to the adjudicator.[382] At the same time, despite or perhaps because of its imperfections, reasonableness constitutes a pillar of the architecture of the international (investment) regime.

382 Ortino, 'Investment Treaties, Sustainable Development and Reasonableness Review', 88.

5. Standards of review in investment treaty arbitration

INTRODUCTION

The concept of standard of review can be defined as the intensity of review or the degree of deference or judicial restraint that an adjudicator grants to lawmakers and decision-makers.[1] At the domestic level, the standards of review govern relations among the legislative, judicial and executive powers. Some deference or self-restraint prevents the adjudicator 'from substituting [his/her] own opinion for the opinion of the legislator who has the authority to make the political decisions'.[2] In turn, an intrusive review 'constitutes a violation of the separation of powers, which blurs the roles of the judiciary and the legislature'.[3] At the domestic level, deference is principally due to the three distinct albeit related arguments of (1) separation of powers, (2) epistemic superiority and (3) judicial economy.[4]

At the international level, the notion of standard of review can be defined as the intensity of review or the degree of deference that an international adjudicator grants to national authorities.[5] In this context, the depth of review is influenced by the interpretation and application of the relevant international obligations.[6] Under international law, states have a relative flexibility in the way they implement their international

---

[1] See e.g. J. Bohanes and N. Lockhart, 'Standard of Review in WTO Law', in D. Bethlehem, D. McRae, R. Neufeld and I. van Damme (eds), *The Oxford Handbook of International Trade Law* (OUP 2010) 379–433.

[2] X. Contiades and A. Fotiadou, 'Social Rights in the Age of Proportionality: Global Economic Crisis and Constitutional Litigation' (2012) 10 IJCL 660–86, 668.

[3] Ibid.

[4] L. Gruszczynski and W. Werner, 'Introduction', in L. Gruszczynski and W. Werner (eds), *Deference in International Courts and Tribunals* (OUP 2014) 1–15, 2.

[5] Bohanes and Lockhart, 'Standard of Review in WTO Law', 379.

[6] C.E. Foster, 'Adjudication, Arbitration and the Turn to Public Law Standards of Review' (2012) 3 JIDS 525–58, 535.

law obligations; yet, they have to comply with them, and international adjudication 'must be objective'.[7] At the international level, deference is grounded in the three distinct albeit related arguments of: (1) self-determination; (2) subsidiarity (that is, 'governments are better placed to make complex factual determinations and political choices than international tribunals');[8] and (3) judicial economy. At the same time, arguments for objective assessment of state conduct also matter; they principally relate to: (1) the primacy of international law over domestic law;[9] (2) the principle of *pacta sunt servanda*;[10] and, more generally, (3) the functioning of international relations and the recognition of international law as a legal system. International law prevails over municipal law for functional reasons; to constrain the unbridled exercise of sovereignty and promote peaceful relations among nations.[11]

What standards of review have arbitral tribunals adopted vis-à-vis state regulation aimed to protect fundamental interests and values? Can ideas regarding the standards of review be borrowed from other legal systems; and if so, which one should be selected? Or, rather, due to the hybrid nature of international investment law and arbitration, should this field develop its own standards of review?

The debate on the standards of review to be applied in investment arbitration has both practical and theoretical relevance. On the one hand, the debate on the standards of review can have practical implications as it 'may answer the ultimate question of which party prevails in a dispute'.[12] In fact, the intensity of review that an arbitral tribunal employs 'can be dispositive of the outcome'.[13] Depending on the selected standards of review, the outcome of the given dispute may vary. Adjudicators could decide analogous cases in different ways, if there was no agreement in the way to adjudicate such cases. Ultimately, lack of analytical thinking

---

[7] Ibid. 536.

[8] Gruszczynski and Werner, 'Introduction', 3.

[9] See, *ex multis*, *Alabama claims of the United States of America against Great Britain*, Award, 14 September 1872, RIAA 29 (1871) (insufficient legal means cannot justify failure of due diligence); Vienna Convention on the Law of Treaties (VCLT), adopted 23 May 1969, in force 27 January 1980, 1155 UNTS 331, Article 27 (providing that a State may not invoke the provisions of its internal law as justification for its failure to perform a treaty).

[10] VCLT, Article 26.

[11] See generally Hersch Lauterpacht, *The Function of Law in the International Community* (OUP 2011).

[12] T.J. Gunn, 'Deconstructing Proportionality in Limitations Analysis' (2006) 19 *Emory International LR* 465–98, 477–8.

[13] Ibid. 480.

and reflection on standards of review could lead to a violation of the principle of equality as adjudicators would approach and adjudicate similar cases differently. In turn, this lack of consistency could fuel criticism against investment treaty arbitration. Lack of predictability could also foster the criticism that investment treaty arbitration constitutes an uneven playing field, rather than a fair dispute-settlement mechanism. Moreover, lack of systemic discussion about standards of review can leave arbitrators without any guidance as to the required level of scrutiny, thus making their task more difficult. Finally, the application of overly deferential or intrusive review can either undermine the effectiveness of the investment arbitration mechanism or compromise its legitimacy.

On the other hand, discussion on the standards of review has theoretical relevance. Such discourse goes to the heart of international adjudication and can contribute to the mutual supportiveness between public international law and international investment law, reinforcing the capacity of the latter to contribute to the harmonious development of the former, and vice versa. Investigating the standards of review adopted by arbitral tribunals and other international courts and tribunals also helps identify the eventual coalescence of best practices, judicial dialogue and the cross-pollination of concepts among international courts and tribunals. Analysis of the relevant arbitral awards can provide arbitrators and practitioners with a roadmap of what has been done in the past, to allow them a sensible choice of the best way to follow among different adjudicatory paths to address current needs. It can also reinforce the perceived legitimacy of international investment arbitration and its capacity to contribute to the commonweal. Finally, investigating these questions can contribute to the effectiveness of international investment law and arbitration, spurring state compliance with arbitral awards.[14] Especially in the decentralized international investment system that lacks a central international investment court, such reflection seems essential. Despite its practical and theoretical importance, discussion on the standards of review in investment arbitration 'remains undertheorized'.[15]

---

[14] L.R. Helfer and A.-M. Slaughter, 'Toward a Theory of Effective Supranational Adjudication' (1997) 107 *Yale LJ* 273–391.

[15] E. Shirlow, 'Deference and Indirect Expropriation Analysis in International Investment Law: Observations on Current Approaches and Frameworks for Future Analysis' (2014) 29 *ICSID Review* 595–626, 609.

This chapter illuminates the standards of review developed by arbitral tribunals, and investigates whether there are convergences and/or divergences between such standards and those adopted by different international courts and tribunals. It proceeds as follows. First, it defines the concept of standards of review and discusses its main aims, objectives and features. Second, it examines the various degrees of self-restraint amidst deference and control. Third, it briefly explores the standards of review adopted by international courts and tribunals, focusing on the International Court of Justice (ICJ). Fourth, it discusses the standards of review adopted by the World Trade Organization (WTO) 'courts'. Fifth, it scrutinizes the margin of appreciation doctrine elaborated by the European Court of Human Rights (ECtHR). Sixth, it explores the extent to which a discourse on the standards of review has emerged in doctrinal discussions concerning international investment law and in the arbitral jurisprudence. As most international investment agreements (IIAs) do not mention the standard of review let alone mandate specific approaches in this regard, examining how arbitral tribunals have approached the issue is crucial. The chapter highlights that arbitral jurisprudence has not developed a systematic approach to the standards of review. At the same time, arbitral tribunals have shown a certain familiarity with the reasoning of other international courts and tribunals. While only a few arbitral tribunals have adopted the margin of appreciation doctrine, some have generically referred to some deference. Finally, the chapter shows that there is no uniform approach to the issue of the standards of review across these jurisdictions. The chapter concludes that while a completely deferential review of state conduct would go against the very purpose of international investment law, an intrusive standard of review that is used by some arbitration tribunals is also ill-advised as international arbitrators should not assume the functions of national legislators and decision-makers. Therefore, the chapter calls for an intermediate solution, an objective assessment that combines scrutiny and respect for the regulatory autonomy of states.

5.1 THE CONCEPT OF THE STANDARDS OF REVIEW

The standard of review is the intensity of review or the level of scrutiny adopted by adjudicators when reviewing state conduct.[16] It determines the pervasiveness of the adjudicators' review into the lawfulness of state

---

[16] S.R. Tully, 'Objective Reasonableness as a Standard for International Judicial Review' (2015) 6 JIDS 546–67, 555.

conduct. It also sets the level of deference a tribunal accords to state authorities.[17] The standard of review does not replace treaty interpretation; it does not alter the applicable law.[18] It is a reference point implicit in any adjudication and the inherent powers of international courts and tribunals.[19]

While standards of review are the essential grammar of international adjudication, both scholars and practitioners have 'difficulty explaining standards of review consistently and often resort to using metaphors and analogies to describe their purpose'.[20] 'Like a telescope, [the standards] of review [offer] either a narrow aperture to limit the breadth of judicial scrutiny, thereby increasing the area of agency discretion, or a wider lens to expand judicial oversight, thereby decreasing agency discretion.'[21]

The concept expresses the need to balance the competing values of control and restraint.[22] On the one hand, control is driven by the desire to uphold the rule of law and safeguard the rights and interests protected under the applicable law. On the other hand, restraint is based on various rationales. In domestic adjudication, as mentioned, restraint is based on: (1) the theory of separation of powers; (2) the perceived limits of judicial review or subsidiarity;[23] and (3) judicial economy. First, calibrating the scope of judicial review over state conduct reflects the allocation of power between the legislative, executive and judicial branches.[24] This structural deference expresses the idea that unelected judges should not second-guess the decisions taken by democratic institutions. Rather, 'courts are only charged with reviewing decisions, not making them'.[25] Second, parliaments and governments are often better equipped to deal with certain issues than judges are.[26] They have time, information and

---

17 Shirlow, 'Deference and Indirect Expropriation Analysis in International Investment Law', 600.

18 Tully, 'Objective Reasonableness as a Standard for International Judicial Review', 553–4.

19 C. Henckels, *Proportionality and Deference in Investor–State Arbitration: Balancing Investment Protection and Regulatory Autonomy* (CUP 2015) 33.

20 A. Peters, 'The Meaning, Measure and Misuse of Standards of Review' (2009) 13 *Lewis & Clark LR* 233–77, 234.

21 P.R. Verkuil, 'An Outcomes Analysis of Scope of Review Standards' (2002–2003) 44 *William & Mary LR* 679–735, 682.

22 D.R. Knight, 'Mapping the Rainbow of Review: Recognizing Variable Intensity' (2010) NZLR 393–431, 411–12.

23 Ibid. 412.

24 Verkuil, 'An Outcomes Analysis of Scope of Review Standards', 682.

25 Knight, 'Mapping the Rainbow of Review', 412.

26 Ibid.

expertise to address given issues. Third, standards of review enable some judicial economy, protecting the court's 'valuable time and resources'.[27]

In transnational adjudication, including investor–state arbitration, the ability of international courts to set applicable standards of review arguably is based on the inherent power of international judicial bodies to determine their own procedures and to effectively exercise their jurisdiction.[28] It is generally held that 'it [is] for international courts to determine whether deference to national authorities is warranted and to what extent'.[29] At the transnational level, the standards of review have three principal functions: (1) they reflect the allocation of power between national governments and international institutions;[30] (2) they reflect the 'relative institutional knowledge and expertise' of international courts and state actors;[31] (3) they enable adjudicators to adopt consistent patterns of jurisprudence. Let us examine these three factors in more detail.

First, the standards of review reflect the allocation of power between international courts and state authorities. Such relationship is often expressed in the concept of subsidiarity.[32] State authorities are arguably 'better suited to adopt general policies'; they have the time and resources to gather information, analyse data and consult experts. They can consider a variety of different interests, and 'anticipate the entire gamut of implications deriving from specific decisions'.[33] Instead, courts adjudicate 'specific dispute[s] on the basis of information supplied to them by the parties, and through the prism of [existing] legal norms'.[34]

---

27 Peters, 'The Meaning, Measure and Misuse of Standards of Review', 240.

28 Y. Shany, 'Towards a General Margin of Appreciation Doctrine in International Law' (2005) 16 EJIL 907–940, 911 (referring to the Convention on the Settlement of Investment Disputes between States and Nationals of Other States, 18 March 1965, 575 UNTS 159, Article 44).

29 Ibid. 914.

30 S.P. Croley and J.H. Jackson, 'WTO Dispute Procedures, Standard of Review, and Deference to National Governments' (1996) 90 AJIL 193–213, 194.

31 Shirlow, 'Deference and Indirect Expropriation Analysis in International Investment Law', 601.

32 A. von Staden, 'The Democratic Legitimacy of Judicial Review beyond the State: Normative Subsidiarity and Judicial Standards of Review' (2012) 10 IJCL 1023–1049; A von Bogdandy and I. Venzke, 'In Whose Name? An Investigation of International Courts' Public Authority and Its Democratic Justification' (2012) 23 EJIL 7–41.

33 Shany, 'Towards a General Margin of Appreciation Doctrine in International Law', 918.

34 Ibid.

Second, state actors generally, albeit not always, seem to be better situated than international courts to appreciate domestic conditions.[35] When international courts and tribunals assess state compliance with international law, they are inevitably detached from the local circumstances underlying the dispute at hand.[36] If international courts assumed intrusive standards of review, they might 'misunderstand the complexities of the conflict, misapply the law to the facts or set totally unrealistic legal standards'.[37] Some self-constraint prevents international courts from determining issues that they are 'ill-equipped, ill-informed or otherwise not designated … to address'.[38]

On the other hand, 'international courts are typically better situated than national actors to identify and interpret the relevant norms of international law' and must ensure the conformity of state decision-making with international law.[39] By striking an appropriate balance between control and deference, international courts and tribunals are 'architects of their own success',[40] contributing in a significant way to their efficiency, effectiveness and perceived legitimacy.[41]

Third, the adoption of consistent standards of review enables adjudicators to treat similar cases alike, potentially enhancing the perceived fairness, coherence and predictability of the system. In turn, lack of consideration of the relevant standards of review can lead to inconsistencies, treating similar issues in a different fashion.[42] These three functions are complementary and work together to guarantee the efficiency, effectiveness and legitimacy of the system.

---

35 Ibid. 919.

36 Ibid.

37 Ibid.

38 Shirlow, 'Deference and Indirect Expropriation Analysis in International Investment Law', 601–602.

39 Shany, 'Towards a General Margin of Appreciation Doctrine in International Law', 919.

40 Helfer and Slaughter, 'Toward a Theory of Effective Supranational Adjudication', 277.

41 Shany, 'Towards a General Margin of Appreciation Doctrine in International Law', 919.

42 J.F. Colares and J.W. Bohn, 'NAFTA's Double Standards of Review' (2007) 42 *Wake Forest LR* 199–246 (reflecting on the North American Free Trade Agreement (NAFTA) Ch. 19).

In the context of investor–state arbitration, the issue concerning standards of review is particularly relevant because the field has competing aims and objectives. In the clash between investment protection and the pursuit of public interest objectives by the host state, intensity of scrutiny adopted by arbitral tribunals in reviewing state conduct influences the outcome of the proceedings.[43] The adoption of appropriate standards of review can enhance the coherence, effectiveness and perceived legitimacy of investment treaty arbitration, potentially 'mitigat-[ing] some elements of the frequently asserted "legitimacy crisis" of ... investment arbitration'.[44]

The standards of review can move along a 'sprectrum of review'.[45] They can range from full deference, where the substantive determinations of the decision-makers are not questioned (and the review focuses on mere procedural compliance), to *de novo* review, which amounts to a new trial, where the reviewing body reprocesses and re-evaluates the evidence, and takes the decision anew.[46] As mentioned, at the international level, deference is grounded in the three distinct albeit related arguments of: (1) self-determination; (2) subsidiarity; and (3) judicial economy. At the same time, arguments for objective assessment of state conduct principally relate to: (1) the primacy of international law over domestic law; (2) the principle of *pacta sunt servanda*; and, more generally, (3) the functioning of international relations and the recognition of international law as a legal system.

What are the difficulties inherent in the application of standards of review? The standards of review are elusive: they are difficult not only to

---

[43] C. Henckels, 'Indirect Expropriation and the Right to Regulate: Revisiting Proportionality Analysis and the Standard of Review in Investor–State Arbitration' (2012) 15 JIEL 223–55, 238 (highlighting that 'the standard of review utilized by tribunals in their assessment of host state measures may be the most important factor governing liability and hence allocation of risk between host states and investors').

[44] A. von Staden, 'Deference or no Deference, that is the Question: Legitimacy and Standards of Review in Investor–State Arbitration' (2012) 4 ITN 3, 3.

[45] Shirlow, 'Deference and Indirect Expropriation Analysis in International Investment Law', 600.

[46] S.W. Schill, 'Deference in Investment Treaty Arbitration: Re-conceptualizing the Standard of Review through Comparative Public Law', SIEL Working Paper No. 33/2012, 6; R. Becroft, *The Standards of Review in WTO Dispute Settlement: Critique and Development* (Edward Elgar 2012) 7; M. Oesch, *Standards of Review in WTO Dispute Resolution* (OUP 2003) 15.

define, but also to apply in practice.[47] Critics contend that standards of review 'defin[e] moods, rather than … legal boundaries'.[48] As a former Justice of the US Supreme Court, Justice Felix Frankfurter once noted, standards of review express a paradox, as they are 'undefined defining terms'.[49] International law scholars and practitioners have also noted the vagueness of the concept.[50]

Because international investment treaties are silent on the issue of the standards of review, arbitral tribunals have interpreted such omission in various ways.[51] While standards of review are and should be flexible to calibrate different levels of deference in different contexts, the same flexibility can be perceived as evidence of inconsistency and unfairness.[52] Moreover, even in consenting that 'it is better to include a discussion of the [relevant] standard of review in an [award] than not to include it, a mechanical recitation of the relevant standard of review, without more, is no more helpful than completely ignoring the standards altogether'.[53] Concerns have arisen that adjudicators formally adopt one standard when they are in fact using another.[54] For instance, while '[m]ost arbitral tribunals emphasize that they are not and that they should not sit as "courts of appeal" reviewing the decisions of municipal courts', 'often they just do that, or something … akin to it'.[55]

De lege ferenda, the standards of review can be specified when states revise their IIAs. As mentioned in Chapter 1, international investment law and arbitration is a matter in flux; at the time of writing, Canada, the EU and UNCITRAL are developing plans to establish a multilateral investment court. The establishment of a multilateral investment court to interpret and apply existing IIAs could include specific reference to the applicable standards of review.

---

47 Peters, 'The Meaning, Measure and Misuse of Standards of Review', 248.

48 Ibid. (reporting this criticism).

49 *Universal Camera Corp v. Nat'l Labor Relations Bd*, 340 US 474, 489 (1951) (Justice Felix Frankfurter).

50 Shirlow, 'Deference and Indirect Expropriation Analysis in International Investment Law', 612.

51 J. Arato, 'The Margin of Appreciation in International Investment Law' (2014) 54 *Virginia JIL* 545–78, 546.

52 Peters, 'The Meaning, Measure and Misuse of Standards of Review', 253.

53 Ibid. 256.

54 Ibid. 257.

55 A.K. Bjorklund, 'Reconciling State Sovereignty and Investor Protection in Denial of Justice Claims' (2004–2005) 45 *Virginia JIL* 809–895, 870 (referring to *Mondev Intl Ltd v. United States*, ICSID Case No. ARB(AF)/99/2, Award, 11 October 2002, para. 126).

De lege lata, arbitral tribunals have oscillated between some self-restraint and control in investor–state arbitration. In fact, the depth of arbitral scrutiny has varied depending on the provision to be applied, the public policy objectives of the host state, the modalities of its action and the relevant context. Arbitral tribunals have accommodated the dynamic tension among these factors in individual arbitrations; therefore, it would be difficult and perhaps ultimately undesirable to attempt devising a unified standard of review to be applied in investor–state arbitration. The calibration of the intensity of review depends on a number of factors, including 'the countervailing principles of vigilance and restraint'. 'More deference is typically accorded to an authority's factual findings as opposed to its determinations of law.'[56]

While the standards of review should theoretically be one of the first and most important considerations when adjudicating investment disputes, the empirical analysis of arbitral jurisprudence shows that while arbitral tribunals rely on standards of review, they often do so implicitly.[57] For instance, in some cases of implicit deference, arbitral tribunals have 'temper[ed] [their] analysis of state acts' by linking state conduct to a broader context, for instance, to economic crisis, or 'circumstances of political and economic transition'.[58]

5.2 AMID DEFERENCE AND CONTROL

Which standard of review should apply to investment treaty arbitration? Should arbitrators second-guess the regulatory choices of the relevant national authorities? Or should they adopt relatively deferential standards of review? As Chen puts it, 'if the arbitrator adopts *de novo* review, ...

[56] Shirlow, 'Deference and Indirect Expropriation Analysis in International Investment Law', 611.

[57] For instance, in *Genin v. Estonia*, the Arbitral Tribunal did not formally consider the standard of review. However, in assessing the state conduct it took the specific circumstances of the country into account. *Alex Genin, Eastern Credit Ltd Inc and A.S. Baltoil v. The Republic of Estonia*, ICSID Case No. ARB/99/2, Award, 25 June 2001, para. 348 (holding that 'the Tribunal considers it imperative to recall the particular context in which the dispute arose, namely, that of a renascent independent state, coming rapidly to grips with the reality of modern financial, commercial and banking practices and the emergence of state institutions responsible for overseeing and regulating areas of activity perhaps previously unknown').

[58] *Saluka Investments BV v. The Czech Republic*, UNCITRAL, Partial Award, 17 March 2006, para. 370.

[he/she] effectively adopts the role of the ultimate *de facto* decision maker of the disputed policy by disregarding the views and determinations of the host governments'.[59] A complete deference, however, would render investment arbitration meaningless, diluting the substance of investment treaty guarantees.[60] Depending on the conceptualization of investor–state arbitration, and the type of dispute in question, the answer varies.[61] As Shirlow points out, 'the selection of a particular standard of review will … be highly dependent upon the tribunal's understanding of its role within a particular system'.[62]

Investor–state arbitration has been compared to different legal systems, including commercial arbitration, domestic administrative review and public international law adjudication.[63] Let us consider how these different conceptualizations require the adoption of different standards of review, and how analogizing investor–state arbitration to different systems can lead arbitrators to adopt different standards of review. This section examines and critically assesses various standards of review models, based on the main conceptualizations of investor–state arbitration as analogous to: (1) commercial arbitration; (2) public international law adjudication; and (3) public law adjudication. Consideration will be given to the view of investor–state arbitration as a hybrid system.

First, if one deemed investment arbitration analogous to commercial arbitration, a standard of review more exacting upon the host state would be favoured. Commercial arbitration presupposes a contract-based horizontal relationship between the parties.[64] Commercial disputes involve private entities, with a tribunal acting as 'impartial referee',[65] and applying the principle of equality of the parties.[66] As Schill aptly puts it,

---

59 T.-F. Chen, 'The Standard of Review and the Roles of ICSID Arbitral Tribunals in Investor–State Dispute Settlement' (2012) 5 *Contemporary Asia Arbitration Journal* 22–43, 28.

60 Ibid.

61 V. Vadi and L. Gruszczynski, 'Standards of Review in International Investment Law and Arbitration: Multilevel Governance and the Commonweal' (2013) 16 JIEL 613–33.

62 Shirlow, 'Deference and Indirect Expropriation Analysis in International Investment Law', 602.

63 See generally V. Vadi, *Analogies in International Investment Law and Arbitration* (CUP 2016); and Chapter 1 above.

64 Schill, 'Deference in Investment Treaty Arbitration', 9.

65 Ibid.

66 A. Roberts, 'Clash of Paradigms: Actors and Analogies Shaping the Investment Treaty System' (2013) 107 AJIL 45–94, 77.

'[p]arty equality ... translate[s] into a "no deference"-paradigm'.[67] According to others, with regard to straightforward commercial claims, 'it would be quite proper for an adjudicator to decide ... applying ordinary commercial dispute resolution principles'.[68] If one considers investment arbitration analogous to commercial arbitration, 'factual findings by tribunals [depend] exclusively ... on the persuasiveness of each party's case; [and] deference to any of the parties has little place'.[69]

Investor–state arbitration and commercial arbitration share some common features, for example the selection of arbitrators by the parties, the confidential nature of the proceedings, and some procedural matters. However, they also differ. International commercial arbitration generally involves private parties and concerns disputes of a commercial nature while investment arbitrations involve private actors and states, and often relate to important public goods.[70] Moreover, it may be difficult to categorize a given claim as 'a straightforward commercial claim'.

For instance, while some scholars have considered the *Malaysian Historical Salvors* case[71] as 'the simplest possible type of investment dispute',[72] others have highlighted the important policy dimensions of the case.[73] As is known, this case concerned the alleged breach of a salvage contract by Malaysia. The underlying contract entitled the company to 70 per cent of the profits earned from the sale of artefacts salvaged from the

---

[67] Schill, 'Deference in Investment Treaty Arbitration', 10.

[68] J.A. Maupin, 'Differentiating Among International Investment Disputes', in Z. Douglas, J. Pauwelyn and J.E. Viñuales (eds), *The Foundations of International Investment Law* (OUP 2014) 467–98, 471.

[69] Y. Fukunaga, 'Standard of Review and Scientific Truths in the WTO Dispute Settlement System and Investment Arbitration' (2012) 3 JIDS 1–18, 12.

[70] See N. Blackaby, 'Investment Arbitration and Commercial Arbitration (or the Tale of the Dolphin and the Shark)', in J.D.M. Lew and L.A. Mistelis (eds), *Pervasive Problems in International Arbitration* (Kluwer Law International 2006) 217–33; J. Paulsson, 'International Arbitration is not Arbitration' (2008) 2 *Stockholm International Arbitration Review* 1–20.

[71] *Malaysian Historical Salvors, SDN, BHD v. The Government of Malaysia*, ICSID Case No. ARB/05/10, Award on Jurisdiction, 17 May 2007; *Malaysian Historical Salvors, SDN, BHD v. The Government of Malaysia*, ICSID Case No. ARB/05/10, Decision on the Application for Annulment, 16 April 2009.

[72] Maupin, 'Differentiating Among International Investment Disputes', 471.

[73] V. Vadi, 'Investing in Culture: Underwater Cultural Heritage and International Investment Law' (2009) 42 *Vanderbilt Journal of Transnational Law* (2009) 853–904.

Diana, a historical shipwreck located in the straits of Malacca.[74] The contract also provided the right of the state to withdraw certain artefacts of significance from sale. A dispute arose with regard to the payment received by the company. The question as to whether the salvage business of the investor could amount to an investment determined the fate of the proceedings. For the sole arbitrator, the salvage activity did not contribute to the investment of the host state; therefore, he dismissed the claim on jurisdictional ground.[75] The Annulment Committee admitted that salvage activities could contribute to the development of the host state and therefore qualify as an investment. Nonetheless, the investor did not move the claim forward due to lack of funding. The case shows that certain claims raise issues of broad public interest (*in casu*, the recovery of underwater cultural heritage, and the possible contribution of the salvor's activities to the development of the host state). These considerations of course do not justify breach of investment treaties, but highlight the complex nature of given cases. As noted by Roberts, 'the failure of some arbitral tribunals to recognize the public nature of investment treaty arbitration, and to allow States a sufficient margin to determine and implement various policy goals, has contributed to the legitimacy crisis in which the investment treaty system currently finds itself'.[76]

Second, if one adopts a public international law paradigm and considers arbitral tribunals as creatures of public international law, the standards of review should 'strike an appropriate balance between state autonomy and the need for compliance with international obligations'.[77] While 'a failure to satisfy requirements of national law does not necessarily violate international law',[78] a state 'may not invoke the provisions of its internal law as justification for its failure to perform a treaty'.[79] Rather, the duty to bring national law into conformity with international law is a

---

74 *MHS v. Malaysia*, Award on Jurisdiction, paras 8–11.

75 Id. para. 151.

76 A. Roberts, 'The Next Battleground: Standards of Review in Investment Treaty Arbitration', in A.J. Van den Berg (ed.), *Arbitration: The Next Fifty Years* (Kluwer 2012) 170–83, 173.

77 C. Henckels, 'Proportionality and the Standard of Review in Fair and Equitable Treatment Cases' (2012) SIEL Working Paper 10.

78 *Gami Investments Inc v. The Government of the United Mexican States*, UNCITRAL Award, 15 November 2004, para. 97.

79 VCLT, Article 27.

well-settled part of customary law,[80] confirmed by consistent jurisprudence.[81] When dealing with national laws and regulations, international courts and tribunals address the question as to whether, in enacting or applying given measures, the state is acting in conformity with its obligations under international law.[82] If the state exercises some 'core non-derogable sovereign functions', or implements higher community norms, 'more deferential review will be favoured'.[83]

Compelling arguments stand in favour of assimilating arbitrators to international judges. International investment agreements are international treaties. They are part and parcel of public international law. Public international law rules and principles govern the arbitral process. Arbitral tribunals interpret and apply treaties according to customary rules of treaty interpretation. Finally, as Crawford puts it, international investment law and arbitration 'bring[s] the state under some measure of control, which is the main aspiration of general international law'.[84]

Third, if one analogizes investment arbitration to 'an internationalized form of judicial review'[85] or to a functional substitute for public law review, then the standard of review 'should be framed as a public law concept connected to the separation of powers doctrine'.[86] Arbitral tribunals should exercise deference when reviewing the conduct of states.[87] In this context, the standards of review reflect and shape the

---

[80] I. Brownlie, *Principles of Public International Law*, 7th edn (OUP 2008) 35.

[81] See e.g. PCIJ, *Treatment of Polish Nationals and other Persons of Polish Origin or Speech in the Danzig Territory*, Advisory Opinion, 4 February 1932 [1931–1932] 6 ILR 209.

[82] See e.g. PCIJ, *German Interests in the Upper Silesia* (*Germany v. Poland*) (Merits) Judgment, 25 May 1926 [1926] PCIJ Rep Series A No. 7, 19.

[83] Shirlow, 'Deference and Indirect Expropriation Analysis in International Investment Law', 602.

[84] J. Crawford, 'International Protection of Foreign Direct Investment: Between Clinical Isolation and Systematic Integration', in R. Hofmann and C.J. Tams (eds), *International Investment Law and General International Law – From Clinical Isolation to Systemic Integration?* (Nomos 2011) 17–28, 22.

[85] Henckels, 'Proportionality and the Standard of Review in Fair and Equitable Treatment Cases', 10.

[86] Schill, 'Deference in Investment Treaty Arbitration', 4.

[87] W.W. Burke-White and A. von Staden, 'Private Litigation in a Public Law Sphere: The Standard of Review in Investor–State Arbitration' (2010) 35 *Yale JIL* 283–346, 285–6; W.W. Burke-White and A. von Staden, 'The Need for Public Law Standards of Review in Investor–State Arbitrations', in S. Schill (ed.), *International Investment Law and Comparative Public Law* (OUP 2010) 689–720, 690.

checks and balances between the legislative, executive and judicial powers.[88] As Henckels puts it, 'decisions about what is in the public interest are primarily political decisions'[89] and adjudicators should not become law makers. After all, arbitrators do not have enough time, resources or even qualifications to undergo *de novo* review, in particular, in those cases involving complex factual determinations, including scientific issues.[90]

International investment law is often compared to a public law system. Certainly, public law has influenced the drafting of certain provisions in IIAs, and constitutional ideas have migrated across boundaries.[91] The public law paradigm brings to light the role of individuals in international investment law and arbitration.[92] Within given limits, it can complement public international law approaches by helping in the identification of general principles of law.[93]

However, investor–state arbitration cannot be reduced to a transnational form of constitutional or administrative review. It is an instrument of public international law, created on the basis of international treaties: arbitral tribunals often apply international law; and within investor–state arbitration, reliance on national constitutional provisions does not justify a violation of public international law. An excessive deference to state action would frustrate the very aims and objectives of international (investment) law.

Finally, scholars have argued that investor–state arbitration is a hybrid system, a unique mixture of various paradigms that require specific consideration.[94] If one accepted this approach, the standards of review would vary depending on the specific features of each investment dispute. If the dispute concerned a purely commercial matter, and the state was acting as a mere commercial actor (*acta iure gestionis*), then the intensity of review would be high; no deference whatsoever would be paid to state action. Instead, if the dispute concerned a public law matter

---

[88] Henckels, 'Proportionality and the Standard of Review in Fair and Equitable Treatment Cases', 9.

[89] Ibid. 20.

[90] Chen, 'The Standard of Review and the Roles of ICSID Arbitral Tribunals', 22, 29.

[91] Vadi, *Analogies in International Investment Law and Arbitration*, 190.

[92] Ibid. 193.

[93] Ibid.

[94] See generally Roberts, 'Clash of Paradigms'.

(for instance, coping with a public health crisis), then the intensity of review would be lower, according to traditional public law criteria.

In conclusion, commentators compare international investment law and arbitration to different domestic and international systems. Depending on the selected analogy, the relevant standards of review can vary, converging and/or diverging to a significant extent. If one adopts a public (international) law paradigm and/or a hybrid paradigm, arbitral tribunals should pay a 'qualified deference' in appropriate circumstances, namely with regard to public policy-related disputes. Such paradigms converge to a significant extent with regard to the question as to whether this category of investment disputes requires some deference on the part of arbitral tribunals. Vice versa, if one adopts a commercial law paradigm, and/or a hybrid paradigm with regard to those investment disputes that concern economic relations between a foreign investor and the host state acting in a purely commercial vein, then no deference should be paid to state action, and the principle of equality of arms should prevail. The various currents may be complementary rather than conflicting; in fact, the different approach would ultimately depend on the inner quality of the dispute.

5.3 STANDARDS OF REVIEW IN INTERNATIONAL LAW

International courts and tribunals have often navigated between the Scylla of excessive deference to, and the Charybdis of excessive intervention into, states' discretion in the implementation of their international law obligations. On the one hand, an excessive deference to states' discretion can jeopardize the effectiveness of international adjudication and of public international law.[95] It can also 'excessively compress, or even defeat, the competing rights and interests' of other states.[96] On the other hand, an excessive control over states' discretion may unduly restrict state sovereignty and undermine the perceived legitimacy and long-term effectiveness of international courts and tribunals.

International courts and tribunals have often acknowledged that states have 'a certain discretion' not only in the manner of implementing their international law obligations, but also in devising and applying 'public policy measures susceptible to interfere with the implementation of

[95] E. Cannizzaro, 'Proportionality and Margin of Appreciation in the Whaling Case: Reconciling Antithetical Doctrines?' (2017) 27 EJIL 1061–9, 1067.

[96] Ibid. 1068.

international obligations'.[97] Judicial self-restraint enables international courts and tribunals to acknowledge 'the reality of pluralism within [the international] legal order, thereby respecting constitutional traditions and national ... policy choices'.[98] In parallel, public international law has developed mechanisms to bridge the gap between the stability of its obligations and the changes of circumstances that states may face. Far from being a static system, public international law is in flux, and it includes a number of derogations, special provisions and even exceptions.

At the same time, international adjudication 'is consistently presented in the essential forms of interpretation and application of the law to the facts'.[99] Far from adopting the notion of 'total deference to the national decision-making process',[100] or 'upholding the absolute discretion of ... states', international courts and tribunals have restated that the compliance with international law obligations has to be carried out 'under international law control'.[101] This approach conforms to the function of international courts and tribunals, that is, to settle disputes 'in conformity with principles of justice and international law'.[102] Not only is the settlement of international disputes desirable because it can restore confidence in the rule of law, but it can also contribute to the maintenance of international peace and security', 'the development of friendly relations ... among nations' and international justice.[103]

In their struggle between deference and control, international courts and tribunals have shaped the contours of a sophisticated system of international review, often relying on an 'objective test' to respect state sovereignty while ensuring compliance with states' international obligations. An objective test checks whether a state regulation is adopted for legitimate reasons, and implemented for its intended purposes. It assesses whether 'the design and implementation' of a measure 'are reasonable in

97 Ibid. 1065.

98 Tully, 'Objective Reasonableness as a Standard for International Judicial Review', 549.

99 Foster, 'Adjudication, Arbitration and the Turn to Public Law', 551.

100 Shany, 'Towards a General Margin of Appreciation Doctrine in International Law', 910.

101 Cannizzaro, 'Proportionality and Margin of Appreciation in the Whaling Case', 1067.

102 VCLT, preamble.

103 Ibid.

relation to achieving the stated ... objectives'.[104] Therefore, the majority of international courts and tribunals have rejected interpretation criteria such as the *in dubio mitius* principle – the principle of restrictive interpretation of treaty obligations in deference to the sovereignty of states.[105] Procedurally, the adoption of such concept would disserve customary rules of treaty interpretation; substantively, such principle would clash with 'the established public international law principle that internal law needs to give way to international obligations'.[106]

In the *Oscar Chinn* case,[107] a case concerning the grant of subsidies to a national company for providing transportation services on the Congo River during the Great Depression, the Permanent Court of International Justice (PCIJ) acknowledged that states enjoy some discretion as 'sole judges of ... critical situation[s]' occurring within their territory and 'of the remedies called for'. However, the Court held that such discretion is not absolute; rather, it must be exercised in compliance with states' international obligations.[108] Analogously, in the *Corfu Channel* case,[109] arising from the damage of two British warships after striking mines in Albanian waters, the ICJ held that while a state can regulate the passage of warships through a strait for security reasons, the imposition of certain modalities of passage should not impair the rights of passage under international law.[110]

In reviewing the legality of the invocation of the necessity defence, the ICJ has clarified that the state is not the only judge of necessity. In the *Nicaragua* judgment,[111] relating to responsibility for military and paramilitary activities in and against Nicaragua, the ICJ held that 'whether a measure is necessary to protect the essential security interests is not ...

---

[104] *Whaling in the Antarctic* (*Australia v. Japan*), Judgment, 31 March 2014 [2014] ICJ Reports 226, para. 97.

[105] J.E. Alvarez, 'Is Investor–State Arbitration Public?' (2016) 7 JIDS 534–76, 552. But see C.J. Larouer, 'In the Name of Sovereignty? The Battle Over *In Dubio Mitius* Inside and Outside the Courts', Cornell Law School Graduate Student Papers Series, Cornell Law Library (2009) 1–49 (noting that the approach remains in the WTO jurisprudence).

[106] Alvarez, 'Is Investor–State Arbitration Public?', 559.

[107] *Oscar Chinn Case* (*Britain v. Belgium*) 1934 PCIJ Series A/B 63, No. 63.

[108] Ibid. 79.

[109] *Corfu Channel* (*United Kingdom of Great Britain and Northern Ireland v. Albania*) Judgment, 9 April 1949 [1949] ICJ Reports 4.

[110] Id. 29.

[111] *Military and Paramilitary Activities in and against Nicaragua* (*Nicaragua v. USA*) Judgment, 27 June 1986 [1986] ICJ Reports 14, para. 282.

purely a question for the subjective judgment of the party'.[112] Analogously, in *Gabcikovo/Nagymaros*,[113] in which the ICJ had to determine whether Hungary was entitled to suspend and then abandon its part of a dam project, the Court stated that the state is not the sole judge of necessity. In particular, the Court held that 'the state of necessity can only be invoked under certain strictly defined conditions which must be cumulatively satisfied: and the State concerned is not the sole judge of whether those conditions have been met'.[114]

In the consular assistance cases, the Court admitted that states have a certain discretion in selecting the means to implement their international obligations; however, it also stated that such discretion is not without qualification. In the *LaGrand* case,[115] concerning violations of the 1963 Vienna Convention on Consular Relations,[116] the ICJ stated that in any future cases, 'if the United States ... should fail in its obligation of consular notification to the detriment of German nationals, an apology would not suffice in cases where the individuals concerned have been subjected to prolonged detention'.[117] Rather, in such cases, the Court held that the United States had the obligation 'to allow the review and reconsideration of the conviction and sentence by taking into account ... the violation of the rights set forth in the Convention'.[118] The Court specified that 'this obligation can be carried out in various ways' and that 'the choice of means must be left to the United States'.[119] Similarly, in *Avena*,[120] also concerning breaches of the Vienna Convention on Consular Relations, the ICJ held that it was for the United States to 'determine the process of review and reconsideration'.[121] However, the ICJ added that 'this freedom in the choice of means for such review and reconsideration is not without qualification'.[122] In conclusion, if international courts

---

112 Ibid. para. 282.

113 *Case Concerning the Gabčíkovo/Nagymaros Project* (*Hungary v. Slovakia*) Judgment, 25 September 1997 [1997] ICJ Reports 7.

114 Ibid. para. 51.

115 *LaGrand (Germany v. United States*) Judgment, 27 June 2001 [2001] ICJ Reports 466.

116 Vienna Convention on Consular Relations, done at Vienna on 24 April 1963, in force 19 March 1967, 596 UNTS 261.

117 *LaGrand* Judgment, para. 125.

118 Ibid.

119 Ibid.

120 *Case Concerning Avena and Other Mexican Nationals (Mexico v. United States*) Judgment, 31 March 2004 [2004] ICJ Reports 12.

121 Ibid. para. 122.

122 Ibid. para. 131.

have granted varying levels of deference to state action, in the light of the public interest at stake, the ICJ has granted limited deference to states in reviewing their compliance with international law.

Against this background, if one admits that investor–state arbitration is analogous to other public international law dispute-settlement mechanisms, then the question arises as to which field of international law is more similar to investor–state arbitration. In fact, international courts and tribunals have adopted different standards of review. Adopting a public international law paradigm, some scholars suggest that arbitral tribunals should generally adopt an intermediate intensity of review, or an objective assessment, and a 'qualified deference' in a selected range of circumstances.[123] Other scholars argue that arbitral tribunals should adopt a (deferential) margin of appreciation doctrine, as adopted by the European Court of Human Rights (ECtHR).[124] The next sections will examine the standards review adopted by the WTO 'courts', the ECtHR and arbitral tribunals respectively.

5.4 STANDARDS OF REVIEW IN INTERNATIONAL TRADE LAW

International trade law oscillates between a 'centrifugal pull towards deference for States' and the centripetal pull of multilateralism.[125] In this field, the issue of standards of review reflects 'a finely drawn balance

---

[123] M. Orellana, 'Science, Risk and Uncertainty: Public Health Measures and Investment Disciplines', in P. Kahn and T. Wälde (eds), *New Aspects of International Investment Law* (Martinus Nijhoff 2007) Ch. 15, 723 (referring to public health-related disputes); L. Gruszczynski and V. Vadi, 'Standard of Review and Scientific Evidence in WTO Law and International Investment Arbitration: Converging Parallels?', in Gruszczynski and Werner (eds), *Deference in International Courts and Tribunals* 152–72 (arguing for some deference in public policy-related disputes); A. von Staden, 'Deference or No Deference, That is the Question: Legitimacy and Standards of Review in Investor–State Arbitration' (2012) 4 ITN 3 (calling for a 'deferential standard of review in appropriate circumstances').

[124] See e.g. M. Orellana, 'The Role of Science in Investment Arbitrations Concerning Public Health and the Environment' (2007) 17 *Yearbook of International Environmental Law* 48–72, 54 (arguing in favour of the adoption of the margin of appreciation doctrine in investment arbitration); Burke-White and von Staden, 'Private Litigation in a Public Law Sphere', 302, 339–43 (calling for the application of the margin of appreciation doctrine and the proportionality test).

[125] Foster, 'Adjudication, Arbitration and the Turn to Public Law Standards of Review', 543.

about where power is located': between the WTO and its members.[126] It expresses 'the particular institutional architecture of the WTO',[127] acknowledging the residual importance of state sovereignty in theory, but building a multilateral trade regime in practice. Although the issue of the standards of review was discussed extensively during the Uruguay Round, the idea of a deferential standard of review has been codified only in the field of trade remedies.[128]

More generally, while members of the WTO have to comply with the covered agreements, some 'deference to domestic regulation is built into the system'.[129] In fact, the Uruguay Round negotiations led to negative rather than positive integration. Member states are not required to adopt common policies;[130] rather, they are required to remove trade barriers and refrain from protectionist behaviour.[131] Therefore, they retain 'policy space for domestic regulatory measures' under the covered agreements.[132] As a result, most covered agreements permit the panels and the Appellate Body (AB) to be 'deferential' towards domestic regulatory policies, as long as they apply such measures equally to foreign and domestic products.[133]

At the same time, the adopted measure must comply with the covered agreement provisions. Article 11 of the Dispute Settlement Understanding (DSU)[134] requires panels to make an 'objective assessment' of the matter before them. In *EC–Hormones*, the AB explained that 'the applicable standard is neither *de novo* review as such, nor total deference,

---

126 M. Ioannidis, 'Beyond Standard of Review – Deference Criteria in WTO Law and the Case for a Procedural Approach', in Gruszczynski and Werner, *Deference in International Courts and Tribunals*, 91–112, 93.

127 Ibid.

128 Agreement on the Implementation of Article VI of the General Agreement on Tariffs and Trade, Marrakesh, 15 April 1994 (Anti-Dumping Agreement), Article 17.6

129 B. Hoekman, 'The World Trade Order: Global Governance by Judiciary?' (2016) 27 EJIL 1083–1093, 1085.

130 Ibid.

131 Ibid.

132 Ibid.

133 Ibid.

134 Understanding on Rules and Procedures Governing the Settlement of Disputes (DSU), 15 April 1994, Marrakesh Agreement Establishing the World Trade Organization, Annex 2, 1869 UNTS 401.

but rather the objective assessment of the facts'.[135] The AB conducts such objective assessment in accordance with customary rules of treaty interpretation.[136] Therefore, the WTO system expresses 'a kind of fundamental equilibrium' between state sovereignty on the one hand, and multilateralism on the other.[137] In this regard, the AB has shaped its own role 'primarily as preserving that equilibrium'.[138]

For instance, in the *Gasoline* case, a dispute arising out of the United States' application of stricter rules on imported gasoline than on domestically refined gasoline, the AB stated that 'WTO Members have a large measure of autonomy to determine their own policies on the environment'.[139] Analogously, in the *Asbestos* case, a dispute arising out of France's ban on asbestos, the AB held that 'it is undisputed that WTO Members have the right to determine the level of protection of health that they consider appropriate in a given situation'.[140] More recently, in the *Seal Products* case, concerning the consistency of the EU ban on seal products with the General Agreement on Tariffs and Trade,[141] the AB relied on the panel's finding that 'members should be given some scope to define and apply for themselves the concept of public moral according to their own system and scales of value'.[142]

While WTO member states have preserved some regulatory autonomy to determine their own policies, the AB has carefully scrutinized 'the rationality of the design of the domestic regulation'.[143] For instance, in

---

[135] *EC Measures concerning Meat and Meat Products (EC – Hormones)*, Appellate Body Report, 13 February 1998, WT/DS26/AB/R, para. 117.

[136] Ibid. paras 117–18.

[137] R. Howse, 'The World Trade Organization 20 Years On: Global Governance by Judiciary' (2016) 27 EJIL 9–77, 44.

[138] A. Lang, 'The Judicial Sensibility of the WTO Appellate Body' (2016) 27 EJIL 1095–1105, 1097.

[139] *United States – Standards for Reformulated and Conventional Gasoline*, Appellate Body Report, 20 May 1996, WT/DS2/AB/R, 634.

[140] *EC – Measures Affecting Asbestos and Asbestos-Containing Products*, Appellate Body Report, 12 March 2001, WT/DS135/AB/R, para. 168.

[141] General Agreement on Tariffs and Trade 1994, 15 April 1994, Marrakesh Agreement Establishing the World Trade Organization, Annex 1A, 1867 UNTS 187, 33 ILM 1153 (1994).

[142] *European Communities – Measures Prohibiting the Importation and Marketing of Seal Products*, Appellate Body Report, 22 May 2014, WT/DS400/AB/R and WT/DS401/AB/R, paras 5.198–9.

[143] Lang, 'The Judicial Sensibility of the WTO Appellate Body', 1098.

US – Tuna II,[144] a dispute arising out of a labelling regime to promote dolphin conservation, the AB reaffirmed the ability of the United States to adopt such labelling scheme, but found against it, on the basis of 'an extremely fine-grained analysis' of regulatory means adopted. Analogously, in *US – Clove Cigarettes*,[145] a dispute arising out of tobacco control measure adopted by the United States, while the AB reaffirmed the importance of the state's ability to adopt tobacco control measures to protect public health, it found the measure discriminatory as it exempted domestically produced menthol cigarettes while it banned the trade of clove cigarettes produced in Indonesia. Again, in the *EC – Seal Products* case, the AB found the EU ban to be inconsistent with WTO law. The AB upheld the Panel's conclusion that the EU Seal Regime was inconsistent with Article I:1 of the GATT 1994 because it did not extend the same market access to Canadian and Norwegian seal products that it accorded to seal products originating from Greenland. If the AB held that the EU Seal Regime was 'necessary to protect public morals' under Article XX(a) of the GATT 1994, it nonetheless found that the EU had not demonstrated that the EU Seal Regime met the requirements of the *chapeau* of Article XX.

With regard to disputes concerning sanitary and phytosanitary measures, the SPS Agreement[146] also attempts to strike a balance between state sovereignty and the preservation of state regulatory autonomy on the one hand, and trade liberalization on the other.[147] While the SPS Agreement 'expressly recognizes the right of members to take SPS measures necessary for the protection of human, animal or plant life or health',[148] it subjects such measures to the requirements of necessity, sufficient scientific evidence and non-discrimination.[149] The Agreement also encourages regulatory harmonization[150] and explicitly includes scientific criteria for assessing the legality of regulatory measures. At the same time, the Appellate Body has clarified the standard of review that

---

144 *United States – Measures Concerning the Importation, Marketing and Sale of Tuna and Tuna Products*, Appellate Body Report, 13 June 2012, WT/DS381/AB/R.

145 *United States – Measures Affecting the Production and Sale of Clove Cigarettes*, Appellate Body Report, 24 April 2012, WT/DS406/AB/R.

146 Agreement on the Application of Sanitary and Phytosanitary Measures (SPS Agreement), entered into force on 1 January 1995, 1867 UNTS 493.

147 P. Van den Bossche and W. Zdouc, *The Law and Policy of the World Trade Organization* 4th edn (CUP 2017) 937.

148 Ibid. 945, SPS Agreement, Article 2.1.

149 Ibid. 945.

150 SPS Agreement, Article 3.

panels must apply. In particular, it held that panels should not assess the correctness of state risk assessments; rather, they should ascertain whether 'coherent reasoning and respectable scientific evidence' support that risk assessment and 'objectively justif[y]' it.[151]

In conclusion, in an attempt to strike the right balance between the competing demands of control and self-restraint, and between the 'economic benefits and political costs of [global] economic integration', the AB has adopted a compromise.[152] While it allows states 'to define and pursue almost any regulatory objective they see fit', it subjects the means chosen to pursue such ends to 'relatively strict international oversight'.[153] This type of objective assessment has raised some doubt as to whether the AB's formal deference to domestic policies has any relevance in practice.[154] The WTO 'courts' do not provide 'margins of appreciation'; rather they adopt a strict scrutiny regarding both factual and legal issues to provide 'security and predictability to the multilateral trading system' and 'preserve the rights and obligations of Members under the covered agreements'.[155]

Certainly, the AB has shown varying degrees of deference; it has been more deferential when reviewing measures relating to the protection of human life and health.[156] Instead, it has adopted 'a more intrusive standard ... when dealing with trade measures (like anti-dumping)'.[157] Oesch highlights that 'panels and the Appellate Body have in general applied intrusive standards of review', but have exercised some self-restraint by adopting 'deferential methods of interpretation'.[158] For instance, they have used the *in dubio mitius* technique of interpretation,

---

151 *US/Canada – Continued Suspension*, DS320, 321, AB Reports, 14 November 2008, para. 590.

152 Lang, 'The Judicial Sensibility of the WTO Appellate Body', 1103.

153 Ibid.

154 P. Mavroidis, 'The Gang that Couldn't Shoot Straight: The Not So Magnificent Seven of the WTO Appellate Body' (2017) 27 EJIL 1107–118, 1112.

155 DSU Article 3.2.

156 M.G. Bloche, 'WTO Deference to National Health Policy: Towards an Interpretive Principle' (2002) 5 JIEL 825–48 (identifying 'an emerging pattern of heightened deference to national authority when member states' health policies conflict with other values protected by trade agreements').

157 Mavroidis, 'The Gang that Couldn't Shoot Straight', 1107.

158 M. Oesch, 'Standards of Review in WTO Dispute Resolution' (2003) 6 JIEL 635–59, 635, 644.

interpreting state obligations restrictively.[159] They have also been more deferential when reviewing state factual conclusions.[160]

5.5 THE MARGIN OF APPRECIATION DOCTRINE

The margin of appreciation doctrine refers to the room for manoeuvre that international adjudicators are willing to accord states in fulfilling their obligations under given international law instruments. Such doctrine has become a key conceptual pillar in the legal architecture of the European Convention on Human Rights (ECHR).[161] While the margin of appreciation is generally considered to be a creation of the European Court of Human Rights (ECtHR), 'there is some dispute as to whether its ultimate origins lie in national or even international doctrines of deference'.[162] Some scholars consider it an emanation of domestic doctrines of deference, migrated to (European) human rights law from the domestic domain;[163] while others consider it to be an emanation of historical international law notions of deference, migrated to the regional realm from the international one.[164]

Whatever the historical origins of the notions, the ECtHR has used the margin of appreciation doctrine to balance the sovereignty of the

---

159 *European Communities – Measures Concerning Meat and Meat Products (EC–Hormones)*, WT/DS26/AB/R, WT/DS48/AB/R, 13 February 1998, para. 165 and fn 154 (considering *in dubio mitius* as a supplementary means of interpretation).

160 Oesch, 'Standards of Review in WTO Dispute Resolution', 658.

161 See generally A. Legg, *The Margin of Appreciation in International Human Rights Law* (OUP 2012); Y. Arai-Takahashi, *The Margin of Appreciation Doctrine and the Principle of Proportionality in the Jurisprudence of the ECHR* (Intersentia 2002).

162 Arato, 'The Margin of Appreciation in International Investment Law', 547.

163 Legg, *The Margin of Appreciation in International Human Rights Law*, 3; H.C. Yourow, *The Margin of Appreciation Doctrine in the Dynamics of European Human Rights Jurisprudence* (Martinus Nijhoff 1996) 14.

164 E. Bjorge, 'Been There, Done That: The Margin of Appreciation and International Law' (2015) 4 CJICL 181–90, 182 (contending that the margin of appreciation doctrine derives from 'the public international law of the early twentieth century') and 184–5 (discussing several factors pointing towards an international genealogy of the concept).

contracting states with the need to secure compliance with the Convention.[165] The margin of appreciation doctrine grants qualified deference to state conduct.[166] Such doctrine differs from the 'general discretion' left to states in how to comply with and implement treaty provisions in their domestic legal system.[167] It is a canon of 'judicial self-restraint'.[168]

On the one hand margin of appreciation secures some latitude for the host state to define and adopt public interest policies and balance public and private interests.[169] According to such doctrine, states maintain a space for manoeuvring in fulfilling their international law obligations and balancing public and private interests due to their social, cultural and historic features[170] and 'their direct and continuous contact with the vital forces of their countries'.[171] In particular, such doctrine allows states a margin of manoeuvre in determining what is in the general interest and how to pursue it, even if that means restricting individual entitlements.

On the other hand the margin of appreciation is a flexible judicial technique enabling the ECtHR to 'navigate a course through … competing considerations'.[172] As such, it has no fixed content. Rather, 'the breadth of [the] margin [of appreciation] varies and depends on a number of factors including the nature of the Convention right in issue, its importance for the individual, the nature of the interference and the

---

[165] Helfer and Slaughter, 'Toward a Theory of Effective Supranational Adjudication', 316–17.

[166] Of jurisprudential origin, the margin of appreciation doctrine has recently been codified. Once ratified by the states parties to the Convention, Protocol 15 will add a direct reference to the concepts of subsidiarity and the margin of appreciation in the preamble to the Convention.

[167] J.A. Sweeney, 'Margins of Appreciation: Cultural Relativity and the European Court of Human Rights in the Post-Cold War Era' (2005) 54 ICLQ 459–74, 462.

[168] D. McGoldrick, 'A Defence of the Margin of Appreciation and an Argument for Its Application by the Human Rights Committee' (2016) 65 ICLQ 21–60, 22.

[169] Sweeney, 'Margins of Appreciation', 462.

[170] E. Benvenisti, 'Margin of Appreciation, Consensus and Universal Standards' (1999) 31 *NYU JIL and Politics* 843–54, 843.

[171] *Handyside v. United Kingdom*, 7 December 1976, Series A No. 24, paras 48–9; *Wingrove v. United Kingdom* (1996) Reports of Judgments and Decisions, 1996-V, para. 58; *Hatton v. United Kingdom* (2003) 37 EHRR 611, 634 (holding that 'the national authorities have direct democratic legitimation and are … in principle better placed than an international court to evaluate local needs and conditions').

[172] Legg, *The Margin of Appreciation in International Human Rights Law*, 58.

object pursued by the interference'.[173] Therefore, the ECtHR 'gives states a wider or narrower space of deference depending on the Convention provision in question – taking into consideration the context and importance of the interests at stake'.[174] For instance, the Court has afforded member states a wide margin of appreciation in the context of 'public emergencies, national security, the protection of public morals, ... interference with private property',[175] 'economic crises', 'social policies' and 'environmental issues'.[176] This greater leeway seems to reflect the adage the safety of the people 'is to be the highest law' (*salus populi suprema lex esto*).[177] After all, '[the state's] first duty [is] to itself. Its own preservation [is] paramount'.[178] Instead, the Court has afforded states a narrow margin of appreciation 'where the right at stake is crucial to the individual's effective enjoyment of ... key rights'.[179] For instance, the Court has expanded its purview in disputes relating to individuals' private lives[180] or concerning the protected rights of historically vulnerable groups in society, such as minorities.[181] Finally, the Court has granted states no margin of appreciation with regard to non-derogable rights such as the rights to life, against torture, slavery and forced labour.[182]

The margin of appreciation has evolved through time. Not only has the court adjusted the margin of appreciation to the particular historical circumstances of states,[183] but it has calibrated it 'in view of a new consensus among the member states as to the meaning or scope of the

---

173 *S. and Marper v. United Kingdom* (2009) 48 EHHR 50, para. 102.

174 Arato, 'The Margin of Appreciation in International Investment Law', 568.

175 Ibid. 568–9.

176 Mcgoldrick, 'A Defence of the Margin of Appreciation', 25.

177 I. De la Rasilla del Moral, 'The Increasingly Marginal Appreciation of the Margin-of-Appreciation Doctrine' (2006) 7 *German LJ* 611–23, 619.

178 France–Venezuela Mixed Claims Commission, *French Company of Venezuelan Railroads Case* (*France v. Venezuela*), 31 July 1905 [1905] 10 RIAA 285, 353.

179 *S. and Marper v. United Kingdom*, para. 102.

180 Arato, 'The Margin of Appreciation in International Investment Law', 569.

181 Mcgoldrick, 'A Defence of the Margin of Appreciation', 25.

182 A. Follesdal, 'Building Democracy at the Bar: the European Court of Human Rights as an Agent of Transitional Cosmopolitanism' (2016) 7 *Transnational Legal Theory* 95–113, 105.

183 Mcgoldrick, 'A Defence of the Margin of Appreciation', 25 (noting that the ECtHR has afforded a wider margin of appreciation to transition economies).

right in question'.[184] In fact, the Court often combines the margin of appreciation with a comparative assessment.[185] When the Court finds that the practice of the majority of European states goes against a given restrictive measure, it narrows the margin of appreciation and widens the intensity of review. After scrutiny, it can oblige the states to abolish such measures.[186] Instead, where the Court finds that 'there is little common ground amongst the member states of the Council of Europe' and 'the law appears to be in a transitional stage', it leaves 'a wide margin of appreciation' to the authorities of each state.[187] In addition, the Court has also revisited the scope of the margin of appreciation in light of the emergence of 'external rules of international law relating to the particular issue'.[188]

The margin of appreciation doctrine has raised three main criticisms. First, some scholars contend that it can fragment the implementation of given treaty regimes, creating 'a variable geometry' of treaty implementation, diluting the power of 'existing jurisprudence and giving undue deference to local conditions, traditions and practices'.[189] For the same reason, the margin of appreciation would lead to an uneven application of international law.[190] Second, the margin of appreciation doctrine can jeopardize the very implementation of given regimes, diluting the power of international treaty obligations and strengthening 'perceptions of international law as non-law ... containing little, if any real constraints on state power'.[191] Similarly, the margin of appreciation would permit given political forces within a country to 'repress their own population'.[192] Third, critics 'fear that states will exploit their discretion under

---

184 Arato, 'The Margin of Appreciation in International Investment Law', 569.

185 Benvenisti, 'Margin of Appreciation, Consensus and Universal Standards', 851.

186 E. Brems, 'Accommodating Diversity in International Human Rights – Legal Techniques', in P. Meerts (ed.), *Culture and International Law* (Hague Academic Press 2008) 63–81, 68.

187 *Fretté v. France* (36515/97), 26 February 2002 [2002] ECHR 156, para. 41.

188 Ibid.

189 Sweeney, 'Margins of Appreciation', 462.

190 Shany, 'Toward a General Margin of Appreciation Doctrine in International Law?', 912 (reporting this criticism).

191 Ibid. (reporting this criticism).

192 Sweeney, 'Margins of Appreciation', 461 (reporting this criticism).

a margin of appreciation doctrine to evade their international responsibilities'.[193] Critics caution that there is a risk of conflating the margin of appreciation doctrine with 'a conservative view of public international law that affords greater respect to state sovereignty' than to individuals.[194] Scholars have noted that an intrinsic contradiction characterizes the margin of appreciation doctrine: on the one hand, it provides states 'a measure of discretion' about how to balance conflicting interests while implementing international obligations; on the other hand, 'the notion of obligation is precisely aimed to curtail the discretion of their addressees'.[195] Finally, critics claim that the ECtHR's use of the margin of appreciation lacks clarity, consistency and predictability.[196]

However, the application of the margin of appreciation doctrine by the ECtHR has also been praised on a number of grounds. First, according to some scholars, not only has the margin of appreciation doctrine not resulted in relativism 'or the lowering of Convention standards', but it has been 'a valuable tool for recognising and accommodating limited local variations within a nevertheless universal model of human rights'.[197] For instance, with regard to the interpretation and application of Article 1 of Protocol 1,[198] the Court has been 'mindful that a democratically elected government must be permitted to make and change policy without being, in effect, held to ransom by a small group of persons who have invested in reliance upon an earlier policy'.[199] As Brigitte Stern points out, 'the purpose of Article 1 of Protocol I is precisely to protect the individual against interference with her property

[193] Shany, 'Towards a General Margin of Appreciation Doctrine in International Law', 924 (reporting this criticism).

[194] Sweeney, 'Margins of Appreciation', 461 (reporting this criticism).

[195] Cannizzaro, 'Proportionality and Margin of Appreciation in the Whaling Case', 1064.

[196] Mcgoldrick, 'A Defence of the Margin of Appreciation', 38 (reporting this criticism).

[197] Sweeney, 'Margins of Appreciation', 474.

[198] Protocol to the Convention for the Protection of Human Rights and Fundamental Freedoms, 20 March 1952, 213 UNTS 263, Article 1 ('Protection of Property').

[199] H. Mountfield, 'Regulatory Expropriations in Europe: The Approach of the European Court of Human Rights' (2002) 11 *NYU Environmental LJ* 136–46, 146.

beyond what the Protocol considers necessary for the satisfaction of the common good in the European democratic framework'.[200]

Second, far from constituting an 'instrument of surrender or abdication', diluting the legal character of international law, the margin of appreciation doctrine has been 'an instrument of supervision'.[201] As the ECtHR is an 'international court', judicial self-restraint reflects subsidiarity (that is, states have the primary responsibility to comply with and implement their treaty obligations),[202] and the 'comparative institutional advantage' of domestic authorities to further compliance with international law within the society in question.[203] Therefore, the doctrine grants qualified deference to governmental regulations and reduces the risk of the Court second guessing democratic authorities.[204]

Third, by fostering 'comity' among state actors and international courts, the margin of appreciation promotes compliance with international law, adopting a gradual approach and boosting the internalization of international norms and values.[205] Moreover, while the Court gives states a wide margin of appreciation to determine the public interest, it uses a proportionality test to assess whether 'a fair balance was struck between the demands of the general interest of the community and the requirements of the protection of the individual's fundamental rights'.[206] In parallel, if the margin of appreciation does not lead to a uniform application of international law, it acknowledges cultural, political and economic divergences among societies and 'leav[es] space for reasonable disagreement, legitimate differences, and ... cultural diversity'.[207] In other words, the margin of appreciation doctrine promotes 'the

---

[200] B. Stern, 'Le droit de propriété, l'expropriation et la nationalisation dans la Convention européenne des droits de l'homme' (1991) 17 *Droit et pratique du commerce international* 394–403, 403 (my translation).

[201] Mcgoldrick, 'A Defence of the Margin of Appreciation', 25.

[202] See e.g. *Buckley v. United Kingdom* (1997) 23 EHRR 101, para. 75 (noting that '[i]t is not for the Court to substitute its own view of what would be the best policy in the planning sphere or the most appropriate individual measure in planning cases').

[203] Mcgoldrick, 'A Defence of the Margin of Appreciation', 32–4.

[204] Orellana, 'Science, Risk and Uncertainty', 675.

[205] Shany, 'Toward a General Margin of Appreciation Doctrine in International Law?', 922.

[206] *Sporrong and Lönroth v. Sweden*, Judgment, 23 September 1982 [1982] ECHR 52, para. 69.

[207] Mcgoldrick, 'A Defence of the Margin of Appreciation', 36–7.

rich cultural, political, and legal diversity across the parties to the Convention'.[208]

In conclusion, as a fluid, flexible and dynamic tool, the margin of appreciation doctrine has enabled the ECtHR to interpret the ECHR in light of the political, social and cultural circumstances of greater Europe and beyond.[209] It expresses deference, subsidiarity, and the idea that states 'are the primary guardians of human rights in Europe'.[210] It also endorses a commitment to the cultural diversity of the member states.[211] As noted by Ratner, 'the Court is perceived as legitimate because of its long history of advancing human rights ... , while respecting state interests through incrementalism, subsidiarity, and the margin of appreciation'.[212]

5.5.1 What Role for the Margin of Appreciation Doctrine in International Law?

The extent of the migration of the margin of appreciation doctrine from European human rights law to public international law in general, and international investment law and arbitration in particular, remains uncertain. While the doctrine has migrated to other human rights systems, including the Inter-American one,[213] it has 'an uncertain status' within the jurisprudence of the ICJ.[214]

While references to the margin of appreciation appeared in early international law cases,[215] more recently, the ICJ has gradually abandoned 'its deferential approach from earlier decades, preferring instead an objective approach'.[216] Nowadays, the Court adopts a cautious if not 'sceptical' stance towards the margin of appreciation doctrine.[217] For

208 Arato, 'The Margin of Appreciation in International Investment Law', 567.

209 Ibid. 570.

210 Ibid.

211 Ibid.

212 S.R. Ratner, 'Regulatory Takings in Institutional Context: Beyond the Fear of Fragmented International Law' (2008) 102 AJIL 475–528, 500.

213 Mcgoldrick, 'A Defence of the Margin of Appreciation', 21.

214 Tully, 'Objective Reasonableness as a Standard for International Judicial Review', 550.

215 Bjorge, 'Been There, Done That', 186.

216 Ibid. 188.

217 Shany, 'Towards a General Margin of Appreciation Doctrine in International Law', 909.

instance, in the *Oil Platform* case,[218] a dispute 'aris[ing] out of the attack [on] and destruction of three offshore oil production complexes ... by several warships of the United States Navy',[219] the Court stated that 'the requirement of international law that measures taken avowedly in self-defence must have been necessary for that purpose is strict and objective, leaving no room for any measure of discretion'.[220]

More recently, in the *Whaling in the Antarctic* case,[221] in which the ICJ assessed the legality of a whaling programme allegedly designed to pursue purposes of scientific research, the Court rejected the defendant's argument that states parties to the Whaling Convention[222] had a margin of appreciation to determine the scope of the scientific research exception.[223] Rather, the Court examined whether 'the programme's design and implementation [were] reasonable in relation to achieving its stated objectives' and added that the standard of review was an 'objective' one.[224] Whether the margin of appreciation has 'a great future behind it' or whether it can contribute to the development of international law jurisprudence remains to be seen.[225]

Therefore, the ECtHR and the ICJ adopt different tools to balance deference and control in international dispute settlement. While the ECtHR couples the deferential margin of appreciation doctrine with proportionality, which is an intensive ground for review, the ICJ does not use such a deferential standard of review, but an objective one, and combines such objective test with reasonableness, which is a more lenient ground for review than proportionality.

With regard to the desirability of the margin of appreciation doctrine in international adjudication, the doctrine is divided. Some scholars suggest that the margin of appreciation doctrine should become a common feature of international adjudication in general,[226] and investment arbitration in particular. The key merits of the margin of appreciation doctrine

---

218 *Case Concerning Oil Platforms* (*Islamic Republic of Iran v. United States of America*) Judgment, 6 November 2003 [2003] ICJ Reports 161.

219 Ibid. paras 1–20.

220 Ibid. para. 73.

221 *Whaling in the Antarctic* (*Australia v. Japan*) Judgment, 31 March 2014 [2014] ICJ Reports 226.

222 International Convention for the Regulation of Whaling, 2 December 1946, in force 10 November 1948, 161 UNTS 72.

223 *Whaling in the Antarctic*, paras 59–60.

224 Ibid. para. 67.

225 Bjorge, 'Been There, Done That', 190.

226 Shany, 'Towards a General Margin of Appreciation Doctrine in International Law', 908 (supporting 'the development of a general margin of

lie in the fact that it enables a 'flexible reading of international law', thus potentially fostering compliance.[227] The margin of appreciation doctrine would be suitable to 'fact-intensive' decisions.[228] Far from advocating a total deference, Shany suggests that adjudicators can accord states 'wider or narrower margins as appropriate'.[229] Other scholars remain cautious.[230] The countries adhering to the European human rights system 'share a common core of social, political, and legal values that ... [are] linked to the effectiveness of the [ECtHR]'.[231] Yet, this factor does not apply to the international community.[232]

5.5.2 The Margin of Appreciation Doctrine in Investment Arbitration

If the margin of appreciation doctrine has been successful in the European human rights system, can it successfully migrate to international investment arbitration? In order to address this question, this section briefly examines the theoretical debate on the promises and pitfalls of such migration, and then scrutinizes and critically assesses the relevant arbitral practice. It highlights that arbitrators rarely rely on the margin of appreciation doctrine in investment arbitration, with varying results.

Given some structural similarities between investment treaty arbitration and human rights adjudication, some scholars have argued that the doctrine of the margin of appreciation can/should migrate to international

---

appreciation doctrine in relation to *some* categories of international law norms governing state conduct').

[227] Ibid. 912.

[228] Ibid.

[229] Ibid.

[230] Bjorge, 'Been There, Done That', 181 (arguing that '[t]he margin of appreciation is, in international law, an aberration'); Arato, 'The Margin of Appreciation in International Investment Law', 547; Kassi D. Tallent, 'The Tractor in the Jungle: Why Investment Arbitration Tribunals Should Reject a Margin of Appreciation Doctrine', in I.A. Laird and T. Weiler (eds), *Investment Treaty Arbitration and International Law* – Vol. 3 (Juris 2010) 124–8 (arguing that 'the margin of appreciation doctrine is, as a general matter, not appropriate for application in the investment arbitration context').

[231] Helfer and Slaughter, 'Toward a Theory of Effective Supranational Adjudication', 276.

[232] Ibid. 277.

investment law and arbitration.[233] At the substantive level, human rights law and international investment law provide for similar standards of protection.[234] Certain human rights standards broadly correspond to given investment law standards.[235] At the procedural level, both international investment law and European human rights law enable individuals to file direct claims against states before an international court/tribunal over the alleged breach of treaty provisions.[236]

However, the regimes retain a number of differences. The European human rights system has a foundational instrument, the ECHR, and a standing Court, the ECtHR, which interprets a single convention among a relatively cohesive number of countries. The margin of appreciation doctrine works well in the context of European human rights adjudication because the ECtHR has developed a remarkable jurisprudence over the course of decades.[237] By contrast, international investment law is a fragmented system that relies on thousands of IIAs. Arbitral tribunals are constituted on a one-off basis and interpret a variety of treaties between different states parties. In investment arbitration, the development of a relatively coherent jurisprudence is still a work in progress. Finally, the ECtHR and arbitral tribunals operate in different geopolitical contexts.

Such key differences explain both the margin's success in the regional field and its marginalization in international investment arbitration.[238]

---

[233] Burke-White and von Staden, 'Private Litigation in a Public Law Sphere', 286 (arguing that 'the most appropriate standard for the resolution of public law arbitrations is the "margin of appreciation" standard as developed by the European Court of Human Rights (ECtHR) and increasingly adopted by other tribunals'); B. Choudhury, 'Recapturing Public Power: Is Investment Arbitration's Engagement of the Public Interest Contributing to the Democratic Deficit?' (2008) 41 VJTL 775–832, 827 (arguing that '[o]verall, use of the margin-of-appreciation doctrine on a case-by-case basis allows for the inclusion of public interest issues into investment treaties').

[234] Vadi, *Analogies in International Investment Law and Arbitration*, 218.

[235] Ibid. (noting the following binary standards: the prohibition of 'denial of justice and the right of a fair trial; full protection and certain aspects of the rights to privacy, liberty and life; [prohibition of unlawful] expropriation and the right to property; fair and equitable treatment and due process; non-discrimination and the right to equality').

[236] Ibid.

[237] Arato, 'The Margin of Appreciation in International Investment Law', 566.

[238] Ibid. 550. See also *Philip Morris Brands Sàrl, Philip Morris Products SA and Abal Hermanos SA v. Oriental Republic of Uruguay*, ICSID Case No. ARB/10/7, Concurring and Dissenting Opinion, Arbitrator Gary Born, 28 June

The doctrine works well in Europe because it builds upon the 'European common heritage of political traditions, ideals, freedom and the rule of law'.[239] By contrast, at the international level there is no such underlying uniformity. Moreover, in investor–state arbitration, the concept of the margin of appreciation can be counterproductive because it may 'creat[e] only an illusion of consistency' while underpinning very different approaches to the question of the appropriate standards of review.[240] The aims, objectives and institutional features of the ECtHR differ from those of arbitral tribunals. This does not mean that the jurisprudence of the Court is irrelevant to the evolution of international law, but that any cross-pollination must consider these historical, institutional and teleological differences.[241]

In investment arbitration, only recently have arbitral tribunals referred to the margin of appreciation doctrine, reaching diverging conclusions on its applicability to the field. Some tribunals have declined to apply the margin of appreciation doctrine to investment arbitration. For instance, in *Quasar de Valores SICAV SA and others v. Russia*,[242] a dispute brought in relation to the shares held by four Spanish investors in the Yukos oil company, the Tribunal held that the 'reliability' of an investment treaty should not be 'diluted' by the margin of appreciation commonly accorded to states in international human rights cases.[243] Analogously, in the *Siemens* arbitration,[244] a dispute arising out of the Argentine government's suspension and subsequent termination of a contract to establish a system of migration control and personal identification, the Tribunal declined to apply the margin of appreciation doctrine. In particular, it noted that 'Article I of the First Protocol to the European Convention on

2016, para. 185 (arguing that 'the margin of appreciation used by the ECtHR reflects 'a specific geographic and historical context', and 'the reasons that led to acceptance of the margin of appreciation in the context of the ECHR are not necessarily transferable to other contexts').

239 ECHR, preamble.

240 Arato, 'The Margin of Appreciation in International Investment Law', 552.

241 Ratner, 'Regulatory Takings in Institutional Context', 501; De la Rasilla del Moral, 'The Increasingly Marginal Appreciation of the Margin-of-Appreciation Doctrine', 623.

242 *Quasar de Valores SICAV SA and others v. Russian Federation*, Award, 20 July 2012, Arbitration Institute of the Stockholm Chamber of Commerce.

243 Ibid. para. 22.

244 *Siemens AG v. Argentine Republic*, ICSID Case No. ARB/02/8, Award, 6 February 2007.

Human Rights permits a margin of appreciation not found in customary international law or the [Germany–Argentina Bilateral Investment] Treaty'.[245]

In *Chemtura v. Canada*,[246] a dispute arising out of a ban of a chemical product, the Tribunal addressed the question as to whether the protection granted under the fair and equitable treatment standard is lessened by a margin of appreciation granted to domestic regulatory agencies and, if so, to what extent.[247] The Tribunal rejected the applicability of such doctrine, holding that:

> [i]n assessing whether the treatment afforded to the Claimant's investment was in accordance with the international minimum standard, the Tribunal must take into account all the circumstances ... This is not an abstract assessment circumscribed by a legal doctrine about the margin of appreciation of specialized regulatory agencies. It is an assessment that must be conducted in concreto.[248]

While the Tribunal did not apply the margin of appreciation doctrine as a formal criterion of deference in investor–state arbitration, it nonetheless exercised some qualified self-restraint when reviewing state conduct. In particular, it noted that 'it [was] not its task to determine whether certain uses of lindane are dangerous' and that it was not its role 'to second-guess the correctness of the science-based decision-making of highly specialized national regulatory agencies'.[249]

Perhaps the *Von Pezold* Tribunal provided the most explicit rejection of the margin of appreciation doctrine in international investment arbitration. In *Von Pezold v. Zimbabwe*,[250] a dispute arising out of a state's seizure of a number of farms without compensation, the Tribunal reasoned that:

> due caution should be exercised in importing concepts from other legal regimes (in this case European human rights law) without a solid basis for doing so. Balancing competing (and non-absolute) human rights and the need to grant States a margin of appreciation when making those balancing

[245] Ibid. para. 354.

[246] *Chemtura Corporation v. Government of Canada*, UNCITRAL, Award, 2 August 2010.

[247] Ibid. para. 123.

[248] Ibid.

[249] Ibid. para. 134.

[250] *Bernhard von Pezold and others v. Republic of Zimbabwe*, ICSID Case No. ARB/10/15, Award, 28 July 2015.

> decisions is well established in human rights law, but the Tribunal is not aware that the concept has found much support in international investment law.[251]

The Tribunal noted that 'there [was] no margin of appreciation qualification within the BITs at issue' and that 'the margin of appreciation doctrine has not achieved customary status'.[252] 'In any case', the Tribunal added, the margin of appreciation doctrine cannot justify unlawful conduct, 'such as a breach of an obligation *erga omnes*.'[253]

Yet, other tribunals have used the margin of appreciation doctrine in public policy-related investment disputes. For instance, in *Philip Morris v. Uruguay*,[254] a case concerning tobacco control measures, the Tribunal rejected all of the claimants' claims for breach of the Switzerland–Uruguay BIT, in relation to a regulation requiring that health warnings comprise 80 per cent of cigarette packaging, and that corporations adopt one single variant of their brand. The Tribunal found plain packaging to be a reasonable measure in light of the margin of appreciation due to states' public policy measures.[255]

Similarly, in *Frontier Petroleum Services Ltd v. Czech Republic*, a dispute concerning the refusal by the host state's judiciary to enforce a commercial arbitral award, the Tribunal used the margin of appreciation doctrine when scrutinizing the Czech courts' conduct.[256] Frontier, a Canadian company, had made an investment in the Czech aircraft production through a joint venture with a local company.[257] When a

---

[251] Ibid. para. 465.

[252] Ibid. para. 466.

[253] Ibid. para. 467.

[254] *Philip Morris Brands Sàrl, Philip Morris Products SA and Abal Hermanos SA v. Oriental Republic of Uruguay*, ICSID Case No. ARB/10/7, Award, 8 July 2016.

[255] Ibid. para. 85 (applying 'a margin of appreciation, derived from ECtHR decisions', and concluding that 'the single presentation requirement was an attempt to address a real public health concern, that the measure taken was not disproportionate to that concern and that it was adopted in good faith) and para. 399 (holding that 'the margin of appreciation is not limited to the context of the ECHR but applies equally to claims arising under BITs, at least in contexts such as public health. The responsibility for public health measures rests with the government and investment tribunals should pay great deference to governmental judgments of national needs in matters such as the protection of public health').

[256] *Frontier Petroleum Services Ltd v. Czech Republic*, UNCITRAL, Final Award, 12 November 2010.

[257] Ibid. para. 26.

dispute arose between Frontier and the Czech company, Frontier commenced and won a commercial arbitration. However, when it sought to enforce the award in the Czech Republic under the New York Convention,[258] the local courts refused enforcement as a matter of public policy, due to the local company's bankruptcy and the need to ensure equality among creditors.[259] Frontier then filed an investment treaty arbitration, claiming that the local courts' refusal to enforce the award amounted to a breach of the fair and equitable treatment standard.[260] The Tribunal stated that states enjoy 'a certain margin of appreciation in determining what their own conception of international public policy is'.[261] It then addressed the question as to whether the local courts' interpretation of the public policy exception under the New York Convention was 'reasonably tenable and made in good faith'.[262] The Tribunal concluded that there was no violation of the fair and equitable treatment standard.

Arbitral tribunals have granted some margin of appreciation to host states for adopting policy measures in times of national emergency. For instance, in *Continental Casualty v. Argentina*,[263] one of the several arbitrations arising out of the Argentine financial crisis, the Tribunal held that states should be granted a 'significant' margin of appreciation when it comes to adopting policy measures in times of national emergency.[264] According to the Tribunal, the margin of appreciation should be viewed as 'a general feature of international law'.[265] For the Tribunal, 'a time of grave crisis is not the time for nice judgments, particularly when examined by others'.[266]

---

[258] United Nations Convention on the Recognition and Enforcement of Foreign Arbitral Awards, 10 June 1958, 330 UNTS 3.

[259] *Frontier v. Czech Republic*, Final Award, para. 29.

[260] Ibid. para. 525.

[261] Ibid. para. 527.

[262] Ibid. para. 527.

[263] *Continental Casualty Co v. Argentine Republic*, ICSID Case No. ARB/03/9, Award, 5 September 2008.

[264] Ibid. para. 181.

[265] Ibid. (holding that '[a] certain deference to such a discretion when the application of general standards in a specific factual situation is at issue, such as reasonable, necessary, fair and equitable, may well be by now a general feature of international law also in respect of the protection of foreign investors under BITs').

[266] Ibid. para. 181.

Analogously, in *Electrabel SA v. Hungary*,[267] the Arbitral Tribunal granted the host state with some margin of appreciation in its compliance with EU law. The facts of the case are as follows. After its accession to the EU, Hungary ceased subsidizing a domestic company, in which Electrabel had invested, in an effort to harmonize Hungarian law with EU law and comply with a decision of the European Commission.[268] Electrabel argued that Hungary should have challenged the Commission's decision, and that by failing to do so, it violated its obligations under the Energy Charter Treaty. The Tribunal rejected the claim, holding that 'Hungary was entitled to a modest margin of appreciation in arriving at its own discretionary decision in regard to such proceedings [under EU law], without thereby committing a breach of the [Energy Charter Treaty's] FET standard'.[269] More interestingly, the Tribunal also used the margin of appreciation doctrine in assessing Hungary's regulation of electricity prices. In particular, it held that the host state enjoyed 'a reasonable margin of appreciation' in regulatory pricing 'before being held to account under the [Energy Charter Treaty's] standards of protection'.[270]

In other arbitrations, arbitral tribunals have afforded the respondent states a margin of appreciation in the exercise of their police powers. For instance, in *Micula v. Romania*,[271] a dispute arising out of the withdrawal of an investment incentive programme due to Romania's then recently acquired membership to the EU, the Tribunal used the margin of appreciation doctrine in ascertaining the nationality of the claimant. The Tribunal held that 'the State conferring nationality must be given a "margin of appreciation" in deciding upon the factors that it considers necessary for the granting of nationality'.[272] In *Saluka v. Czech Republic*,[273] a dispute arising out of events immediately after the privatization of the Czech banking sector, the Tribunal held that the state 'enjoyed a margin of discretion in the exercise of [the] responsibility' of regulating

---

[267] *Electrabel SA v. Republic of Hungary*, ICSID Case No. ARB/07/19, Decision on Jurisdiction, Applicable Law and Liability, 30 November 2012.

[268] Ibid. para. 2.24.

[269] Ibid. para. 6.92.

[270] Ibid. para. 8.35.

[271] *Micula v. Romania*, ICSID Case No. ARB/05/20, Decision on Jurisdiction and Admissibility, 24 September 2008.

[272] Ibid. para. 94.

[273] *Saluka Investments BV v. The Czech Republic*, UNCITRAL/PCA, Partial Award, 17 March 2006.

the bank sector.[274] In *Gemplus SA and Talsud SA v. United Mexican States*,[275] arising out of Mexico's effort to create a national vehicle registry to prevent car theft and organized crime, the Tribunal accorded the state 'a generous measure of appreciation'.[276] The Tribunal 'accept[ed] the Respondent's submissions to the effect that [the] Tribunal should not ... second-guess government decision-making'.[277]

In conclusion, the margin of appreciation is an emerging line of argument by respondent states in investment arbitrations. It draws upon the deference that certain other international courts, such as the ECtHR, accord to governments when ascertaining their compliance with their international obligations. However – at least to date – the margin-of-appreciation doctrine remains an outsider in investment arbitration. It remains to be seen whether these migratory patterns will become more consistent, and be proven by history to be ahead of their time.

5.6 STANDARDS OF REVIEW IN INTERNATIONAL INVESTMENT ARBITRATION

The concept of standards of review is arguably far less developed and consistent in international investment law and arbitration as compared to other areas of public international law.[278] The current state of the art is

---

274 Ibid. para. 272.

275 *Gemplus SA and Talsud SA v. United Mexican States*, ICSID Case Nos ARB(AF)/04/3 and ARB(AF)/04/4, Award, 16 June 2010.

276 Ibid. para. 6.26.

277 Ibid.

278 Only recently has the literature started focusing on standards of review in international investment law and arbitration. See e.g. C. Henckels, 'The Role of the Standard of Review and the Importance of Deference in Investor–State Arbitration', in Gruszczynski and Werner (eds), *Deference in International Courts and Tribunals* 113–34; E.M. Leonhardsen, 'Treaty Change, Arbitral Practice and the Search for Balance: Standards of Review and the Margin of Appreciation in International Investment Law', in Gruszczynski and Werner (eds), *Deference in International Courts and Tribunals*, 135–51; Vadi and Gruszczynski, 'Standards of Review in International Investment Law and Arbitration' 613–33; L. Gruszczynski and V. Vadi, 'Standard of Review and Scientific Evidence in WTO Law and International Investment Arbitration: Converging Parallels?', in Gruszczynski and Werner (eds), *Deference in International Courts and Tribunals*, 152–72; Roberts, 'The Next Battleground: Standards of Review in Investment Treaty Arbitration', 170; Burke-White and von Staden, 'Private Litigation in a Public Law Sphere' 283; Burke-White and von Staden, 'The Need for Public Law Standards of Review in Investor–State Arbitrations', 689–720;

due to a number of factors. First, IIAs generally do not refer to the standards of review. This seems to be a common feature of public international law instruments, with treaties very rarely setting the required level of scrutiny.[279] Typically, it is for international courts to develop such standards. Second, the boom of investment arbitrations is relatively recent, while the jurisprudence of other branches of public international law has a more settled character. Therefore, the jurisprudence developed by arbitral tribunals under IIAs is novel and quantitatively more limited than the jurisprudence developed by other international jurisdictions. Third, arbitral tribunals are constituted on a one-off basis and apply different IIAs. Not only is there no binding precedent in international investment law, but there is no general appeal mechanism within international investment arbitration to ensure the development of a consistent jurisprudence. Therefore, different arbitral tribunals may adopt different standards of review. Finally, different constituencies make up the arbitral community. This includes not only international lawyers but also trade law experts and even public law scholars and commercial lawyers.[280] Therefore, they may approach the issue of the standards of review from different perspectives.

Arbitral tribunals have adopted different standards of review. As Schill highlights, 'arbitral jurisprudence is unsettled on how to conceptualize deference, on what degree of deference to accord when reviewing host state conduct, and on the factors that should influence the appropriate standard of review'.[281] Some arbitral tribunals have shown a low degree of deference, finding liability with regard to host state measures taken in

---

R. Moloo and J.M. Jacinto, 'Standards of Review and Reviewing Standards: Public Interest Regulation in International Investment Law' (2011:2012) *Yearbook of International Investment Law and Policy* 539–67.

[279] But see Agreement on Implementation of Article VI of the General Agreement on Tariffs and Trade 1994 (Anti-Dumping Agreement), 15 April 1994, Marrakesh Agreement Establishing the World Trade Organization, Annex 1A, 1868 UNTS 201, 33 ILM 1125 (1994).

[280] See S. Schill, 'W(h)ither Fragmentation? On the Literature and Sociology of International Investment Law' (2011) 22 EJIL 875–908.

[281] S.W. Schill, 'Deference in Investment Treaty Arbitration: Reconceptualizing the Standard of Review through Comparative Public Law', SIEL Working Paper No. 33/2012, 9.

the public interest.[282] Other tribunals have shown a higher degree of self-restraint, according qualified deference to state conduct with regard to public policy-related disputes.[283]

For instance, in *Glamis Gold v. United States*,[284] a dispute arising out of the requirement of backfilling after mining, the Tribunal declined to adopt the formal criteria of deference, while exercising some self-restraint. The respondent argued that 'in reviewing State agency or departmental decisions and actions, international tribunals as well as domestic judiciaries favor deference to the agency so as not to second guess the primary decision-makers or become "science courts"'.[285] The Tribunal disagreed 'that domestic deference in national court systems is necessarily applicable to international tribunals'. Instead, it found that the standard of deference was already 'present in the [fair and equitable treatment (FET)] standard as stated, rather than being additive to that standard'.[286] Nonetheless, the Tribunal acknowledged that '[i]t is not the role of this Tribunal or any international tribunal, to supplant its own judgment of underlying factual material and support for that of qualified domestic agency'.[287] Rather, the Tribunal held that 'the sole inquiry for the tribunal ... is whether or not there was a manifest lack of reasons for the legislation'.[288] It also acknowledged that 'governments must compromise between the interests of competing parties and, if they were bound to please every constituent ... with each piece of legislation, they would be bound and useless'.[289] Analogously, in *Lemire v. Ukraine*, the Tribunal noted that a breach of a treaty provision does not occur where a national authority 'makes a decision which is different from the one the arbitrators would have made if they were the regulators. The arbitrators are not

---

282 See generally the long stream of investment arbitrations against Argentina relating to the measures the host state had adopted vis-à-vis the economic crisis of 2001–2002. Burke-White and von Staden, 'Private Litigation in a Public Law Sphere', 297–301.

283 See e.g. *Frontier Petroleum Service Ltd v. Czech Republic*, UNCITRAL, Final Award, 12 November 2010, para. 527.

284 *Glamis Gold Ltd v. United States of America*, ICSID Award, 8 June 2009.

285 Ibid. para. 617.

286 Ibid. (emphasizing that 'The idea of deference is found in the modifiers "manifest" and "gross" that make this standard a stringent one; it is found in the idea that a breach requires something greater than mere arbitrariness, something that is surprising, shocking, or exhibits a manifest lack of reasoning').

287 Ibid. para. 779.

288 Ibid. para. 805.

289 Ibid. para. 803.

superior regulators; they do not substitute their judgment for that of national bodies applying national laws'.[290]

Instead, other tribunals have explicitly endorsed notions of deference. For instance, in *Myers v. Canada*,[291] a dispute arising out of Canada's ban on the export of PCB wastes from Canada to the United States, and alleged economic harm to the investor, the Tribunal rejected the claim that such ban on the export of PCB constituted an expropriation because the ban was temporary and there was no transfer of benefits to the host state. The Tribunal affirmed that 'regulatory conduct by public authorities is unlikely to be the subject of legitimate complaint under Article 1110 of NAFTA, although the tribunal does not rule out that possibility'.[292] The Tribunal also held that it was not its task to second-guess the regulatory autonomy of the host state: 'When interpreting and applying the 'minimum standard', arbitral tribunals 'do not have an open-ended mandate to second-guess government decision-making' as 'governments have to make many potentially controversial choices'.[293] The Tribunal also held that a determination that Canada had breached the fair and equitable treatment standard 'must be made in the light of the high measure of deference that international law generally extends to the right of domestic authorities to regulate matters within their own borders'.[294] In fact, the Tribunal noted that:

> [If states] appear to have made mistakes, to have misjudged the facts, proceeded on the basis of a misguided economic or sociological theory, placed too much emphasis on some social values over others and adopted solutions that are ultimately ineffective or counterproductive, [t]he ordinary remedy, if there were one, for [such] errors … is through internal political and legal processes, including elections.[295]

At the same time, arbitral tribunals, like other international tribunals, scrutinize the given national measures and their compliance with the host state international investment law obligations. For example, in *Tza Yap*

---

290 *Joseph Charles Lemire v. Ukraine*, ICSID Case No. ARB/06/18, Decision on Jurisdiction and Liability, 14 January 2010, para. 283.

291 *SD Myers Inc v. Canada*, UNCITRAL/NAFTA, Partial Award, 13 November 2000.

292 Ibid. para. 281.

293 Ibid. para. 261.

294 Ibid. para. 263.

295 *SD Myers Inc v. Government of Canada*, Partial Award, para. 261.

Shum v. Republic of Peru,[296] a dispute arising out of the seizure of the bank account of claimant's due to tax debt, the Tribunal, following the *Myers* Tribunal, held that international law gives a high level of deference to public authorities in the regulation of matters within their jurisdiction.[297] However, the Tribunal also added that such deference is not unlimited. Even when states pursue a legitimate public interest, the Tribunal noted, they are not exempt from liability and must pay compensation if their conduct is arbitrary or discriminatory.[298] Even though the Tribunal acknowledged that 'the regulatory authority of the State deserves deferential treatment', it held that 'it is essential to do so without losing sight of the reasons why such deference is accorded'.[299] Therefore, arbitral tribunals should not pay total deference to national measures, simply accepting the determinations of the relevant national authorities as final.

Analogously, in *Marion Unglaube v. Costa Rica*, the Arbitral Tribunal held that:

> [w]here ... a valid public policy does exist, and especially where the action or decision taken relates to the State's responsibility for the protection of public health, safety, morals or welfare, as well as other functions related to taxation and police powers of states, such measures are accorded a considerable measure of deference in recognition of the right of domestic authorities to regulate matters within their borders.[300]

The Tribunal added that '[t]his deference, however, is not without limits. Even if such measures are taken for an important public purpose, governments are required to use due diligence in the protection of foreigners and will not be excused from liability if their action has been arbitrary or discriminatory'.[301]

Rather, arbitral tribunals must objectively assess whether the competent authorities complied with their international investment law obligations. Such review 'must be conducted *in concreto*',[302] considering 'all the [relevant] circumstances', including 'the fact that certain agencies

---

[296] *Tza Yap Shum v. Republic of Peru*, ICSID Case No. ARB/07/6, Award, 7 July 2011.

[297] Ibid. para. 147.

[298] Ibid. para. 148.

[299] Ibid. para. 196.

[300] *Marion Unglaube v. Republic of Costa Rica*, ICSID Case No. ARB/08/1, Award, 16 May 2012, para. 246.

[301] Ibid. para. 247.

[302] *Chemtura v. Canada*, Award, para. 98.

manage highly specialized domains involving scientific and public policy determinations'.[303] For instance, in *Tecmed v. Mexico*, a case concerning the operation of a hazardous waste landfill, the Tribunal held that 'the analysis starts at the due deference owing to the State when defining the issues that affect its public policy or the interests of society as a whole'.[304] Nonetheless, the Tribunal specified that such deference 'does not prevent the Arbitral Tribunal … from examining … whether such measures are reasonable with respect to their goals, the deprivation of economic rights and the legitimate expectations of who suffered such deprivation'.[305]

In this respect, the evaluation of the evidence will be crucial for determining whether the host country has met its obligations under the relative IIA.[306] Therefore, respondent states will have to show that their regulations aim at achieving legitimate public goals and that they follow due process of law. As one Arbitral Tribunal held: '[the] "public interest" requires some genuine interest of the public. If mere reference to "public interest" can magically [create] such interest … and therefore satisfy this requirement, then such requirement would be rendered meaningless since the Tribunal can imagine no situation where this requirement would not have been met'.[307]

For example, in the *Chemtura* case, the Tribunal investigated whether state authorities reviewed an insecticide in good faith or whether such review breached the due process rights of the claimant.[308] In the Tribunal's view, 'the evidence of the record [did] not show bad faith or disingenuous conduct on the part of Canada'.[309] Rather, such evidence showed that the federal agency responsible for the regulation of pest control products in Canada reviewed the product 'in pursuance of its mandate and as a result of Canada's *international obligations*'.[310] Canada

303 Ibid. para. 123.

304 *Tecnicas Medioambientales Tecmed SA v. The United Mexican States*, ICSID Case No. ARB(AF)/00/2, Award, 29 May 2003, para. 122.

305 Ibid.

306 PCIJ, *German Interests in the Upper Silesia* (*Germany v. Poland*) (Merits) Judgment, 25 May 1926, [1926] PCIJ Rep Series A No. 7, 19.

307 *ADC Affiliate Ltd and ADC & ADMC Management Ltd v. Republic of Hungary*, ICSID Case ARB/03/16, Award, 2 October 2006, para. 432.

308 Ibid. para. 145.

309 Ibid. para. 138.

310 Ibid. para. 138 (emphasis added).

'amply established the existence of [environmental and health] concerns' by discussing relevant international health law instruments.[311]

Even with regard to jurisdictional matters, arbitral tribunals have tended to adopt an objective assessment. For instance, in *PNG v. Papua New Guinea*,[312] a case arising out of an alleged investment in a copper mine, the respondent submitted that in cases of jurisdictional doubt, international tribunals should decline to hear a dispute out of deference to state sovereignty and that there should be a presumption against jurisdiction. The claimant, however, counter-argued that this conception was 'truly a relic of a bygone age'.[313] The Tribunal adopted 'a neutral, objective approach towards jurisdictional objections, without preconceived preferences in one direction or the other'.[314] The Tribunal endorsed the claimant's view that '[i]n investment arbitration, both the interpretive and substantive facets of *in dubio mitius* have been consistently rejected in favour of a neutral (neither restrictive nor expansive) approach'.[315] Analogously, in *Mondev Int'l Ltd v. United States of America*,[316] the Tribunal held that 'there is no principle either of extensive or restrictive interpretation of jurisdictional provisions in treaties'.[317] Rather, it held that treaty provisions establishing the Tribunal's jurisdiction should be 'interpreted in accordance with the applicable rules of interpretation of treaties' as 'set out in Articles 31–33 of the Vienna Convention on the Law of Treaties, which for this purpose can be taken to reflect the position under customary international law'.[318]

With regard to the conduct of domestic courts and tribunals, arbitral tribunals have declined to adopt particular deference. For instance, in *Eli Lilly and Co v. Canada*,[319] a dispute arising in the pharmaceutical sector, the United States intervened in the proceedings under Article 1128 of the NAFTA arguing that 'under international law, the actions of domestic courts are accorded a greater presumption of regularity than legislative or

---

311 Ibid.

312 *PNG Sustainable Development Program Ltd v. Independent State of Papua New Guinea*, ICSID Case No. ARB/13/33, Award, 5 May 2015.

313 Ibid. para. 177.

314 Ibid. para. 257.

315 Ibid.

316 *Mondev Int'l Ltd v. United States of America*, ICSID Case No. ARB(AF)/99/2, Award, 11 October 2002, para. 43.

317 Ibid.

318 Ibid.

319 *Eli Lilly and Co v. Canada*, ICSID Case No. UNCT/14/2, Award, 16 March 2017.

administrative acts are'.[320] For the United States, '[f]oreign nationals have no cause for complaint' under international law about a domestic legal system if such system 'conforms to a "reasonable standard of civilized justice" and is fairly administered'.[321] Accordingly, the United States argued that 'unless there is a denial of justice, international tribunals will defer to domestic courts interpreting matters of domestic law'.[322]

Although the Tribunal did not adjudicate on this point for reasons of judicial economy, it nonetheless noted in an *obiter dictum* that:

> the conduct of the judiciary will in principle be attributable to the State by reference to uncontroversial principles of State responsibility. As a matter of principle, therefore, having regard to the content of the customary international law minimum standard of treatment, the Tribunal is unwilling to shut the door to the possibility that judicial conduct characterized [as anything] other than as a denial of justice may engage a respondent's obligations under NAFTA Article 1105.[323]

This *obiter dictum* seems to conform to public international law. In fact, international courts and tribunals are 'the proper organs' to adjudicate the question as to whether 'a rule of international law has been broken'.[324] National courts are 'instrumentalities of the state, so the state may be judged for the acts or omissions of its courts with respect to aliens'.[325] Because, internationally, the state and its courts are 'a single entity', international law 'does not allow the very party whose compliance is in question to determine whether it is transgressive'.[326]

Similarly, in *Aguas del Tunari SA v. Republic of Bolivia*,[327] the Tribunal noted that 'the Vienna Convention represents a move away from the canons of interpretation previously common in treaty interpretation'.[328] For instance, the Tribunal noted, 'the Vienna Convention does

---

[320] Ibid. para. 204.
[321] Ibid.
[322] Ibid.
[323] Ibid. para. 223.
[324] C.F. Amerasinghe, *State Responsibility for Injuries to Aliens* (Clarendon 1967) 215.
[325] J. Paulsson, *Denial of Justice in International Law* (CUP 2005) 4.
[326] Ibid.
[327] *Aguas del Tunari SA v. Republic of Bolivia*, ICSID Case No. ARB/02/03, Decision on Jurisdiction, 21 October 2005.
[328] Ibid. para. 91.

not mention the canon that treaties are to be construed narrowly, a canon that presumes States cannot have intended to restrict their range of action'.[329]

In *Loewen v. United States of America*, a case concerning an investment in the funeral business, the Tribunal did not accept 'the Respondent's submission that NAFTA is to be understood in accordance with the principle that treaties are to be interpreted in deference to the sovereignty of states'. Rather, it endorsed the view that 'NAFTA is to be interpreted in good faith in accordance with the ordinary meaning to be given to its terms in their context and in the light of its object and purpose'.[330]

5.7 CONVERGING STANDARDS OF REVIEW?

Is achieving a unified standard of review, a one-size-fits-all solution, desirable within and across different legal systems at the domestic and international levels? Perhaps counter-intuitively, this section argues that a unified standard of review may not be as desirable as it might seem at first glance. At the national level, different legal systems express different political, historical and cultural contexts. At the international level, while international legal instruments do not generally provide any guidance on the standards of review, international courts and tribunals have navigated between the Scylla of an excessive deference to, and the Charybdis of an excessive control over, state actions, using different degrees of self-restraint.

A certain variation of the standards of review across legal systems is not only inevitable, but perhaps also desirable, as it can endorse the necessary flexibility to better respond to the specific needs of each branch of law.[331] Such variation is part and parcel of the judicial method, being rooted in a number of national and international legal cultures. Not

---

[329] Ibid.

[330] *Loewen Group Inc and Raymond L. Loewen v. United States of America*, ICSID Case No. ARB(AF)/98/3, Decision on Hearing of Respondent's Objection to Competence and Jurisdiction, 5 January 2001, para. 51.

[331] For a similar position, see Arato, 'The Margin of Appreciation in International Investment Law', 553; Shirlow, 'Deference and Indirect Expropriation Analysis in International Investment Law', 625 (calling for 'a shift in standards of review analysis away from a unitary notion of deference towards a more nuanced approach'). See also D.R. Knight, 'Mapping the Rainbow of Review: Recognizing Variable Intensity' (2010) NZLR 393–431, 397 and 411 (noting that 'there are polar views on the desirability of variable intensity of review' at the domestic level).

only can 'different standards of review ... be appropriate in different circumstances',[332] but they also enable different calibrations of the competing values of restraint and control. For instance, the adoption of emergency measures in the context of an economic crisis or the adoption of public health measures in the context of pandemics can require higher deference than the pursuit of economic activities of an essentially commercial nature undertaken by a state.[333] If the adoption of a given standard of review is 'adequately explained', then arbitral tribunals can adopt 'different standards of review in different cases'.[334]

Judicial dialogue can help arbitral tribunals and other international law courts and tribunals to deal with similar issues.[335] In investor–state arbitration, the standards of review 'coalesce gradually through well-reasoned arbitral practice, knitted together over time through a rich judicial dialogue'[336] not only with other arbitral tribunals, but also with other international courts and tribunals. While there is no binding precedent in international (investment) law, persuasive precedents matter.[337]

In investment arbitration, the intensity of review varies widely. Respondent states have increasingly invoked the margin of appreciation in the context of investor–state arbitrations.[338] While some arbitral tribunals have borrowed the doctrine from the jurisprudence of the ECtHR, others have expressly rejected it. Therefore, the question as to whether the margin of appreciation doctrine has migrated to international investment law and arbitration remains open. While some arbitral tribunals have referred to the more general notion of deference, at least in public policy-related disputes, other tribunals have rejected the idea that any deference should be afforded to host states.

---

332 Arato, 'The Margin of Appreciation in International Investment Law', 565.

333 L. Gruszczynski and V. Vadi, 'Standard of Review and Scientific Evidence in WTO Law and International Investment Arbitration: Converging Parallels?', in Gruszczynski and Werner, *Deference in International Courts and Tribunals*, 152–72.

334 Arato, 'The Margin of Appreciation in International Investment Law', 573.

335 Ibid. 547.

336 Ibid. 553.

337 Ibid. 574.

338 *Biwater Gauff (Tanzania) Ltd v. United Republic of Tanzania*, ICSID Case No. ARB/05/22, Award, 24 July 2008, para. 436 (recalling that the respondent state referred to 'the margin of appreciation under international law', but ultimately not addressing the issue).

The variety of approaches is fundamentally due to the hybrid nature of international investment law and arbitration. If investor–state arbitration is considered to be a sub-species of international commercial arbitration, then no deference should be paid to state action to respect parties' equality of arms.[339] If one considers investor–state arbitration as a form of public law adjudication, arguments for deference abound.[340] If one considers investor–state arbitration as a form of international public law adjudication, then relevant analogies can be drawn from the jurisprudence of the ICJ, the ECtHR and the WTO panels and Appellate Body.

There is no uniform approach to the issue of the standards of review in international law. The ICJ has tended to reject the margin of appreciation doctrine in favour of a more demanding objective standard of review, characterized by a parlance of 'interpretation and application' of the law to the facts of the case. The ECtHR has elaborated the margin of appreciation doctrine, to foster its perceived legitimacy, efficiency and effectiveness. In turn, WTO panels and the AB have formally used deferential terminology while concretely adopting searching standards of review.

Can one detect general trends within the emerging arbitrations? Arbitral tribunals align themselves with the field of public international law rather than regional law. Arbitral jurisprudence oscillates between deference and control. On the one hand, arbitral tribunals have increasingly shown some self-restraint – albeit not a total deference – when reviewing public policy-related regulatory measures.[341] This development is a positive one for a number of reasons. First, public policy-related regulation lies at the very heart of state sovereignty. Public policy-related disputes, such as health/environment-related disputes, differ from other investment disputes, due to their impact on public welfare. A perceived lack of consideration for paramount public policy concerns might fuel the so-called 'legitimacy crisis' of investment arbitration.

Second, arbitral tribunals have specialized epistemic competence to assess the compliance of a state measure with international law rather than the correctness of the relevant scientific evidence. Arbitrators are international law experts but may not have expertise in scientific matters. Specialized domestic regulatory agencies usually assess scientific evidence before adopting policy-related measures. Arguably, in most cases,

---

339 S.W. Schill, 'Deference in Investment Treaty Arbitration: Re-conceptualizing the Standard of Review' (2012) 3 JIDS 577–607, 587.

340 Burke and Von Staden, 'Private Litigation in a Public Law Sphere', 287.

341 See generally V. Vadi, *Public Health in International Investment Law and Arbitration* (Routledge 2012).

those agencies may be better placed than international adjudicators to assess risk or to undertake other public policy-related enquiry.

Third, risk regulation has a hybrid nature in that it involves both scientific and legal aspects.[342] Yet, the governance of risk 'cannot be left to scientists alone'.[343] Rather, when regulating scientific matters, regulators will have to take into account the specific preferences of their constituency depending on the specific socio-cultural conditions of their country and the existence of international standards. It is not up to international tribunals to challenge the level of risk that given societies are willing to take.

The examined awards seem to confirm that international investment arbitration should be regarded as a dispute-settlement mechanism among those available under international law, thus calling for the standards of review characterizing public international law adjudication. The examined investment arbitrations also indicate that this mechanism can gradually become responsive to societal concerns.

The *Chemtura* case is a paradigmatic example of this approach. The Chemtura Tribunal showed some self-restraint by clarifying that arbitral tribunals should not 'second-guess the correctness of the science-based decision-making of highly specialised national regulatory agencies'.[344] At the same time, the Tribunal objectively assessed the conduct of the respondent state, noting that it would not apply an abstract level of deference; rather, it would weight all the circumstances. First, it considered 'the fact that certain agencies manage highly-specialized domains involving scientific and public policy determinations'.[345] Second, it weighted the fact that many countries had taken steps to ban and restrict the use of lindane and referred to multilateral environmental agreements (MEAs), implicitly confirming the view that international investment law does not constitute a self-contained regime; rather it must be interpreted in the light of public international law. While the existence of MEAs did not shield the state measures from review, it constituted evidence of the government's good faith. Having said that, the *Chemtura* Tribunal exercised judicial economy and mentioned certain theoretical elements only in passing.

---

342 For a seminal study, see L. Gruszczynski, *Regulating Health and Environmental Risks under WTO Law. Critical Analysis of the SPS Agreement* (OUP 2010) 147–55.

343 Ibid. 13.

344 *Chemtura v. Canada*, Award, para. 134.

345 Ibid. para. 123.

Therefore, the practice of international investment tribunals and other international courts and tribunals presents some notable convergences. Although both international law and international investment law do not explicitly endorse an abstract and general standard of deference (for example in the form of the margin of appreciation doctrine) that should apply to national determinations, they reject the idea of an intrusive *de novo* review, arguably acknowledging the limits of their jurisdiction. With regard to public policy-related disputes, arbitral tribunals usually refrain from second-guessing decisions adopted by local scientific authorities, especially when such measures appear to be reasonable, and adopted in good faith to address major public policy issues. The reasonableness of such measures is verified with reference to actual, verifiable local circumstances, taking into account international legal instruments regulating the field. Overall, the relevant practice seems to indicate a preference for some self-restraint in public policy-related investment disputes.

On the other hand, the practice of international investment tribunals and other international courts and tribunals also diverge, in particular with regard to the issue of optimal design of the judicial scrutiny over national regulation measures. Investment tribunals are concerned with the quality of the regulatory process – for example reviewing the good faith, reasonableness, transparency and inclusiveness of the regulatory processes.[346] WTO panels, on the other hand, tend to show a distinct interest in the internal (scientific) legitimacy of measures. This dissimilarity is due to the textual difference of the applicable law in the relevant disputes. Moreover, while the ECtHR systematically applies the margin of appreciation doctrine, arbitral tribunals have adopted various approaches to the issue.

CONCLUSIONS

Standards of review are 'methodological devices for determining the degree of deference' that international courts (should) grant to the conduct of states in their implementation of international treaties.[347] What standards of review are appropriate in investor–state arbitration?

---

346 See e.g. Grand River Enterprises Six Nations Ltd and others v. United States of America, ICSID/UNCITRAL, Award, 12 January 2011, para. 212.

347 Tully, 'Objective Reasonableness as a Standard for International Judicial Review', 550.

Most investment treaties do not mandate specific standards of review. Rarely have arbitral tribunals explicitly mentioned the issue of standards of review. While other international and domestic jurisdictions have adopted increasingly sophisticated approaches to the issue, only recently has the debate on standards of review touched upon international investment law and arbitration.

Far from being a purely theoretical matter, identifying the appropriate standards of review in investment treaty arbitration touches the heart of international investment arbitration as a legitimate, efficient and effective international dispute-settlement mechanism. In fact, investigating this key issue holds the promise of reinforcing the perceived legitimacy, coherence and effectiveness of international investment law and arbitration. It can also affect the outcomes of given arbitrations. As argued elsewhere, '[t]he important benefits, but also the pressing dangers implicit in the selection of the relevant standards of review' demand an 'in depth reflection' on this issue 'by the arbitral community, policy makers and practitioners' alike.[348]

While an intensive standard of review can strengthen the rule of law and good governance, an overly intrusive review may undermine state regulatory autonomy and the pursuit of legitimate public policy objectives. In turn, this may fuel the alleged 'legitimacy crisis' of the international investment law regime and undermine its coherence with public international law and, ultimately, its effectiveness. By the same token, some deference enables regulatory evolution and the adjustment of municipal law to evolving circumstances. Yet, too deferential of an approach may jeopardize state compliance with its international law obligations, and the effectiveness of international investment law and arbitration.

Depending on the selected conceptualization of investment arbitration and the type of investment dispute, the standards of review can vary. If investor–state arbitration is seen as a form of public law adjudication, arguments for deference abound. Such an approach is particularly suitable to cover public policy-related disputes. Conversely, if one adopts a commercial law paradigm, then arbitral tribunals should pay no deference to state action. Such an approach suits investment disputes that concern economic relations between a foreign investor and the host state acting in a purely commercial vein (*iure gestionis*). Finally, if investor–state arbitration is seen as a form of international public law adjudication, then

---

[348] Vadi and Gruszczynski, 'Standards of Review in International Investment Law and Arbitration', 632.

relevant analogies can be drawn from the jurisprudence of the ICJ, the ECtHR and the WTO panels and Appellate Body.

A fruitful way to reconcile these apparently diverging approaches to the standard-of-review issue is to conceptualize international investment arbitration as a hybrid system whose identity shifts depending on circumstances. If one adopts the hybrid conceptualization of investor–state arbitration, the above-mentioned approaches to the standard-of-review issue appear complementary rather than conflicting. In fact, the intensity of review would ultimately depend on the inner quality of the dispute, the provision to be applied, and the circumstances of the case – whether it deals with the exercise of state police powers (*acta iure imperii*) or activities of a commercial nature carried out by a state (*acta jure gestionis*). The intensity of the review in public policy-related investment disputes will be lower than in commercial disputes. Such approach combines scrutiny and self-restraint. Vice versa, with regard to those disputes merely presenting a contractual nature with the state acting *jure gestionis*, arbitral tribunals would grant no deference to the respondent state. Yet, because it may be difficult to qualify a dispute as merely commercial, the chapter argued that the default paradigm should be that of public international law.

Can one detect general trends within the emerging arbitrations? Arbitral tribunals have increasingly shown some self-restraint – albeit not a total deference – when reviewing public policy-related regulatory measures. They generally accept that they should not conduct an intrusive *de novo* review with regard to such disputes. This development is a positive one for a number of reasons. First, public policy-related regulation lies at the very heart of state sovereignty. Second, arbitral tribunals have little, if any, epistemic competence to assess the correctness of the relevant scientific evidence. Third, risk regulation has a hybrid nature in that it involves both scientific and legal aspects. When regulating scientific matters, regulators will have to take into account the specific preferences of their constituency and the existing international standards. It is not up to international tribunals to challenge the level of risk that societies are willing to take.

Judicial dialogue and cross-fertilization can help arbitral tribunals and other international law courts and tribunals to deal with similar issues. In investor–state arbitration, as in other legal fields, the appropriate standards of review are coalescing gradually through a rich judicial dialogue not only with other arbitral tribunals, but also with other international courts and tribunals. While there is no binding precedent in international investment law, arbitral tribunals often refer to prior awards and international decisions with mixed outcomes.

The practice of international investment tribunals and other international courts and tribunals presents some notable convergences. Although both international law and international investment law do not formally endorse an abstract and general standard of deference (for example in the form of the margin of appreciation doctrine) that should apply to national determinations, they reject the idea of an intrusive *de novo* review. With regard to public policy-related disputes, arbitral tribunals usually refrain from second-guessing decisions adopted by local scientific authorities, especially when such measures appear reasonable and adopted in good faith to address major public policy issues. The reasonableness of such measures is verified *in concreto*, by considering the local circumstances, but also by taking into account international legal instruments regulating the field. Overall, the relevant practice seems to indicate a preference for some self-restraint in public policy-related investment disputes.

On the other hand, the practice of international investment tribunals and that of other international courts and tribunals also diverge, in particular with regard to the issue of optimal design of the judicial scrutiny over national regulation measures. Investment tribunals are concerned with the quality of regulatory process – for example reviewing the good faith, reasonableness, transparency and inclusiveness of the regulatory processes. WTO panels, on the other hand, tend to show a distinct interest in the internal (scientific) legitimacy of measures. This dissimilarity is due to the textual difference of the applicable law in the relevant disputes. Moreover, while the ECtHR systematically applies the margin of appreciation doctrine, arbitral tribunals have adopted various approaches to the issue. For instance, while some arbitral tribunals have borrowed the doctrine from the jurisprudence of the ECtHR, others have expressly rejected it. Therefore, the question as to whether the margin of appreciation doctrine has successfully migrated from human rights law to international investment law remains open.

In conclusion, a unified standard of review may not be desirable within and across different legal systems. Rather, a certain variation of the standards of review across legal systems would be preferable, as such dynamism and flexibility better respond to the specific needs of each branch of law. Moreover, a certain variation of the standards of review within investor–state arbitration can be appropriate to deal with different types of disputes.

6. Proportionality, reasonableness and standards of review in investment treaty arbitration

Quis custodiet ipsos custodes?[1]

Juvenal

INTRODUCTION

What is the linkage between proportionality and reasonableness, on the one hand, and standards of review, on the other? This chapter connects the dots and maps the interaction between proportionality, reasonableness and standards of review. A scrutiny of the arbitral jurisprudence reveals that these elements do interact in a variety of different ways. A range of combinations, approximations and even intersections are possible between proportionality, reasonableness and standards of review. The existence of multiple arrangements requires some comprehensive analysis to find the best combination of these factors. In fact, proportionality and reasonableness can be tested for more or less intensively.[2]

Whatever the method of review selected by the arbitrators – be it proportionality or reasonableness – the intensity of review is one of the main tools to calibrate it. Because of the strict scrutiny imposed by the proportionality test, a more deferential standard of review should be adopted when applying such test.[3] International courts and tribunals adopting the proportionality analysis generally complement it with some

[1] Juvenal, *The Satires* (N. Rudd, trans) (OUP 1992) satire VI, lines 347–8 ('who will guard the guardians?').

[2] J. Rivers, 'Proportionality and Variable Intensity of Review' (2006) 65 *Cambridge LJ* 174–207.

[3] C. Henckels, *Proportionality and Deference in Investor–State Arbitration: Balancing Investment Protection and Regulatory Autonomy* (CUP 2015) 172; V. Vadi, 'Proportionality, Reasonableness and Standards of Review in Investment Treaty Arbitration', in A. Bjorklund (ed.), *Yearbook of International Investment Law and Policy* (2013–2014) 201–228.

deference. For instance, the European Court of Human Rights has elaborated the doctrine of the margin of appreciation to attenuate the problems inherent in proportionality. Conversely, because the structure of the reasonableness test is more lenient, it may require a more intense standard of review. International courts and tribunals adopting reasonableness as a method of review usually complement it with an objective assessment. For instance, the International Court of Justice complements the reasonableness criterion with a standard of objective review.

At first glance, reflection on proportionality, reasonableness and standards of review seems 'a perspective that is grounded more in public than in public international law'.[4] Concepts such as these belong to the domestic lexicon. At the same time, they also permeate the language of public international law albeit to varying extents. Not only do they increasingly appear in international legal instruments and doctrinal writings, but also in the decisions of international courts and tribunals. Because of the vagueness of treaty provisions, arbitral tribunals often use specific legal tools, such as proportionality and reasonableness, to review state measures under international investment treaties. In parallel, arbitral tribunals use the standards of review to identify 'the degree of deference that is granted to states in their implementation of international legal obligations'.[5]

Moreover, the emerging debate on the role of proportionality, reasonableness and standards of review expands possibilities, and can contribute to the further theorization and development of the field of international investment law. Not only does an examination of the eventual migration of elements of constitutional discourse to the public international law realm offer a working hypothesis – a possible lens through which to examine the field of international investment law and arbitration,[6] highlighting the multiple points of interaction between the domestic and the international level – but it also concerns the question as to what role arbitral tribunals should play in the international legal system, and the question concerning the ultimate aims of international investment law.

4 C.E. Foster, 'Adjudication, Arbitration and the Turn to Public Law Standards of Review' (2012) 3 JIDS 525–58, 525.

5 L. Gruszczynski and W. Werner, 'Introduction', in L. Gruszczynski and W. Werner (eds), *Deference in International Courts and Tribunals* (OUP 2014) 1–15, 1.

6 J.P. Trachtman, 'The Constitutions of the WTO' (2006) 17 EJIL 623–46, 624.

Reflecting on the use of proportionality, reasonableness and standards of review by arbitral tribunals goes to the heart of the investment treaty system.

Therefore, reflecting on proportionality, reasonableness and standards of review in international investment law and arbitration is both timely and important. It is timely, because international investment law is an expanding area of international law, but remains under-theorized. It is important, because international investment law is a vital area of international law, with great political, social and economic relevance, which can foster peaceful and prosperous relations among nations.

At the same time, this book cautions against the mechanical transposition of domestic law concepts in international law because this can undermine the adjudicatory function under public international law.[7] For this reason, the migration of proportionality analysis to international investment law is not recommended *a priori* (that is, on the basis of theoretical deduction rather than from observation or experience). The current investment treaty system lacks the sort of institutional density necessary to make proportionality analysis plausible, if not desirable. As proportionality presupposes 'the fundamentals of constitutional grammar',[8] it may be suitable to those regimes that have a certain constitutional density. In particular, it may not be suitable to investor–state arbitration due to the latter's current lack of constitutional density. That being said, this does not mean that proportionality might not be useful in the future, if an international agreement established a multilateral investment court or contributed to some further institutionalization in the field. Nonetheless, if arbitral tribunals adopted proportionality analysis as a method of review, some deference would be needed to attenuate the intrusiveness of such analysis. For the time being, reasonableness may be a more appropriate criterion of review, one that arbitral tribunals and other international courts have used extensively. Reasonableness already belongs to the grammar of international law, being part and parcel of a number of international law instruments, and the jurisprudence of the respective international courts and tribunals. If arbitral tribunals adopt reasonableness as a method of review, an objective scrutiny is required to maintain fidelity to the treaty text.

---

7 C.E. Foster, 'International Adjudication – Standard of Review and Burden of Proof' (2012) 21 RECIEL 80–91. See also V. Vadi, *Analogies in International Investment Law and Arbitration* (CUP 2016) 241.

8 C.E. Foster, 'A New Stratosphere? Investment Treaty Arbitration as "Internationalized Public Law"' (2015) 64 ICLQ 461–85, 471.

Despite its importance for the field, the state of the art on the interplay between proportionality, reasonableness and the intensity of arbitral review in investment arbitration remains limited. This chapter aims to address this gap in the existing literature. In order to find the best combination between proportionality, reasonableness and standards of review, this chapter suggests that consideration of the 'object and purpose' of the treaty may be crucial. In this regard, customary rules of treaty interpretation, as restated in the Vienna Convention on the Law of Treaties (VCLT),[9] require the interpreters to interpret treaty provisions in light of their object and purpose. The preambles of IIAs often express the aim of such treaties and can provide the interpreter with a useful centre of gravity to find the equilibrium among proportionality, reasonableness and standards of review. This is particularly the case when the given preamble requires an appropriate balance between the promotion of foreign direct investments and the sustainable development of the host state.[10] As noted by Ortino, '[w]hile investment treaties focus on investment protection, they are fundamentally aimed at achieving broader objectives, such as prosperity, development and in particular today, sustainable development'.[11] Therefore, IIAs should be interpreted as requiring protection of foreign investors and their investments and promoting the prosperity and well-being of the states parties, while preserving the state 'authority … to regulate in the public interest'.[12]

This chapter proceeds as follows. First, it briefly summarizes the promises and pitfalls of proportionality analysis in investor–state arbitration. Second, it discusses the pros and cons of the use of reasonableness in investor–state arbitration. Third, it connects the dots between proportionality, reasonableness and standards of review. Fourth, it discusses the question as to whether arbitral review can be conceived as a dialogue between arbitral tribunals, treaty makers and foreign investors. The conclusions sum up the key findings of the chapter.

---

9 Vienna Convention on the Law of Treaties (VCLT), adopted 23 May 1969, in force 27 January 1980, 1155 UNTS 331.

10 Vadi, 'Proportionality, Reasonableness and Standards of Review', 226–7; F. Ortino, 'Investment Treaties, Sustainable Development and Reasonableness Review: A Case Against Strict Proportionality Balancing' (2017) 30 *Leiden JIL* 71–91, 75–87.

11 Ortino, 'Investment Treaties, Sustainable Development and Reasonableness Review', 90.

12 Ibid. 91 (internal citations omitted).

6.1 PROPORTIONALITY: PROMISES AND PITFALLS

The concept of proportionality can be understood as a methodological framework for balancing conflicting values. The proportionality test is usually articulated in four main phases: (1) legitimacy, (2) suitability, (3) necessity, and (4) proportionality.[13] First, the legitimacy test requires that the adopted measure pursues a legitimate objective. Second, the suitability test requires that the adopted measure be suitable to achieve the stated objectives. There must be a rational, logical and causal relationship between the measure and its objectives. Third, the necessity test aims at verifying that the measure was the least restrictive available alternative or that no less drastic means were available. Fourth, the proportionality test in the narrow sense requires adjudicators to ascertain that the benefit gained from realizing the objective exceeds the harm caused by the adopted measure.

The notion of proportionality has spread over different national, regional and international adjudicative systems, due to a variety of reasons. First, its supporters contend that proportionality can bring order and coherence to legal systems. Proportionality analysis delimits the legitimate exercise of state authority. It also delimits the expectations of foreign investors and enables adjudicators to adopt nuanced decisions rather than 'all-or-nothing' approaches,[14] and to structure their analysis in a robust framework that 'may produce better and more convincing reasoning' of tribunals, thus enhancing predictability.[15] Proportionality analysis can also 'reduc[e] the sense of defeat for the losing party. As such, it is consensus-oriented because it acknowledges explicitly that there are valid constitutional arguments on both sides'.[16] Furthermore, the adoption of this type of analysis can facilitate dialogue in the global community of judges, providing 'a common language that transcends

---

[13] See J.H. Jans, 'Proportionality Revisited' (2000) 27 *Legal Issues of Economic Integration* 239–65, 240–41.

[14] B. Kingsbury and S.W. Schill, 'Public Law Concepts to Balance Investors' Rights with State Regulatory Actions in the Public Interest: The Concept of Proportionality', in S.W. Schill (ed.), *International Investment Law and Comparative Public Law* (OUP 2010) 75–105, 79.

[15] Ibid. 103.

[16] W. Sadurski, 'Reasonableness and Value Pluralism in Law and Politics', in G. Bongiovanni, G. Sartor and C. Valentini (eds), *Reasonableness and Law* (Springer 2009) 129–46, 145.

national borders'.[17] Finally, its proponents argue that 'proportionality analysis can constitute a gateway for non-investment law principles to enter into the argumentative framework of investment treaty arbitration and thereby help to overcome the fragmentation of international law'.[18]

However, the viability of proportionality as the main tool for balancing different interests and values in investment arbitration has been challenged on five different grounds: (1) institutional competences; (2) incommensurability; (3) scale of values; (4) textual hook; and (5) propertization.

First, critics contend that proportionality empowers courts and tribunals to second-guess the decisions of the host state.[19] By considering different alternatives to given measures under the necessity test, and by balancing competing interests under the proportionality test (in the narrow sense), the adjudicator can be perceived as interfering with the regulatory autonomy of states, replicating the original decision-making process. The proportionality test requires arbitrators 'to behave as legislators'.[20] In particular, the necessity test would – almost without exception – invalidate the given measure since the arbitral tribunal can always envisage alternatives with the benefit of hindsight.

Second, proportionality assumes measurability; to be balanced, two competing principles should be based on a common denominator.[21] However, some values are not necessarily commensurable to others.[22] It is argued that cost-benefit analysis is flawed with respect to public sector decisions due to the incommensurability of certain values. Moreover, the proportionality test does not explain 'what must be proportionate to what'.[23]

Third, proportionality analysis tells us nothing about the scale of values that will determine the final outcome, potentially leaving the

---

[17] M. Cohen-Eliya and I. Porat, 'Proportionality and the Culture of Justification' (2011) 59 AJCL 463–90, 472.

[18] Kingsbury and Schill, 'Public Law Concepts to Balance Investors' Rights', 104.

[19] I. Porat, 'Why All Attempts to Make Judicial Review Balancing Principled Fail?,' paper presented at the VII World Congress of the International Association of Constitutional Law, Athens, 11–15 June 2007, 7.

[20] A. Stone Sweet and J. Mathews, 'Proportionality Balancing and Global Constitutionalism' (2008) 47 *Columbia Journal of Transnational Law* 73–164, 88.

[21] A. Barak, *Proportionality: Constitutional Rights and their Limitations* (CUP 2012) 482–4.

[22] See generally C. Sunstein, 'Incommensurability and Valuation in Law' (1994) 92 *Michigan LR* 779–861.

[23] Jans, 'Proportionality Revisited', 239.

adjudicator free to select his/her own value system.[24] As value systems vary from one country to another, and what may be relatively sensible to the constituency of one country may appear nonsensical to that of another, proportionality analysis might not be suitable to investment arbitration, as arbitrators may not be familiar with the context of a given policy measure.

Fourth, in several systems in which proportionality analysis is consistently applied by adjudicators, it is based on a textual hook. One could argue that the lack of a textual hook shows that the treaty-makers did not envisage a specific concept to be part of the treaty. Accordingly, proportionality should not be part of the system. Yet, in other fields of law, proportionality has emerged as a jurisprudential concept, despite the lack of any textual hook. Moreover, the formation of consistent jurisprudence can lead to the codification of the concept in the text of treaties. For instance, in EU law, proportionality has achieved a treaty status, after a consistent jurisprudence of the Court of Justice of the European Union has coalesced, considering it to be a general principle of such law.[25]

Finally, one may wonder whether the mechanical transposition of proportionality analysis from domestic law to investment treaty arbitration could tip the balance in favour of investment promotion. Certainly, the promotion of foreign direct investment is one of the key objectives of investment treaties, as often stated in the relevant preambles. Yet, there is an ongoing battle of ideas as to the aims and objectives of international investment law.[26] Scholars have pointed out that 'as most preambles reveal, the promotion and protection of investment is the means to an end, the end being the maximization of welfare, development and prosperity of the home and host state'.[27] Thus, 'promoting foreign investments is 'a qualified rather than absolute goal'.[28] In parallel, arbitral tribunals have also highlighted that 'the object and purpose of the

---

[24] Stone Sweet and Mathews, 'Proportionality Balancing and Global Constitutionalism', 89.

[25] See Chapter 3, section 3.4.

[26] *Malaysian Historical Salvors SDN BHD v. Malaysia*, ICSID Case No. ARB/05/10, Dissenting Opinion of Judge Mohamed Shahabuddeen, 19 February 2009, para. 62 (referring to 'a titanic struggle between ideas, and correspondingly between capital exporting countries and capital importing ones' with regard to the question as to whether the contribution to the development of the host state is a requirement of the notion of investment).

[27] A. Van Aaken, 'Interpretational Methods as an Instrument of Control in International Investment Law' (2014) 108 *ASIL Proceedings* 196–8, 198.

[28] A. Roberts, 'Triangular Treaties: The Extent and Limits of Investment Treaty Rights' (2015) 56 *Harvard ILJ* 353–417, 379 (pinpointing that '[o]n a

[applicable bilateral investment] Treaty is not to protect foreign investments per se, but as an aid to the development of the domestic economy'.[29] Therefore, the application of the proportionality test requires further thinking on the underlying culture of international investment law. The use of the proportionality analysis in an uncritical fashion risks neglecting the existence of the different aims of the field.

While reference to proportionality used to be rare in investment arbitration, in the past decade, arbitral tribunals have increasingly relied on some form of proportionality analysis. In a few cases, the concept has been used to define substantive standards of protection, including the protection against unlawful expropriation, fair and equitable treatment, and non-discrimination. Other cases referred to proportionality as it was required under the applicable national law. In other cases, proportionality was used to define the ambit of application of given exceptions. Finally, proportionality has also been used with regard to procedural matters.

In conclusion, proportionality – like any other doctrinal framework – is not a neutral process; rather it is based on the primacy and priority of individual entitlements over the exercise of public powers.[30] The diffusion of the proportionality analysis highlights 'a shift from a culture of authority to a culture of justification', which is connected, *inter alia*, to the rise of the human rights movement that developed after World War II.[31] The concept has had an extraordinary success in a number of constitutional and even regional systems; it certainly belongs to several fields of international law, such as that of countermeasures. Yet, the question as to whether the proportionality doctrine has successfully migrated to international investment law remains open. If the notion has gradually appeared in arbitral awards, a critical mass of them consistently using such concept is still missing. Moreover, questions remain as to the desirability of the concept in international investment law due to the lack of constitutional density of the field.

---

domestic level, no state protects investments to the exclusion of all other interests. One should not expect the outcome to be different at the international level').

[29] *Joseph Charles Lemire v. Ukraine*, ICSID Case No. ARB/06/18, Award on Jurisdiction, 14 January 2010, para. 273.

[30] M. Sakellaridou, 'La généalogie de la proportionalité,' paper presented at the VII World Congress of the International Association of Constitutional Law, Athens, 11–15 June 2007, 20.

[31] Cohen-Eliya and Porat, 'Proportionality and the Culture of Justification', 463.

However, this may change in the near future, due to the current tectonic shifts in investment law and arbitration. Not only have states begun to explicitly refer to human rights in their treaties,[32] but there are ongoing discussions to reform investor–state arbitration. In light of these developments, the existing architecture of the system will likely undergo some sensible change. In a more structured context, with a quasi-constitutional density, proportionality might play a useful role in the elusive search for harmonious balance between the protection of foreign investment and the promotion of the (sustainable) development of the host state in conformity with principles of justice and international law.

6.2 REASONABLENESS: PROMISES AND PITFALLS

Reasonableness has become an increasingly common interpretive tool in investment treaty arbitration and is used in a variety of different contexts. A concept *à géométrie variable*,[33] reasonableness allows law to adapt to changing circumstances,[34] constituting the link or *trait d'union* between the treaty-makers and the adjudicators.

In the context of investment treaty arbitration, reasonableness has a tripartite structure and delimits and defines the role of the three relevant actors: (1) the host state; (2) the investor; and (3) the adjudicators. First, it is an implied condition on the grant of every power that the power will be exercised reasonably. In this field, 'reasonableness functions as a normative yardstick to control the exercise of discretionary powers by States that may have an adverse impact on the flow of goods and capital across States'.[35] State measures must be reasonable.

The issue consists precisely in identifying 'what regulatory action is to be considered reasonable and what is not'.[36] The concept of

---

[32] See e.g. Morocco–Nigeria BIT, signed 3 December 2016, preamble and Article 15.

[33] N. MacCormick, 'On Reasonableness', in C. Perelman and R. Van der Elst (eds), *Les notions à contenu variable en droit* (Bruylant 1984) 131–56, 131.

[34] O. Corten, *L'utilisation du raisonnable par le juge international. Discours juridique, raisons et contradictions* (Bruylant 1997) 150–51.

[35] F. Ortino, 'From "Non-discrimination" to "Reasonableness": A Paradigm Shift in International Economic Law?' (2005) *NYU Jean Monnet Working Paper* 01/05, 33.

[36] G. Verhoosel, 'Foreign Direct Investment and Legal Constraints on Domestic Environmental Policies: Striking a "Reasonable" Balance between Stability and Change' (1997–1998) 29 *Law & Policy in International Business* 451–78, 478.

reasonableness can take a concrete form by reference to international standards.[37] Arbitrators can evaluate the reasonableness of state action in the light of state practice and/or general principles of law.[38] If given regulatory measures are in tune with international practice – be it in the form of international treaties and/or specialized agency guidelines – they should be presumed to be reasonable. Such a reference to international standards would not only provide legal certainty but would also allow arbitrators to define a reasonableness standard with greater ease. In this context, reasonableness can contribute to the consistency, unity and coherence of international law.[39]

Second, reasonableness can be conceived to be 'the essence of investors' legitimate expectations'.[40] As an Arbitral Tribunal pointed out, 'the concept of "legitimate expectations" relates … to a situation where a Contracting Party's conduct creates reasonable and justifiable expectations on the part of an investor (or investment) to act in reliance on said conduct, such that a failure by the [state] to honour those expectations could cause the investor (or investment) to suffer damages'.[41] Accordingly, 'tribunals should consider whether the alleged expectation is that of a diligent or prudent investor, that is, an investor that has taken into account all circumstances surrounding the investment, including the political, socioeconomic, and historical conditions prevailing in the host State'.[42] An expectation will be unreasonable if it conflicts with laws, policies, or practices that were in place at the time of the investment, and which were, or ought to have been, known to the investor before making the investment.[43] Furthermore, it would be reasonable to expect a foreign investor to comply with international standards.

Third, reasonableness can constitute a limit to the subjectivity of the adjudicator.[44] In fact, all awards and decisions must be supported by

---

37 Ibid. 460.

38 M. Atienza, 'On Reasonableness in Law' (1990) 3 *Ratio Juris* 148–58, 158.

39 Corten, *L'utilisation du raisonnable par le juge international*, 220.

40 F. Mutis Tellez, 'Conditions and Criteria for the Protection of Legitimate Expectations under International Investment Law' (2012) 28 *ICSID FILJ Review* 432–42, 432–5.

41 *Thunderbird Gaming Corporation v. The United Mexican States*, NAFTA/UNCITRAL, Award, 26 January 2006, paras 147–8.

42 Tellez, 'Conditions and Criteria', 3.

43 *Thunderbird v. The United Mexican States*, Award, paras 148, 164.

44 Ibid. para. 162.

reasons.[45] Failure to state the reasons on which a given award is based is a ground for annulment of the award.[46] Furthermore, according to customary law canons of treaty interpretation, as restated in the VCLT, interpretation must be reasonable.[47]

Some international investment agreements (IIAs) expressly provide a textual hook for reasonableness. In particular, some IIAs prohibit states from adopting 'unreasonable or discriminatory measures' 'that impair ... the management, maintenance, use, enjoyment, extension, sale and ... liquidation' of foreign investments.[48] Such ban proscribes unreasonable state conduct even in the absence of discrimination.[49] Reasonableness has also been conceived as an articulation of (or partially coinciding with) the principle of non-discrimination.[50] According to this view, the principle of non-discrimination is infringed when identical and reasonably similar factual situations are treated differently. Other treaties link reasonableness to full protection and security[51] and/or fair and equitable treatment. Yet other treaties use reasonableness as a tool to detect indirect expropriation.[52] More broadly, as mentioned, reasonableness belongs to the lexicon of treaty interpretation. Customary rules of treaty interpretation as restated in Article 32 of the VCLT enable adjudicators to use 'supplementary means of interpretation', if the methods of treaty interpretation lead to 'manifestly absurd or unreasonable' outcomes.[53] Finally, the reasonableness criterion may be part of the (applicable) national law.

However, several criticisms can (and have) be(en) raised against the reasonableness criterion. First, some authors consider it to be intrinsically vague, lenient and opaque. Without given parameters – these authors argue – reasonableness leaves state authority (and adjudicators) unbound,

---

45 T. Landau, 'Reasons for Reasons: The Tribunal's Duty in Investor–State Arbitration', in A.J. Van den Berg (ed.), *50 Years of the New York Convention* (Kluwer 2009) 187–205.

46 ICSID Convention, Article 52(1).

47 VCLT, Article 32.

48 See e.g. Agreement between the Government of the United Kingdom of Great Britain and Northern Ireland and the Government of Argentina on the promotion and protection of investments, Article 2.2.

49 Verhoosel, 'Foreign Direct Investment and Legal Constraints on Domestic Environmental Policies', 477.

50 See generally Ortino, 'From "Non-discrimination" to "Reasonableness"'.

51 Energy Charter Treaty, opened for signature 17 December 1994, in force 16 April 1998, (1995) 34 ILM 360, Article 10.

52 Harvard Law School, Draft Convention on the International Responsibility of States for Injuries to Aliens (1961) 55 AJIL 548–84, Article 10(5).

53 VCLT, Article 32.

as this criterion does not provide a structured analytical framework.[54] In turn, the vagueness of the reasonableness criterion would lead to inconsistent and unpredictable awards.

Second, critics note that the concept of reasonableness is of only apparent simplicity. As Professor Craig points out, 'insofar as incommensurability is a problem for proportionality, it also poses analogous difficulties for reasonableness review'.[55]

Third, adopting a restrictive or minimalist interpretation of reasonableness, such criterion can be reduced to a procedural assessment concerning the deliberation process of a given measure. Yet, one may wonder whether scrutiny based on argumentative patterns can be sufficient to detect indirect forms of discrimination, expropriation and similar measures. This interpretation dilutes the relevant standards of protection, as it would detect only direct/evident forms of misbehaviour by state authorities. Instead, adopting an expansive or maximalist notion of reasonableness, there is a risk of arbitral activism, that is, a risk that arbitral tribunals substitute their judgments for that of states. In fact, such criterion would lead to a substantive assessment of the given measure.

Finally, the distinction between reasonableness and proportionality remains ambiguous, asymmetrical and yet potentially complementary. There is uncertainty as to whether one concept implies, partially coincides with, or expands the other. Certainly, reasonableness and proportionality are asymmetrical. For instance, given measures may be considered to be reasonable but may in fact be disproportionate. Conversely, given measures may be considered to be proportionate but may be unreasonable. In some cases, reasonableness and proportionality overlap, despite their conceptual differences. In other cases, they can be complementary as adjudicators often consider reasonableness and proportionality together, assessing the 'reasonable proportionality' or 'proportionate reasonableness' of given measures. The adoption of one test or another does not seem to make the other criterion redundant in practice; what can be perfectly proportionate may be unreasonable, and what is reasonable may be disproportionate. This assessment very much depends on circumstances.

---

54 A. Barak, *Proportionality: Constitutional Rights and their Limitations* (CUP 2012) 375.

55 P. Craig, 'The Nature of Reasonableness Review' (2013) 66 *Current Legal Problems* 131–67, 132.

6.3 PROPORTIONALITY, REASONABLENESS AND STANDARDS OF REVIEW

Proportionality and reasonableness constitute methods for reviewing state measures. Standards of review measure the intensity of such review. Although proportionality and reasonableness, on the one hand, and standards of review, on the other, are often treated separately, they require a joint assessment to achieve a fuller understanding of: (1) arbitral review, generally; (2) proportionality and reasonableness as tests of review; and (3) the intensity of review. This section illustrates the way in which proportionality and reasonableness can (and have) interact(ed) with standards of review.

Arbitral tribunals have adopted varied approaches in order to calibrate private and public interests in international investment arbitration. In this context, arbitral tribunals have used the concept of reasonableness and, albeit to a more limited extent, that of proportionality. Such argumentative structures provide a starting point for investigating whether state measures are lawful. Proportionality and reasonableness have both similar and dissimilar features. Both proportionality and reasonableness tests require a reasoned analysis from the decision-maker and the adjudicators. Both tests foster a culture of justification, under which states and adjudicators must provide reasons for their actions and decisions respectively. However, they also have dissimilar properties.

Because of its peculiar features, the proportionality test is usually a strict test that enables adjudicators to review the merits of the solution devised by the state authorities. It 'go[es] beyond the more traditional and narrower concept of a reasonableness review of the initial decision'.[56] If arbitral tribunals coupled the proportionality test with strict scrutiny, this would likely curtail state power to adopt measures in the public interest. For the same reason, the combination of the strict proportionality test with a strict scrutiny would likely establish a government of arbitrators in which arbitrators pay little or no deference to state authorities and *de novo* review given state measures.

The reasonableness test, on the other hand, appears to have a lighter touch. If arbitral tribunals coupled the reasonableness test with lenient scrutiny, this would likely expand state power to adopt measures in the

---

[56] M. Andenas and S. Zleptnig, 'Proportionality: WTO Law in Comparative Perspective' (2006–2007) 42 *Texas ILJ* 371–423, 382.

public interest to such an extent as to nullify its international law obligations. For the same reason, the combination of the reasonableness test with a lenient scrutiny would likely prevent any meaningful check on state conduct and ultimately jeopardize compliance with, and the effectiveness of, international (investment) law.

Such argumentative structures provide a starting point for investigating whether state measures are lawful and raise the question of what standards of review should be used. The current theoretical inquiry on the relative merits and pitfalls of proportionality and reasonableness as grounds of review needs to be complemented by an investigation of the intensity with which such grounds are applied. In fact, the intensity of review can calibrate the reach of the proportionality and reasonableness tests respectively.[57] Whatever the test selected by the arbitrators – be it proportionality or reasonableness among others – depending on the intensity of review, the outcome of a given dispute may differ. Here the challenge lies in formulating a theory of intensity of review that can both comply with the international law framework introduced by IIAs and accommodate the state right to regulate in the public interest.

Because of the strict scrutiny imposed by the proportionality test, a more deferential standard of review should be adopted when applying such test. Proportionality is a 'very searching form of review'[58] that leaves considerable discretion to courts. Therefore, there is considerable agreement as to why adjudicators should have regard for the views of states and adopt some self-constraint when testing for proportionality. On the one hand, international courts and tribunals 'are not suitable bodies for resolving polycentric questions affecting a large number of disparate

---

[57] Another tool for calibrating proportionality and reasonableness is the burden of proof. International law generally requires that the person who makes an assertion must prove that assertion (*actori incumbit probatio*) and that a given fact be proven beyond reasonable doubt. *Bosnia and Herzegovina v. Serbia and Montenegro* (*Case Concerning the Application of the Convention and Punishment of the Crime of Genocide*) Judgment, 26 February 2007, [2007] ICJ Reports 43, para. 204 (holding that 'on the burden or onus of proof, it is well established in general that the applicant must establish its case and that a party asserting a fact must establish it'). However, international courts and tribunals still enjoy some 'degree of flexibility', 'in relation to the allocation of the burden of proof'. Foster, 'International Adjudication – Standard of Review and Burden of Proof', 87.

[58] G. Nolte, 'General Principles of German and European Administrative Law' – A Comparison in Historical Perspective' (1994) 57 MLR 191–212, 205.

interests'.[59] On the other hand, reasons of subsidiarity – meant as 'a need to allocate competence in a principled way among multiple different levels of authority' – indicate that the implementation of a treaty is primarily a responsibility of the state and that international courts play a 'subsidiary role' 'with respect to sovereign, territorial, nation states'.[60] Intervention of the courts is made necessary by the alleged failure of the state to implement its treaty obligations.[61] While 'there is no distinctive role for concept of deference or self-restraint' in the first two stages of proportionality (that is, the assessment of the legitimacy and adequacy of a given measure), deference may be appropriate in the last two stages of proportionality (that is, necessity and proportionality in the strict sense stages).[62] Courts using the proportionality analysis generally reduce the intensity of their review at these stages.

While proportionality provides the courts with an intensive and 'far reaching ground of review', in practice its application depends on how strictly a court applies the test and how far it defers to the choices of the state.[63] Constitutional courts generally 'combine proportionality analysis with institutional considerations, including deference'.[64] The European Court of Human Rights (ECtHR) complements the proportionality analysis with a deferential standard of review, that is, the margin of appreciation doctrine.[65] EU courts apply proportionality 'with varying

---

59 J. Rivers, 'Proportionality and Variable Intensity of Review' (2006) 65 *Cambridge LJ* 174–207, 175–6 (referring to domestic courts).

60 P.G. Carozza, 'The Problematic Applicability of Subsidiarity to International Law and Institutions' (2016) 61 *American Journal of Jurisprudence* 51–67, 51–2.

61 Ibid.

62 Rivers, 'Proportionality and Variable Intensity of Review', 202.

63 T. Tridimas, 'Proportionality in Community Law: Searching for the Appropriate Standard of Scrutiny', in E. Ellis (ed.), *The Principle of Proportionality in the Laws of Europe* (Hart Publishing 1999) 65–84, 69.

64 V.C. Jackson, 'Being Proportional about Proportionality' (2004) 21 *Constitutional Commentary* 803–859, 858.

65 Y. Arai-Takahashi, *The Margin of Appreciation Doctrine and the Principle of Proportionality in the Jurisprudence of the ECtHR* (Intersentia 2002) 14 (describing the margin of appreciation doctrine as 'the other side of the principle of proportionality'); E.M. Leonhardsen, 'Looking for Legitimacy: Exploring Proportionality Analysis in Investment Treaty Arbitration' (2012) 3 JIDS 95–136, 116 (noting that 'proportionality analysis can be regarded as the corollary to [the ECtHR's] lenient standard of review known as the margin of appreciation doctrine, which is crucial to the relation between proportionality analysis and legitimacy of international judicial review'); F. Matscher, 'Methods of Interpretation of the Convention', in R. St. John Macdonald, F. Matscher and H. Petzold

degrees of intensity, ranging from a deferential approach to a rigorous and searching examination of the justification for a measure which has been challenged'.[66] The sliding scales of review depend on the subject matter of the dispute,[67] and the primary decision-makers. In particular, EU courts have exercised some self-restraint in their review of measures by the European Commission and, albeit to a lesser extent, of decisions by domestic governments.[68] Some self-constraint may cause the proportionality test to converge with reasonableness.[69] In conclusion, courts adopting the proportionality analysis generally complement it with some deference 'to soften its apparent impact'.[70]

In investor–state arbitration, scholars and practitioners advocate the use of the proportionality analysis in tandem with deferential approaches.[71] However, the investment treaty regime lacks 'the constitutional density' of the other examined systems such as domestic constitutional systems and the EU, the latter being a quasi-constitutional, *sui generis* international order.[72] Moreover, while several investment tribunals have adopted a proportionality analysis similar to that adopted by the ECtHR, only a few have adopted a deferential standard of review (in a way that

(eds), *The European System for the Protection of Human Rights* (Martinus Nijhoff 1993) 63–82, 79 (describing the concept of proportionality as 'corrective and restrictive of the margin of appreciation').

66 P. Craig, 'Proportionality, Rationality and Review' (2010) NZLR 265–301, 268.

67 Ibid. 291.

68 G. Van Harten, *Sovereign Choices and Sovereign Constraints: Judicial Restraint in Investment Treaty Arbitration* (OUP 2013) 32.

69 Rivers, 'Proportionality and Variable Intensity of Review', 178.

70 J. Rivers, 'Proportionality and Discretion in International and European Law', in N. Tsagourias (ed.), *Transnational Constitutionalism: European and International Models* (CUP 2007) 107–132, 107.

71 See generally C. Henckels, *Proportionality and Deference in Investor–State Arbitration: Balancing Investment Protection and Regulatory Autonomy* (CUP 2015) (advocating the use of the proportionality analysis and deference); S. Schill, 'Deference in Investment Treaty Arbitration: Re-conceptualizing the Standard of Review' (2012) 3 JIDS 577–607 (also advocating the use of proportionality and some deference in investor–state arbitration); W. Burke-White and A. von Staden, 'Private Litigation in a Public Law Sphere: The Standard of Review in Investor–State Arbitrations' (2010) 35 *Yale JIL* 283–346, 343 (considering that in investor–state arbitration there should be a low intensity review and that state conduct should be endorsed unless 'the balance struck by the national government is blatantly unreasonable or out of proportion').

72 I borrow the term 'constitutional density' from Carozza, 'The Problematic Applicability of Subsidiarity to International Law and Institutions', 66.

would be comparable to the margin of appreciation doctrine). Therefore, 'the balancing of interests by [arbitral] tribunals has tended to favour investment rights'.[73] If the proportionality test is adopted, the parallel self-restraint is crucial for fostering the perceived legitimacy of international judicial review.[74]

Conversely, because the structure of the reasonableness test is more lenient, it may require a more intense standard of review. National courts endorsing the reasonableness analysis have simultaneously developed a heightened or 'hard look' scrutiny.[75] Analogously, at the international level, the International Court of Justice (ICJ) complements the reasonableness criterion with a standard of objective review. This enables the ICJ to meaningfully and effectively review state measures to assess their compliance with their international law obligations. When an international tribunal uses a concept like 'reasonableness' for reviewing state measures, an objective scrutiny is (as it should be) applied to the test.[76]

For instance, whereas 'reasonableness' found its place in the Optional Protocol[77] to the International Covenant on Economic, Social and Cultural Rights (ICESCR),[78] the proposal to add a margin of 'appreciation' to the Protocol was rejected, as it would have diluted the Protocol to such an extent as to undermine its function.[79] As is known, the Protocol permits individuals to make complaints to the UN Committee on Economic, Social and Cultural Rights for alleged breaches of the

---

[73] B. Choudhury, 'Recapturing Public Power: Is Investment Arbitration's Engagement of the Public Interest Contributing to the Democratic Deficit?' (2008) 41 VJTL 775–832, 826.

[74] Leonhardsen, 'Looking for Legitimacy', 116.

[75] Wouter and Duquet, 'The Principle of Reasonableness in Global Administrative Law', 15.

[76] G.K. Freund, 'Look up in the Sky, it's a Bird, it's a Plane ... it's Reasonableness' (1991) 20 *Southwestern University LR* 195–218, 217; but see O. Corten, 'Reasonableness in International Law', in R. Wolfrum (ed.), *Max Planck Encyclopaedia of Public International Law* (OUP 2013) para. 3 (considering reasonableness as 'a general limiting factor upon States' margin of appreciation').

[77] Optional Protocol to the International Covenant on Economic, Social and Cultural Rights (OP-ICESCR), GA Res 63/117, opened for signature 10 December 2008, in force 5 May 2013, A/RES/63/117.

[78] International Covenant on Economic, Social and Cultural Rights, opened for signature 16 December 1966, in force 3 January 1976, 993 UNTS 3.

[79] B. Griffey, 'The "Reasonableness" Test: Assessing Violations of State Obligations under the Optional Protocol to the International Covenant on Economic, Social and Cultural Rights' (2011) 11 *Human Rights LR* 275–327, 295.

Covenant.[80] The Protocol constitutes a significant milestone in the history of international law, as it will enable the development of the first case-based jurisprudence on compliance with economic, social and cultural rights in the UN human rights system. Article 8(4) of the Protocol requires that 'the Committee shall consider the reasonableness of the steps taken by the State Party'.[81] If the provision reflects a 'hard won consensus', at the same time, commentators have pointed out that it 'requires a robust standard of review of the steps taken by the State Party to realise Covenant rights'.[82]

The nexus between proportionality and reasonableness, on the one hand, and standards of review, on the other, moves beyond traditional notions of the Euclidean geometry.[83] As is known, for the Greek mathematician Euclid (325–270 BC), given two points, one and only one straight line can join them.[84] This axiom presupposed a particular geometrical model, which Euclid believed to underlie physical reality. The Euclidean geometry remained in use practically unchanged for more than 2,000 years. Since the second half of the nineteenth century, however, an 'away from Euclid' movement began, which led to the appearance of a multitude of geometrical approaches, the so-called non-Euclidean geometries. Non-Euclidean geometries have constituted a paradigm shift in the history of science as they proposed other descriptions of the real.[85] First identified by Carl Friedrich Gauss (1777–1855) and then developed by Janos Bolyai (1802–1860), Nicolai Ivanovich Lobachevskij (1792–1856) and Barnhard Riemann (1826–1866), non-Euclidean geometries, including hyperbolic and elliptic geometries, have overcome Euclid's fifth postulate, the parallel postulate, and offered

---

[80] OP-ICESCR, Article 2.

[81] OP-ICESCR, Article 8(4).

[82] B. Porter, 'Reasonableness and Article 8(4)', in M. Langford, B. Porter, R. Brown and J. Rossi (eds), *The Optional Protocol to the International Covenant on Economic, Social and Cultural Rights: A Commentary* (University of Pretoria Press 2016) 173–202, 174.

[83] Euclidean geometry is named after the Greek mathematician Euclid who lived in the fourth century BC. See generally M.J. Greenberg, *Euclidean and Non-Euclidean Geometries: Development and History*, 4th edn (W.H. Freeman 2007); M. Kline, *Mathematical Thought from Ancient to Modern Times* (OUP 1972) 861–81.

[84] VV.AA. 'Euclidean Geometry', *Encyclopaedia Britannica* (2014), <http://www.britannica.com/EBchecked/topic/194901/Euclidean-geometry> accessed 24 October 2017.

[85] M. Livio, *The Golden Ratio: The Story of Phi, The World's Most Astonishing Number* (Broadway Books 2002) 248.

rational, consistent and yet alternative mathematical models of space. In fact, while Euclidean geometry is two-dimensional and modelled by a flat plane, as it turns out, the universe itself is not flat. Non-Euclidean geometries acknowledge that the space is three-dimensional and that in the actual physical space, there may be many lines between two points in a curved space – even an infinite number. Non-Euclidean geometries seem to offer a better model, and their impact has gone far beyond the boundaries of geometry.[86]

Arbitral jurisprudence reveals that proportionality, reasonableness and standards of review interact in a variety of different ways. At times, proportionality, reasonableness and standards of review appear in the form of parallels (in the form of straight lines between proportionality and standards of review, on the one hand, and a straight line between reasonableness and standards of review, on the other). But more often they appear in the forms of hyperbolic and elliptic figures, in which a variety of combinations, approximations and even intersections are possible between proportionality, reasonableness and standards of review. The existence of multiple combinations – or non-Euclidean geometries – impels scholars and practitioners to rethink this complex interplay and to investigate the best combination or triangulation of these factors.

What is the appropriate methodology for determining the intensity of review? The intensity with which arbitral tribunals apply proportionality and/or reasonableness depends on the specific provision that is being applied, the subject matter of the dispute, the objective of state action and the modalities of the same. The identification of a centre of gravity helps in finding the best combination of these elements. In this regard, this book argues that gravity grounds the international investment law system within the universe of international law.[87] No investment treaty exists in a normative vacuum; rather, it belongs to the universe of public international law. As any other treaty, it must be interpreted in good faith and according to customary rules of treaty interpretation. The aims of investor–state arbitrations are similar to those of other international courts and tribunals, as expressed in the preamble of the VCLT. As is

[86] For instance, Albert Einstein used non-Euclidean geometries as models of the physical space for formulating its theory on relativity. See generally D.M. Burton, *The History of Mathematics: An Introduction* (MacGraw-Hill 2007) Ch. 11.

[87] M. Lennard, 'Navigating by the Stars: Interpreting the WTO Agreements' (2002) 5 *Journal of International Economic Law* 17–89; B. Simma and D. Pulkowski, 'Of Planets and the Universe: Self-contained Regimes in International Law' (2006) 17 *European Journal of International Law* 483–529.

known, such preamble acknowledges that 'disputes concerning treaties, like other international disputes, should be settled by peaceful means and in conformity with the principles of justice and international law.'[88]

6.4 ARBITRAL REVIEW AS DIALOGUE BETWEEN DIFFERENT ACTORS

The current international investment regime does not express a 'linear narrative' but is the outcome of a complex historical interaction between states, arbitral tribunals and foreign investors.[89] This section proposes the conceptualization of arbitral review as a dialogue among different actors and examines the role of arbitral tribunals, states and foreign investors.

Arbitral tribunals engage in a sort of 'dialectical review' of state conduct;[90] they compel respondent states into a process of reasoned engagement. Once an investor has filed an arbitration alleging the breach of one or more investment treaty provisions, states have to defend themselves. At the heart of the arbitral process is the scrutiny of reasons. In turn, by interpreting and applying international investment law, arbitral tribunals contribute to the progressive development of international law.[91] Well-reasoned arbitral awards can promote state compliance, the implementation of international law norms, and the effectiveness of the system. They can contribute to the gradual emergence of a *jurisprudence constante*.[92] The increasing publicity of arbitral awards has also facilitated a dialogue between arbitral tribunals, states and investors.

There is an ongoing dialogue between arbitral tribunals on the one hand and other international tribunals and courts on the other. While there is no binding precedent in international law, arbitral tribunals refer to previous awards. The arbitral jurisprudence contributes to, and benefits

---

[88] VCLT, preamble.

[89] J.E. Alvarez, 'Is Investor–State Arbitration Public?' (2016) 7 JIDS 534–76, 575.

[90] R.B. Ahdieh, 'Between Dialogue and Decree: International Review of National Courts' (2004) 79 NYULR 2029–163, 2034 (offering a model of 'dialectical review', that is, 'a pattern of judicial review, yet one with dialogue at its core').

[91] C. Schreuer, 'The Development of International Law by ICSID Tribunals' (2016) 31 *ICSID Review* 728–39, 739.

[92] A.K. Bjorklund, 'Investment Treaty Arbitral Decisions as Jurisprudence Constante', in C. Picker, I. Bunn and D. Arner (eds), *International Economic Law: The State and Future of the Discipline* (Hart Publishing 2008) 265–80.

from, a pool of persuasive precedents.[93] In addition, arbitral tribunals have also established a dialogue with other international courts and tribunals, thus contributing to the cross-fertilization of concepts and ideas and the potential coalescence of general principles of law and customary law.[94] Arbitral tribunals belong to a 'global community of courts'.[95] Persuasive arbitral awards can influence subsequent arbitral tribunals, as well as other international courts and tribunals.[96] Clearly, such dialogue has a merely persuasive character, because there is no hierarchy among international tribunals.

A dialogue between arbitral tribunals and domestic courts has also emerged. Such dialogue has a more structured and hierarchical nature, as arbitral tribunals' role is to hold governments to account. In some cases, arbitral tribunals have approvingly cited domestic courts' decisions; in other cases, they have had to assess whether such domestic decisions infringed given investment treaty provisions, such as the fair and equitable treatment standard and the prohibition of denial of justice. In conclusion, the reasoning of arbitral tribunals is crucial to maintain, and ideally to enhance, the perceived effectiveness, legitimacy and justice of the system.

Because of their role-splitting (*dédoublement fonctionnel*), states are both the makers and receivers of international (investment) law norms.[97] States play a dual role in investor–state arbitration 'as treaty parties (with an interest in interpretation) and actual or potential respondents in investor–state disputes (with an interest in avoiding liability)'.[98] As treaty parties, states can establish a 'constructive dialogue' with investment tribunals.[99] They can also fine tune or renegotiate investment treaty

---

[93] See generally V. Vadi, *Analogies in International Investment Law and Arbitration* (CUP 2016).

[94] S. Puig, 'Emergence and Dynamism in International Organizations: ICSID, Investor–State Arbitration and International Investment Law' (2013) 44 *Georgetown JIL* 531–608, 547.

[95] A.-M. Slaughter, 'A Global Community of Courts' (2003) 44 *Harvard ILJ* 191–219.

[96] Schreuer, 'The Development of International Law by ICSID Tribunals', 739.

[97] G. Scelle, 'Le phénomène juridique du dédoublement fonctionnel', in W. Schätzel and H.-J. Schlochauer (eds), *Rechtsfragen der Internationalen Organisation – Festschrift für H. Wehberg* (Klostermann 1956) 324–42.

[98] A. Roberts, 'Power and Persuasion in Investment Treaty Interpretation: The Dual Role of States' (2010) 104 AJIL 179–225, 180.

[99] Ibid. 225.

provisions in light of the relevant arbitral jurisprudence.[100] The more recent IIAs display a number of features that are clearly in reaction to arbitral practice.[101] More drastic courses of actions include withdrawing state consent to arbitrate, denouncing international treaties, restricting investors' access to investor–state arbitration, and excluding investor–state arbitration from the text of future treaties.[102] If states are to retain investor–state arbitration in their IIAs it is because they are persuaded that it is a sensible mechanism for settling disputes. Therefore, the reasoning of arbitral tribunals is crucial to maintain, and ideally to enhance, the perceived legitimacy and effectiveness of the system. As actual or potential respondents in investor–state disputes, states must justify their measures. They can also try to influence the development of customary international law, by adopting a consistent stance on given legal issues. Most countries comply with arbitral awards,[103] essentially for purposes of maintaining a good reputation.[104]

Arbitral review also establishes a dialogue between arbitral tribunals and foreign investors. Investor–state arbitration enables private actors to free themselves from the strains and vagaries of diplomatic protection, and empowers them to assert their rights and interests before an international tribunal.[105] In this manner, foreign investors have direct access to international justice. At the same time, unreasonable and/or disproportionate expectations do not belong to the language of international law, and should be rejected by arbitral tribunals. Because investor–state arbitration has been conceptualized as a tool to protect foreign investors from injustice, it should not become a means to prevent legitimate regulation by the host state.

---

100 Ibid. 221.

101 Schreuer, 'The Development of International Law by ICSID Tribunals', 737.

102 L.E. Trakman and D. Musayelyan, 'The Repudiation of Investor–State Arbitration and Subsequent Treaty Practice: The Resurgence of Qualified Investor–State Arbitration' (2016) 31 *ICSID Review* 194–218.

103 T. Mizushima, 'The Role of the State after an Award is Rendered in Investor–State Arbitration', in S. Lalani and R. Polanco Lazo (eds), *The Role of the State in Investor–State Arbitration* (Brill 2015) 274–92, 274.

104 A.T. Guzman, 'A Compliance-Based Theory of International Law' (2002) 90 *California LR* 1823–80, 1880.

105 Roberts, 'Triangular Treaties', 353 (arguing that 'investment treaties should be reconceptualized as triangular treaties, i.e. agreements between sovereign states that create enforceable rights for investors as non-sovereign, third-party beneficiaries').

In conclusion, only by creating well-reasoned arbitral jurisprudence can arbitral tribunals (and, if established, an International Investment Court) enhance their legitimacy, fulfill the aims and objectives of international investment law and contribute to its development in conformity with international law.

6.5 CRITICAL ASSESSMENT

Like other international courts and tribunals, arbitral tribunals have to interpret and apply international law provisions. Reflection on proportionality, reasonableness and standards of review can help adjudicators to interpret and apply vague investment treaty provisions and settle investment disputes in a more coherent and predictable fashion, potentially attuning the international investment regime to other fields of public international law and ideally enhancing its effectiveness, legitimacy and justice.

Both proportionality and reasonableness are 'meaningless without some ... calibration of intensity'.[106] Therefore, the interplay between proportionality and reasonableness, on the one hand, and standards of review, on the other, is of critical importance. Arbitral tribunals combine proportionality, reasonableness and standards of review in various ways. As proportionality transposes 'the fundamentals of constitutional grammar' from constitutional law into the international domain,[107] it suits those integrated regimes that have a certain constitutional density. While the current investment treaty system lacks the sort of constitutional density that can make proportionality analysis plausible, if not desirable, this does not mean that proportionality may not become part of international investment law and arbitration in the future, if an agreement on a multilateral investment court, or further institutionalization, is achieved. International investment law and arbitration is still developing and

[106] D.R. Knight, 'Mapping the Rainbow of Review: Recognizing Variable Intensity' (2010) NZLR 393–431, 397; M. Taggart, 'Proportionality, Deference, *Wednesbury*' (2008) NZLR 423–50, 450 (suggesting that the 'proportionality doctrine is no more monolithic than ... [r]easonableness ... [It] respond[s] ... to the same contextual and deference factors as ... [r]easonableness').

[107] Foster, 'Investment Treaty Arbitration as "Internationalized Public Law"', 471.

undergoing some structural changes.[108] In particular, the proposed establishment of a World Investment Court may lead to the coalescence of an integrated jurisprudence, in which proportionality could be used.

For the time being, reasonableness seems a more appropriate criterion of review, one that arbitral tribunals and other international courts have used extensively. Reasonableness already belongs to the grammar of international law, being part and parcel of a number of international law instruments, as well as part of the jurisprudence of international courts and tribunals.

Whether or not arbitral tribunals opt for proportionality and/or reasonableness, what is really crucial is the standard of review that accompanies their choice. As shown in Chapter 5, there are shifting standards of review, and there is no one-size-fits-all standard of review in either national or international adjudication. As argued in Chapter 5, a unitary standard of review is not desirable because the intensity of review must be flexible to adapt to the functional diversification and specialization of international courts and tribunals. In selecting the appropriate standards of review, arbitral tribunals should take into account different factors including the applicable law, the political, social and cultural context, the complexity of the policy questions involved, and the structure of the processes and institutions that have generated the measure under review. Arbitrators should carefully select the appropriate standards of review to enhance the perceived legitimacy and effectiveness of investor–state arbitration as an important part of public international law.

In this regard, proportionality embodies some distrust of state authorities: it derives from post-war European political culture that state measures affecting individuals' entitlements must be treated with suspicion.[109] Tribunals use the proportionality concept, expanding rather than constraining their authority.[110] Unless proportionality is calibrated with some deference, it can lead to an arbitral race to the top in the protection of investors' entitlements. Reasonableness tends to be more

---

[108] Arguably, with the EU becoming a major player in the field, it may gradually introduce the concept of proportionality, which is a general principle of EU law, in its IIAs. See e.g. EU-Singapore FTA, Article 11.36 (requiring the parties to 'provide for the measures, procedures and remedies under their respective domestic law, against acts of infringement of intellectual property rights', taking into account, *inter alia*, 'the need for proportionality between the seriousness of the infringement and the interests of third parties').

[109] M. Cohen-Eliya and I. Porat, *Proportionality and Constitutional Culture* (CUP 2012) 123.

[110] Van Harten, *Sovereign Choices and Sovereign Constraints*, 68.

flexible than proportionality. Yet, it risks providing loose standards of protection unless calibrated with an objective review, such as that adopted by the ICJ.

That being said, both proportionality and reasonableness are vague notions whose contents are indeterminate and which remain ones of overall judgment. The use of such concepts risks emphasizing the power of international arbitral tribunals vis-à-vis that of national policy makers. There is a risk that when applying these terms, tribunals prioritize their view of proportionality and reasonableness, reducing the autonomy of the state in addition to and beyond what is required by investment treaties.[111] As the content of proportionality and reasonableness 'will be determined primarily through the arbitral process',[112] they risk enabling arbitral tribunals to second guess governmental policies, and to establish a *gouvernment des arbitres*.[113] This gives rise to the question of: who will guard the guardians (*quis custodiet ipsos custodes*)? While this book leaves the task of evaluating the pros and cons of adopting proportionality and/or reasonableness to policy makers and adjudicators, it has offered a solid starting point for such assessment, providing a much-needed contextualization of these concepts by setting them against their intellectual, cultural and legal background.[114]

CONCLUSIONS

This chapter connects the dots and maps the interaction between proportionality, reasonableness and standards of review. While each of these themes has been examined at greater length in previous chapters,[115] this chapter juxtaposes them to pinpoint the merits and limits of their joint use.

Conceived as logical methods or analytical tools to assist arbitrators in drawing a fair balance between public and private interests, the concepts of proportionality and reasonableness have attracted increasing attention

111 E. Guntrip, 'Self-Determination and Foreign Direct Investment: Reimagining Sovereignty in International Investment Law' (2016) 65 ICLQ 829–57, 837.

112 Foster, 'Investment Treaty Arbitration as "Internationalized Public Law"', 470.

113 Guntrip, 'Self-Determination and Foreign Direct Investment', 838.

114 Cohen-Eliya and Porat, *Proportionality and Constitutional Culture*, 158.

115 See Chapter 3 (on proportionality), Chapter 4 (on reasonableness) and Chapter 5 (on standards of review).

from scholars, practitioners and policy makers alike. Proportionality and reasonableness can be used to ascertain the consistency between a certain measure and its objectives, delimit investors' expectations and review state conduct. Both proportionality and reasonableness allow the scrutiny of public authority and the consideration of different legal interests and values. Both foster a culture of justification.

Proportionality and reasonableness, however, have a different structure and ethos. The proportionality test has a well-articulated framework of analysis. Yet, the exacting nature of the proportionality analysis can make its use inappropriate for arbitral tribunals because it would permit arbitrators to second-guess the decisions of the host state by replicating the original decision-making process. Reasonableness can (but not necessarily does) provide an alternative analytical framework. Reasonableness seems to require a fluid, flexible and qualitative analysis, emphasizing logic, rationality and coherence. However, reasonableness can provide too vague a criterion if it is not accompanied by adequate standards of review.

More importantly, the adoption of proportionality and/or reasonableness is not a neutral process as it may have important consequences. The book has provided a much-needed contextualization of these concepts by setting them against their intellectual, cultural and legal background. In particular, the fact that the proportionality concept has been successful in constitutional contexts does not necessarily entail that it can be useful, successful or desirable in systems that, for the time being, lack such constitutional density, such as investment arbitration. The adoption of the proportionality analysis can determine a race to the top of investment treaty standards, while the adoption of the reasonableness standard implies a slightly less intrusive scrutiny of state conduct.

Far from advocating the use of proportionality or reasonableness in investment arbitration, this book examines the various arguments in favour of and against such use, and concludes that while the migration of proportionality to international investment law and arbitration is far from being settled, reasonableness seems to be part and parcel of it. This book does not aim at advocating the use of proportionality or reasonableness; rather, it aims at enabling the reader to make informed choices.

Whatever the test selected by the arbitrators – be it proportionality or reasonableness – the intensity of review is one of the main tools to calibrate it. Because of the strict scrutiny imposed by the proportionality test, a more deferential standard of review should be adopted when applying such test. Courts and tribunals adopting the proportionality analysis generally complement it with some deference. Conversely, because the structure of the reasonableness test is more lenient, it may require a more intense standard of review. For instance, the ICJ complements the reasonableness criterion with a standard of objective review.

Undoubtedly, the debate will continue so as to address the scope/intensity of arbitral review of state measures and the method through which this should be expressed, whether that be reasonableness or proportionality. This chapter contributed to the emerging debate stressing the importance of scrutinizing proportionality and/or reasonableness analysis in conjunction with the standards of review.[116] This degree of deference in turn depends on the selected paradigm through which investment treaty arbitration is conceptualized. In conclusion the discussion about proportionality, reasonableness and standards of review concerns the question as to what role arbitral tribunals should play in the international legal system and the ultimate aims of international investment law.

[116] For analogous reasoning in the WTO context, see P. Van den Bossche, 'Looking for Proportionality in WTO Law' (2008) 35 *Legal Issues of Economic Integration* 283–94, 284.

Conclusions

International investment law and arbitration is an area of international law whose nature is debated and in flux. The adhesion to IIAs necessarily involves the limitation of state sovereignty in exchange for certain benefits. In this regard, however, IIAs are more intrusive than trade agreements as foreign investment takes place within the borders of a state. In addition, investment treaties provide foreign investors with direct access to investor–state arbitration. While developing countries have deemed investment treaty arbitration politically biased against them, industrialized countries have expressed some concerns about this mechanism as well. In particular, there is uncertainty over the relevance or irrelevance of norms protecting non-economic values within investment treaty arbitration. Taking into account and responding to such criticisms on the functioning of investment treaty arbitration in relation to public goods is crucial to allow international investment law to develop in accordance with, and contribute to the evolution of, public international law.

De lege ferenda, as city planners periodically revise zoning plans to achieve the desired ideal city, several states are now revising their investment policies and practices to attract foreign direct investments, foster sustainable development and protect key non-economic values. States are gradually recalibrating their treaties through the inclusion of exceptions, carve-outs and more precise standards of treatment. However, major procedural reforms are also under way, as discussions on the establishment of an International Investment Court are moving forward.

De lege lata, just as architects and engineers must comply with all of the relevant building and zoning codes, as well as current laws, in order to plan, design and review the construction of buildings, similarly international arbitrators must also interpret and apply international investment law in order to adjudicate investment disputes. International investment law and arbitration is more polychromatic than it may look at first sight. A number of mechanisms are built into the system to protect the state right to regulate and address tensions between investor and host state interests under existing treaties. International investment law is not a self-contained system, but is part of international law.[1] Customary rules of treaty interpretation, as restated by the Vienna Convention on the Law of Treaties, require arbitrators to interpret IIAs in consonance with international law.[2]

This book has investigated whether – in the arsenal of interpretive tools arbitrators have to build their jurisprudence – proportionality, reasonableness and standards of review can constitute the cornerstones of their interpretive construction. Adjudicators have used such tools increasingly at the domestic, regional and international levels. The migration of constitutional ideas to other legal fields can offer concrete solutions to emerging conceptual dilemmas. However, adopting an international law approach to the matter, the book highlights that there cannot be mechanical migrations of concepts from the domestic legal field to the international one. Legal transplants are cultural transplants, thus calling for the development of context-sensitive methodologies. Therefore, not only should one verify whether the item that would migrate has proven satisfactory in its domestic legal system of origin, but one should consider whether it would be suitable to the recipient international legal system. Therefore, the book proposes a critical approach to the migration of constitutional ideas to the international realm. It then examines the role that ideas such as proportionality, reasonableness and standards of review play in international investment law and arbitration.

Conceived as an analytical tool to assist adjudicators in determining the interaction between public and private interests, the concept of proportionality has attracted growing attention by scholars and policy makers alike, and has migrated from constitutional law to a number of other legal fields. Proportionality expresses the idea that there should be a balance between competing objectives or values. It offers a structured method of reasoning that can restrain the exercise of public powers, shape adjudication and manage private actors' expectations. Often depicted as an ideal mechanism for balancing opposing interests and thus creating equilibrium between private and public interests, it expresses the eternal search for beauty, precision and perfection.

This book investigated the question as to whether, and if so to what extent, proportionality has migrated from constitutional law to EU law, WTO law, and international investment law respectively. Undoubtedly,

---

[1] *Asian Agricultural Products Ltd v. Republic of Sri Lanka*, ICSID Case No. ARB/87/3, Award, 27 June 1990, para. 21.

[2] Vienna Convention on the Law of Treaties, signed 23 May 1969, in force 27 January 1980, 1155 UNTS 331, Article 31(3)(c).

the migration of proportionality to EU law has been successful. Not only is proportionality analysis part and parcel of EU law, but it has become one of its general principles. While the migration of proportionality to WTO law remains a work in progress, some of its elements already belong to the international trade regime. On the other hand, no consensus seems to have arisen with regard to the legal status of proportionality in international investment law.

De lege lata, most investment treaties do not refer to proportionality. Therefore, an examination of the arbitral practice is of critical relevance for ascertaining whether, and if so how, proportionality has migrated to investment treaty arbitration. In the past decade, arbitral tribunals have increasingly relied on some form of proportionality analysis for delimiting substantive standards of protection, clarifying procedural matters and even quantifying damages and legal fees. Yet, the proportionality analysis is not yet used consistently in investment treaty arbitration. Rather, arbitral tribunals have used the proportionality concept in different contexts, in different ways, and for different purposes. While most tribunals have not adopted it at all, other tribunals have mentioned it in passing, or together with other notions such as reasonableness. More importantly, in the context of investment arbitration, proportionality analysis lacks the clear and consistent structure it has in other fields of law. In conclusion, while generic reference to proportionality has increased in the awards rendered in the past decade, a critical mass of awards relying on this test is missing. It remains to be seen whether the growing frequency of reference to proportionality is evidence of a proper migration.

If proportionality were a general principle of law, or constituted an element of customary law, it could eventually be used in international investment law and arbitration as part of the applicable law or as a matter of treaty interpretation. Arbitrators could refer to proportionality in their awards as either part of the applicable law, under Article 42 of the Convention on the Settlement of Investment Disputes between States and Nationals of Other States (ICSID Convention),[3] or as a rule of international law applicable in the relations between the parties under Article 31(3)(c) of the VCLT.[4] In the uncertainty as to the legal status of proportionality in international law, the legal grounds for considering proportionality in investor–state arbitration can be problematic. Certainly, if the applicable law is that of the host state, and this law includes the

[3] ICSID Convention, Article 42.
[4] VCLT, Article 31(3)(c).

proportionality principle, such principle becomes relevant in the context of investment treaty arbitration. In conclusion, more comparative and international law studies are needed to ascertain the legal status of proportionality in international law.

A corollary question is whether proportionality *should* migrate to international investment law. The doctrine is divided. A number of prominent scholars argue that proportionality is, and/or should be, part of the international investment law regime.[5] For them, proportionality analysis constitutes 'the best available doctrinal framework with which to meet the present challenges' to the investment treaty system.[6] Adopting a utilitarian/functionalist approach, proponents of proportionality argue that proportionality aims to address universal legal problems, and that therefore it can be transplanted from one field to another. In their view, proportionality analysis can be a useful tool of judicial governance to calibrate conflicting interests in international investment law.[7]

Yet, critics contest the use of proportionality analysis in investor–state arbitration on a number of grounds. The legal systems in which proportionality has flourished present more cohesion, integration and uniformity than international investment law and arbitration. In particular, constitutional law systems are integrated expressions of a given constituency. In parallel, EU law has a constitutional dimension. It is a system of its own kind, whose aims go beyond pure economic integration to include the protection of human rights and fundamental freedoms. While WTO law does not have the same constitutional density as constitutional law and EU law, its covered agreements include articulated exceptions that enable the WTO panels and Appellate Body to balance economic and non-economic values. Instead, international investment law is composed of different IIAs, and lacks a centralized dispute-settlement mechanism. Moreover, most IIAs govern state conduct and do not address investor obligations. The fact that arbitrators can take other instruments of international law into account when interpreting investment treaties under

---

[5] See e.g. A. Stone Sweet, 'Investor–State Arbitration: Proportionality's New Frontier' (2010) 4 LEHR 46–76.

[6] Ibid. 48.

[7] See e.g. B. Kingsbury and S.W. Schill, 'Public Law Concepts to Balance Investors' Rights with State Regulatory Actions in the Public Interest: The Concept of Proportionality', in S.W. Schill (ed.), *International Investment Law and Comparative Public Law* (OUP 2010) 75–105.

Article 31(3)(c) of the VCLT does not expand their jurisdiction.[8] Proportionality does not clarify the scale of values to be used in order to evaluate competing objectives, thus leaving the adjudicator free to select the relevant criteria.[9] In particular, there are concerns that the application of proportionality in investment arbitration could lead to the over-protection of foreign investments.

Even in accepting that proportionality can be used as a mere methodology, without any need for further investigation of its legal status, questions remain as to whether it is suitable for transposition in investor–state arbitration. At an analytical level, one may legitimately wonder whether proportionality can contribute to better awards given the specific features of international investment law. While proportionality analysis can work perfectly well in given domestic constitutional contexts, and in systems with constitutional density such as EU law, this does not necessarily mean that it can do so in the international investment regime. Proposals to use only some parts of the proportionality test do not seem persuasive: such proposals are not referring to proportionality, but to something different.

In conclusion, that proportionality is a sophisticated theory of adjudication that works well in a number of constitutional systems and other systems with constitutional density is uncontroversial. Its transposability from constitutional law to other legal systems is also uncontroversial, as the concept can (and has) migrate(d) from constitutional law to other legal systems such as EU law. However, this book shows that the debate as to whether proportionality analysis has migrated and/or should migrate to (and be part of) international investment law remains open, and in fact, is currently far from being settled. Certainly, from an international law perspective, more studies are needed to address the question as to whether proportionality is a general principle of international law and/or an emerging rule of customary international law. If arbitral tribunals are to use proportionality to form their interpretation of particular provisions, they must ensure that they master the relevant methodological risks and opportunities.

That being said, *de lege ferenda*, the fact that international investment law lacks constitutional density does not mean that it cannot acquire this in the future, through treaty making – in particular, through the insertion

8 S.L. Karamanian, 'The Place of Human Rights in Investor–State Arbitration' (2013) 17 *Lewis & Clark L Review* 423–47, 437.

9 A. Stone Sweet and J. Mathews, 'Proportionality Balancing and Global Constitutionalism' (2008) 47 *Columbia Journal of Transnational Law* 73–164, 89.

of non-economic considerations in the preambles, and in the text of international investment agreements. Recent investment agreements have included references to labour rights, the rights of indigenous peoples and other non-economic concerns. Future reforms of the international investment regime in general, and the eventual creation of a World Investment Court in particular, may also lead to some appreciation of proportionality analysis. Moreover, proportionality can become a general principle or even customary law in the future.

Reasonableness is a common canon of judicial review at both the domestic and international levels. While the concept of reasonableness remains vague, its open-endedness makes it particularly fit for use in evolving legal systems because it enables such systems to adapt to emerging circumstances. Reasonableness is a flexible, pragmatic and contextual standard that has a distinct evaluative character and can deliver 'just results in individual cases'.[10] Like proportionality, reasonableness expresses a culture of justification: it requires states to offer reasons for their actions and to adopt measures that can be considered to be reasonable, taking into account different interests and values. It requires adjudicators to clarify vague treaty provisions, review state action, and provide reasoned decisions, helping them to bridge the gap between treaty law and the concrete circumstances of each case. Finally, it asks investors to behave reasonably and have only reasonable expectations. Reasonableness requires a more qualitative analysis and relies on a more fluid structure than proportionality. However, it can provide too vague a criterion if it is not accompanied by adequate standards of review.

Reasonableness is part and parcel of international law in general and international investment law and arbitration in particular. It appears in both international investment agreements and arbitral awards. Far from being a purely theoretical tool, reasonableness has acquired practical relevance, helping arbitrators to reach some sensible outcomes. Therefore, the claim that there is no better alternative to proportionality is overstated with regard to the specific field of investor–state arbitration. Despite or perhaps because of its imperfections, reasonableness constitutes a pillar of the current architecture of the international investment regime. In the absence of explicit provisions about which ground of

---

[10] J. Wouters and S. Duquet, 'The Principle of Reasonableness in Global Administrative Law' (2013) 12 *Jean Monnet Working Paper* 1–42.

review is applicable, the choice of which parameter to apply is left to the adjudicator.[11]

Whatever ground of review arbitrators adopt, a crucial matter is the standards of review, that is, the degree of deference granted by arbitral tribunals to the conduct of states in their implementation of international treaties. While other international and domestic jurisdictions have adopted increasingly sophisticated approaches to the issue, only recently has the debate on standards of review touched upon international investment law and arbitration. Identifying the appropriate standards of review is key to making investment arbitration a legitimate, efficient and effective international dispute-settlement mechanism.

While an objective standard of review can strengthen the rule of law and good governance, an overly intrusive review may undermine state regulatory autonomy and the pursuit of legitimate public policy objectives. In turn, this may fuel the alleged 'legitimacy crisis' of the international investment law regime, its coherence with public international law, and ultimately its effectiveness. By the same token, some self-restraint enables regulatory evolution and the adjustment of municipal law to evolving circumstances. Yet, too deferential of an approach may jeopardize state compliance with its international law obligations, and the effectiveness of international investment law and arbitration.

Given the contested nature of international investment law and arbitration, several approaches to the standard-of-review issue can be envisaged. If one adopts a public law paradigm, arbitral tribunals should adopt a 'qualified deference' in appropriate circumstances. Conversely, if one adopts a commercial law paradigm, then no deference should be paid to state action. If one adopts the hybrid conceptualization of investor–state arbitration, the two above-mentioned approaches to the standard-of-review issue are complementary rather than conflicting. In fact, the intensity of review would ultimately depend on the inner quality of the dispute, the provision to be applied and the circumstances of the case – whether it deals with the exercise of state police powers (*acta iure imperii*) or activities of a commercial nature carried out by a state (*acta jure gestionis*). If one adopts an international law paradigm, then a scrutiny of how international courts and tribunals have dealt with the issue of standards of review is in order. Thus, the book explores how international courts and tribunals, such as the International Court of

---

11 F. Ortino, 'Investment Treaties, Sustainable Development and Reasonableness Review: A Case against Strict Proportionality Balancing' (2017) 30 *Leiden JIL* 71–91, 88.

Justice, WTO 'courts' and the European Court of Human Rights have dealt with the issue of standards of review, and concludes that such standards vary from one jurisdiction to another. A unified standard of review may not be desirable within and across different legal systems. Rather, a certain variation of the standards of review across legal systems may be preferable, as such approach endorses the necessary flexibility to better respond to the specific needs of each subfield of international law.

A certain variation of the standards of review within investor–state arbitration can also be appropriate, so as to address different types of disputes. The book shows that arbitral tribunals have increasingly demonstrated some self-restraint – albeit not a total deference – when reviewing public policy-related regulatory measures. In such cases, arbitral tribunals have avoided conducting an intrusive *de novo* review.

Far from advocating the use of proportionality or reasonableness in investment arbitration, this book examines the various arguments in favour of and against such use, and concludes that while the migration of proportionality to international investment law and arbitration is far from being settled, reasonableness seems to be part and parcel of it. The book does not aim at advocating the use of proportionality or reasonableness; rather, it aims at enabling the reader to make informed choices. Whatever the test selected by the arbitrators – be it proportionality or reasonableness – the intensity of review is one of the main tools to calibrate it. Because of the strict scrutiny imposed by the proportionality test, a more deferential standard of review should be adopted when applying such test. Conversely, because the structure of the reasonableness test is more lenient, it may require a more intense standard of review.

Undoubtedly, the debate will continue to address the scope/intensity of arbitral review of state measures and of the method through which this should be expressed, whether that be reasonableness or proportionality. This book contributes to the emerging debate stressing the importance of scrutinizing proportionality and/or reasonableness analysis in conjunction with the standards of review. In conclusion, the discussion about proportionality, reasonableness and standards of review concerns the question as to what role arbitral tribunals should play in the international legal system.

Bibliography

Adinolfi, A. 'The Principle of Reasonableness in European Union Law', in G. Bongiovanni, G. Sartor and C. Valentini (eds), *Reasonableness and Law* (Springer 2009) 381–404.

Ahdieh, R.B. 'Between Dialogue and Decree: International Review of National Courts' (2004) 79 NYULR 2029–163.

Alberti, L.B. *On the Art of Building in Ten Books* (J. Rykwert, N. Leach and R. Tavernor, trans) [*De Re Aedificatoria*, 1450] (MIT Press 1988).

Alexy, R. 'The Reasonableness of Law', in G. Bongiovanni, G. Sartor and C. Valentini (eds), *Reasonableness and Law* (Springer 2009) 3–15.

Alexy, R. 'Constitutional Rights and Proportionality' (2014) 22 *Revus* 51–65.

Allott, P. 'Language, Method and the Nature of International Law' (1971) 45 *British YIL* 79–135.

Alschner, W. 'Regionalism and Overlap in Investment Treaty Law: Towards Consolidation or Contradiction?' (2014) 17 JIEL 271–98.

Alston, P. 'Resisting the Merger and Acquisition of Human Rights by Trade Law: A Reply to Petersmann' (2002) 13 EJIL 815–44.

Alvarez, J.E. 'Constitutional Interpretation in International Organizations', in J.M. Coicaud and V. Heiskanen (eds), *The Legitimacy of International Organizations* (UN University Press 2001) 104–120.

Alvarez, J.E. 'Contemporary Foreign Investment Law: An Empire of Law or the Law of Empire?' (2009) 60 *Alabama LR* 943–75.

Alvarez, J.E. 'A BIT on Custom' (2010) 42 *NYU JIL & Policy* 17–80.

Alvarez, J.E. 'The Evolving BIT', in I.A. Laird and T. Weiler (eds), *Investment Treaty Arbitration and International Law* (Juris 2010) Ch. 1.

Alvarez, J.E. *The Public International Law Regime Governing International Investment* (Hague Academy of International Law 2011).

Alvarez, J.E. 'The Return of the State' (2011) 20 *Minnesota JIL* 223–64.

Alvarez, J.E. 'Beware: Boundary Crossings – A Critical Appraisal of Public Law Approaches to International Investment Law' (2016) 17 JWIT 171–228.

Alvarez, J.E. 'Is Investor–State Arbitration Public?' (2016) 7 JIDS 534–76.

Amerasinghe, C.F. *State Responsibility for Injuries to Aliens* (Clarendon 1967).

Andenas, M. and Fairgrieve, D. 'Intent on Making Mischief: Seven Ways of Using Comparative Law', in P.G. Monateri (ed.), *Methods of Comparative Law* (Edward Elgar 2012) 25–60.

Andenas, M. and Zleptnig, S. 'Proportionality: WTO Law in Comparative Perspective' (2006–2007) 42 *Texas ILJ* 371–423.

Anghie, A. *Imperialism, Sovereignty and the Making of International Law* (CUP 2005).

Arai-Takahashi, Y. *The Margin of Appreciation Doctrine and the Principle of Proportionality in the Jurisprudence of the ECHR* (Intersentia 2002).

Arai-Takahashi, Y. 'Proportionality', in D. Sheldon (ed.), *Oxford Handbook of International Human Rights Law* (OUP 2013) 446–68.

Arato, J. 'The Margin of Appreciation in International Investment Law' (2014) 54 *Virginia JIL* 545–78.

Atienza, M. 'On Reasonableness in Law' (1990) 3 *Ratio Juris* 148–58.

Atienza, M. *El derecho como argumentacion* (Ariel 2006).

Baetens, F. (ed.) *Investment Law Within International Law: Integrationist Perspectives* (CUP 2013).

Banakar, R. 'Power, Culture and Method in Comparative Law' (2009) 5 *International Journal of Law in Context* 69–85.

Barak, A. *Purposive Interpretation in Law* (Princeton University Press 2005).

Barak, A. 'Proportionality and Principled Balancing' (2010) 4 LEHR 1–18.

Barak, A. *Proportionality: Constitutional Rights and their Limitations* (CUP 2012).

Barnes, W.R. 'Contemplating a Civil Law Paradigm for a Future International Commercial Code' (2004–2005) 65 *Louisiana LR* 677–774.

Bartels, L. 'The Separation of Powers within the WTO: How to Avoid Judicial Activism' (2004) 53 ICLQ 861–95.

Bassiouni, M.C. 'A Functional Approach to "General Principles of International Law"' (1990) 11 *Michigan JIL* 768–818.

Batlan, F. 'Law in the Time of Cholera: Disease, State Power, and Quarantines Past and Future' (2007) 80 *Temple LR* 53–122.

Bean, V. and Beauvais, J.C. 'The Global Fifth Amendment? NAFTA's Investment Protection and the Misguided Quest for an International Regulatory Takings Doctrine' (2003) 78 NYULR 30–143.

Beatty, D.M. *The Ultimate Rule of Law* (OUP 2003).

Beatty, D.M. 'Law's Golden Rule', in G. Palombella and N. Walker (eds), *Relocating the Rule of Law* (Hart Publishing 2009) 99–115.

Becroft, R. *The Standards of Review in WTO Dispute Settlement: Critique and Development* (Edward Elgar 2012).

Behn, D. 'Legitimacy, Evolution and growth in Investment Treaty Arbitration: Empirically Evaluating the State of the Art' (2015) 46 *Georgetown JIL* 363–415.

Behrens, P. 'Towards the Constitutionalization of International Investment Protection' (2007) 45 *Archiv des Völkerrechts* 153–79.

Bell, J. 'Comparing Public Law', in A. Harding and E. Orücü (eds), *Comparative Law in the 21st Century* (Kluwer Law International 2002) 235–48.

Bendor, A.L. and Sela, T. 'How Proportional is Proportionality?' (2015) 13 IJCL 530–44.

Benvenisti, E. 'Margin of Appreciation, Consensus and Universal Standards' (1999) 31 *NYU JIL and Politics* 843–54.

Benvenisti, E. 'Reclaiming Democracy: The Strategic Uses of Foreign and International Law by National Courts' (2008) 102 AJIL 241–74.

Benvenisti, E. 'Sovereigns as Trustees of Humanity: On the Accountability of States to Foreign Stakeholders' (2013) 107 AJIL 295–333.

Bermann, G.A. 'Comparative Law and International Organizations', in M. Bussani and U. Mattei (eds), *The Cambridge Companion to Comparative Law* (CUP 2012) 241–54.

Bernal Pulido, C. 'The Migration of Proportionality across Europe' (2013) NZJPIL 483–515.

Besson, S. 'State Consent and Disagreement in International Law-Making. Dissolving the Paradox' (2016) 29 *Leiden JIL* 289–316.

Bhagwati, J. 'Why Multinationals Help Reduce Poverty' (2007) 30 *World Economy* 211–28.

Binder, C., Kriebaum, U., Reinisch, A. and Wittich, S. (eds) *International Investment Law for the 21st Century* (OUP 2009).

Bjorge, E. 'Been There, Done That: The Margin of Appreciation and International Law' (2015) 4 CJICL 181–90.

Bjorge, E. and Williams, J.R. 'The Protean Principle of Proportionality: How Different is Proportionality in EU Contexts?' (2016) *Cambridge LJ* 186–9.

Bjorklund, A.K. 'Reconciling State Sovereignty and Investor Protection in Denial of Justice Claims' (2004–2005) 45 *Virginia JIL* 809–895.

Bjorklund, A.K. 'Investment Treaty Arbitral Decisions as Jurisprudence Constante', in C. Picker, I. Bunn and D. Arner (eds), *International Economic Law: The State and Future of the Discipline* (Hart Publishing 2008) 265–80.

Bjorklund, A.K. 'National Treatment', in A. Reinisch (ed.), *Standards of Investment Protection* (OUP 2008) 29–58.

Blackaby, N. 'Investment Arbitration and Commercial Arbitration (or the Tale of the Dolphin and the Shark)', in J.D.M. Lew and L.A. Mistelis

(eds), *Pervasive Problems in International Arbitration* (Kluwer Law International 2006) 217–33.
Blauberger, M. and Schmidt, S.K. 'The European Court of Justice and its Political Impact' (2017) *West European Politics* 1–12.
Bloche, M.G. 'WTO Deference to National Health Policy: Towards an Interpretive Principle' (2002) 5 JIEL 825–48.
Bobek, M. 'Reasonableness in Administrative Law: A Comparative Reflection on Functional Equivalence', in G. Bongiovanni, G. Sartor and C. Valentini (eds), *Reasonableness and Law* (Springer 2009) 311–26.
Bohanes, J. and Lockhart, N. 'Standard of Review in WTO Law', in D. Bethlehem, D. McRae, R. Neufeld and I. van Damme (eds), *The Oxford Handbook of International Trade Law* (OUP 2010) 379–433.
Bomhoff, J. 'Balancing, the Global and the Local: Judicial Balancing as a Problematic Topic in Comparative (Constitutional) Law' (2008) 31 *Hastings International and Comparative LR* 555–86.
Bomhoff, J. 'Beyond Proportionality: Thinking Comparatively About Constitutional Review and Punitiveness' (2016) 12 *LSE Law, Society and Economy Working Papers*, 1–22.
Bongiovanni, G., Sartor, G. and Valentini, C. 'Introduction', in G. Bongiovanni, G. Sartor and C. Valentini (eds), *Reasonableness and Law* (Springer 2009) xi– xiii.
Bongiovanni, G., Sartor, G. and Valentini, C. (eds) *Reasonableness and Law* (Springer 2009).
Bonnitcha, J., Skovgaard Poulsen, L.N. and Waibel, M. *The Political Economy of the Investment Treaty Regime* (OUP 2017).
Borsi, F. *Leon Battista Alberti* (Harper & Row 1977).
Brabcová, A. 'Accession of the European Union to the European Convention on Human Rights Examining the CJEU's Approach in the Opinion 2/13 the Future of the EU-ECHR Accession Process', Charles University in Prague Faculty of Law Research Paper No. 2016/I/4.
Brems, E. 'Accommodating Diversity in International Human Rights – Legal Techniques', in P. Meerts (ed.), *Culture and International Law* (Hague Academic Press 2008) 63–81.
Brierly, J.L. *The Law of Nations: An Introduction to the International Law of Peace*, 6th edn (H. Waldock, ed.) (OUP 1963).
Brower, C.N. and Schill, S.W. 'Is Arbitration a Threat or a Boom to the Legitimacy of International Investment Law?' (2008) *Chicago JIL* 471–98.
Brown, C. 'Reasonableness and the Law of the Sea: The Prompt Release of the Volga' (2003) 16 *Leiden JIL* 621–30.
Brownlie, I. *Principles of Public International Law*, 7th edn (OUP 2008).
Brownlie, I. *Principles of Public International Law*, 8th edn (OUP 2012).

Bücheler, G. *Proportionality in Investor–State Arbitration* (OUP 2015).

Burke, E. *Enquiry into the Origin of Our Ideas of the Sublime and the Beautiful* (1757).

Burke-White, W.W. and von Staden, A. 'Private Litigation in a Public Law Sphere: The Standard of Review in Investor–State Arbitrations' (2010) 35 *Yale JIL* 283–346.

Burke-White, W.W. and von Staden, A. 'The Need for Public Law Standards of Review in Investor–State Arbitrations', in S. Schill (ed.), *International Investment Law and Comparative Public Law* (OUP 2010) 689–720.

Burton, D.M. *The History of Mathematics: An Introduction* (MacGrawHill 2007).

Bussani, M. and Mattei, U. (eds) *The Cambridge Companion to Comparative Law* (CUP 2012).

Calamita, N.J. 'The Principle of Proportionality and the Problem of Indeterminacy in International Investment Treaties', in A. Bjorklund (ed.), *Yearbook of International Investment Law and Policy* (2013–2014) 157–200.

Cannizzaro, E. *Il principio della proporzionalità nell'ordinamento internazionale* (Giuffré 2000).

Cannizzaro, E. 'The Role of Proportionality in the Law of International Countermeasures' (2001) 12 EJIL 889–916.

Cannizzaro, E. 'Proportionality and Margin of Appreciation in the Whaling Case: Reconciling Antithetical Doctrines?' (2017) 27 EJIL 1061–1069.

Cappelletti, M. 'Repudiating Montesquieu? The Expansion and Legitimacy of "Constitutional Justice"' (1985) 35 *Catholic University LR* 1–32.

Caron, D.D. 'Investor–State Arbitration: Strategic and Tactical Perspectives on Legitimacy' (2009) 32 *Suffolk Transnational LR* 513–24.

Carozza, P.G. 'The Problematic Applicability of Subsidiarity to International Law and Institutions' (2016) 61 *American Journal of Jurisprudence* 51–67.

Cass, D.Z. *The Constitutionalization of the World Trade Organization: Legitimacy, Democracy, and Community in the International Trading System* (OUP 2005).

Cassese, S. 'Beyond Legal Comparison' (2012) *Annuario di diritto comparato e di studi legislativi* 387–95.

Chen, T.-F. 'The Standard of Review and the Roles of ICSID Arbitral Tribunals in Investor–State Dispute Settlement' (2012) 5 *Contemporary Asia Arbitration Journal* 23–43.

Cheng, B. *General Principles of Law as Applied by International Courts and Tribunals* (CUP 1953).

Choudhury, B. 'Recapturing Public Power: Is Investment Arbitration's Engagement of the Public Interest Contributing to the Democratic Deficit?' (2008) 41 VJTL 775–832.

Choudry, S. 'Migration as a New Metaphor in Comparative Constitutional Law', in S. Choudry (ed.), *The Migration of Constitutional Ideas* (CUP 2006) 1–25.

Choudry, S. (ed.) *The Migration of Constitutional Ideas* (CUP 2006).

Christiansen, T. and Reh, C. *Constitutionalizing the European Union* (Palgrave Macmillan 2009).

Christoffersen, J. *Fair Balance: A Study of Proportionality, Subsidiarity and Primarity in the European Convention on Human Rights* (Martinus Nijhoff 2009).

Clark, M. 'Venezuela's Withdrawal from the ICSID Convention', *Association for International Arbitration Bulletin*, October 2012, 2.

Cohen, M.A. *Beyond Beauty: Reexamining Architectural Proportion* (Marsilio 2013).

Cohen-Eliya, M. and Porat, I. 'Proportionality and the Culture of Justification' (2011) 59 AJCL 463–90.

Cohen-Eliya, M. and Porat, I. *Proportionality and Constitutional Culture* (CUP 2012).

Cohen-Eliya, M. and Porat, I. 'Proportionality and Justification' (2014) 64 *University of Toronto LJ* 458–77.

Coicaud, J.M. *Legitimacy and Politics* (CUP 2002).

Colares, J.F. and Bohn, J.W. 'NAFTA's Double Standards of Review' (2007) 42 *Wake Forest LR* 199–246.

Comeaux, P. and Kinsella, N. *Protecting Foreign Investment under International Law* (Oceana Publications 1997).

Contiades, X. and Fotiadou, A. 'Social Rights in the Age of Proportionality: Global Economic Crisis and Constitutional Litigation' (2012) 10 IJCL 660–86.

Coomans, F. 'Reviewing Implementation of Social and Economic Rights: An Assessment of the "Reasonableness" Test as Developed by the South African Constitutional Court' (2005) 65 *Heidelberg JIL* 167–96.

Cordero Moss, G. 'Full Protection and Security', in A. Reinish (ed.), *Standards of Investment Protection* (OUP 2009) 131–50.

Corten, O. *L'utilisation du raisonnable par le juge international. Discours juridique, raisons et contradictions* (Bruylant 1997).

Corten, O. 'The Notion of Reasonable in International Law: Legal Discourse, Reason and Contradictions' (1999) 48 ICLQ 613–25.

Corten, O. 'Reasonableness in International Law', in R. Wolfrum (ed.), *Max Planck Encyclopedia of Public International Law* (OUP 2013).

Craig, P. *Administrative Law*, 6th edn (Sweet and Maxwell 2008).

Craig, P. 'Proportionality, Rationality and Review' (2010) NZLR 265–301.
Craig, P. 'The Nature of Reasonableness Review' (2013) 66 *Current Legal Problems* 131–67.
Craig, P. and De Búrca, G., *EU Law*, 5th edn (OUP 2011).
Crawford, J. 'International Protection of Foreign Direct Investment: Between Clinical Isolation and Systematic Integration', in R. Hofmann and C.J. Tams (eds), *International Investment Law and General International Law: From Clinical Isolation to Systemic Integration?* (Nomos 2011) 17–28.
Crawford, J. (ed.) *Brownlie's Principles of Public International Law*, 8th edn (OUP 2012).
Croley, S.P. and Jackson, J.H. 'WTO Dispute Procedures, Standard of Review, and Deference to National Governments' (1996) 90 AJIL 193–213.
Daly, P. *A Theory of Deference in Administrative Law – Basis, Application and Scope* (CUP 2012).
Dattu, R. 'A Journey from Havana to Paris: The Fifty-Year Quest for the Elusive Multilateral Agreement on Investment' (2000–2001) 24 *Fordham ILJ* 275–316.
Dawson, M., De Witte, B. and Muir, E. (eds) *Judicial Activism at the European Court of Justice* (Edward Elgar 2013).
Daza-Clark, A.M. *International Investment Law and Water Resources Management* (Brill 2016).
De Brabandere, E. *Investment Treaty Arbitration as Public International Law: Procedural Aspects and Implications* (CUP 2014).
De Brabandere, E. and Gazzini, T. (eds) *International Investment Law: The Sources of Rights and Obligations* (Martinus Nijhoff 2012).
De Búrca, G. 'The Principle of Proportionality and its Application in EC Law' (1993) 13 *Yearbook of European Law* 105–150.
De Búrca, G. 'After the EU Charter of Fundamental Rights: The Court of Justice as a Human Rights Adjudicator?' (2013) 14 *Maastricht Journal of European and Comparative Law* 168–84.
De la Rasilla del Moral, I. 'The Increasingly Marginal Appreciation of the Margin-of-Appreciation Doctrine' (2006) 7 *German LJ* 611–23.
De Vittor, F. and Cannizzaro, E. 'Proportionality in the European Convention on Human Rights', in R. Kolb and G. Gaggioli (eds), *Research Handbook on Human Rights and Humanitarian Law* (Edward Elgar 2013) 125–45.
De Wet, E. and Vidmar, J. (eds) *Hierarchy in International Law: The Place of Human Rights* (OUP 2012).
Del Vecchio, G. *Sui principi generali del diritto* (Giuffré 1958).
Desmedt, A. 'Proportionality in WTO Law' (2001) 4 JIEL 441–80.

DiMascio, N. and Pauwelyn, J. 'Non-Discrimination in Trade and Investment Treaties: Worlds Apart or Two Sides of the Same Coin?' (2008) 102 AJIL 48–89.

Dolzer, R. and Schreuer, C. *Principles of International Investment Law*, 2nd edn (OUP 2012).

Domingo, R. *The New Global Law* (CUP 2010).

Douglas, Z. 'The Hybrid Foundations of Investment Treaty Arbitration' (2003) 74 BYIL 151–289.

Douglas, Z. 'Can a Doctrine of Precedent be Justified in Investment Arbitration?' (2010) 25 *ICSID Review – FILJ* 104–110.

Douglas, Z., Pauwelyn, J. and Viñuales, J.E. (eds) *The Foundations of International Investment Law: Bringing Theory into Practice* (OUP 2014).

Douglas, Z. 'International Responsibility for Domestic Adjudication: Denial of Justice Reconstructed' (2014) ICLQ 1–34.

Dugan, C., Rubins, N., Wallace, D. and Sabahi, B. *Investor–State Arbitration* (OUP 2008).

Dupont, C. and Schultz, T. 'Towards a New Heuristic Model: Investment Arbitration as a Political System' (2016) 7 JIDS 3–30.

Dupuy, P.-M., Francioni, F. and Petersmann, E.-U. (eds) *Human Rights in International Investment Law and Arbitration* (OUP 2009).

Eeckhout, P. 'The Scales of Trade – Reflections on the Growth and Functions of the WTO Adjudicative Branch' (2010) 13 JIEL 3–26.

Ellis E. (ed.) *The Principle of Proportionality in the Laws of Europe* (Hart Publishing 1999).

Ellis, J. 'General Principles and Comparative Law' (2011) 22 EJIL 949–71.

Emiliou, N. *The Principle of Proportionality in European Law: A Comparative Study* (Kluwer Law International 1996).

Endicott, T. 'Proportionality and Incommensurability', *Oxford Legal Research Paper* 40 (2012).

Epstein, A.L. 'The Reasonable Man Revisited: Some Problems in the Anthropology of Law' (1972–1973) 7 *Law & Society R* 643–64.

Fassbender, B. 'The Meaning of International Constitutional Law', in N. Tsagourias (ed.), *Transnational Constitutionalism: International and European Models* (CUP 2007) 837–51.

Fassbender, B. *The United Nations Charter as the Constitution of the International Community* (Brill 2009).

Feldman, D. 'Modalities of Internationalisation in Constitutional Law' (2006) 18 *European Review of Public Law* 131–58.

Fellman, D. 'Constitutionalism', in P.P. Wiener (ed.), *Dictionary of the History of Ideas: Studies of Selected Pivotal Ideas* vol. 1 (Charles Scribner's Sons 1973) 485.

Feyerabend, P.K. *Against Method: Outline of an Anarchistic Theory of Knowledge* (Verso 1978).

Fish, M.J. 'An Eye for an Eye: Proportionality as a Moral Principle of Punishment' (2008) 28 OJLS 57–71.

Focarelli, C. *International Law as Social Construct: The Global Struggle for Justice* (OUP 2012).

Follesdal, A. 'Building Democracy at the Bar: the European Court of Human Rights as an Agent of Transitional Cosmopolitanism' (2016) 7 *Transnational Legal Theory* 95–113.

Fontanelli, F. 'The Mythology of Proportionality in Judgments of the Court of Justice of the European Union on Internet and Fundamental Rights' (2016) 36 OJLS 630–60.

Foster, C.E. 'Adjudication, Arbitration and the Turn to Public Law Standards of Review' (2012) 3 JIDS 525–58.

Foster, C.E. 'International Adjudication – Standard of Review and Burden of Proof' (2012) 21 RECIEL 80–91.

Foster, C.E. 'A New Stratosphere? Investment Treaty Arbitration as "Internationalized Public Law"' (2015) 64 ICLQ 461–85.

Francioni, F. 'Compensation for Nationalisation of Foreign Property: The Borderland between Law and Equity' (1975) 24 ICLQ 255–83.

Francioni, F. 'Access to Justice, Denial of Justice and International Investment Law' (2009) 20 EJIL 729–47.

Franck, S.D. 'The Legitimacy Crisis in Investment Treaty Arbitration: Privatizing Public International Law Through Inconsistent Decisions' (2005) 73 *Fordham LR* 1521–625.

Franck, S.D. 'Development and Outcomes of Investment Treaty Arbitration' (2009) 50 *Harvard ILJ* 435–89.

Franck, T.M. 'On Proportionality of Countermeasures in International Law' (2008) 102 AJIL 715–67.

Franck, T.M. 'Proportionality in International Law' (2010) 4 LEHR 230–42.

Frankenberg, G. 'Critical Comparisons: Re-thinking Comparative Law' (1985) 26 *Harvard ILJ* 411–55.

Frankenberg, G. 'Comparing Constitutions: Ideas, Ideals, and Ideology – Toward a Layered Narrative' (2006) 4 IJCL 439–59.

Frankenberg, G. 'Comparative Constitutional Law', in M. Bussani and U. Mattei (eds), *Cambridge Companion to Comparative Constitutional Law* (CUP 2012) 171–90.

Freund, G.K. 'Look up in the Sky, it's a Bird, it's a Plane … it's Reasonableness' (1991) 20 *Southwestern University LR* 195–218.

Fukunaga, Y. 'Standard of Review and Scientific Truths in the WTO Dispute Settlement System and Investment Arbitration' (2012) 3 JIDS 1–18.

Gaja, G. 'Principi generali del diritto (Diritto internazionale)' (1986) 36 *Enciclopedia diritto* 533–8.
Gao, J. 'Reasonableness of the Bond Under Article 292 of the LOS Convention: Practice of the ITLOS' (2008) 7 *Chinese JIL* 115–42.
Gardam, J.G. 'Proportionality and Force in International Law' (1993) 87 AJIL 391–413.
Garrido-Muñoz, A. 'Managing Uncertainty: The International Court of Justice, "Objective Reasonableness" and the Judicial Function' (2017) 30 *Leiden* JIL 1–18.
Gaubatz, K.T. and MacArthur, M. 'How International is International Law?' (2001) 22 *Michigan JIL* 239–82.
Gentili, A. *De iure belli* [1598] (John C. Rolfe trans) (Clarendon Press 1933).
González Jácome, J. 'El uso del derecho comparado como forma de escape de la subordinación colonial' (2006) 7 *International Law: Revista Colombiana de Derecho Internacional* 295–338.
Gordon, R. 'Two Dogmas of Proportionality' (2011) *Judicial Review* 182–91.
Gordon, S. *Controlling the State: Constitutionalism from Ancient Athens to Today* (Harvard University Press 1999).
Greenberg, M.J. *Euclidean and Non-Euclidean Geometries: Development and History*, 4th edn (W.H. Freeman 2007).
Griffey, B. 'The "Reasonableness" Test: Assessing Violations of State Obligations under the Optional Protocol to the International Covenant on Economic, Social and Cultural Rights' (2011) 11 *Human Rights LR* 275–327.
Gruszczynski, L. *Regulating Health and Environmental Risks under WTO Law. Critical Analysis of the SPS Agreement* (OUP 2010).
Gruszczynski, L. and Vadi, V. 'Standard of Review and Scientific Evidence in WTO Law and International Investment Arbitration: Converging Parallels?', in L. Gruszczynski and W. Werner (eds), *Deference in International Courts and Tribunals: Standard of Review and Margin of Appreciation* (OUP 2014) 152–72.
Gruszczynski, L. and Werner, W. (eds) *Deference in International Courts and Tribunals* (OUP 2014).
Gruszczynski, L. and Werner, W. 'Introduction', in L. Gruszczynski and W. Werner (eds), *Deference in International Courts and Tribunals* (OUP 2014) 1–15.
Guild, E., Gortázar Rotaeche, C. and Kostakopoulou, D. (eds) *The Reconceptualization of European Union Citizenship* (Brill 2014).
Gunn, T.J. 'Deconstructing Proportionality in Limitations Analysis' (2006) 19 *Emory International LR* 465–98.

Guntrip, E. 'Self-Determination and Foreign Direct Investment: Re-imagining Sovereignty in International Investment Law' (2016) 65 ICLQ 829–57.

Gutteridge, H.C. 'Comparative Law and the Law of Nations' (1944) 21 *British YIL* 1–10.

Guzman, A. 'Explaining the Popularity of Bilateral Investment Treaties: Why LDCs Sign Treaties that Hurt Them' (1997) 38 *Virginia JIL* 639–88.

Guzman, A.T. 'A Compliance-Based Theory of International Law' (2002) 90 *California LR* 1823–80.

Habermas, J. *The Crisis of the European Union. A Response* (C. Cronin, trans) (Polity Press 2012).

Hallward-Driemeier, M. 'Do Bilateral Investment Treaties Attract Foreign Direct Investment? Only a Bit … And They Could Bite', Policy Research Working Paper No. 3121 (World Bank 2003).

Harbo, T.I. 'The Function of the Proportionality Principle in EU Law' (2010) 16 *European LJ* 158–85.

Harbo, T.I. *The Function of the Proportionality Analysis in European Law* (Brill 2015).

Helfer, L.R. and Slaughter, A.-M. 'Toward a Theory of Effective Supranational Adjudication' (1997) 107 *Yale LJ* 273–391.

Henckels, C. 'Indirect Expropriation and the Right to Regulate: Revisiting Proportionality Analysis and the Standard of Review in Investor–State Arbitration' (2012) 15 JIEL 223–55.

Henckels, C. 'Proportionality and the Standard of Review in Fair and Equitable Treatment Cases' (2012) SIEL Working Paper 10.

Henckels, C. 'The Role of the Standard of Review and the Importance of Deference in Investor–State Arbitration', in L. Gruszczynski and W. Werner (eds), *Deference in International Courts and Tribunals* (OUP 2014) 113–34.

Henckels, C. *Proportionality and Deference in Investor–State Arbitration: Balancing Investment Protection and Regulatory Autonomy* (CUP 2015).

Hickman, T. 'Problems for Proportionality' (2010) NZLR 303–326.

Higgins, R. *Problems and Process: International Law and How We Use It* (OUP 1994).

Hilf, M. 'Power, Rules and Principles – Which Orientation for WTO/GATT Law?' (2001) 4 JIEL 111–20.

Hirsch, M. 'Investment Tribunals and Human Rights: Divergent Paths', in P.-M. Dupuy, F. Francioni and E.-U. Petersmann (eds), *Human Rights in International Investment Law and Arbitration* (OUP 2008) 97–114.

Hirsch, M. 'Sources of International Investment Law', in A.K. Bjorklund and A. Reinisch (eds), *International Investment Law and Soft Law* (Edward Elgar 2012) 9–38.

Hirschl, R. *Towards Juristocracy: The Origins and Consequences of the New Constitutionalism* (Harvard University Press 2004).

Hirschl, R. 'The Question of Case Selection in Comparative Constitutional Law' (2005) 53 AJCL 125–56.

Hoekman, B. 'The World Trade Order: Global Governance by Judiciary?' (2016) 27 EJIL 1083–1093.

Howse, R. 'The World Trade Organization 20 Years On: Global Governance by Judiciary' (2016) 27 EJIL 9–77.

Howse, R. and Nicolaidis, K. 'Legitimacy Through "Higher Law"'? Why Constitutionalizing the WTO is a Step Too Far', in T. Cottier and P.C. Mavroidis (eds), *The Role of the Judge in International Trade Regulation: Experience and Lessons for the WTO* (University of Michigan Press 2003) 307–348.

Hsu, L. 'Applicability of WTO Law in Regional Trade Agreements: Identifying the Links', in L. Bartels and F. Ortino (eds), *Regional Trade Agreements and the WTO Legal System* (OUP 2006) 525–52.

Husa, J. 'Methodology of Comparative Law Today: From Paradoxes to Flexibility?' (2006) 4 *Revue Internationale de droit comparé* 1095–1117.

Ioannidis, M. 'Beyond Standard of Review – Deference Criteria in WTO Law and the Case for a Procedural Approach', in L. Gruszczynski and W. Werner (eds), *Deference in International Courts and Tribunals* (OUP 2014) 91–112.

Jackson, J. *The World Trading System* (MIT Press 2002).

Jackson, V.C. 'Being Proportional About Proportionality' (2004) 21 *Constitutional Commentary* 803–859.

Jackson, V.C. 'Constitutional Law in an Age of Proportionality' (2015) 124 *Yale LJ* 3094–3193.

Jackson, V.C. and Tushnet, M. (eds) *Defining the Field of Comparative Constitutional Law* (Praeger 2002).

Jacob, M. *Precedents and Case-based Reasoning in the European Court of Justice* (CUP 2014).

Jans, J.H. 'Proportionality Revisited' (2000) 27 *Legal Issues of Economic Integration* 239–65.

Jovanović, S. *Restriction de compétences discrétionnaires des Etats en droit international* (Pédone 1988).

Judson, L. 'Aristotle on Fair Exchange' (1997) 15 *Oxford Studies in Ancient Philosophy* 147–75.

Juvenal, *The Satires* (N. Rudd, trans) (OUP 1992).

Kahn-Freund, O. 'On Uses and Misuses of Comparative Law' (1974) 37 MLR 1–27.

Kalicki, J. and Medeiros, S. 'Investment Arbitration in Brazil' (2008) 24 *Arbitration International* 423–45.

Kapterian, G. 'A Critique of the WTO Jurisprudence on Necessity' (2010) 59 ICLQ 89–127.

Karamanian, S.L. 'The Place of Human Rights in Investor–State Arbitration' (2013) 17 *Lewis & Clark L Review* 423–47.

Kaufmann-Kohler, G. 'Arbitral Precedent: Dream, Necessity or Excuse?' (2007) 23 *Arbitration International* 357–78.

Kaufmann-Kohler, G. and Podestà, M. 'Challenges on the Road toward a Multilateral Investment Court', 201 *Columbia FDI Perspectives*, 5 June 2017.

Kennedy, D. 'Political Ideology and Comparative Law', in M. Bussani and U. Mattei (eds), *The Cambridge Companion to Comparative Law* (CUP 2012) 35–56.

Kilcup, J. 'Proportionality in Customary International Law: An Argument Against Aspirational Laws of War' (2016) 17 *Chicago JIL* 244–72.

Kingsbury, B. and Schill, S. 'Investor–State Arbitration as Governance: Fair and Equitable Treatment, Proportionality and the Emerging Global Administrative Law', in A.J. van den Berg (ed.), *50 Years of the New York Convention* (Kluwer Law International 2009) 5–68.

Kingsbury, B. and Schill, S. 'Investor–State Arbitration as Governance: Fair and Equitable Treatment, Proportionality and the Emerging Global Administrative Law', New York University School of Law, Public Law & Legal Theory Research Paper Series, Working Paper No. 09-46 (2009) 1–56.

Kingsbury, B. and Schill, S. 'Public Law Concepts to Balance Investors' Rights with State Regulatory Actions in the Public Interest: The Concept of Proportionality', in S. Schill (ed.), *International Investment Law and Comparative Public Law* (OUP 2010) 75–105.

Kingsbury, B. and Straumann, B. (eds) *The Roman Foundations of the Law of Nations* (OUP 2010).

Klabbers, J., Peters, A. and Ulfstein, G. (eds) *The Constitutionalization of International Law* (OUP 2009).

Kläger, R. 'Fair and Equitable Treatment: A Look at the Theoretical Underpinnings of Legitimacy and Fairness' (2010) 11 JWIT 435–42.

Kläger, R. *Fair and Equitable Treatment in International Investment Law* (CUP 2011).

Klatt, M. and Meister, M. *The Constitutional Structure of Proportionality* (OUP 2012).

Kleinheisterkamp, J. 'Investment Treaty Law and the Fear of Sovereignty: Transnational Challenges and Solution' (2015) 78 MLR 793–825.

Kline, M. *Mathematical Thought from Ancient to Modern Times* (OUP 1972).

Knight, D.R. 'Mapping the Rainbow of Review: Recognizing Variable Intensity' (2010) NZLR 393–431.

Kriebaum, U. and Schreuer, C. 'The Concept of Property in Human Rights Law and International Investment Law', in S. Breitenmoser (ed.), *Liber Amicorum Luzius Wildhaber: Human Rights Democracy and the Rule of Law* (Nomos 2007) 743–62.

Kriebaum, U. 'The Relevance of Economic and Political Conditions for Protection under Investment Treaties' (2011) 10 *The Law and Practice of International Courts and Tribunals* 383–404.

Kulick, A. *Global Public Interest in International Investment Law* (CUP 2012).

Kumm, M. 'Constitutional Rights as Principles: On the Structure and Domain of Constitutional Justice' (2004) 3 IJCL 574–96.

Kumm, M. 'The Legitimacy of International Law: A Constitutionalist Framework of Analysis' (2004) 15 EJIL 907–931.

Kumm, M. 'The Idea of Socratic Contestation and the Right to Justification: The Point of Rights-Based Proportionality Review' (2010) 4 LEHR 141–75.

Kurtz, J. 'Australia's Rejection of Investor–State Arbitration: Causation, Omission and Implication' (2012) 27 *ICSID Review* 65–86.

Kurtz, J. *The World Trade Organization and International Investment Law: Converging Systems* (CUP 2016).

Lacey, N. and Pickard, H. 'The Chimera of Proportionality' (2015) 78 MLR 216–40.

Lalive, P. 'On the Reasoning of International Arbitral Awards' (2010) 1 JIDS 55–65.

Landau, T. 'Reasons for Reasons: The Tribunal's Duty in Investor–State Arbitration', in A.J. Van den Berg (ed.), *50 Years of the New York Convention* (Kluwer 2009) 187–205.

Lang, A. 'The Judicial Sensibility of the WTO Appellate Body' (2016) 27 EJIL 1095–1105.

Larouer, C.J. 'In the Name of Sovereignty? The Battle Over *In Dubio Mitius* Inside and Outside the Courts', Cornell Law School Graduate Student Papers Series, Cornell Law Library (2009) 1–49.

Lauterpacht, H. *Private Law Sources and Analogies of International Law: With Special Reference to International Arbitration* (Longmans, Green and Co Ltd 1927).

Lauterpacht, H. *The Function of Law in the International Community* (OUP 2011).
Legg, A. *The Margin of Appreciation in International Human Rights Law* (OUP 2012).
Legrand, P. 'How to Compare Now?' (1996) 16 *Legal Studies* 232–42.
Legrand, P. 'The Impossibility of Legal Transplants' (1997) 4 *Maastricht Journal of European and Comparative Law* 111–24.
Legrand, P. 'On the Singularity of Law' (2006) 47 *Harvard ILJ* 517–30.
Lennard, M. 'Navigating by the Stars: Interpreting the WTO Agreements' (2002) 5 *Journal of International Economic Law* 17–89.
Leonhardsen, E.M. 'Looking for Legitimacy: Exploring Proportionality Analysis in Investment Treaty Arbitration' (2012) 3 JIDS 95–136.
Leonhardsen, E.M. 'Treaty Change, Arbitral Practice and the Search for Balance: Standards of Review and the Margin of Appreciation in International Investment Law', in L. Gruszczynski and W. Werner (eds), *Deference in International Courts and Tribunals* (OUP 2014) 135–51.
Levi Montalcini, R. *In Praise of Imperfection* (Basic Books 1989).
Livio, M. *The Golden Ratio: The Story of Phi, The World's Most Astonishing Number* (Broadway Books 2002).
Loughlin, M. 'What is Constitutionalization?', in P. Dobner and M. Loughlin (eds), *The Twilight of Constitutionalism?* (OUP 2010) 47–69.
Lowe, V. 'The Politics of Law-Making: Are the Method and Character of Norm Creation Changing?', in M. Byers (ed.), *The Role of Law in International Politics: Essays in International Relations and International Law* (OUP 2000) 207–26.
Lowe, V. 'Regulation or Expropriation?' (2002) 55 *Current Legal Problems* 447–66.
Lowenfeld, A.F. *International Litigation and the Quest for Reasonableness – Essays in Private International Law* (OUP 1996).
MacCormick, N. 'On Reasonableness', in C. Perelman and R. Van der Elst (eds), *Les notions à contenu variable en droit* (Bruylant 1984) 131–56.
Malmström, C. 'In Davos, Discussing Investment Disputes', *European Commission Blog*, 19 January 2017.
Mann, H. 'The Right of States to Regulate and International Investment Law: A Comment', in UNCTAD, *The Development Dimension of FDI: Policy and Rule-Making Perspectives* (UN 2003) 211–23.
Matscher, F. 'Methods of Interpretation of the Convention', in R. St. John Macdonald, F. Matscher and H. Petzold (eds), *The European System for the Protection of Human Rights* (Martinus Nijhoff 1993) 63–82.

Maupin, J.A. 'Differentiating Among International Investment Disputes', in Z. Douglas, J. Pauwelyn and J.E. Viñuales (eds), *The Foundations of International Investment Law* (OUP 2014) 467–98.

Mavroidis, P., Meagher, N., Prusa, T.J. and Yanguas, T., 'Ask for the Moon, Settle for the Stars. What is a Reasonable Period to Comply with WTO Awards?' *EUI Working Paper* RSCAS 2016/45 (2016) 1–23.

Mavroidis, P. 'The Gang that Couldn't Shoot Straight: The Not So Magnificent Seven of the WTO Appellate Body' (2017) 27 EJIL 1107–118.

McGoldrick, D. 'A Defence of the Margin of Appreciation and an Argument for Its Application by the Human Rights Committee' (2016) 65 ICLQ 21–60.

McIntyre, O. 'The Principle of Equitable and Reasonable Utilisation', in A. Tanzi, O. McIntyre, A. Kolliopoulos, A. Rieu-Clarke and R. Kinna (eds), *The UNECE Convention on the Protection and Use of Transboundary Watercourses and International Lakes* (Brill 2015) 146–59.

McLachlan, C. 'The Principle of Systemic Integration and Article 31(3)(c) of the Vienna Convention' (2005) 54 ICLQ 279–320.

McLachlan, C. 'Investment Treaties and General International Law' (2008) 57 ICLQ 361–401.

McLachlan, C., Shore, L. and Weiniger, M. *International Investment Arbitration* (OUP 2007).

McRae, D. 'Proportionality and the Gulf of Maine Maritime Boundary Dispute' (1981) 19 *Canadian YIL* 287–302.

McRae, D. 'The World Trade Organization and International Investment Law: Converging Systems – Can the Case for Convergence be Made?' (2014) 9 *Jerusalem Review of Legal Studies* 13–23.

Michaels, R. 'The Functional Method of Comparative Law', in M. Reimann and R. Zimmermann (eds), *The Oxford Handbook of Comparative Law* (OUP 2006) 339–82.

Miles, K. 'Investor–State Dispute Settlement: Conflict, Convergence and Future Directions' (2016) *European Yearbook of International Economic Law* 273–308.

Mitchell, A.D. 'Proportionality and Remedies in WTO Disputes' (2007) 17 EJIL 985–1008.

Mizushima, T. 'The Role of the State after an Award is Rendered in Investor–State Arbitration', in S. Lalani and R. Polanco Lazo (eds), *The Role of the State in Investor–State Arbitration* (Brill 2015) 274–92.

Möller, K. 'Proportionality: Challenging the Critics' (2012) 10 IJCL 709–731.

Moloo, R. and Jacinto, J.M. 'Standards of Review and Reviewing Standards: Public Interest Regulation in International Investment Law' (2011:2012) *Yearbook of International Investment Law and Policy* 539–67.

Monateri, P.G. 'Black Gaius – A Quest for the Multicultural Origins of the "Western Legal Tradition"' (1999–2000) 51 *Hastings LJ* 479–556.

Monateri P.G. (ed.) *Methods of Comparative Law* (Edward Elgar 2012).

Montt, S. *State Liability in Investment Treaty Arbitration: Global Constitutional and Administrative Law in the BIT Generation* (Hart Publishing 2009).

Moorhead, T. 'European Union Law as International Law' (2012) 5 EJLS 125–44.

Morrone, A. 'Constitutional Adjudication and the Principle of Reasonableness', in G. Bongiovanni, G. Sartor and C. Valentini (eds), *Reasonableness and Law* (Springer 2009) 215–22.

Mountfield, H. 'Regulatory Expropriations in Europe: The Approach of the European Court of Human Rights' (2002) 11 *NYU Environmental LJ* 136–46.

Mutis Tellez, F. 'Conditions and Criteria for the Protection of Legitimate Expectations under International Investment Law' (2012) 28 *ICSID Review–FILJ* 432–42.

Nadavukaren Schefer, K. *International Investment Law* (Edward Elgar 2013).

Newcombe, A. and Paradell, L. *Law and Practice of Investment Treaties* (Kluwer Law International 2009).

Newton, M. and May, L. *Proportionality in International Law* (OUP 2014).

Nolte, G. 'General Principles of German and European Administrative Law – A Comparison in Historical Perspective' (1994) 57 MLR 191–212.

Nolte, G. 'Thin or Thick? The Principle of Proportionality in International Humanitarian Law' (2010) 4 LEHR 245–55.

Oesch, M. *Standards of Review in WTO Dispute Resolution* (OUP 2003).

Oesch, M. 'Standards of Review in WTO Dispute Resolution' (2003) 6 JIEL 635–59.

O'Keefe, R. 'Proportionality', in J. Crawford, A. Pellet and S. Olleson (eds), *The Law of International Responsibility* (OUP 2010) 1157–68.

Olynyk, S. 'A Balanced Approach to Distinguishing Between Legitimate Regulation and Indirect Expropriation in Investor–State Arbitration' (2012) 15 *International Trade and Business LR* 254–96.

Orellana, M.A. 'Science, Risk and Uncertainty: Public Health Measures and Investment Disciplines', in P. Kahn and T.W. Wälde (eds), *New Aspects of International Investment Law* (Martinus Nijhoff 2007) Ch. 15.

Orellana, M.A. 'The Role of Science in Investment Arbitrations Concerning Public Health and the Environment' (2007) 17 *Yearbook of International Environmental Law* 48–72.

Ortino, F. 'From "Non-discrimination" to "Reasonableness": A Paradigm Shift in International Economic Law?' (2005) *NYU Jean Monnet Working Paper* 01/05.

Ortino, F. 'Investment Treaties, Sustainable Development and Reasonableness Review: A Case against Strict Proportionality Balancing' (2017) 30 *Leiden JIL* 71–91.

Paparinskis, M. 'Analogies and Other Regimes of International Law', in Z. Douglas, J. Pauwelyn and J.E. Viñuales (eds), *The Foundations of International Investment Law: Bringing Theory into Practice* (OUP 2014) Ch. 3.

Paulsson, J. *Denial of Justice in International Law* (CUP 2005).

Paulsson, J. 'Indirect Expropriation: Is the Right to Regulate a Risk?' (2006) TDM 1–9.

Paulsson, J. 'International Arbitration is not Arbitration' (2008) 2 *Stockholm International Arbitration Review* 1–20.

Pauwelyn, J. 'At the Edge of Chaos? Foreign Investment Law as a Complex Adaptive System' (2014) 29 *ICSID Review* 372–418.

Peng, S. 'How Much Time is Reasonable – The Arbitral Decisions under Article 21.3(c) of the DSU' (2008) 26 *Berkeley JIL* 323–51.

Perelman, C. 'Le raisonnable et le déraisonnable en droit' (1978) 23 *Archives de Philosophie du droit* 35–42.

Perelman, C. 'The Rational and the Reasonable', in C. Perelman (ed.), *The New Rhetoric and the Humanities: Essays on Rhetoric and Its Applications* (Reidel 1979) 117–23.

Perelman, C. *Le raisonnable et le déraisonnable en droit* (Libraire Générale de Droit et de Jurisprudence 1984).

Peters, A. 'The Meaning, Measure and Misuse of Standards of Review' (2009) 13 *Lewis & Clark LR* 233–77.

Petersen, N. *Proportionality and Judicial Activism* (CUP 2017).

Peterson, L.E. *The Global Governance of Foreign Direct Investment: Madly Off in All Directions* (Friedrich Ebert Stiftung Publisher 2005).

Picciotto, S. 'Linkages in International Investment Regulation: The Antinomies of the Draft Multilateral Agreement on Investment' (1998) 19 *University of Pennsylvania JIEL* 731–68.

Picker, C.B. 'International Law's Mixed Heritage: A Common/Civil Law Jurisdiction' (2008) 41 *Vanderbilt Journal of Transnational Law* 1083–1140.

Picker, C.B. 'International Investment Law: Some Legal Cultural Insights', in L. Trakman and N. Ranieri (eds), *Regionalism in International Investment Law* (OUP 2013) 27–58.

Pila, J. 'Pluralism, Principles and Proportionality in Intellectual Property' (2014) 34 OJLS 181–200.

Pirker, B. *Proportionality Analysis and Models of Judicial Review* (Europa Law Publishing 2013).

Poiares Maduro, M. 'How Constitutional Can the EU Be? The Tension between Intergovernamentalism and Constitutionalism in the EU', in J.H.H. Weiler and C.L. Eisgruber (eds), *Altneuland: The EU Constitution in a Contextual Perspective*, Jean Monnet Working Paper No. 5/04, 2004.

Poirier, M.R. 'The NAFTA Chapter 11 Expropriation Debate through the Eyes of a Property Theorist' (2003) 33 *Environmental Law* 851–928.

Poole, T. 'Proportionality in Perspective' (2010) NZLR 369–91.

Porat, I. 'Why All Attempts to Make Judicial Review Balancing Principled Fail?', paper presented at the VII World Congress of the International Association of Constitutional Law, Athens, 11–15 June 2007.

Porat, I. 'Some Critical Thoughts on Proportionality', in G. Bongiovanni, G. Sartor and C. Valentini (eds), *Reasonableness and Law* (Springer 2009) 234–50.

Porter, B. 'Reasonableness and Article 8(4)', in M. Langford, B. Porter, R. Brown and J. Rossi (eds), *The Optional Protocol to the International Covenant on Economic, Social and Cultural Rights: A Commentary* (University of Pretoria Press 2016) 173–202.

Portuese, A. 'Principle of Proportionality as Principle of Economic Efficiency' (2013) 19 *European LJ* 612–35.

Puig, S. 'Emergence and Dynamism in International Organizations: ICSID, Investor–State Arbitration and International Investment Law' (2013) 44 *Georgetown JIL* 531–608.

Puig, S. 'Recasting ICSID's Legitimacy Debate: Towards a Goal-Based Empirical Agenda' (2013) 36 *Fordham ILJ* 465–504.

Puig, S. 'No Right Without a Remedy: Foundations of Investor–State Arbitration' (2013–2014) 35 *University of Pennsylvania JIL* 829–61.

Puig, S. 'The Merging of International Trade and Investment Law' (2015) 33 *Berkeley JIL* 1–59.

Raimondo, F. *General Principles of Law in the Decisions of International Criminal Courts and Tribunals* (OUP 2008).

Ranjan, P. 'Using the Public Law Concept of Proportionality to Balance Investment Protection with regulation in International Investment Law: A Critical Appraisal' (2014) 3 CJICL 853–83.

Ratner, S.R. 'Regulatory Takings in Institutional Context: Beyond the Fear of Fragmented International Law' (2008) 102 AJIL 475–528.

Raustiala, K. 'Rethinking the Sovereignty Debate in International Economic Law' (2003) 6 JIEL 841–78.

Rautenbach, I.M. 'Proportionality and the Limitation Clauses of the South African Bill of Rights' (2014) 17 *Potchefstroom Electronic LJ* 2228–67.

Reich, A. 'From Diplomacy to Law: The Juridicization of International Trade Relations' (1996–97) 17 *Northwestern JIL & Business* 775–849.

Reich, N. 'How Proportionate is the Proportionality Principle? Some Critical Remarks on the Use and Methodology of the Proportionality Principle in the Internal Market Case Law of the ECJ', Working Paper, presented at the Oslo conference on 'The Reach of Free Movement', 2011.

Reimann, M. and Zimmermann, R. (eds) *The Oxford Handbook of Comparative Law* (OUP 2006).

Reiner, C. and Schreuer, C. 'Human Rights and International Investment Arbitration', in P.-M. Dupuy, F. Francioni and E.-U. Petersmann (eds), *Human Rights in International Investment Law and Arbitration* (OUP 2008) 82–96.

Reinisch, A. *Standards of Investment Protection* (OUP 2008).

Reitz, J.C. 'How to do Comparative Law' (1998) 46 AJCL 617–36.

Repetto, G. *Argomenti comparativi e diritti fondamentali in Europa. Teorie dell'interpretazione e giurisprudenza sovranazionale* (Iovene 2011).

Ripinsky, S. 'Venezuela's Withdrawal from ICSID: What it Does and Does Not Achieve', ITN, 13 April 2012.

Rivers, J. 'Proportionality and Variable Intensity of Review' (2006) 65 *Cambridge LJ* 174–207.

Rivers, J. 'Proportionality and Discretion in International and European Law', in N. Tsagourias (ed.), *Transnational Constitutionalism: European and International Models* (CUP 2007) 107–132.

Rivers, J. 'The Presumption of Proportionality' (2014) 77 MLR 409–433.

Roberts, A. 'Power and Persuasion in Investment Treaty Interpretation: The Dual Role of States' (2010) 104 AJIL 179–225.

Roberts, A. 'The Next Battleground: Standards of Review in Investment Treaty Arbitration', in A.J. Van den Berg (ed.), *Arbitration: The Next Fifty Years* (Kluwer 2012) 170–83.

Roberts, A. 'Clash of Paradigms: Actors and Analogies Shaping the Investment Treaty System' (2013) 107 AJIL 45–94.

Roberts, A. 'Triangular Treaties: The Extent and Limits of Investment Treaty Rights' (2015) 56 *Harvard ILJ* 353–417.

Roberts, A. 'The Shifting Landscape of Investor–State Arbitration: Loyalists, Reformists, Revolutionaries and Undecideds', *International Economic Law and Policy Blog*, 15 June 2017.

Roy, S. 'Privileging (Some Forms of) Interdisciplinarity and Interpretation: Methods in Comparative Law' (2014) 12 IJCL 786–807.

Ryan, C.M. 'Meeting Expectations: Assessing the Long-Term Legitimacy and Stability of International Investment Law' (2008) 29 *University of Pennsylvania JIL* 725–62.

Ryngaert, C. *Jurisdiction in International Law* (OUP 2008).

Sabahi, B. *Compensation and Restitution in Investor–State Arbitration* (OUP 2011).

Sacerdoti, G. 'Precedent in the Settlement of International Economic Disputes: The WTO and Investment Arbitration Models', in A. Rovine (ed.), *Contemporary Issues in International Arbitration and Mediation* (Martinus Nijhoff 2010) 225–46.

Sacerdoti, G. 'Trade and Investment Law: Institutional Differences and Substantive Similarities' (2014) 9 *Jerusalem Review of Legal Studies* 1–12.

Sacerdoti, G., with Acconci, P., Valenti, M. and De Luca, A. (eds) *General Interests of Host States in International Investment Law* (CUP 2014).

Sadurski, W. 'Reasonableness and Value Pluralism in Law and Politics', in G. Bongiovanni, G. Sartor and C. Valentini (eds), *Reasonableness and Law* (Springer 2009) 129–46.

Sakellaridou, M. 'La généalogie de la proportionalité', paper presented at the VII World Congress of the International Association of Constitutional Law, Athens, 11–15 June 2007.

Salacuse, J.W. 'The Emerging Global Regime for Investment' (2010) 51 *Harvard ILJ* 427–74.

Salacuse, J.W. *The Law of Investment Treaties* (OUP 2010).

Salacuse, J.W. and Sullivan, N.P. 'Do BITs Really Work? An Evaluation of Bilateral Investment Treaties and their Grand Bargain' (2005) 46 *Harvard ILJ* 67–130.

Salles, L.E. *Forum Shopping in International Adjudication* (CUP 2014).

Salmon, J. 'Le concept de raisonnable en droit international public', in P. Reuter (ed.), *Mélanges offerts à Paul Reuter. Le droit international: unité et diversité* (Pedone 1982) 447–78.

Sartor, G. 'Doing Justice to Rights and Values: Teleological Reasoning and Proportionality' (2010) 18 *Artificial Intelligence and Law* 175–215.

Sartor, G., Bongiovanni, G. and Valentini, C. 'Reasonableness in International Law', *Oxford Bibliographies* (OUP 2016) 1–20.

Sauter, W. 'Proportionality in EU Law: A Balancing Act?' TILEC Discussion Paper (2013) 1–31.

Scelle, G. 'Le phénomène juridique du dédoublement fonctionnel', in W. Schätzel and H.-J. Schlochauer (eds), *Rechtsfragen der Internationalen Organisation – Festschrift für H. Wehberg* (Klostermann 1956) 324–42.

Schill, S.W. *The Multilateralization of International Investment Law* (CUP 2009).

Schill, S.W. (ed.) *International Investment Law and Comparative Public Law* (OUP 2010).

Schill, S.W. 'International Investment Law and Comparative Public Law: An Introduction', in S.W. Schill (ed.), *International Investment Law and Comparative Public Law* (OUP 2010) 3–38.

Schill, S.W. 'Public Law Concepts to Balance Investors' Rights with State Regulatory Actions in the Public Interest – The Concept of Proportionality', in S. Schill (ed.), *International Investment Law and Comparative Public Law* (OUP 2010) 75–105.

Schill, S.W. 'Enhancing International Investment Law's Legitimacy: Conceptual and Methodological Foundations of a New Public Law Approach' (2011) 52 *Virginia JIL* 57–102.

Schill, S.W. 'System-Building in Investment Treaty Arbitration and Lawmaking' (2011) 12 *German LJ* 1083–1110.

Schill, S.W. 'W(h)ither Fragmentation? On the Literature and Sociology of International Investment Law' (2011) 22 EJIL 875–908.

Schill, S.W. 'Cross-regime Harmonization through Proportionality Analysis: The Case of International Investment Law, the Law of State Immunity and Human Rights' (2012) 27 *ICSID Review* 87–119.

Schill, S.W. 'Deference in Investment Treaty Arbitration: Re-conceptualizing the Standard of Review through Comparative Public Law', SIEL Working Paper No. 33/2012.

Schill, S.W. 'Deference in Investment Treaty Arbitration: Re-conceptualizing the Standard of Review' (2012) 3 JIDS 577–607.

Schill, S.W. 'General Principles of Law and International Investment Law', in T. Gazzini and E. de Brabandere (eds), *International Investment Law: The Sources of Rights and Obligations* (Martinus Nijhoff 2012) 133–81.

Schlesinger, R.B. 'Research on the General Principles of Law Recognized by Civilized Nations' (1957) 51 AJIL 734–53.

Schlink, B. 'Proportionality', in M. Rosenfeld and A. Sajó (eds), *The Oxford Handbook of Comparative Constitutional Law* (OUP 2012) 719–36.

Schlink, B. 'Proportionality in Constitutional Law: Why Everywhere But Here?' (2012) 22 *Duke J of Comparative & International Law* 291–302.

Schneiderman, D. 'NAFTA's Takings Rule: American Constitutionalism Comes to Canada' (1996) 46 *U. Toronto LJ* 499–538.

Schneiderman, D. *Constitutionalizing Economic Globalization: Investment Rules and Democracy's Premise* (OUP 2008).

Schneiderman, D. 'Investing in Democracy? Political Process and International Investment Law' (2010) 60 *University of Toronto LJ* 909–940.

Schneiderman, D. 'Legitimacy and Reflexivity in International Investment Arbitration: A New Self-Restraint?' (2011) 2 JIDS 471–95.

Schor, M. 'Mapping Comparative Judicial Review' (2008) 7 *Washington University Global Studies LR* 257–87.

Schreuer, C. 'The Concept of Expropriation under the ETC and other Investment Protection Treaties' (2005) 2 TDM 1–10.

Schreuer, C. 'The Development of International Law by ICSID Tribunals' (2016) 31 *ICSID Review* 728–39.

Sedlak, D. 'ICSID's Resurgence in International Investment Arbitration: Can the Momentum Hold?' (2004) 23 *Penn State International LR* 147–71.

Selzer, M. *The Symmetry Norm and the Asymmetric Universe* (Keep Ahead 2015).

Shalakany, A. 'Arbitration and The Third World: A Plea for Reassessing Bias Under the Specter of Neoliberalism' (2000) 41 *Harvard ILJ* 419–68.

Shan, W., Simons, P. and Singh, D. (eds) *Redefining Sovereignty in International Economic Law* (Hart Publishing 2008).

Shany, Y. 'Towards a General Margin of Appreciation Doctrine in International Law?' (2005) 16 EJIL 907–940.

Shelton, D. 'Form, Function, and the Powers of International Courts' (2009) 9 *Chicago JIL* 537–71.

Shihata, I.F.I. 'Toward a Greater Depoliticization of Investment Disputes: The Roles of ICSID and MIGA' (1986) 1 *ICSID Review–FILJ* 1–25.

Shirlow, E. 'Deference and Indirect Expropriation Analysis in International Investment Law: Observations on Current Approaches and Frameworks for Future Analysis' (2014) 29 *ICSID Review* 595–626.

Shlomo-Agon, S. 'Clearing the Smoke: The Legitimation of Judicial Power at the WTO' (2015) 49 JWT 539–89.

Shoenbaum, T.J. 'International Trade and Protection of the Environment: The Continuing Search for Reconciliation' (1997) 91 AJIL 269–76.

Siems, M. 'The End of Comparative Law' (2007) 2 *Journal of Comparative Law* 133–50.

Siems, M.M. 'The Curious Case of Overfitting Legal Transplants', in M. Adams and D. Heirbaut (eds), *The Method and Culture of Comparative Law: Essays in Honour of Mark Van Hoecke* (Hart Publishing 2014) 133–45.

Simma, B. 'Foreign Investment Arbitration: A Place for Human Rights?' (2011) 60 ICLQ 573–96.

Simma, B. and Pulkowski, D. 'Of Planets and the Universe: Self-contained Regimes in International Law' (2006) 17 *European Journal of International Law* 483–529.

Skovgaard Poulsen, L.N. 'Bounded Rationality and the Diffusion of Modern Investment Treaties' (2014) 58 *International Studies Quarterly* 1–14.

Slaughter, A.-M. 'Judicial Globalization' (2000) 40 *Virginia JIL* 1103–124.

Slaughter, A.-M. 'A Global Community of Courts' (2003) 44 *Harvard ILJ* 191–219.

Sohn, L.B. and Baxter, R.R. 'Responsibility of States for Injuries to the Economic Interests of Aliens' (1961) 55 AJIL 548–84.

Sornarajah, M. *The Settlement of Foreign Investment Disputes* (Kluwer Law International 2000).

Sornarajah, M. 'The Clash of Globalizations and the International Law on Foreign Investment' (2003) 12 *Canadian Foreign Policy* 1–32.

Sornarajah, M. 'Right to Regulate and Safeguards', in UNCTAD, *The Development Dimension of FDI: Policy and Rule Making Perspectives* (UN 2003).

Sornarajah, M. 'A Coming Crisis: Expansionary Trends in Investment Treaty Arbitration', in K.P. Sauvant (ed.), *Appeals Mechanism in International Investment Disputes Law* (OUP 2008) 39–80.

Sornarajah, M. *The International Law on Foreign Investment*, 3rd edn (CUP 2010).

Sornarajah, M. *Resistance and Change in the International Law on Foreign Investment* (CUP 2015).

Sourgens, F.G. 'Law's Laboratory: Developing International Law on Investment Protection as Common Law' (2014) 34 *Northwestern JIL & Business* 181–247.

St. John MacDonald, R. and Johnston, D.M. (eds) *Towards World Constitutionalism: Issues in the Legal Ordering of the World Community* (Martinus Nijhoff 2005).

Starner, G.M. 'Taking a Constitutional Look: NAFTA Chapter 11 as an Extension of Member States' Constitutional Protection of Property' (2002) 33 *Law & Policy International Business* 405–436.

Stein, E. 'Lawyers, Judges, and the Making of a Transnational Constitution' (1981) 75 AJIL 1–27.

Stern, B. 'Le droit de propriété, l'expropriation et la nationalisation dans la Convention européenne des droits de l'homme' (1991) 17 *Droit et pratique du commerce international* 394–403.

Stern, B. 'In Search of the Frontiers of Indirect Expropriation', in A. Rovine (ed.), *Contemporary Issues in International Arbitration and Mediation* (Martinus Nijhoff 2008) 29–51.

Stewart, R.B. 'Remedying Disregard in Global Regulatory Governance: Accountability, Participation, and Responsiveness' (2014) 108 AJIL 211–70.

Stoll, P.-T. 'Constitutional Perspectives on International Economic Law', in M. Cremona, P. Hilpold, N. Lavranos, S.S. Schneider and A.R. Ziegler (eds), *Reflections on the Constitutionalisation of International Economic Law* (Brill 2014) 201–213.

Stone Sweet, A. 'Investor–State Arbitration: Proportionality's New Frontier' (2010) 4 LEHR 46–76.

Stone Sweet, A. and Brunell, T.L. 'Trustee Courts and the Judicialization of International Regimes' (2013) *Journal of Law and Courts* 61–88.

Stone Sweet, A. and Della Cananea, G. 'Proportionality, General Principles of Law, and Investor–State Arbitration: A Response to José Alvarez' (2014) *NYU JIL and Politics* 911–54.

Stone Sweet, A. and Mathews, J. 'Proportionality Balancing and Global Constitutionalism' (2008) 47 *Columbia Journal of Transnational Law* 73–164.

Subedi, S. *International Investment Law: Reconciling Policy and Principle*, 3rd edn (Hart Publishing 2016).

Sunstein, C. 'Incommensurability and Valuation in Law' (1994) 92 *Michigan LR* 779–861.

Sweeney, J.A. 'Margins of Appreciation: Cultural Relativity and the European Court of Human Rights in the Post-Cold War Era' (2005) 54 ICLQ 459–74.

Taggart, M. 'Proportionality, Deference, *Wednesbury*' (2008) NZLR 423–50.

Tallent, K.D. 'The Tractor in the Jungle: Why Investment Arbitration Tribunals Should Reject a Margin of Appreciation Doctrine', in I.A. Laird and T. Weiler (eds), *Investment Treaty Arbitration and International Law* – Vol. 3 (Juris 2010) 124–8.

Tesauro, G. 'Reasonableness in the European Court of Justice Case Law', in A. Rosas, E. Levits and Y. Bots (eds), *The Court of Justice and the Construction of Europe* (Springer 2013) 307–327.

Teubner, G. 'Global Bukowina: Legal Pluralism in the World Society', in G. Teubner (ed.), *Global Law without a State* (Dartmouth 1997) 3–30.

Teubner, G. 'Fragmented Foundations: Societal Constitutionalism beyond the Nation State', in P. Dobner and M. Loughlin (eds), *The Twilight of Constitutionalism?* (OUP 2010) 327–41.

Timmermans, C. 'The Constitutionalization of the European Union' (2002) 21 *Yearbook of European Law* 1–11.

Tobin, J. and Rose-Ackerman, S. 'Foreign Direct Investment and the Business Environment in Developing Countries: The Impact of Bilateral Investment Treaties' (2005) Yale Law and Economics Research Paper No. 293, 1–52.

Tomuschat, C. 'The European Court of Human Rights and Investment Protection', in C. Binder, U. Kriebaum, A. Reinisch and S. Wittich (eds), *International Investment Law for the 21st Century: Essays in Honour of Christoph Schreuer* (OUP 2009) Ch. 34.

Trachtman, J.P. 'Trade and ... Problems, Cost-Benefit Analysis and Subsidiarity' (1998) 9 EJIL 32–85.

Trachtman, J.P. 'The Constitutions of the WTO' (2006) 17 EJIL 623–46.

Trakman, L.E. and Musayelyan, D. 'The Repudiation of Investor–State Arbitration and Subsequent Treaty Practice: The Resurgence of Qualified Investor–State Arbitration' (2016) 31 *ICSID Review* 194–218.

Tremblay, L.B. 'An Egalitarian Defence of Proportionality-based Balancing' (2014) 12 IJCL 864–90.

Tridimas, T. *The General Principles of EU Law* (OUP 1998).

Tridimas, T. 'Proportionality in Community Law: Searching for the Appropriate Standard of Scrutiny', in E. Ellis (ed.), *The Principle of Proportionality in the Laws of Europe* (Hart Publishing 1999) 65–84.

Tridimas, T. *The General Principles of EU Law*, 2nd edn (OUP 2006).

Tridimas, T. 'Precedent and the Court of Justice: A Jurisprudence of Doubt?', in J. Dickson and P. Eleftheriadis (eds), *The Philosophical Foundations of EU Law* (OUP 2012) 307–330.

Tsakyrakis, S. 'Proportionality: An Assault on Human Rights?' (2009) 7 IJCL 468–93.

Tully, S.R. 'Objective Reasonableness as a Standard for International Judicial Review' (2015) 6 JIDS 546–67.

Tushnet, M. 'Some Reflections on Method in Comparative Constitutional Law', in S. Choudry (ed.), *The Migration of Constitutional Ideas* (CUP 2006) 67–83.

Twining, W. 'Globalization and Comparative Law' (1999) 6 *Maastricht Journal of European and Comparative Law* 217–43.

Urbina, F.J. 'A Critique of Proportionality' (2012) 57 *American Journal of Jurisprudence* 49–80.

Urbina, F.J. *A Critique of Proportionality and Balancing* (CUP 2017).

Vadi, V. 'Investing in Culture: Underwater Cultural Heritage and International Investment Law' (2009) 42 *Vanderbilt Journal of Transnational Law* 853–904.

Vadi, V. 'Critical Comparisons: The Role of Comparative Law in Investment Treaty Arbitration' (2010) 39 *Denver JIL & Policy* 67–100.

Vadi, V. 'Converging Divergences: The Rise of Chinese Outward Foreign Investment and Its Implications for International (Investment) Law' (2012) *Yearbook of International Investment Law* 705–724.

Vadi, V. *Public Health in International Investment Law and Arbitration* (Routledge 2012).

Vadi, V. 'The Migration of Constitutional Ideas: The Strange Case of Proportionality in International Investment Law and Arbitration', in A.K. Bjorklund (ed.), *Yearbook on International Investment Law and Policy* (2013–2014) 337–60.

Vadi, V. 'Proportionality, Reasonableness and Standards of Review in Investment Treaty Arbitration', in A.K. Bjorklund (ed.), *Yearbook of International Investment Law and Policy* (2013–2014) 201–228.

Vadi, V. *Cultural Heritage in International Investment Law and Arbitration* (CUP 2014).

Vadi, V. 'Jus Cogens in International Investment Law and Arbitration' (2015) 46 *Netherlands YIL* 357–88.

Vadi, V. 'The Migration of Constitutional Ideas to Regional and International Economic Law: The Case of Proportionality' (2015) 35 *Northwestern Journal of International Law and Business* 557–89.

Vadi, V. *Analogies in International Investment Law and Arbitration* (CUP 2016).

Vadi, V. 'A History of Success? Proportionality in International Economic Law', in A. Segura Serrano (ed.), *The Reform of International Economic Governance* (Routledge 2016) 171–92.

Vadi, V. and Gruszczynski, L. 'Standards of Review in International Investment Law and Arbitration: Multilevel Governance and the Commonweal' (2013) 16 JIEL 613–33.

Vadi, V. and Gruszczynski, L. 'Standards of Review and Scientific Evidence in WTO Law and International Investment Arbitration: Converging Parallels?', in L. Gruszczynski and W. Werner (eds), *Deference in International Courts and Tribunals* (OUP 2014) 152–72.

Van Aaken, A. 'Interpretational Methods as an Instrument of Control in International Investment Law' (2014) 108 *ASIL Proceedings* 196–8.

Van den Bossche, P. 'Looking for Proportionality in WTO Law' (2008) 35 *Legal Issues of Economic Integration* 283–94.

Van den Bossche, P. and Zdouc, W. *The Law and Policy of the World Trade Organization* 4th edn (CUP 2017).

Vandevelde, K.J. 'A Unified Theory of Fair and Equitable Treatment' (2010) 43 *NYU JIL & Politics 43–106.*

Van Harten, G. *Investment Treaty Arbitration and Public Law* (OUP 2007).

Van Harten, G. 'The Public–Private Distinction in the International Arbitration of Individual Claims Against the State' (2007) 56 ICLQ 371–94.

Van Harten, G. *Sovereign Choices and Sovereign Constraints: Judicial Restraint in Investment Treaty Arbitration* (OUP 2013).

Van Harten, G. and Loughlin, M. 'Investment Treaty Arbitration as a Species of Global Administrative Law' (2006) 17 EJIL 121–50.

Van Harten, G. and Scott, D.N. 'Investment Treaties and the Internal Vetting of Regulatory Proposals: A Case Study from Canada' (2016) 7 JIDS 92–116.

Van Hoecke, M. 'Deep Level Comparative Law', in M. Van Hoecke (ed.), *Epistemology and Methodology of Comparative Law* (Hart Publishing 2004) 165–74.

Vanhonnaeker, L. *Intellectual Property Rights as Foreign Direct Investments* (Edward Elgar 2015).

Veel, P.-E. 'Incommensurability, Proportionality, and Rational Legal Decision-Making' (2010) 4 LEHR 178–230.

Verhoosel, G. 'Foreign Direct Investment and Legal Constraints on Domestic Environmental Policies: Striking a "Reasonable" Balance between Stability and Change' (1997–1998) 29 *Law & Policy in International Business* 451–78.

Verkuil, P.R. 'An Outcomes Analysis of Scope of Review Standards' (2002–2003) 44 *William & Mary LR* 679–735.

Viñuales, J.E. *Foreign Investment and the Environment in International Law* (CUP 2012).

Viñuales, J.E. 'Sovereignty in Foreign Investment Law', in Z. Douglas, J. Pauwelyn and J.E. Viñuales (eds), *The Foundations of International Investment Law* (OUP 2014) 317–62.

Voigt, C. 'The Role of General Principles in International Law and Their Relationship to Treaty Law' (2008) 31 *Retfærd Årgang* 3–25.

Von Bogdandy, A. and Venzke, I. 'In Whose Name? An Investigation of International Courts' Public Authority and Its Democratic Justification' (2012) 23 EJIL 7–41.

Von Staden, A. 'Deference or no Deference, that is the Question: Legitimacy and Standards of Review in Investor–State Arbitration' (2012) 4 ITN 3.

Von Staden, A. 'The Democratic Legitimacy of Judicial Review beyond the State: Normative Subsidiarity and Judicial Standards of Review' (2012) 10 IJCL 1023–1049.

Voon, T. 'Consolidating International Investment Law: the Mega-Regionals as a Pathway towards Multilateral Rules' (2017) *World Trade Review* 1–31.

Voon, T. and A.D. Mitchell, 'Denunciation, Termination and Survival: The Interplay of Treaty Law and International Investment Law' (2016) 31 *ICSID Review* 413–33.

VV.AA. 'Euclidean Geometry', *Encyclopaedia Britannica* (2014), <http://www.britannica.com/EBchecked/topic/194901/Euclidean-geometry> accessed 26 October 2013.

Waibel, M., Kaushal, A., Chung, K.-H.L. and Balchin, C. (eds) *The Backlash Against Investment Arbitration: Perceptions and Reality* (Kluwer Law International 2010).

Waibel, M., Kaushal, A., Chung, K.-H.L. and Balchin, C. 'The Blacklash against Investment Arbitration: Perceptions and Reality', in M. Waibel, A. Kaushal, K.-H.L. Chung and C. Balchin (eds), *The Blacklash Against Investment Arbitration: Perceptions and Reality* (Kluwer Law International 2010) xxxviii.

Wälde, T. 'The "Umbrella" (or Sanctity of Contract/Pacta Sunt Servanda) Clause in Investment Arbitration: A Comment on Original Intentions and Recent Cases' (2004) 1 TDM 1–13.

Waldron, J. 'Some Models of Dialogues between Judges and Legislators' (2004) 23 *Supreme Court LR* 7–37.

Waldron, J. 'Foreign Law and the Modern Jus Gentium' (2005) 119 *Harvard LR* 129–45.

Watson, A. 'Comparative Law and Legal Change' (1978) 37 *Cambridge LJ* 313–36.

Watson, A. *Legal Transplants: An Approach to Comparative Law* (University of Georgia Press 1994).

Webber, G.C.N. 'Proportionality, Balancing, and the Cult of Constitutional Rights Scholarship' (2010) 23 *Canadian J of Law and Jurisprudence* 179–202.

Weiler, J.H.H. '*Fin-de-siecle* Europe: Do the New Clothes have an Emperor?', in J.H.H. Weiler, *The Constitution of Europe: 'Do the New Clothes Have an Emperor?' and Other Essays on European Integration* (CUP 1999) 238–63.

Weiler, J.H.H. *The Constitution of Europe* (CUP 1999).

Weiler, J.H.H. 'The Rule of Lawyers and the Ethos of Diplomats: Reflections on the Internal and External Legitimacy of WTO Dispute Settlement' (2001) 35 JWT 191–207.

Weiß, W. 'Human Rights in the EU: Rethinking the Role of the European Convention on Human Rights after Lisbon' (2011) 7 *European Constitutional LR* 64–95.

Wellhausen, R. 'Recent Trends in Investor–State Dispute Settlement' (2016) 7 JIDS 117–35.

Wittkower, R. *Architectural Principles in the Age of Humanism* (Warburg Institute 1949).

Wittkower, R. 'The Changing Concept of Proportion' (1960) 89 *Daedalus* 199–215.
Wolfrum, R. 'Legitimacy of International Law from a Legal Perspective: Some Introductory Considerations', in R. Wolfrum and V. Roeben (eds), *Legitimacy in International Law* (Springer 2008) 1–24.
Wouters, J. and Duquet, S. 'The Principle of Reasonableness in Global Administrative Law' (2013) 12 *Jean Monnet Working Paper* 1–42.
Xiuli, H. 'On the Application of the Principle of Proportionality in ICSID Arbitration and Proposals to Government of the People's Republic of China' (2006) 13 *James Cook University LR* 233–58.
Xiuli, H. 'The Application of the Principle of Proportionality in *Tecmed v. Mexico*' (2007) 6 *Chinese JIL* 635–52.
Young, E.A. 'The Constitution Outside the Constitution' (2007) 117 *Yale LJ* 408–473.
Young, S.P. 'Introduction', in S.P. Young (ed.), *Reasonableness in Liberal Political Philosophy* (Routledge 2014) 1–6.
Yourow, H.C. *The Margin of Appreciation Doctrine in the Dynamics of European Human Rights Jurisprudence* (Martinus Nijhoff 1996).
Zammit Borda, A. 'Comparative Law and Ad Hoc Tribunals: The Dangers of a Narrow Inquiry' (2012) 40 *International Journal of Legal Information* 22–38.
Zumbansen, P. 'Comparative Law's Coming of Age? Twenty Years after *Critical Comparisons*' (2005) 6 *German LJ* 1073–1084.
Zumbansen, P. 'Transnational Comparisons: Theory and Practice of Comparative Law as a Critique of Global Governance' (2012) *Osgoode Hall Law School, Research Paper* No. 1/2012.
Zweigert, K. 'Méthodologie du droit comparé', in *Mélanges J. Maury* (Dalloz-Sirey 1960) 579–96.

DOCUMENTS OF INTERNATIONAL ORGANIZATIONS

Economic and Social Council, Commission on Human Rights, Sub-commission on the Promotion and Protection of Human Rights, Report of the High Commissioner for Human Rights, Human Rights, Trade and Investment, E/CN.4 /Sub.2/2003/9, 2 July 2003.
European Commission, Recommendation for a Council Decision authorising the opening of negotiations for a Convention establishing a multilateral court for the settlement of investment disputes, 13 September 2017, COM (2017) 493 final.

ILC, Fragmentation of International Law: Difficulties Arising from the Diversification and Expansion of International Law, Report of the Study Group (Martti Koskenniemi) UN Doc. A/CN.4/L.682 (13 April 2006).

OECD, 'Indirect Expropriation and the Right to Regulate in International Investment Law', Working Paper on International Investment 4/2004.

UNCITRAL, Possible Future Work in the Field of Dispute Settlement: Reforms of Investor–State Dispute Settlement (ISDS) Note by the Secretariat, 20 April 2017, A/CN.9/917.

UNCTAD, *World Investment Report 2016* (UN 2016).

Index